BLUES ALL DAY LONG

MUSIC IN AMERICAN LIFE

*A list of books in the series appears
at the end of this book.*

BLUES ALL DAY LONG

THE JIMMY ROGERS STORY

Wayne Everett Goins

Foreword by Kim Wilson

UNIVERSITY OF ILLINOIS PRESS
Urbana, Chicago, and Springfield

Library of Congress Cataloging-in-Publication Data
Goins, Wayne E., author.
Blues all day long : the Jimmy Rogers story /
Wayne Everett Goins ; foreword by Kim Wilson.
pages cm. — (Music in American life)
Includes bibliographical references, discography, and index.
ISBN 978-0-252-03857-0 (hardcover : alk. paper) —
ISBN 978-0-252-08017-3 (pbk. : alk. paper) —
ISBN 978-0-252-09649-5 (e-book)
1. Rogers, Jimmy. 2. Guitarists—United States—Biography.
3. Jazz musicians—United States—Biography. I. Title.
ML419.R613G65   2014
787.87'1643092—dc23   2014007477
[B]

For my father, William Earl Goins,
who gave me the gift of music.
They called him Bill.

For "Uncle Jimmy" Jones, my first blues guitar hero.
I still hear that Fender Jaguar.

For Uncle John Lewis Goins, who gave my dad
the first real guitar I ever owned. Oh, look at what you did.

CONTENTS

PART II. RISING FROM THE ASHES
(1970–1989)

PART III. FATHERS AND SONS
(1989–1997)

FOREWORD

Kim Wilson

Jimmy Rogers—oh, man. It's so hard to tell you what he meant to me. Was he my father? My uncle? Big brother? I don't know. Maybe he was all of them. One thing's for sure, though—he was definitely my hero. When you were around him, everything seemed to flow in an effortless, natural kind of way. And his music was just like his personality—with Jimmy, there was no need for rehearsal. He struck me as a really nice cat. Despite whatever he'd been through, he was always a happy, confident, and generous guy. I think it's because he knew where he stood in the grand scheme of things, which obviously was as one of the most important players in the history of the blues—not just in Chicago, but the world. You don't know how good it felt the first time he turned and looked at me with that Cheshire cat grin of his, sweat dripping down his face, and said to me, "Muthafucka, you can *play* that shit!"

When you first meet someone like this, they are like gods to you, and you're in awe of them. But then you get to know them and they become more like family. It becomes like a big party. You play jokes on each other. You laugh, and you cry together—from laughter. We did a lot of great gigs, and the whole time we were out there I never heard one negative thing out of him. Jimmy was a fun-loving guy, and sometimes he was an instigator, which he loved when it came to getting me in trouble! I was like a son to him—he'd say that to me all the time. We also were drinking buddies, and whenever I'd go to the bar, he'd get a smile on his face and say, "Get one for you, and one for *me*!" That was one of his favorite sayings. Our conversations were about everyday life, not a bunch of deep philosophical talk about our approach to playing guitar and harp. It was just about having a ball. Sometimes Muddy would get in-depth about the music, but Jimmy didn't. All that mattered to Jimmy was that when we played together, I knew where to put things behind him, and he really enjoyed that.

Of course, Jimmy had his favorite songs he liked to play, and many of them became mine as well because of him. "Chicago Bound" was one he loved to crank up, and "Gold Tailed Bird" was another one he really liked to perform; he was such a master at playing those greasy licks, making them just drip at that slow tempo. Sometimes he would play things that I never heard him do before. I was on a bandstand once at Antone's on a night when there were a lot of guitarists on-stage for some reason—I think it was for the club's twentieth-anniversary party. Buddy Guy, Rusty Zinn, Derek O'Brien, Luther Tucker—all the cats were there. I heard someone behind me doing some serious B. B. King–type stuff, and I'm looking around for who it was that was doing it. I'm thinking it's Luther, Buddy, or maybe Rusty. I turn around to look, and it's Jimmy, standing there smiling with that same Cheshire cat grin. It was the only time I ever heard him do that.

I remember one particular gig when he was in Austin, and I decided to drop by his hotel and hang out. I walked up to the Stephen F. Austin Hotel and headed up to his room. I guess the smoke alarms weren't working, because there was a layer of smoke on the whole floor. I followed the smoke and it led me straight to Jimmy's room. The drummer, Richard "Hubcap" Robinson, always shared a room with Jimmy when they were on the road. I knock on the door, and when it opened, there was Jimmy with smoke billowing all around his head. They had a huge deep fryer they'd stashed in the trunk of the car and brought along for the road trip. They'd been frying fish in the room, and there was Hubcap scraping the fish carcasses down the toilet, saying, "Oh, man, you just missed it—we been fishin'!" I just fell out laughing.

You wanna talk about someone who loved him some Jimmy? That was Clifford Antone. Clifford bought Jimmy one of the nicest guitars he ever had, and Jimmy named her Ludella. Antone always kept Ludella there for him, and that beautiful red guitar was always available when Jimmy arrived. Antone always looked out for Jimmy and treated him like royalty whenever he came to town, which was about three or four times a year, and he usually stayed for about a week. And he always found time to go fishing when he got there, which is how he and Hubcap got theirs when they filled the floor with smoke. Hell, that room probably *still* smells like fish. Jimmy and Pinetop—another one of his great fishing buddies—were really good friends, both on and off the stage. "Perk" Perkins is what he would call him. One night I was in San Jose taking the place of Hubert Sumlin, and we wound up rooming together, the three of us. I remember Pinetop's feet were hanging over the edge of the bed directly above my head while I was lying on the floor (I gave those guys the bed). It was like we were three kids at camp, with the lights out and Jimmy laughing his ass off in the dark at things that Pinetop was saying. God, I thought Jimmy would have a heart attack, he was laughing so hard with the two of them cutting up that night. You see, it was never deep with Jimmy, just funny as hell. When and where it got deep was on the bandstand.

People knew how much Jimmy loved me, and I've been asked a lot about things he might have told me about the "good old days" at Chess. The answer might be a bit disappointing, I'm afraid, but the truth is that Jimmy was all about the present and future; he wouldn't dwell on the past much at all. Once, though, he did tell about a rare occurrence: he said he used an entire horn section on some things he recorded that never came out during the Chess days. I think he probably thought he was somewhat overlooked in the past, because all of his sessions were offshoots of Muddy's sessions. I think it made him feel like he was on the backburner. I've always felt he deserved better than that. I produced what I thought was one of Jimmy's better albums, called *Ludella*. That record was, at least for me, the beginning of doing something really credible. It's not very often you get a chance to give back a little bit to the people who were your inspiration. I couldn't give him what he gave me in a hundred lifetimes, but that was one thing I *could* do. It was a lotta pressure to come up with something good, because I wanted it to be an album he could really be proud of. What I saw Jimmy do in the studio for that album was amazing. He'd do a song three times in a row, and all the while he was editing while he was playing! At different points while we were listening to the playback in the control room, he'd say to me, "You can snip it right there and put a tail on it!"

Jimmy was one of the inventors of amplified Chicago blues. I appreciated the fact that he pushed the envelope while he was building his legacy—like, for example, the way he wrote "My Baby Don't Love Me No More." How many times did you hear that kinda thing back then? I think he was looking forward; he was leaning more on the R & B stuff—he had more of a modern mind. Had someone nurtured it, I do believe that could have gone in a *lot* of different directions. Jimmy is still one of the most underrated blues artists to ever pick up a guitar, and I don't think people dwell on him enough. He never got the credit he deserved, and he should be in the Rock and Roll Hall of Fame. Those records of him on Chess prove that he is every bit as valid as Little Walter, Muddy, Leonard Chess, Hubert Sumlin, Howlin' Wolf, Willie Dixon—he should be right alongside them. He was barely mentioned in *Cadillac Records*, a movie that should have been a miniseries on HBO—you can't tell a story that big in two hours, man. Maybe then they would have gotten it right and included Jimmy Rogers as he should have been all along.

Jimmy took me under his wing and treated me like I was one of them. I'm not sure I even deserved that, but that's what he did. Knowing him was one the greatest experiences of my life.

ACKNOWLEDGMENTS

Thanks to the Rogers family for allowing me to tell their story: Angela Lane, Cordero Lane, Deborah Lane, Jackie Lane, James D. Mosely, Jimmy D. Lane, and Willie Miller. Extra special thanks to Cordero, who introduced me to all of these family members, who each contributed in their own special way.

I am grateful to all the contributors who gave me materials for the development of this manuscript: Steve Balkin, Frank "Right Hand" Bandy, Ken Bays, Scotty "Bad Boy" Bradbury, Billy Branch, Tom Brill, Gordon "Buzz" Brown, Mark Camarigg, "Good Rockin'" Derral Campbell, George Case, Randy Chortkoff, Edward Chmelewski, Dave Clark, Jeanette Clarke-Lodovici (for William Clarke), Bob Corritore, James Cotton, Steve Cushing, Bill Dahl, Norman Darwen, Scott Dirks, Ola Dixon, Keith Doder, Ronnie Earl, Steve F'dor, Billy Flynn, James Fraher, Bill Gilmore, "Barrelhouse Chuck" Goering, Henry Gray, Steve Guyger, Per Hansen, Ted Harvey, Joe Harley, Jerry Haussler, Mark Hoffman, David Horwitz, Andrew Huff, Mark Hummel, Charlie Hussey, Chris James, Greg Johnson, Paul Kahn, Jim Kahr, Chad Kassem, Rich Kirch, John Koenig, Mark "Madison Slim" Koenig, Bob Koester, Edward Komara, Dave Krull, Willy Leiser, Andy Loesche, Bill Lupkin, Bob Maglinte, Tony Mangiullo, Ben Manilla and Dan Aykroyd and the *House of Blues Radio Hour*, Eli Marcus, "Steady Rollin'" Bob Margolin, Dave Maxwell, John May, Andy McKaie, Danny Morrison, Nick Moss, James "The Blues Hound" Nagel, "Tony O" Melio, Ray Norcia, Derek O' Brien, Paul Oscher,

"Piano Willie" O'Shawny, Holger Peterson, Rod and Honey Piazza, Jerry Pillow, Tom Radai, Robert Pruter, Eomot Rasun, Dave Rubin, James Segrest, Matthew Skoller, Willie "Big Eyes" Smith (rest in peace), John Stedman, Ray Stiles, Bob Stroger, Richie Untenberger, Jimmie Vaughan, Dave Waldman, Michael "Mudcat" Ward, Michael "Junior" Watson, Jody Williams, Kim Wilson, Richie "Little Rich" Yescalis, and Rusty Zinn.

A ton of gratitude to the Inner Circle—my special advisory council, the all-star team of Dick Shurman, Mary Katherine Aldin, Jim O'Neal, and Charlie Musselwhite. Dick, your willingness to take the time out of your personal schedule to continually stand over my shoulder to make sure I got it right was a luxury I could never expect and never repay. I will always owe you one, and I cannot put into words how you went so far above and beyond the call of duty to help me preserve the Rogers legacy. Mary Katherine, I struggle to find words to fully account for the impact you have made on my life. To have you in my corner—from the very beginning—has been such a blessing to me. You have been my beacon and guiding light, and I am always striving to make you proud. Jim, let's just say that your spirit is in every page; your contribution to this book is colossal. The unfettered access you gave me to every issue of *Living Blues*—and allowing me to sit at your table and absorb your knowledge and wisdom—cannot be overestimated. The blues gods will smile on your soul forever. And Charlie, you epitomize what it means to be a bluesman. You have given me what every researcher dreams of having—friendship, sound advice, and, most of all, honesty. You are the stuff that legends are made of, and I am honored to have played with you in San Francisco when I was on tour with Ichiban Records back in '93. Little did we know our paths would cross again for such a worthy cause.

To one of the unsung Chicago blues trailblazers, Bob Riedy, I can only say that the abundance of material you gave me when I needed to capture both the riots of the late '60s and the evolution of blues on the North Side at the start of the '70s was so riveting—only a reporter on the ground could give such an accurate account. You were there through it all, and you lived to tell the story—but most important, you were there to provide a musical haven for Jimmy when he finally reemerged after ten long years. I hope you are happy with the results of my efforts to tell your part of the story along with his.

To Susan Antone and the entire crew down there in Austin, Texas—thank you for allowing me to talk with you all about Jimmy's legacy at Antone's. I am incredibly grateful to Kim Wilson for allowing me to get onstage with him and sit in that night with the Fabulous Thunderbirds. He gave me the rare opportunity to play in the spot where Jimmy stood, and it was awesome. Proper thanks go to

Robert Pruter and Robert Campbell and the entire team who continually update the important work on the Red Saunders Research Foundation website. Thank you so much for acknowledging my little contribution to the Parkway Records mystery that is forever unraveled—things of that nature are what keep us going.

Thanks to members of the administration at Kansas State University—Provost April Mason; Dean Brian Spooner; my Department Head of Music, Gary Mortenson; and all of my colleagues in the Department of Music for encouragement and support while I was away on sabbatical to work on this project.

Authors who served as role models and encouraged me to do honorable research are Robert Gordon (*Can't Be Satisfied: The Life and Times of Muddy Waters*), James Segrest and Mark Hoffman (*Moanin' at Midnight: The Life and Times of Howlin' Wolf*), and especially Scott Dirks (*Blues with a Feeling: The Little Walter Story*), who played such a crucial role during the early phase of my research. Thanks so much for all the lively banter during the many phone calls and e-mails; you are the epitome of blues scholarship. Other books worthy of mention that I leaned upon heavily during this project are Michael Ruppli's *The Chess Labels: A Discography, Vol. 1*; Mike Rowe's *Chicago Blues: The City and the Music*; and *The Blues Discography, 1943–1970*, by Les Fancourt and Bob McGrath.

I would like to thank Laurie Matheson for giving me the opportunity to publish this book, and for hanging in there with me and waiting so patiently while I worked to get it right; Laurie and the entire publishing staff at the University of Illinois Press have made this dream a reality. To my editor, Robin Mosher, who spent many days and nights reading the manuscript and encouraging me to push onward and upward, thank you so much for your time and talent. And to my copyeditor, Jill R. Hughes, you did a tremendous job fine-tuning this book during the final phase of preparation—thanks for having incredible "eyes and ears" for rhythm in writing.

I'd like to pay an extra special debt of gratitude to Dawn Durante, my appointed assistant acquisitions editor at the University of Illinois Press. Dawn, I can truly say that without your help, this book would not have been completed. You were the guiding force that steered me the remainder of the way through, and you were absolutely superb when it came time to grab the baton that Laurie passed to you. Not only did you run the most excellent race, but you also held my hand firmly and pulled me across the finish line. If this book proves to be a winner, it is because of you.

I had a couple of very special friends who also supported me, particularly Walter Dodds, who read early versions of the manuscript and offered good advice on how to make the book better, and Adam Gussow, whose enthusiasm for the project and belief that this story needed to be told helped me keep the faith. Harriett Ottenheimer was always a role model for doing good blues research, and her support and supplemental materials helped me move my project forward at the outset. Roberto Prieto Ruguera was a tremendous source for me early on, and Bruce Iglauer was honest and forthright with his helpful comments. Phillip Williams from Houston has always been a reliable resource.

Thanks go out to my entire Goins family in Chicago, with extra special thanks to two of my brothers, Garrett and Barnard, who assisted me so well when I went on my first round of interviews on the Chicago leg of the tour; and to my Manhattan family—my daughters, Jasmine and Cherry—for unwavering love and support.

The most special thanks of all are saved for my wife, Deborah. Were it not for her, this project would have never seen the light of day. Her love, patience, and endurance on my behalf are immeasurable. Everyone should be this lucky.

INTRODUCTION

The blues wasn't born in Chicago, but it sure was raised there—just like me. For all of my life, I've had a direct and powerful connection to the blues. My father, William Earl Goins, knew and hung out with Little Walter (they were drinking buddies) and could mimic his harp style with ease. When he was in a Jimmy Reed mood, my dad could play harp that way too, or Big Walter's style when he felt like it. He also taught me my first blues guitar licks in the key of E, and I listened to all the classic Chess sides almost daily when my family was at 2713 West Jackson on the West Side of Chicago and throughout my teens while I lived on Sixty-fourth and Laflin Street on the Southwest Side. Even before I could read, I knew the names of the tunes my dad put on the turntable, because I'd memorized the colors on the label imprints of the 45s and LPs that he had. This is how I was introduced to the music of some of the main men of Chess Records: Muddy, Little Walter, Chuck Berry, and Howlin' Wolf. Looking back, I realize that I was so close to the music of Jimmy Rogers without even knowing it.

Indeed, Jimmy was an unknown soldier to me then. Unlike today's liner notes, the Chess album covers back then didn't list the sidemen and all the intricate details of which songs they played on, and of course the disc itself shed no light beyond the name of the song, the artist, and the record label. Unbeknownst to me, I was getting regular doses of Jimmy Rogers through Muddy's songs when my dad wore the grooves out on the 1958 Chess LP *The Best of Muddy Waters*, the first collection of Muddy tunes. Jimmy's intricate guitar lines are inextricably linked to the legendary sound, his licks slowly sizzling on the vinyl surface of those tracks my father spun religiously.

As a young teen I played in my first blues band with my uncle Jimmy Jones and was onstage with him when Hound Dog Taylor sat in with us at one of my first gigs on Rush Street. He took my guitar that night and told me, "This is how you do it, son." At the time I had just discovered Jimi Hendrix and was playing a Stratocaster and wearing a Hendrix-style headband with another scarf around my left thigh like Jimi did. Taylor took one look at me and knew I still had things to learn about the roots of Hendrix and rock, which is, of course, the blues. I watched him in awe as he kicked his leg in the air while he played greasy licks in that smoky room that had a smell I can't even begin to describe here. I was getting closer.

I had no idea at the time, but I lived only seven blocks across from Jimmy and his family. When I attended Lindblom Technical High School, my walking route to school was to go down to Sixty-third Street off Ashland Avenue and head west, right past his house on the left side of the street, in five minutes' time. For four years straight I did this, until I moved away to college. So close . . .

After years of blues and jazz gigs, and an academic career that started more than thirty-five years ago, I found myself at Kansas State University in Manhattan, Kansas, where I became the director of Jazz Studies. But the blues, it won't leave me alone. As luck would have it, Cordero Lane, the trombonist in one of my jazz bands, turned out to be the grandson of Jimmy Rogers. Unbelievable.

Standing in my office, "Cody" called his aunt (Jimmy's daughter Angela) at her home, and I spoke to her briefly. Then he told me his uncle—Jimmy Rogers's youngest son, Jimmy D. Lane (also known as "Little Jimmy")—lived only forty minutes away, in nearby Salina. With Cody in tow, my wife and I traveled down to Jimmy D.'s house in late January 2008 with a tape recorder (and a basket of home-fried chicken to loosen things up a bit). I told him how honored I was to meet the prodigal son who carried the blues torch. "It's all good," said Jimmy D., who reminded me immediately of a perfect blend of Jimi Hendrix and Stevie Ray Vaughan in both attire and manner when I met him and listened to his music. Legacy, indeed.

I eventually met most of Jimmy's other children. I asked them all the same question: why hasn't Jimmy received his turn to be lauded for his achievements in the form of a definitive biography like Muddy, Wolf, Little Walter, Jimmy Reed, and Hubert Sumlin? After all, he was a co-founder of the classic Delta blues–based post–World War II Chicago sound. Anyone who has heard the music of

Muddy Waters during his most essential period—from roughly 1949 to 1960, it is argued here—knows that the classic sound that drove blues lovers crazy was first founded upon the seamless interaction that existed between *two* guitars, with the second guitar providing the lower layer, drums providing the basic pulse, and a sharp harp to provide the colorful embellishments.

Without the presence of that second, sympathetic, subtle, gentle, and understated guitar to provide an incessant countermelody to the stinging lead, the sonic structure is incomplete. Even after one considers the substantial role of Otis Spann on piano—whose driving, yet ornate "call-and-response" style filled the void Rogers left upon his departure from the Waters band—the legendary body of '50s Chess work under the Muddy Waters banner would not have existed without it. Jimmy Rogers helped to shape the Muddy Waters sound and, in the process, defined an entire style that influenced generations of guitarists over the next fifty years and beyond. Indeed, Jimmy's sonic imprint on the trajectory that was Muddy Waters's career remains significant. Just listen to "Still a Fool," "Honey Bee," "Baby, Please Don't Go," "Mad Love," "I'm Ready," "Mannish Boy," "I Want You to Love Me," and, most of all, "Hoochie Coochie Man." These were some of Muddy's biggest hits, and Jimmy played a crucial role in the development of those tunes.

During the course of his own solo career, his very first Chess single was a hit, with "That's All Right" and "Ludella" crashing the airwaves in 1950 just as hard as Muddy's "I Can't Be Satisfied" had done previously. "That's All Right" remains one of his most covered blues songs, while Jimmy's biggest hit—"Walkin' by Myself"—not only made an immediate impact on the U.S. charts but also was embraced overseas in such large numbers that the tune is still performed as a classic standard by blues bands around the globe, along with a number of others from Jimmy's recorded catalog.

In addition to his rare and standard-setting empathy as an accompanist and an exceptionally lyrical style on the guitar that made his sound unique, Jimmy had the ability to take previously crafted songs and reshape them into his own by putting that distinct touch on them to such a polished degree that his versions practically rendered the original one obsolete. His gentle yet persuasive vocal style, combined with his melodic sensibilities, created a truly enduring sound that has made a direct impact on every generation that followed, including the current round of guitarists who have benefited from emulating his musical approach. He has made contributions both large and small to the blues canon as an accompanist and style setter on guitar, as well as an accomplished composer and interpreter of music. No other blues guitarist of his era is due more credit for capturing the essence of weaving both the melodic rhythm and lead patterns quite like he did. Jimmy Rogers deserves proper recognition for his significant contribution to blues history.

You can imagine my surprise, then, when I asked around about why a definitive biography on Jimmy's life hadn't yet been published, and no clear answers came forth. *Maybe nobody cared to take the time to do it*, I thought to myself. And it was true—all those years had gone by, and when I looked back I saw no book written on his life, almost as if it weren't as important to chronicle than some others. What about Jimmy's character led to his invisibility? Did he not make a big enough splash to last a lifetime?

Indeed, he did not portray the moxie of Muddy Waters, who, when moved to do so, would shove a bottle of beer down his pants, shake it up by gyrating his hips, and watch the foam spill to the thrill of the ladies in the crowd. He didn't have the temper and cockiness of Little Walter, whose fiery and aggressive personality offstage was as notorious as the beautiful music he created onstage and in the studio. He wasn't physically large in stature and status like Willie Dixon. He never howled, growled, and prowled like Wolf. He wasn't tall and lean and wearing dapper two-toned suits and bowler hats like Sonny Boy Williamson II. And he never learned to duckwalk while singing about fast cars—or even faster girls.

But then you look a bit closer and you suddenly figure it out: although he was right in the middle of it all, Jimmy's personality was unlike any of the others around him. His goodness lay in his democracy, in his allowing so many people around him to have a voice. He was less concerned with dominating any scene with his own musical voice at the expense of another. Every band member who worked with him (and I have interviewed scores of them) says he never failed to share his limelight with his band members—to a fault, some of his sidemen have said. A few music critics also thought his good-natured disposition hindered his career to some degree (one interviewer even said he wished that Jimmy would get mad—just for once, about *anything*—during the Q & A session). Personally, that kind of thinking makes me feel a bit uncomfortable, like nice guys finish last. Well, that just wouldn't do, as far as I was concerned. I had to get closer.

So I forged ahead and asked for the family's blessing to put Jimmy's legacy where it belongs: right on the front line with the rest of his friends in the blues fraternity. I viewed the absence of a biography about his musical journey as a sign of good luck for me, an opportunity of a lifetime to make a lasting contribution. The Rogers family embraced the idea. They gave me support, and I was honored to be the one to take the plunge. After all, Jimmy had a story to tell.

He was *there*. His voice—his story—should be told from his perspective, from beginning to end.

So I dove in with both arms and started digging. And wouldn't you know it? In searching for Jimmy Rogers, I found myself. I found the best opportunity to fulfill one of life's greatest callings: to be a storyteller. At long last the Jimmy Rogers story is being told, here and now. The research for this book *literally* brought me back home. Back to that same old place . . .

PART I

FROM MINTER CITY TO MADISON STREET (1924–1960)

1

MONEY, MARBLES, AND CHALK

My mother was Grossie Jackson. My father's name
was Roscoe . . . He was from Georgia, around
Atlanta. So he came up there in Mississippi,
workin', I guess. They got together and I was born.

—Jimmy Rogers

Jimmy Rogers was born James A. Lane on June 3, 1924, in Ruleville, Mississippi, to Grossie Jackson and Walter "Roscoe" Lane. Roscoe was from an area near Atlanta, Georgia (little is known about what brought him to the South). While there is almost no information about his father's background, much more is known about Jimmy's mother. Grossie Jackson, born on January 17, 1905, was from the small town of Maben, Mississippi; she was one of seven children born to LeAnna Miller and William Jackson.

After a whirlwind romance, eighteen-year old Grossie discovered that she was pregnant, possibly to the surprise of both her and Roscoe's parents. As was the custom of the day among black folk in rural towns in the early 1920s, any circumstance that would have led to a woman giving birth out of wedlock was frowned upon, placing heavy expectations upon the soon-to-be father to protect his family name. According to the 1930 U.S. Census Bureau statistics, Grossie Jackson was nineteen when she married Roscoe and became Grossie Lane. Shortly after, the couple and their new baby returned to Roscoe's hometown of Atlanta.

Roscoe got a job working at a sawmill plant, "one of what you call 'groundhog' sawmills," Jimmy once explained.[1] Though few details are known about the circumstances surrounding what took place at the job site, there was evidently a physical encounter between Roscoe and another worker at the plant, and Roscoe got the worst of it: he was killed at his worksite.[2] The entire event is shrouded in mystery. Even today no one knows what the scuffle was about, how Roscoe died, whether any charges were filed, or whether the culprit was ever brought to justice. What is certain, however, is that while Jimmy was just a toddler, his dad died in what more than likely amounted to some senseless fight that broke out between him and another person at the sawmill.[3]

Grossie, no doubt distraught over the loss of her husband, did not stay long in the town that had brought such tragedy to her family. After the funeral she immediately gathered her belongings and brought her infant son, James, back to Mississippi—not to Ruleville, but to the nearby town of Vance, where her mother was anxiously waiting. "I left Atlanta in 1926," Jimmy said.[4] He was two and a half years old.

Grossie found that being both a widow and a single parent at the tender age of twenty-one was not conducive to establishing a stable environment for either herself or her son. A female with little education and no particular job skills had few options in the 1920s, and being a Negro woman in the South definitely didn't help matters. It is not surprising, then, that not long after her return to Mississippi in 1926, she met a man—Henry Hall from Minter City—and struck up an immediate relationship with this handsome, brown-skinned gentleman who was at least thirteen years her senior. Their union blossomed quickly, and within the next year Grossie had a baby girl, LeAnna Hall (born in 1928), named after her mother. Not yet six years old, Jimmy now had a half sister who was about three years younger than himself. By 1930 (according to the census report) they were all living under the same household in Sunflower County.

At some point a decision was made to restructure the living arrangements in the family. Maybe Grossie and her husband decided it; maybe it was Grossie and her mother's idea. Whatever the case, someone thought it best that Jimmy live with his grandmother LeAnna Jackson on a permanent basis. Over the next twenty years Grossie and Henry Hall had a total of eleven children, all of whom were raised on a plantation owned by Arthur Sturdivant in Minter City, Mississippi, where they sharecropped until around 1957. In chronological order, the children were LeAnna, Avery, John, Lula, Georgia (who died before 1940 at age two of pneumonia), Elizabeth, Henry Jr. (known as "Brother"), Iguster, Gertrude, David, and Mary.

Meanwhile, Jimmy was relocated thirty miles down the highway in Vance to live in the home of Grossie's mother, where he would spend the next few years. In LeAnna Jackson's home, Jimmy was raised and treated as her son. Also living there were his three aunts—Annie Lou, Mary, and Sarah—who Jimmy often referred to as his sisters. (This arrangement would eventually become a source of great confusion for interviewers in later years.)

According to an interview with Jimmy, LeAnna Jackson's young looks belied her actual age. Jimmy said, "People thought my grandmother [LeAnna] was my mother, and [thought] my aunt, [Grossie's sister] Annie Lou, was my sister. She [Annie] was four years older than me."[5] Annie Lou was nine years old at the time of Grossie's marriage to Henry, while Jimmy was approaching the age of five. Jimmy's grandmother LeAnna had a brother named William "Willie" Miller who worked for the Illinois Central Railroad as a porter, traveling to Memphis, Detroit, and Chicago. Whenever he could, he helped get LeAnna jobs cleaning the railroad cars, which required her to travel to wherever the train's destination happened to be. As he grew up, Jimmy traveled right along with her. Unlike most other children of his age, he didn't get much time to work on the farm, spending a relatively limited amount of time milking cows and retrieving eggs from the chicken coop.

As a result of traveling with his grandmother, the time Jimmy spent playing with his childhood friends was spotty: "I'd be goin' and comin'," he said. "I would stay for a while. Then they wouldn't see me for the next couple of years."[6] Unfortunately, all the travel meant that Jimmy missed a great deal of school in his formative years in Vance, which he later regretted. It left an indelible mark on him, and years later he would work doubly hard to ensure that his own children had as thorough an education as possible. (Research into Jimmy's childhood is complicated by the fact that he did not live under the same roof as his half brothers and sisters.) As a consequence of being under his grandmother's guardianship, he was subject to the conditions at home created by her particular line of work. Thus he was forced to lead what can only be described as a nomadic lifestyle; her job as a train porter, by definition, required that she travel both frequently and far away.

It comes as no surprise, then, that not much is known about Jimmy's developmental years between the ages of five and twelve, because he was constantly in motion, traveling around the country by railroad car under the arm of his grandmother, who did what she had to do to make ends meet. To be sure, the circumstances were less than ideal, and one can only imagine the trepidation that LeAnna felt whenever she had to remove Jimmy from school to take him along with her on these long and frequent journeys. She knew full well that this was not the ideal life for a child; Jimmy should have been at home, squatting in the backyard in his dirty knee pants with a whole mess of other kids his own age, shooting marbles, or romping through Mississippi mud just for the fun of it. Jimmy's aunt Annie Lou (LeAnna's youngest daughter) was not old enough to look after Jimmy herself, which was probably why LeAnna opted to take him with her. Then again, maybe she just needed the company.

Jimmy's home life was further complicated around 1950 when his grandmother LeAnna (now well into her fifties) met Henry Rogers, a light-skinned handsome man. Most likely, LeAnna (who had reclaimed her maiden name of Miller by then since her husband, William Jackson, had passed) moved her family, along with Jimmy, to Charleston, Mississippi, where she married Henry Rogers and became LeAnna Rogers. This union led to an entirely new set of stepbrothers and stepsisters for Jimmy, who was raised as *their* brother. This was the family that Jimmy came to know, and Charleston was the city where he would eventually discover the blues as a teenager. While he had the stability of living with his grandmother, step-grandfather, aunts, and possibly Henry's children, he saw little of his own mother, brothers, and sisters.

Getting to the roots of Jimmy Rogers's family tree is a difficult task at best. And Jimmy eventually added yet another layer to the degree of complexity—as if the roots of his lineage weren't already complicated enough. In an attempt to establish his own identity as a teenager, he pondered how he wanted to be referred to. He had several options: first, the surname of his biological father, Roscoe *Lane*, was a possibility; second, he could choose his stepfather, Henry *Hall*'s surname; a third consideration was the surname of his grandmother LeAnna's husband, Henry *Rogers*.

What he ended up with would be a combination of the first and third options. Initially Jimmy chose to retain the last name Lane in order to keep the surname of the man who was his actual blood relative, passing up the opportunity to be James Hall or even James Rogers. "I had always been going under Lane," he admitted. "I got my social security card under that one and came on through that way."[7] Thus, as an adolescent, he was known to all as James Lane. As an adult, however, he reconsidered his initial choice and became Jimmy Rogers. "I grabbed his name when I became a professional musician," Jimmy explained.

More than likely this decision was made because Henry Rogers actually spent more time raising Jimmy than either his actual father, Roscoe Lane, or his mother's husband, Henry Hall. Clearly, LeAnna and Henry Rogers had treated Jimmy like their son, not their grandson, and raised him as the older brother in the family. Consequently, he viewed his Rogers "aunts and uncles" as his own younger siblings. Jimmy stated, "Well, I had that name because of my sisters and brothers [in actuality, they were his step-aunts and -uncles]. My stepfather [i.e., step-grandfather] was a Rogers, and they used to call me a Rogers, too."

Even so, Jimmy never did sign his name that way, from childhood throughout adulthood. "I sign it 'J. A. Lane,'" Jimmy told a reporter in a 1972 interview.[8]

Indeed, out of hundreds of interviews over the illustrious career of the man who became known as Jimmy Rogers, he never spoke of any significant influence on his life by the person who would have played the role of his step-grandfather. Only his choice of the name Rogers might indicate such an influence. Whatever the case may be, what is certain is that despite the interruptions in his schooling, Jimmy did love the frequent trips on the train and looked forward to them; they offered the kind of adventure children rarely experience. And although he could not have realized it at the time, the long hours and thousands of miles he logged during his early years on the road would serve as superb training for the life that lay ahead of him.

Jimmy never ran with a large group when he was younger, but he did have two especially close pals in Vance: Moody Jones and James "Snooky" Pryor. Jimmy met Snooky (then known to Jimmy as "Bubba") in 1934. Jimmy was just beyond ten years old. Destined to become a Chicago harp legend, Snooky Pryor grew up about five miles outside of Vance and became one of Jimmy's closest childhood friends when he was around nine years old. He and Jimmy would go rabbit hunting together, Jimmy with his .22 rifle and Snooky with his three-foot stick, which he used to "tap" the rabbits. According to Jimmy, Snooky was an amazing talent when it came to using his home-fashioned stick to kill wild game: "Man, he could throw that stick. He didn't need no gun . . . he'd have four, five, six rabbits. We'd take 'em to my grandmother at home . . . I'd skin 'em, wash 'em . . . she'd salt 'em, put him in a pan with a little vinegar and let him sit there for a few hours . . . Taste better than chicken."[9] Snooky, even in his later years, was proud of his accomplishments during the times he and Jimmy wandered in the woods. "They had rifles," he recalled, "but I'd kill as many as they did with a stick this long. I'd trim the end, put a metal tap on it, put a nail up in it so the tap wouldn't come out. I'd kill a rabbit runnin' with that tap stick. I'd shoot birds out of the air with a slingshot, too."[10]

There are few remaining stories that exist about the people and places near Vance or Charleston that shaped Jimmy's life. Apparently his natural tendencies were to keep to himself socially. This temperament, combined with the strict principles of his grandmother, led to limited outside activity beyond maintaining his daily routine of schoolwork and household chores. Consequently, he developed into somewhat of a loner, although there was never a clear indication that he was *lonely*. From what can be gathered, his involvement with music served as a fair companion and kept him in good company in the early days. He always had Snooky, and his other good friend, Moody, to look forward to seeing at school—when he was there. There was, however, another particular young man who grew up in the same neighborhood when Jimmy lived in Vance. He stood out in Jimmy's childhood memory as an older kid who sought the affections of one of his relatives. His name was John Lee Hooker.

Evidently, John Lee (born August 22, 1917) had a thing for Jimmy's aunt Annie Lou, who, like her mother LeAnna, looked a lot younger than she actually was. "Most people thought she was my sister but she was my baby aunt. She was about three [or four] years older than me. He liked *her*, so he protected *me*. In fact, the last time I saw him, he asked about her . . . [Annie Lou] never did like him too tough durin' that time," Jimmy later recalled.[11]

While Jimmy's physical stature was unimposing for his age, John Lee's build was even more so, with a lean, taut frame that would remain the same throughout his lifetime. "I was something like maybe 12 or 13," Jimmy explained, "and he was much older than me [nearly seven years] but he was a small guy, you know, so he would be around with me and some more boys who were my age." Because of John Lee's size and gentle demeanor, he was thought to be easy prey for the bullies in the area. According to Jimmy, they were sadly mistaken: "He was a real hard little fella! Y'know, boys'll pick on you if they don't like you and he was small . . . But see, he was old and hard so he could fight! He'd win most of the fights he was in 'cause he was older than the guy who was attackin'.' That's why we got to be real good friends, 'cause he was a good boxer, good with his fists. Me, I never like to fight."[12]

From early 1936 to early 1938, when Jimmy was between the ages of twelve and fourteen, he left Vance for almost two years when he went with his grandmother to West Memphis, Arkansas, which was where he first encountered James Peck Curtis, Joe Willie Wilkins, and Robert Junior Lockwood. Although Jimmy wasn't as mature as they were, they allowed him to accompany the group, due to his persistence and fascination with the blues life. "They recognized me and respected me as a young musician tryin' to learn," he said, "and I appreciate all those guys for that."[13]

This was an important, formative period in Jimmy's musical life. About the West Memphis days, Jimmy said, "It was swingin' over there, man. At the roller rink it was a club there . . . they'd get together and throw the big balls." In addition to slide guitar wizard Houston Stackhouse and the harp shark Sonny Boy Williamson II, other young artists in the West Memphis area were gradually maturing, and Jimmy saw them all on a fairly regular basis. Three faces in particular—Junior Parker, B. B. King, and Little Milton—were singing spiritual songs during that time, well before they began their secular life of blues.[14]

Jimmy spent a good part of his early years—when he wasn't traveling—going to school part-time and listening to music full-time. Barely a teenager by now, he realized that music would play a major role his life. "As far back as I can remember, I always liked music," he said. "I first started playing music in Charleston. I was about 13 years old. I was listening to records such as Roosevelt Sykes, Memphis Slim, Peetie Wheatstraw, the original 'Sonny Boy' [Williamson]."[15]

Jimmy and his grandmother returned to Charleston after her job on the train was completed. During the second half of 1938, when he was about fourteen, Jimmy met several players in Vance whom he would later encounter in Chicago; one of them was Theodore Roosevelt Taylor. The young man who oddly had six fingers on both of his hands would later become better known in Chicago as "Hound Dog" Taylor, but once had a different nickname. It was "Nitter" when he and Jimmy knew each other in Vance.[16]

LeAnna Rogers was a hardworking, churchgoing woman, who lived her life "according to the Good Book." She prayed and attended worship services dutifully and tuned in regularly to the gospel radio programs that kept the soulful strains of the spiritual quartets and choirs wafting through the air as she went about her daily duties at home. Sundays, of course, were sacred, and she faithfully attended church to keep herself bound in the service of her Lord and Savior. In the typical fashion of the deeply religious black Christians of the South, she could not reconcile herself to what was widely considered the "devil's music." For LeAnna Rogers, listening to the blues was a sacrilegious act that was simply not tolerated in her household. *Playing* the blues was unthinkable.

As a teenager Jimmy would have much preferred to live with his mother. He knew that Grossie was nowhere near as strict as his grandmother LeAnna, who had little tolerance for the worldly ways of those who were clearly on the path of sin. She gave Jimmy very little latitude when it came to making time for music. Her home was an environment he didn't necessarily appreciate, as he so desperately wanted to spend more time roaming the streets with his two buddies, catching up on the latest sounds coming out of the juke joints, and maybe even running into one of the bluesmen as they stumbled out of one joint and into the next.

Jimmy found ways to sneak beyond his grandmother's grasp and get the blues feeling any way he could, no matter what the risk. According to Jimmy, "I['d] just taken it up on my own and by chances I would go over to a friend's house that had guitar, piano, something like that. They taken me behind their back and jam a while, you know what I mean." As far as Jimmy knew, there was not a strong legacy of blues musicians in his family's history. Instead, his family maintained a deeply religious background in the Delta: "They's really against music—blues, period."[17] Childhood friend Snooky Pryor grew up with the same circumstances in his household, saying he also had to sneak around just to get a chance at trying to blow a few notes. Had he gotten caught, he later said, "my old man would have killed me . . . he hated that kind of music . . . told me that was the devil's music."[18]

Jimmy gives his grandmother credit for keeping his head on straight and helping him stay out of trouble during those times. According to his memory, she "kept me clean of bein' with police records and stuff . . . she taught me to respect the ladies, too." When it came to discipline, his grandmother didn't hesitate to tan his backside when it came to teaching Jimmy the difference between right and wrong: "She would get this hide [his rear end] . . . she'd break those switches together and get that butt, boy. And they hurt. So I was a pretty good guy."[19] Still, Jimmy couldn't resist the urge to make music. Unlike his grandmother, he loved the blues from the start and would not be denied the chance to recreate the sounds he heard on the radio, even if it meant taking the risk of catching a beating. Around the age of fourteen he experimented with the harmonica, saying, when trying to recall the year that he tried to imitate his harp heroes, it "musta been 'long about 1937–38."[20]

The next couple of years would also find Jimmy exploring the sounds of the guitar, an instrument he was attracted to almost as much as the harmonica. It was 1939 and he was almost sixteen years old. Like dozens of other aspiring blues babies, Jimmy had seen many of the older guys handcraft their own instruments, using baling wire to form a resonator from the taut string. His first guitar, then, was what was known as a "diddley bow," a simple wire that was nailed against the outside of the house wall.[21] "I used to have a broom wire with a sweeping broom holding it together," Jimmy said. "I had that sort of thing. I'd get a bottle and run it up and down, get different sounds."[22] Crude though it may have been, in the world of social dissonance that typified the black experience in the Deep South during the late 1930s, it was all the sound he needed to quench the craving for something melodic. As often as he could, and at the risk of his own hide, Jimmy sought out the sound of his lyrical companion. "At night the wind would be blowin' and the wire would be singin', 'woooo,'" Jimmy remembered. "I had to wrap a rag around it to keep my grandmother from hearin'. When she'd leave in the mornin', man, I'd go wild. I'd be havin' a ball and she never did know what I'd been doin' all day."[23]

Indeed, Jimmy much preferred to be totally ensconced in his favorite pastime, which was music, all the time. He grew up listening to the local favorite, John Lee "Sonny Boy" Williamson—the *original* Sonny Boy, who was from Jackson, Mississippi. Many still refer to him as Sonny Boy I.[24] Jimmy's closest childhood friend, Snooky Pryor, reminisced:

> Yeah, me and Jimmy Rogers growed up together. He was a couple of years younger than me . . . I used to walk over to his house to get him. It took me, aw, shit, a hour, maybe two hours walkin' to get there. Then we'd both walk on to get the rest of 'em. There were about six of us little fellas doin' it. Myself, Jimmy Rogers, a little boy called Kitten, one called Go, one called Brother-hood, and one called Jack. We used to all get in a circle there [in Vance] and we *aaaall* used to try to play harmonica.[25]

In the early days Jimmy and Snooky would travel together on foot to find good live music to listen to at the nearest juke joint. Often this meant walking for long distances. According to Snooky, "It wouldn't be nothin' for us to walk five or eight miles together . . . to get to where the hot spot was!" Jimmy, Snooky, and Moody Jones were ecstatic if they as much as caught a glimpse of Sonny Boy, or even heard a rumor about his being in town. They were all listening to the music of Roosevelt Sykes, Memphis Slim, and Peetie Wheatstraw. During the time Jimmy and his pals ran the streets together, it was actually Jimmy who was well known as "Snooky," a name given to him by his grandmother and cousins. "And they was calling me 'Snook' then," Rogers recalled. "My grandmother gave me that nickname . . . I didn't know why she started callin' me that."[26] Pryor, on the other hand, was simply known as "Bubba." The nicknames would be com-pletely switched some years later, as "Bubba" would take "Snooky" as his new nickname when Jimmy left for Chicago and Pryor went into the military. Pryor said he took it because he admired Jimmy's harmonica playing so much and wanted to be like him. Jimmy didn't mind at all, and they would both get a big laugh out of it many years later.[27]

Jimmy introduced Snooky to his friends, who were all interested in play-ing harmonica at the time. Three of them formed a harmonica trio, and each purchased a harp for the princely sum of fifty cents. Jimmy's brand preference was the Hohner Marine Band: it always won out over the American Ace, which he regarded as a cheap instrument. Soon, Snooky and Jimmy, and two other pals Jimmy had picked up—Levi "Gold" Lee and his brother, Marion "Kitten" Lee—formed a harmonica quartet. "We'd noise the whole neighborhood," he said. The four friends did their best imitation of Sonny Boy's style when they had their regular harp huddles. Of the entire group, Jimmy was the best of them and won both the admiration and envy of Snooky Pryor. "[Snooky] used to be jealous of me with the harmonica," Jimmy recalled. "I was pretty good with it. I don't know how good, but he said he wished he could play like me."[28]

One day word spread that Sonny Boy Williamson II—Aleck "Rice" Miller— was coming through Vance, much to the delight of the boys. At the time, he was traveling under the name of Sonny Boy Miller. Jimmy remembered it well: "He had a bunch of us followin' him around, man . . . He had some harmonicas around his waist. He'd get out there and play—sit on a corner, store fronts, any- where he could make him a few quarters. His playin' sounded pretty to me."[29] Snooky agreed with Jimmy, saying Sonny Boy II "used to be standin' up there on top of an old money chest or somethin' like that . . . standin' there for every- body to see him, and he's blowin' like hell and have him a shoebox of money . . . and in those days and times he was the best goin'. I mean, he had a style that nobody else had, and in those days and times—like we make these harps squeal now—couldn't nobody do it. Nobody but him."[30]

Rice Miller was in many ways somewhat of a gunslinger back in those days, because he was on a mission: to leave no question as to who was the heaviest player around. Whenever he played he tried to make such a lasting impression that every person who saw him would go slack-jawed after the first phrase he blew. He did it all with the highest degree of showmanship, something the local townspeople had never seen before. "He was callin' hisself 'Little Boy Blue,'" said Snooky. "I know the reason he did it. [The original] Sonny Boy's records were sellin' . . . they wasn't publishin' the pictures and things on records, well, he could fool anybody. And so he was gettin' more publicity than [the real] Sonny Boy was." When asked just how talented Sonny Boy II was when it came to directly imitating the original Sonny Boy or any other competition around, Pryor was definitive in his response, saying, "He could do 'em all. Only one difference: he could do 'em better."[31]

Jimmy and Snooky also listened to an albino named John Blissett play house parties, and, according to Pryor, Blissett could really play the harp: "He couldn't play but two things—*Highway 51* and *Mississippi Dragline*, but let me tell you, he could blow the piss out of 'em."[32] For Pryor, Blissett showed real promise and outranked even other contemporaries whom he and Jimmy thought were top- shelf players. "I think he was a little bit better than Sonny Terry," Pryor said.[33]

Because he was still underage, Jimmy usually had to sneak into the juke joints to see his favorite artists, which included Son House, Hound Dog Taylor, Robert Petway, and Tommy McClennan (who Jimmy claims got "ripped off" by Little

Richard when he sang the *wop-bob-a-lu-bop-a-lop-bam-boom* vocal riff on the 1950s hit "Tutti Frutti"). Beyond that, Jimmy liked to hang around outside of local watering holes and strain his ears to listen attentively to the jukeboxes, known locally as "Seabirds," a substituted vernacular for the actual brand name of Seeburg. "We'd be standing around out there under the lights, just be practicin' our harps," said Jimmy. "They'd be playin' one record after another."

Tampa Red, Memphis Minnie, Big Bill Broonzy, Memphis Slim—they were all the rage at the time, and patrons of the juke joints would be guzzling corn whiskey and swinging to the music, doing the latest local dance crazes like the jitterbug, Lindy Hop, and what Jimmy remembered as "Pullin' the Skiff."[34] The artists Jimmy heard on the shellac 78s were his main influences, and he dreamed of someday having the opportunity to share the stage with them. Before long he realized that being an accomplished blues musician had become a recurring dream of his—not while he was asleep, but while he was actively doing his daily chores around the house. His thoughts would soon turn to action as he gradually gravitated toward what would soon become his early life as a bluesman.

He was still too young to get inside the juke joints that he so desperately wanted to enter just to mingle with the grownups, lean against the Seeburg, and eyeball some slick chick who could really take a spin on the dance floor. He and his young homeboys would always resort to finding a willing accomplice who could go inside, get them a drink, and hustle it out the door so that they could steal away and pass the bottle in private. Jimmy and his boys pooled their money together and bought their half-pint for twenty-five cents and got their brief buzz from the one or two shots apiece. After talking stuff like the grownups did, the trio would break up their little party, and he'd head for home, hoping that his grandmother was still clinging to the lie he'd told about being at his friend Leroy's house the whole time he was away.

When Arthur Johnson (the uncle of famed Chicago bluesman Luther "Guitar Junior" Johnson) heard rumors that Jimmy was getting pretty proficient on the guitar, he set out to prove that he, Johnson, was the best in the area. He came from Minter City and went looking for Jimmy, who was about to encounter his first showdown. Johnson was a huge fan of the music of Arthur "Big Boy" Crudup's blues style. His showdown with Jimmy finally took place. "He was supposed to been a very fine guitar man durin' that time, and he heard about me," Jimmy recalled. "And he wanted to cut my head, as they say, you know. So he came over to our house and he heard me play." As it turned out, Jimmy had little to worry about. "He was gonna show me something, but instead I showed *him*!" Jimmy crowed years later. "I had found my way how to tune in different keys and stuff. I really surprised him. Then he wanted to be with me then to play gigs and he started takin' me to gigs with him, and like that."[35] Arthur Johnson, later known as Little Arthur, eventually moved to Chicago (not to be confused with harmonica player Little Arthur Duncan, also in Chicago).

While Jimmy had never met or heard much of John Lee Williamson—Sonny Boy I—he got regular exposure to Rice Miller (the eventual Sonny Boy II) as he listened for him on the radio when they played the *King Biscuit Time*, the most popular radio program among blacks in the South. "I would run home and listen to his records every day around 12:00 to hear him," Jimmy exclaimed. "It came on at 12:45, and I'd be digging every *inch* of his sounds."[36]

Jimmy got his first big break when he ran into Miller when he came to play a gig in Phillip, which was about ten miles away from Vance. Jimmy, Snooky, and the rest of the gang all wanted to hitch a ride in Arthur Johnson's pickup truck, which couldn't hold them all comfortably. That never deterred the boys, who surely looked like a motley crew. "We'd all get on the back, get on the fenders, everywhere," Jimmy remembered fondly. "We were just hangin' on there, man, *ridin*."[37] Miller's gig was especially significant to Jimmy; even though he'd seen Rice come through town and blow his harp on the streets alone, it was Jimmy's first time ever to actually see a live performance of a full band.

The venue was a typical juke joint, with the small room in front serving as the main club space, with tables and chairs in the back. Surprisingly, the acoustics in these haunts were typically excellent—after all, they were always located out in the open country. While there were few other architectural obstructions to contend with during the late 1930s in the Delta region, the night sounds would travel for several yards down the road in any direction. "You would get a big enough sound to hear and play okay," Jimmy remembered. "If the party was a nice size bedroom, they'd move all the stuff out, put it in another room somewhere . . . and when you'd sing somethin', it would sound. You could hear it soundin' *real* good, an echo sound."[38]

The cost of entry was one or two quarters apiece, and the boys could afford that. The band would be hot that night: Rice Miller, backed by Robert Junior Lockwood (guitar), Joe Willie Wilkins (guitar), Peck Curtis (drums), and Robert "Dudlow" Taylor (piano), a huge man affectionately known as "Five-by-Five," a moniker used—just like Count Basie's vocalist Jimmy Rushing—to jokingly hint that Taylor was as wide as he was tall. He was characterized as "a man that had no personality, nothing whatsoever but a good mind for the blues, a good heart and a good pair of hands. He didn't know an A-minor chord from a B-flat."[39] Robert Junior Lockwood, whose mother had been heavily courted by the legendary blues guitarist Robert Johnson, was born on March 27, 1915, and raised on his grandfather's 160-acre farm not too far from Helena, Arkansas.[40] Jimmy heard Rice Miller's band regularly on KFFA out of Helena on the popular show *King Biscuit Time*, which started near the end of 1941. Now he would get to hear it live.

Jimmy first met Marion Walter Jacobs somewhere between 1942 and 1943 when the two met in Helena, both tagalongs, hanging around Lockwood, Miller, and guitarist Robert Nighthawk (whose real name was Robert Lee McCollum; he also went by McCoy, his mother's maiden name).[41] This would prove to be the place and time where Rogers would learn the appropriate lessons for how to accompany harmonica players, and also how to hold down the second-line guitar part securely.

Born in Marksville, Louisiana, on May 1, 1930, Marion Jacobs (better known by his middle name, Walter) was only twelve or thirteen at the time he introduced himself to Jimmy, who described Walter at that time as looking like "a little squirrel-faced boy."[42] Originally a devout copycat of Sonny Boy Williamson I, Walter got a full dose of Sonny Boy II and was forever changed. But during this early period, he was virtually invisible to the veterans, who had little use for him. He made an impression on Jimmy, who said, "He was a little boy then [around 1942]. I was maybe around 17 or 18 years old . . . he was kinda on the same musical route like I did . . . They didn't want to recognize him, but he was learnin' something, see."[43] Walter got his opportunity to play with the veterans in much the same manner as Jimmy: you waited until the stars of the show wanted to go and gamble in the back room, and that's when you got your shot on the stage.

Jimmy remembered when the man who became known as "Little Walter" was still in the shadow of "Big Walter" Horton back in Memphis, well before he would dominate the entire blues world in Chicago. Horton, who was thirteen years Walter's senior, would try to pass on the experience and wisdom he earned the hard way. But Walter wasn't interested, or at least it appeared that way. According to Rogers, "Big Walter would tell him this and that, and Little Walter just throw his hat off." Still Jimmy knew that Walter was listening and noticed that he'd slink off and "practice it by himself, then come back and it'd work. Big Walter showed Little Walter lots of cuts but he wouldn't admit to it."[44]

Helena proper and West Helena were places where the blacks congregated on a regular basis, where they felt comfortable letting their hair down to get their boogie on. Right along with that came the typical roughnecks and violence that often accompanied the good-time party atmosphere that drew them all there. "Beer was served in cups. Whiskey you had to drink out of the bottle," guitarist

Johnny Shines remembered. "See, they couldn't use mugs in there because the people would commit mayhem, tear people's heads up with those mugs. Rough places they were."[45] Indeed, these places were the exact type of environment that Jimmy learned to hate and ultimately spent the rest of his life trying to avoid. To Jimmy, violence was simply bad for his health.

Fighting never did interest Jimmy. More important to him was the gambling room in the back, where the heavy action took place. As expected, Sonny Boy Williamson II would kick off the evening by playing a hot set. Then he'd sneak off to the back room and join the crap game already in full swing. This was how Jimmy got a chance to play for his first audience—Sonny Boy handed the instrument to Jimmy when he wanted a backroom break. "Sonny Boy liked me 'cause I could blow that harmonica and flail the guitar," Jimmy recalled.[46]

Jimmy also recalled that there were a few really good slide guitar players during that time. "One of the best, they called him [Houston] Stackhouse," Jimmy recalled. "And then the next real good slide man down there was Robert Nighthawk. He was about the finest out of the whole bunch."[47] Eventually Joe Willie joined the fray, and Robert Junior Lockwood too, although he was there just to monitor the situation, which usually got out of hand after a while. Jimmy remembered the nights vividly: "People was dangerous about fightin' and stuff around with gamblin'. I didn't think about, 'I could get killed.' But I *would* think, 'if my grandmother knew I was there, boy, I was in *big* trouble.' So I would stay out there where the dance was goin' on."[48]

There would be a real benefit to staying out on the floor that particular night: Jimmy got to play with the band in Joe Willie's place, because Joe Willie was too busy in the back room with Sonny Boy. According to Jimmy, "We'd be on the stage just playin', and I'd take Joe Willie's guitar . . . I wasn't afraid or ashamed to play it. Whatever they was playin' I was just jumpin' in and playin' what I knew about it and keep up with it."[49]

Jimmy's first big break was significant for yet another reason: it was his first direct encounter with six strings being amplified. "Freakiest sound I'd ever heard," he said. "I had never played an electric guitar, and I didn't play one again until I got to Chicago."[50] He obviously made a pretty good impression, because shortly thereafter he began picking up gigs with his once-rival Arthur Johnson, who now fully accepted Jimmy as a legitimate contender on the local scene, and the two chose to team up rather than cut each other down. The act always went well, until the alcohol would gradually catch up with Arthur, leading him to shift gears from being a performer to being a backroom gambler. It didn't take long for Jimmy to routinely accept the role of guitarist, dropping his harmonica and picking up Johnson's acoustic guitar. Eventually Jimmy found himself being drawn more to the guitar than the harmonica. He had his reasons: "To get the girls, man. That's what it was about."[51]

As the 1930s wore on, Jimmy began doing more gigs in Vance and surrounding areas, and eventually he traveled in higher circles within the fraternity of blues musicians. His efforts to expand his reputation paid off; he went on his first road gig with some of the best musicians in the area, including Sonny Boy, Joe Willie Wilkins, and Chester Burnett—better known as Howlin' Wolf. The group traveled on a regular basis to Memphis, Tennessee, which had a curfew requiring all patrons to be off the streets by a certain time if they wanted to avoid problems with the police. West Memphis did not have such restrictions; it was, as Jimmy put it, "wide open." The band traveled by both car and bus to make their regular paying gigs, playing first at a roller rink in Memphis and then on to West Memphis to perform at a club called the Baby Grand. "Sometimes we'd get $3 a night, $5 at most, a drink of whiskey and $2. But this was something I wanted to *do*. I wanted to learn."[52]

As to where he felt he first earned his reputation, Jimmy said, "I had my first becoming to be known in the blues field, it [was] really in Memphis. That's where I really was known, through Robert Junior Lockwood, through Willie Wilkins, and Sonny Boy . . . that's where I met all those guys . . . and that was just what I liked, the type of music that they were playing, you know. I felt at home doing that."[53] Nevertheless, the road was always a stern taskmaster, and Jimmy was gradually learning how to deal with less than ideal conditions when the band hit the highway.

Adjusting to sometimes strained situations included finding the best way to silently suffer the various personalities the band boasted. Chester "Howlin' Wolf" Burnett was uniquely gifted with a double-barrel blast of country blues that emanated from his voice like a man possessed. He was a consummate showman, even if his harmonica skills were relatively marginal compared to the heavyweights like Sonny Boy. To some, Howlin' Wolf came across as ignorant in the purely academic sense. Others felt like he was playing it up and actually was a lot smarter than he let on. But there was one thing all musicians agreed about when it came to dealing with the man: Wolf had one of the strongest personalities when it came to being strict and stubborn about how he wanted his music to be presented to the public.

The problem was, Wolf was fairly irregular when it came to his vocal phrases. In the course of performing a typical twelve-bar blues, Wolf would get the beat "turned around," so to speak, making his entries sometimes in the middle of a phrase, one beat short, two or three beats beyond the phrase, or anywhere in between. It drove most backing musicians crazy trying to follow him. To complicate matters even further, Wolf always blamed the backing band members for the disruptive, uneven patterns he caused; the tune always felt like it was about to fall apart at any minute. Remarkably, it almost always hung together, even if it wasn't pretty. Jimmy would find himself doing his best to follow Wolf's patterns, which required every bit of his focused attention, lest he be blamed for being the cause of it all. As Jimmy explained:

> Wolf's timing was bad. Maybe mine wasn't the best in the world but it was pretty good. His timin', he would try to lay on his pattern. He'd follow the pattern through. If it were four beat or six beat he would really try to lay as close to it as he could and it was up to the band to keep him straight; if they don't keep him straight and follow what he's doin', things are gonna goof up and then you got a problem out of Wolf. I found that out at a real early stage there. He was kind of a hard guy to try to get through to because you didn't understand where he was coming from and he couldn't explain to you where he wanted you to go.[54]

Since Jimmy's grandmother still worked as a porter for the Illinois Central Railroad, cleaning the traveling cars, he continued his travels to St. Louis, a routine he'd established since 1938 and would continue off and on for several years. He had no regular work as a gigging musician there, though not for lack of trying. The gigs just weren't that plentiful in St. Louis, and those musicians who had gigs weren't in the mood to share. Jimmy would typically wander across the bridge out of St. Louis proper into East St. Louis, where the black clubs were. By this time his grandmother had stopped wondering where he was drifting to; she well knew what his passion was, and she also knew she was powerless to stop him. She wisely abandoned the switch after Jimmy grew substantially larger in physical stature. "She'd always say, 'I better leave him alone, but he done sold hisself to the devil!'"[55]

According to Jimmy, "After I got of age, my grandmother, she just seen the place where she wasn't gonna be able to stop me from tryin' to play, so she just give me up. Said, 'well, OK, you can do what you want to as far as that's concerned.'"[56] After finally receiving her blessings, Jimmy pursued his passion with a vengeance, practicing along with records, and chose not to spend too much time participating in the small, loose jam sessions that took place. This would be a theme that would follow him the rest of his life: the preference for a more controlled, disciplined atmosphere where the musical experience could unfold at the apex.[57]

When he was fifteen, in 1939, Jimmy traveled with his grandmother to Chicago and stayed for a year, then went to Memphis, then back to Mississippi. Jimmy had cousins, aunts, and uncles everywhere, a situation that would serve him well in later years when he turned professional and was running up and down the road, exhausting his resources and needing a resting place. He also discovered musical talent among his relatives: "I had quite a few of my relatives scattered around the South—Georgia. Some in Texas, and I met some boys in Mississippi—they're musicians now. One, they call him Homesick James . . . I met him while I was visiting my aunt, as a child, maybe 13, 14."[58] James (born in Somerville, Tennessee, on May 3, 1914) was a slide guitarist who claimed to be the cousin of Elmore James, bought him his first guitar, and even taught James how to play slide.

During this period, Robert Junior Lockwood and Sonny Boy were tag-teaming pretty well while they performed together across the South as a guitar-harp duo. But then an incident occurred between the two veterans. According to Jimmy, "Something happened between Sonny Boy and Robert Junior, and he had Robert Nighthawk to replace him on guitar." Thus, when Jimmy was around twenty-two, he played right beside both of his idols onstage: he joined Rice Miller's band and played along with Robert Nighthawk. His opportunity came when Miller wanted to go and gamble in the back room. "I got to talkin' with Sonny Boy [Miller] and some of the fellows in the group there," Jimmy said. "And he wanted to hear what I sound like, so he put me on the stage when he was in the back room gambling."[59]

During this time the KFFA broadcast in Helena made the town the hottest place to be for any serious bluesman. The radio show was the drawing card for musicians all around to converge upon the town, and it could be heard throughout Mississippi, Arkansas, Missouri, and Tennessee. If you got some airplay, you knew it was the best promotional material anywhere, and there would soon be bookings to follow. The financial rewards reaped after each broadcast kept blues musicians coming from everywhere. "That's where the whole bunch were, right there in Helena," Jimmy reminisced, citing Willie Love, Elmore James, and a teenage Little Walter Jacobs. Although Jimmy never got an opportunity to play over the airwaves on the *King Biscuit* radio show with either Sonny Boy or Robert Nighthawk, eventually Little Walter would have his chance.[60] Indeed, Walter increased his position when he landed the gig at the KFFA radio station with a sponsor of Mother's Best Flour.

By 1940 Jimmy shuttled regularly between St. Louis and Chicago in search of regular gigs in either city. He soon realized that on the Missouri side there were "mostly piano players and a few harmonica players" but very little work for struggling guitarists. In East St. Louis he would camp out at Ned Love's, where he'd run into Roosevelt Sykes and Walter Davis, who would allow him to sit in, though he wasn't given any money. He also realized that the St. Louis scene could get pretty rough. "They'd fight in a minute down there. And that would be the end of me when they start fightin', I'd get to goin'," Jimmy would say, thinking about his longevity and how senseless it would be to ruin his career early on to some idiot who had nothing to lose. "I want to die in my old age, you know?"[61]

2

CHICAGO BOUND

We knew we were doing something different, but
we never knew how good we really were. We took
the blues of Big Bill Broonzy, Memphis Minnie,
and Tampa Red and we put it on the beat.

—Jimmy Rogers

The impact that Jimmy Rogers, Muddy Waters, and Little Walter had on the history of Chicago blues was so huge that many people actually believe there wasn't much of a blues scene happening before their arrival in the mid-1940s. Nothing could be further from the truth. There was so much happening then that Jimmy, Muddy, and Little Walter all had to earn their way into an already thriving scene in Chicago. Indeed, it was serendipitous that the artists who had the town sewn up just happened to be the same ones Jimmy had worshipped back in Mississippi, when he heard recordings blaring out of the juke joints, or when he was fortunate enough to have personal encounters with them while he was earning his stripes as a novice in West Memphis, Helena, or St. Louis.

All of the famous names Jimmy acknowledged as a child were booked in whichever Chicago bars would have live music: Tampa Red, Big Maceo Merriweather, Lonnie Johnson, Big Bill Broonzy, Memphis Slim, Memphis Minnie, Sleepy John Estes, and John Lee "Sonny Boy" Williamson—the *original* Sonny Boy. Williamson lived in Jackson, Tennessee, but then arrived in Chicago in 1937 and joined the Bluebird label in May of that year to record with Joe Williams and Robert Nighthawk. Jimmy had already met Sonny Boy II back in the Mississippi Delta hotspots of Helena and West Memphis; now he was trying to get on the inside track with Sonny Boy I. He had made an exploratory journey to Chicago as early as 1943, arriving by train with his grandmother. After taking a look around, he decided he liked it, but he wasn't able to stay, because his grandmother moved them to St. Louis for approximately two years, between 1943 and 1945. It was there that he spent time trying to fit into the club scene, sitting in with legendary local pianists Roosevelt Sykes and Walter Davis.[1] Jimmy learned quickly that some of his musical colleagues in the St. Louis area weren't as willing to share their time, talent, or resources as those he had encountered back at home in Mississippi. Due to the closed ranks of the working musicians there, he would have to try to augment his income as a young professional by taking as many road gigs as he could. It was on one of these numerous trips that he first met his future wife, Dorothy Turner. Jimmy had an engagement in South Bend, Indiana, when he met her in the bar where he was performing. The introverted Dorothy had been encouraged to show up at the venue as a blind date for Jimmy through a mutual friend. "Young and beautiful" was how Jimmy described her. "Dorothy was kind of shy. Her girlfriend put it together for us."[2] The two would eventually marry two decades later.

While Jimmy was sharpening his skills in St. Louis, another Delta-born guitarist was making his way toward the Windy City: McKinley Morganfield, known as Muddy Waters. What Muddy saw when he pulled out of the train depot could not have been too different from what Jimmy witnessed when he had first set eyes upon the bustling urban sprawl that was Chicago. "It looked like this was the fastest place in the world: cabs dropping fares, horns blowing, the peoples walking so fast," Muddy later recalled.[3] He arrived in the Windy City at the age of thirty with high hopes, mingled with amazement; he'd never been in a city with the magnitude and intensity of Chicago. But others had made the transition and met with success, so Muddy was determined to do the same, even if success—or anything else, for that matter—wasn't there to meet him as he emerged from the Illinois Central train station at Twelfth Street and Michigan Avenue in May 1943.[4]

When he first started out, Muddy had already narrowed down the life paths he wanted to pursue, knowing early on that there were few viable options for a black man in the South. "Back then there was three things I wanted to be: a heck of a preacher, a heck of a ballplayer or a heck of a musician," Muddy remembered. Muddy had his own early experiences with the rural South juke joints. In fact, he, unlike Jimmy Rogers, was old and bold enough to run one himself. "I had my little crap table going in the back," Muddy recalled. "I'd put coal oil in bottles, take a rope and hang 'em up there on the porch to let people know my dance was going on, and I had a lot of them lights for people to gamble by. It's pretty hard to see the dice sometimes in that lamplight. They had some fast boys with the dice down there; you had to have good eyes."[5]

In Chicago there would also be ample opportunities to participate in crap games, but only after Muddy learned his way around the city. For now, there was little familiarity with the faces and places he encountered. "I had some people there, but I didn't know where they was," he said. "I didn't know nothing."[6] Fortunately for Muddy, his cousin Dan Jones and Dan's wife were eagerly awaiting his arrival at their South Side apartment, located on the fourth floor at 3656 Calumet Avenue, in a tenement building situated in a primarily black neighborhood that was rough, to say the least. Once Muddy found his relatives, he assumed a fairly lowbrow position in their living quarters: he slept on the couch.[7]

Meanwhile, even though Jimmy's primary residence was in St. Louis, he found every opportunity to ride the train back to Chicago. One of those return trips to the city would help convince him to move there permanently. Near the end of 1944, he realized that the relatively few gigs he was getting in St. Louis were both too infrequent and too unrewarding financially. Although he had made several extended visits earlier, it was not until early 1945 that he made the permanent move to Chicago. His grandmother made sure he was in good hands, putting him in the care of her brother, Willie Miller. "Uncle Willie" lived on Lake Street and had sons about the same age as Jimmy. It wasn't too long, however, before Jimmy found his own place on Peoria Street, located near the famed Maxwell Street area, well known among musicians throughout Chicago as a bustling haven for a wide range of street performers who were there to sharpen their craft.[8] Jimmy felt more comfortable than ever now, surrounded by relatives who were numerous and scattered across several cities, including St. Louis; Detroit; and South Bend, Indiana. It was a perfect setup for Jimmy because it meant he had a place to lay his head whenever he traveled on the road, which was his preferred lifestyle during these lean years.

Now that he had settled into his own apartment, Jimmy wasted no time looking for a day gig to make ends meet. He eventually landed a job working for Sonora Radio and Cabinet Company, where he was responsible for sawing and sanding the wood for cabinets before assembly.[9] It was here that he met Jesse Jones, the brother of Dan Jones. Jesse, also a cousin of Muddy Waters, was a mutual blues fan who held a managerial position at the Sonora plant. Always looking out for Jimmy, Jesse soon promoted him to a higher level that was less risky: spray-painting. Jimmy's new job was to apply the first coating of varnish to the wood after assembly. Jesse Jones "got me into that part where my hands wouldn't get cut off," Jimmy said."[10]

Still, Jimmy did not find himself well suited for the regular nine-to-five lifestyle. "Getting up early in the morning to punch a clock wasn't my style," he quipped years later, showing definite signs that he had a bad case of the blues-man's disease. "I would like to go to bed at four o'clock and sleep 'til noon."[11] At night Jimmy would play little gigs here and there to try to keep himself in the blues game while trying to make ends meet. Along the way he met several fellow musicians who, like himself, were trying to keep afloat musically. He also met non-musicians who actively supported his cause. One particular gentleman, who went by the name of Zene, served as a patron saint for Jimmy whenever weekend gigs were available. "He protected me from guys who wanted to fight, and bought me whiskey," Jimmy recalled.[12]

Because he lived near Maxwell Street, Jimmy could always catch whatever action was going on during the busiest period of the week, Saturdays and Sundays. As early as seven or eight in the morning, dozens of blues artists used Maxwell Street as the official gathering place to socialize with their buddies, participate in extensive all-day jam sessions, and eat the best Polish sausages in the world. The area, known as "Jewtown," was the marketplace for individual entrepreneurs to set up their cardboard tables and hawk their wares, which ranged from cheap watches, to tube socks, to matching sets of hubcaps. Jimmy once said of Maxwell Street, "Jewtown, on Saturdays and Sundays from around eleven o'clock to about five in the evening, you could make more money with three or four guys than you could make in a club in the whole week. Man, there'd be hundreds of peoples around."[13] He said Jewtown was like a carnival every weekend. "After nine o'clock, oh, man, that place was swamped with people and it'd be that way until five, six o'clock in the evening. It's full, like Mardi Gras," he mused.[14]

Maxwell Street represented a legitimate alternative means of making money for the blues artists who couldn't get regular booking at the clubs. There were numerous musicians who got their start as a direct result of being "discovered" on Maxwell Street. There was a certain protocol that was to be maintained between the patrons, the artists, and the residents who actually lived on the city blocks that were converged upon on a weekly basis. "We'd have some guy, give him a couple of bucks if he'd drop a cord out his window down the sidewalk down there," Jimmy recounted. "Two bucks for some juice . . . Then we'd get some crates or maybe he'd give you a chair or box to sit on."[15]

According to Jimmy, the hippest spots to set up shop were at the corners of Maxwell and Peoria, Fourteenth and Peoria, or Halsted and Maxwell. Once a musician established one of those areas as his regular spot, everybody else acknowledged it as such, and no one hassled you about it; you owned that zone for the three or four hours of prime time when blues music filled the streets. People flung open their windows, sat inside the frames with cool drinks on hot days, and soaked up the sun and sound as the shattered glass from old broken bottles shimmered against the sunlight.

As one might expect, the festival atmosphere of Chicago was teeming with musicians who wanted to be discovered by someone who could further their careers. Indeed, there were many aspiring artists whose ultimate desire was to hear themselves on wax for an inexpensive price. Many of the more talented ones discovered that they could get a "dub," or an acetate master copy, from one local entrepreneur, Bernard Abrams, who took advantage of the opportunity to record them. Jimmy spent time down on Maxwell Street working with what was his first band: Jimmy on guitar, John Henry Barbee, Eddie "Porkchop" Hines on drums, Claude Smith on guitar, and a piano player called "King" (according to Jimmy's recollection). Around that same time, local piano legend Sunnyland Slim helped Jimmy and his boys get their first regular gigs at the Club 21, aptly named for its location at 21 North Western Avenue.[16]

Jimmy was now building his reputation and getting better known on both Maxwell Street and in a few clubs. Yet he still hadn't met the man who would become an integral part of his blues future—Jesse Jones's cousin Muddy Waters. Muddy had already arrived in Chicago two years earlier and was pretty much doing the same thing as Jimmy: trying to break into the club scene. Jesse happened to mention that he had a cousin who had come to Chicago from Mississippi. "He just wanted to meet me," said Jimmy.[17] After months of hype about Muddy's talent, Jesse eventually introduced Muddy to Jimmy. Even though he was eleven years older than Jimmy, Muddy appeared—at least from Jimmy's perspective—to be very shy when he arrived at Jimmy's house that day, still a bit intimidated about the fast life in the city. "He came from the South, and he get to Chicago, that's a big city to him and he's afraid of gangsters, Al Capone and all those guys was around," Jimmy recalled. "He was trying to stay away from all that stuff."[18] Still, the two hit it off, and both instinctively knew there was an immediate kind of chemistry between them.

At that time Muddy was living in the 1800 block of Thirteenth Street with his uncle Dan Jones Sr., who had invited him up to Chicago. This was only ten minutes away from where Jimmy lived, so he made a regular routine of visiting Muddy for little two-way jam sessions during times when the house was empty and while everyone who had day jobs was off to work. Jimmy remembered it this way:

> Wouldn't be nobody home but us musicians. We come in, plug up the amp, get us one of these half-pint or pint bottles and get some ideas. We'd run through

a few verses and move on to something else and keep on. Finally, after maybe three or four days fooling around, you'd be done built a number. On weekends, we'd buy a few drinks and play guitar. So we decided then that we'd start this house-party deal over again here in Chicago.[19]

These get-togethers quickly evolved into a series of well-organized, disciplined rehearsals. Soon, however, Muddy's uncle, who managed an apartment building, helped Muddy find his own place in the building. Muddy's new apartment was located on the same block, right up the street from his uncle. He moved up to the second floor into a spacious four-room furnished pad at 1851 West Thirteenth Street for only thirty-five dollars a month and was expected to pay his own light and gas bills.[20] Dan and Jesse Jones's father, Dan Jones Sr., also worked in the furniture business and helped to make Muddy's life a bit more comfortable. Jimmy said, "Old Man Jones fixed Muddy up. Muddy had furniture all through that house, bed and dressers, end tables, stove, refrigerator, a little radio, and a record player."[21]

Jimmy felt a sense of instant familiarity when he met and played with Muddy. He just understood Muddy's personal demeanor and musical sensibility. It was something he'd experienced with several players back when he paid his dues in Helena and West Memphis. "Muddy was a little older and he was the most like ol' Robert Johnson's style with the slide guitar," Jimmy said. "I understood the slide style quite well—I learned guitar in the Delta—so I could back him up good."[22] It was during this period that Jimmy began thinking seriously about making the permanent switch to guitar, and he was toting an acoustic that had been electrified by mounting a DeArmond pickup underneath the strings near the tailpiece. He would adjust his volume and tone from the amplifier to get a sound that rose above the din permeating the black clubs on the South Side, which were usually packed with hard-partying patrons fit tightly inside the low-ceilinged, poorly ventilated establishments.

Now that the two men had found common ground and gotten to know each other well, Jimmy took it upon himself to try to upgrade Muddy's instrument of choice and to get him better adjusted to the rigors of urban musicianship. According to Jimmy's recollection, "He had a Gretsch hollow-box."[23] He explained further: "Muddy had a hollow 'S' curve like the Gene Autry guitar, and I took him to 18th and Halsted and got him a DeArmond pickup put on his guitar, got him a little amplifier, and then you could get a sound out of it."[24]

Because both Muddy and Jimmy had strong family ties to Mississippi, their musical tastes were quite similar, and their philosophical approaches to what good country blues should be also ran along similar lines. It didn't take long for a strong bond to form between the two, and their rehearsals increased in frequency and intensity, to the delight of both men. They meticulously shaped their sound so that the melodic, harmonic, and rhythmic phrases were perfectly sculpted and arranged. The musical lines were practically inseparable, if not for the fact that Muddy focused on developing his slide technique, while Jimmy mastered his single-note countermelodies and rhythmic support. They were slowly cooking up a batch of blues that both West and South Sides would want to taste, and they knew they were onto something that hadn't been done before.

The practice routine evolved into a relationship that emerged as one that was somewhere between two ballet dancers and two heavyweight boxers: They could sling each other around the room and never lose faith in one's ability to catch the other. They could throw hard jabs at each other yet never catch a blow to the body. It was a perfectly choreographed blues dance. They strove for perfection, wanting it to be flawless when they hit the streets with this new groove, so they pushed even harder. "We would just rehearse all the time," Jimmy recalled. "That's all we would do, just lay around and practice, run through songs and build songs and sounds and tones. He [Muddy] was a good bass player and I could play the lead to fit in and we just kept on buildin' that way. Finally we came up with something."[25]

Muddy's cousin Dan got Muddy a job working at Westerngrade Venetian Blind Suppliers, delivering venetian blinds. While he worked the day job—and rehearsed at Jimmy's house—Muddy was doing the same as Jimmy was in order to stay on top of the blues scene: he was out and about, hitting the streets, meeting people, and rubbing elbows with the rest of the blues cats. "It was about a year before he got hooked up with anybody else to do any gigging," Jimmy recalls.[26] Rogers talked in detail about the "scabbin'" method he and a few of his musical associates used in order to make ends meet: "You hit here, you set up with asking this guy that owns the club if he wouldn't mind you playing a few numbers—quite naturally it was good for his business, he would say okay. You'd play a number or two, they'd like it—you'd pick up a buck here, a buck there, y'know."[27]

During this time both Jimmy and Muddy were working diligently to sharpen their skills on guitar. Jimmy concentrated on the urban approach of a single-note, fingerpicking method, while Muddy focused on the rural slide technique. About Muddy's sound, Jimmy said, "He was showin' me some licks that he was doin'—He didn't say this, but this was just sense to me from knowing the background of this style of music. See, it was Son House and Robert Johnson there. He was mostly relying on Robert Johnson's style with the slide."[28] Muddy described himself a bit more accurately: "I call my style *country* style. Big Bill was the daddy of country-style blues singers. When I got here, he was the top man."[29]

Jimmy concurred, saying, "Big Bill Broonzy . . . that was one of my favorites. I liked his guitar and I liked the way he played, so I'd get a few licks out of [him]."[30] Jimmy remembered the impact Broonzy made when he first encountered him. "I was just beginnin' to get somethin' together a little then, and he was playin' Lake Street for Ruby Gatewood's here in Chicago. That was his home stand and he was in the city. He would play on Lake Street for her all the time. And that's where I met him and from then on I would see him. He was a fine fellow. He'd give me a lot of advice about life, and about music and about different things like that, and it paid off. The old man was telling the truth, you know."[31] Indeed, the place affectionately known as "The Gate" was where Broonzy had held court since the mid-1930s, and Memphis Minnie hosted what were known as "Blue Monday" parties there as well.[32]

Jimmy had learned to take heed and learn from the experience of others he respected, trying his best not to make unnecessary mistakes in the business that those who came before him had already made. Indeed, Muddy felt the same reverence for Broonzy: "Big Bill, he don't care where you from. He didn't look over you 'cause he been on records for a long time. 'Do your thing, stay with it, man; if you stay with it, you going to make it.' That's what Big Bill told me. Mostly I try to be like him."[33]

A few years after Muddy had arrived in Chicago in 1943, his grandmother passed away. She remembered Muddy in her will, and Muddy suddenly found himself with an unexpected bundle of cash that allowed him a bit of breathing room for a spell. After he took care of the financial affairs involved with laying his grandmother to rest, he used the remaining money to get himself a car, an item that very few in his circle of friends had. His new set of wheels was a two-door, rust-colored 1940 Chevrolet. As one might expect, his stature rose among the blues players who needed transportation to and from local gigs, especially among those whose gigs were out of town.

In 1946 "almost nobody didn't have a car," Jimmy said, when describing the mobility of blues musicians who needed to get to work. There were several three-day-weekend engagements they had in Peoria, Illinois; Detroit, Michigan; or Gary, Indiana, where club owners often imported Chicago bluesmen to set the standard for what good-time music should sound like. Jimmy recalled, "It was me and Muddy and Sonny Boy and Sunnyland and [drummer] Baby Face Leroy [Foster]. We'd get about ten or fifteen dollars apiece when we'd get a night there . . . For years and years we'd go up there on weekends [in Gary, Indiana]."[34] Jimmy and Muddy would regularly go tooling all about town in that two-door Chevy—the "clean machine"—and after a while they'd be settled down, parked in front of the apartment, passing whiskey in a brown paper bag back and forth. They'd practice all afternoon, cruise around town in the evenings, take more than a few swigs of whiskey between the two of them, and the next day they'd start the routine all over again.

Muddy's car was instrumental in helping him get his foot in the door. "Whenever they had to go out of town, someplace they couldn't ride a bus or get a cab reasonable, then they'd call Muddy—like Gary, or some place like that," Jimmy explained. If Williamson (Sonny Boy I) went along, he would typically drink so much that he would pass out, leaving the lion's share of the work to Muddy and Jimmy. "We'd go on over there and John Lee, Sonny Boy'd get high and I'd play the harp, and Muddy was bumping the bass on the guitar, Sunnyland Slim would bring in the piano and we'd make the gig," said Jimmy.[35]

Muddy's sound was rough around the edges to the ears of some urban blues artists, who much rather preferred that Muddy's glass slide stay in his pocket. They couldn't afford to insult him, though, because they needed his transportation to make it to the gigs. In other words, no Muddy, no money. "They didn't recognize him as a musician, but they would use him because he had the car," Jimmy observed.

Still, Muddy's guitar playing remained too rural for the modern style of Chicago, and the natives were restless when it came to the country blues he had to offer. "They'd get Muddy to plunk along on the bass," Jimmy said. The brazen musical attack of Muddy Waters hadn't yet won over the likes of some of the younger musicians, who hadn't been exposed to the origins of his sound. "The steel that Muddy used on his finger, didn't too many guys try to do that, they didn't really care for it too much," Jimmy recalled. "It was a nice sound for him, but didn't too many guys try to pick up on that style of slide. Son House and Robert Nighthawk helped Muddy to learn what little slide he knew."[36]

Jimmy and Muddy had regular rounds they would make to keep their faces in the places they needed to be seen in order to keep gigging. Clubs located on the South Side could be found at Forty-seventh and Cottage Grove (708 Club), Thirty-fifth and Indiana (Smitty's Corner), or Forty-seventh and South Park (Club De Lisa). Memphis Slim was holding a gig down on the West Side at a club called the Triangle Inn, located at the intersection of the north-south Racine Street and the adjacent Blue Island Avenue, with the east-west Roosevelt Road completing the triangle. Sonny Boy, on harp, was a main attraction for Memphis Slim's gig, which drew large numbers of people who came out just to see him. Almost like clockwork, Sonny Boy would get way too drunk and start a bar brawl, leading to the inevitable tussle that would just about tear the whole building apart with knives and bottles—no guns.[37] Jimmy was the one who bailed him out onstage almost every time, switching from guitar to harp to finish the show.

Now that Jimmy and Muddy were officially a team, they worked almost exclusively as a duo until one of the Jones boys once again arranged a meeting that would have a significant impact on their musical direction. After a chance encounter at a music store, Jesse Jones invited guitarist Claude Smith to Muddy's apartment and introduced the two of them. Claude "Blue Smitty" Smith, from Marianna, Arkansas, had a melismatic, single-string guitar style that, according to blues historian Mike Rowe, was "an awkward compendium of such diverse influences as Crudup, Yank Rachell, and Charlie Christian."[38] "Smitty and I were dealin' together when Muddy came to Chicago," Jimmy recalled. "We was playin' around little parties and different things like that. Smitty was real good at the time, he sure was. Back then he was playing pretty durn good. He had the style you know—most guys was doin' a style thing then—he had his own little thing, ya know."[39]

Smitty was a guitarist whom some regarded as one of the next stars on the blues horizon. Jimmy remembers when Smitty and Muddy were introduced. "I was playing with Smitty and I got a few ideas from him," said Jimmy. "When Muddy came to Chicago, we started hanging around together, him and Smitty and myself."[40] Just like Jimmy, Smitty's encounter with Muddy was one where he tried to offer what knowledge he could to modernize Muddy's musical methodology. Smitty offered a few standard and alternate tunings that might freshen Muddy's sound. "I don't know anything about that other tuning, I play with slide all the time," Muddy told Smitty.[41]

Smitty could only watch as Muddy demonstrated the style and technique he'd spent his entire lifetime mastering while he honed his skills down in Rolling Fork and Clarksdale, Mississippi. "I tried to get him away from that slide 'cause I could play single-note picking," Smitty said. "And I would teach him how to play the bass to what I was playing." Muddy acknowledged Smitty's helpful hints, saying, "He really learnt me some things on guitar . . . I played mostly bottleneck until I met Smitty. It was a very, very good improvement he did for me, because I didn't have to try to develop everything with the slide by itself."[42]

Jimmy stood back and watched the entire session unveil, and he quickly realized how committed Muddy was to the use of his beloved slide. For his part, Muddy knew Jimmy and Smitty meant well when they tried to alter his basic technique. At the same time, however, Muddy was stubborn and had no intention of abandoning the sound he loved so well. It was that glass slide against those metal strings that he was accustomed to, and it was almost as if Robert

Johnson were standing over his shoulder, whispering, "Don't ever let it go, man—it'll be your salvation, I swear!"

Muddy clung to his style more tightly than ever. Jimmy remembers a rarely told story about how devoted Muddy was to the unique sound that he achieved with the special slide he carried with him at all times, as well as the panic that ensued when he eventually lost it.

> So as soon as he would strike out, he had a bottleneck, a Coca Cola bottleneck he was usin'. So he eventually lost it somewhere. He had a hole in his coat pocket. Oh, man, he'd rather lost a hundred dollars than lost that piece of bottleneck! And it was a long time before he could get another piece of steel that would work. He tried a whole lotta bottles, trying to find one with the neck like that but they had changed styles of the bottles, and he couldn't ever find a bottle with that long slick part to it. So he started usin' a steel slide. And he never did get that piece of steel to work for him like he did using that bottleneck.[43]

Ultimately they managed to merge all their efforts and fine-tune the music in a way that still allowed room for each of the three men to be who they needed to be individually. Muddy appreciated what Jimmy and Smitty did for him. Likewise, Smitty appreciated Muddy's efforts. "He always had a good sense of timing," Smitty said. "And from then on, every week, sometimes four or five times a week, in the evenings, we'd get together."[44] Indeed, Jimmy and Smitty did engage in house parties, with one guitar tuned regularly and the other tuned to "Spanish," or open G, for Muddy's slide work.

Though Smitty sang frequently, he wasn't known as a singer of any considerable skills. Of the three of them, Muddy was the best when it came to belting out the gritty stuff that Memphis Minnie, Sunnyland Slim, and Tampa Red were using with authority to dominate the club scene. Even the record labels like Columbia, Brunswick, and Vocalion were looking for the next rough-and-tumble blues shouter to bring that "Mississippi thing." In fact, volume levels were getting so loud that the instruments themselves would require amplification to evenly match the aggressive singing style that was the new Chicago blues.

The boys decided to follow suit. "Pretty soon Smitty and I just put Muddy through as the leader, because he would do most of the rough blues singing," Jimmy said.[45] Thus, the duet routine that Jimmy and Muddy had first arranged was now augmented with Smitty's musical contribution. The trio now worked toward neatly weaving Smitty's vocals and flashy guitar work between Muddy's stinging, sliding guitar work and Jimmy's complementary harmonica work.

The three of them sharpened their sound until they were ready to try their luck at performing publicly as a cohesive unit. They landed a gig at the Chicken Shack (located at Polk Street and Ogden), playing Friday through Sunday for five dollars a night. The band was so successful that the owner wanted them to extend their performances to Thursdays as well. "That place stayed jam packed," said Smith. "Jimmy Rogers was blowing harmonica then, I was playing first guitar and Muddy was playing second. And this one boy was playing, had a bass string hooked up to this washtub . . . We played there for him, oh, I guess all that year."[46] Whenever Smitty couldn't—or wouldn't—make the gig, Jimmy switched over to the guitar.

The opportunity finally arrived for the group to start making better money, and it arrived through the auspices of Eddie Boyd, a pianist and singer who was a well-known backing musician for Sonny Boy I and Tampa Red on the popular Bluebird label. Boyd offered the trio a chance to play at a club called the Flame, telling Jimmy and Muddy that he knew someone who wanted them to play there on a regular basis, with one condition: they had to be full-fledged union members; neither of them were at that time, and so they joined. Jimmy and Muddy's new association with Boyd gave them a chance to make the first decent money since their arrival on the scene: fifty-two dollars per week.[47] Muddy was still trying to find his sound when Boyd tried to direct him his way. "Eddie [Boyd] wanted me to play like Johnny Moore," Waters said. "He wanted it to be a sweet kind of blues."[48] Muddy ultimately chose to stop trying to be something he clearly was not, instead opting to devote himself purely to refining his natural, God-given gift of serving it up raw and uncut.

Boyd handled the financial affairs for them, and soon both Jimmy and Muddy served as backup musicians to Eddie Boyd at the club. According to Smitty's recollection, at some point during this stretch Jimmy fell out of the band because of some personal problems with a woman. Smitty described it as "girl trouble" and hinted that Jimmy's personal issues might have interfered with the band's success at the time. Shortly thereafter, Eddie Boyd suddenly abandoned the gig for what he thought was a more prosperous proposition offered to him by Sonny Boy I to play for steel mill workers in Gary, Indiana.[49] By the time Boyd left, Jimmy had evidently gotten his act together and was back in the saddle.

It was at this point that Muddy and Jimmy had first met Albert Luandrew, better known as Sunnyland Slim. Sunnyland was a seminal figure whose presence would repeatedly have a major impact on the direction of the careers of both Muddy Waters and Jimmy Rogers. Sunnyland promptly took over the gig when Eddie Boyd left the Flame club. Sunnyland (whose nickname came from a song he wrote about the popular train that traveled from Memphis to St. Louis) had the hippest hangout after a long night's work. His home, located at Twenty-sixth and Prairie, was a blues musician's dream and not unlike the country juke joints he had frequented while growing up in Mississippi. Meanwhile, two other fellow harp-blowing musicians from Jimmy's Southern roots were soon to join him in Chicago and share the benefits of Sunnyland's generosity—David "Honeyboy" Edwards and Marion "Little Walter" Jacobs.

Honeyboy Edwards was sometimes a guest on the KFFA radio show Little Walter hosted back in Helena, Arkansas, and the two struck up a relationship that grew tighter as the years went by. They both loved the wild life and hoboing on trains, and the two of them traveled everywhere together as a team, playing harp and guitar as a duo. They hopped trains throughout the South, including the cities of Ruleville, Memphis, and New Orleans, and became, as they say, thick as thieves. "I never did get so close to nobody in my life like Little Walter. He was my partner," Honeyboy said.[50] Independently, they both eventually decided to cash in their chips and head north for a better life in the North.

One day, while staying with Big Walter Horton during the summer of '43 in Memphis, Horton told Honeyboy he was leaving for St. Louis. Honeyboy joined him a little while later and they teamed up, playing gigs in St. Louis. Then in Caruthersville, Missouri, in '44 they teamed up with Sunnyland Slim to form a trio and played together at Sunnyland's regular gig for a guy known as Juke. And now, somewhere between May and June of 1945, Honeyboy had arrived in Chicago with Little Walter. The two had hoboed first, then earned enough money by playing in the train depot in Decatur, Illinois, to catch the train properly and head straight into Union Station.[51] The first place they hit was the blues mecca of Maxwell Street. Edwards was totally shocked not only at how many jobs were available but also at how much music-making and merriment took place down there. "Everybody had a job," Edwards crowed, adding, "they didn't ever sleep!" Honeyboy was duly impressed with the intensity and devotion that the patrons displayed as they listened to the musicians play the blues. "They'd come to Jewtown, listen to the blues all day long, on a Monday," he said. "Go to work at four o'clock, get off at twelve. Or come to work at eight o'clock in the morning, get off at eight, make it to Jewtown—somebody'd probably be sitting around playing. Boy, it'd be something!"[52]

It didn't take long for Honeyboy and Little Walter to jump right in.

We went out in the street and made more money than we ever made before—made about $20 apiece, emptied out our cigar box four or five times. We had the biggest crowd around us. People chucking quarters and dollars at us. Money was floating then. Take that hamburger stand on Maxwell and Halsted, sitting in the same spot now, open every day. You get a polish sausage there for a dime, pork chop sandwich, get that for twenty cents. Stacked all up with meat and onions. Get one, feed two people. We was making money then.[53]

Not long after they arrived, Honeyboy just happened to bump into Jimmy while down on Maxwell Street. He remembered seeing Jimmy wearing a suit and a straw top hat, with a woman who was carrying a baby (most likely the woman was Jimmy's common-law wife, Mattie; the baby was Jimmy's son Robert).[54] Jimmy lived only a half block from the center of Maxwell Street activities. On a weekend morning in June 1945, he had his window raised, as always, listening to the blues call. He suddenly heard a sound that was unfamiliar to his ears, yet entirely captivating.

I heard this strange harp sound. I got up and put my clothes on and went down there, and there was Little Walter there. He just had come here from St. Louis . . . He was on Maxwell Street in Chicago, maybe a block, a block and a half from my house there on Peoria Street. And I heard this harmonica one Sunday morning—woke me up! . . . I got up, put my clothes on, went down in the crowd on Maxwell Street there, and got up where I could hear him. He was still blowin', and I was listenin'. He had a band with him. He had a bass player and a guitar, and a drum was playing with him. But the only thing that was really standing out to me was the harmonica. That's what I wanted to hear, and I knew how to back it up. And I sat in with them, and well, we had a wonderful time down there. That's the way we really met—*communicating*.[55]

Like almost every person who encountered the young genius harp player, Jimmy Rogers's life was changed forever after he met Little Walter again, in Chicago. When they finished playing, Jimmy formally reintroduced himself to Walter, whom he hadn't seen since the days they spent in Memphis with Sonny Boy Williamson II. They had a lively conversation on the streets for about an hour. Jimmy knew instantly that there was something special about this kid. They could have played all day and night, and probably would have if the weather hadn't taken a sudden turn for the worse. The boys scrambled to seek shelter, and since Jimmy lived right around the corner and up the street, he decided that the two should retreat back to his apartment. By the time they arrived, they both were drenched. "It started raining that Sunday evening," Jimmy recalled, "and he left with me and got wet, we both got wet. We ran up to my place. He and I could wear the same clothes at the time, and he put on some of my dry clothes, and he found out where I lived and he'd come to my house every day. He'd wake me up and we'd talk and sit down and rehearse." Jimmy told friend and interviewer Tom Townsley about the early days when he first met Little Walter, and how he was the one to give Walter his first alcoholic beverage—a screwdriver. Before that drink, Walter was eating either Stage Plank cookies or Vanilla Wafers, along with drinking Carnation milk straight from the can to wash the cookies down.[56]

They began playing together as a duo, and Walter quickly became a fixture in Jimmy's group as well.[57] The ensemble had a regular routine of going from club to club, playing for the tips, collecting money in the kitty—a blown-glass bowl in the shape of a cat—which sat on the floor in front of the group and had an open head where coins and bills could be dropped as patrons passed by. "We were out by 8:00 at night," Jimmy recalled, "and different taverns started around 9, so by the time the taverns closed at 2:00, we maybe done hit four or five, maybe six taverns, and we had a pocket of money apiece, maybe $15, $20 apiece. That's pretty good money back during that time. *Extra* good money for a musician."[58]

Relatively speaking, it wasn't the ideal way to earn a living—they would have rather had something more dependable. "We started doin' that," Jimmy added, "not because I really like it that way. I wanted a steady job someplace, steady gig."[59] Still, things could have been worse—at least they were working. When the music was really grabbing the audiences on Maxwell Street, Jimmy would often leave with somewhere near fifty dollars, and that was after the entire pot was divided up among his band members, which usually included Eddie "Porkchop" Hines, John Henry Barbee, and newcomer and Maxwell devotee Little Walter.[60]

By August 1945, however, Honeyboy had left Walter, citing the sudden on-slaught of cold weather that predicted a harsh winter arriving. He left Walter in cold Chicago to fend for himself. This proved to be more difficult than before; many of the faithful patrons weren't coming as much these days because of "the Hawk"—that vicious Lake Michigan wind that cut straight across the horizon and right into your skull, with temperatures sometimes dropping down to nearly thirty below zero. One of Walter's sisters, Marguerite, said, "He suffered a lot in Jewtown. He was cold, hungry. He used to drink RC Cola, and he told me he used to eat Stage Plank cake, which is sorta like ginger cake, has an icing on it. He used to have to put tape on his jacket to keep out of the cold, and had to stay with a woman old enough to be his mother."[61]

Snooky Pryor, Jimmy's boyhood friend from Vance, Mississippi, had already endured the Hawk since he'd arrived in town five years before Jimmy made the permanent move there. "I left Lambert in 1936," Snooky said. "I come to Chicago in 1940." (Five years later Jimmy would stumble across Snooky's music on Maxwell Street. "He had this 'Snooky and Moody' thing out," Jimmy remembered, "and I'd looked at the record. I said, 'Who's named Snooky? It's not me. Who is this?'" After finally catching up with Moody Jones and asking if he'd made a record with a guy named Snooky, Jones answered affirmatively with, "'Yeah, Snooky Pryor.' And I come to thinkin', I said, 'Pryor—I bet that's Bubba!' And when I did see him, it was him . . . He taken my nickname.'")[62]

Pryor, who was twenty-four years old, had recently completed four years in the army after being stationed in Fort Sheridan and had received an honorable discharge. He still had his uniform on when he first arrived at Maxwell Street. He went right to work, bringing his performance skills that had been honed in the military. Pryor asserted that, contrary to popular belief, he had pioneered the use of a microphone well before Little Walter ever set foot in Chicago. According to Snooky, "I used to play all the [bugle] calls on this great big old army P.A. microphone . . . After I played taps and stuff in the evenin' time, one night I decided to try my harmonica through there. It sound just like a saxophone— ya know what I mean . . . I was playin' *Flyin Home*, Woody Herman stuff. That's where I get all those licks from."[63]

Pryor played with several prominent artists, including Memphis Minnie, who had an outgoing personality onstage and otherwise. Pryor described her as a "bombshell. Oh, she was a nice lady . . . but she drinked pretty heavy . . . She used to talk real loud . . . She'd drink and then she'd dip snuff and then she'd put tobacco in her mouth all at the same time . . . And boy could she talk some talk. She could say words that weren't even invented . . . Used to talk about me like hell too."[64] It was inevitable that the old pals, Snooky and Jimmy, would bump into each other at the most popular gathering place for blues musicians. Pryor remembered, "It was around December of 1945 that I met him at that little hot dog place that they used to have in there . . . Me and my wife, we was in there, and I see this guy standing over there not too far from us. I believe he was drinking a coke. I say, 'I know him.' So I goes up, still have a uniform on. I says, 'Wha cha know, Snook.' He didn't know who I was."[65]

Once Jimmy recognized Snooky, the two embraced and caught up on old times. Pryor told of his military exploits, and Jimmy shared his latest activities since he'd just recently made his permanent move to town. Pryor recalled:

> Yeah, that was just about the time when he started playin' guitar in Chicago. Now he was a damn good harmonica player. He had a tone out of this world. He was just like Old Man Rice Miller [who] had a tone that nobody didn't

have, and so Jimmy was the same way. I asked him why he give it up. I said "if you could prove yourself like you did back when we was kids together, then I wouldn't mess with you on harmonica." I wasn't as heavy as him on harmonica, but I could sing better and I could blow louder.[66]

By 1945 Pryor was already on the fast track to establishing himself as one of the preeminent blues harp players in Chicago. He wasn't intimidated by Sonny Boy I, or any of the others, and was making inroads into what would be one of the first small-scale recording labels available to the "minor league" players in town such as Snooky and Moody. Chester Scales told Pryor, "'Well, good as you sound, I can get you recorded inside of a week." With that, Pryor said, "We just went in and cut it. Without a contract or anything. Just go in and blow."[67] Scales had an outfit not too far from Maxwell Street, on Sedgwick, where they could lay down a few tracks. In reference to his song lyrics, Pryor said, "That's how come I was talkin' about Sedgwick Street, that's where I was at." Eventually "Snooky and Moody Blues" was born. The song is a narrative that chronicles Pryor's need to boogie as he roams the streets of Chicago.

Jimmy never played with Snooky then but could typically be found playing on one of the opposite corners. "The ones that blowed the loudest and had the best music, that's who got the crowd and that's who got the biggest kitty," Pryor said.[68] As he had not yet fully established himself as a guitar player, Jimmy, at the time, was developing his harp skills right alongside his pal Snooky. "Jimmy was real good with the harmonica," Snooky admitted. "Now I'll tell you, he's got a different style. He had a hell of a style. If he'd a kept on, I think he would have been tops at harmonica, yeah. I mean . . . he even had a different tone from any harmonica I've heard yet."[69] Once the three old friends reunited in Chicago, the good times were rolling just as they did back in Vance. Jimmy was more inspired than ever to book gigs that gave them opportunities to jam the way they did before the boyhood trio went their separate ways as their lives took them in different directions.

One of the musicians Jimmy found work with was also one of his childhood heroes, Tampa Red, whose music Jimmy had listened to on the radio as he dreamed of playing with such musicians. Now his dreams were becoming reality. "I worked with Tampa several gigs," Jimmy recalled. "Me, Little Johnny Jones [piano], and Tampa Red. We used to play over at the Purple Cat on Madison Street. And over on Lake Street around California, we played there together." According to Jimmy, they also played songs on Tampa's set: "Don't You Lie to Me," "Let Me Play with Your Poodle," and "When Things Go Wrong." "He'd just play straight old blues," Jimmy remembered.[70] From Tampa he learned very valuable lessons about how to survive:

> I used to go over to Tampa Red's house with Johnny Jones. Tampa was a quiet type-person . . . He would treat you real nice. He would give you points on what you were trying to learn. We used to go over there and he would tell us stories about different places that he played and how to react in different situations. You know, the straight way how to take care of yourself and conduct yourself with the public—and that's what I did . . . Tampa would tell us, "if you live fast, you get in trouble fast. So you soon get it over real fast" . . . I guess that's why I don't get into trouble now. Because I learned from good guys who would tell me how to conduct myself. Big Bill and Tampa, people like that would tell you.[71]

Along with Jimmy and some of his cohorts, like Dan and Jesse Jones, you could easily find the heaviest hitters on the blues scene enjoying themselves at Sunnyland's place in an atmosphere that must have felt much like a boys club environment: Little Walter, Lee Brown, Floyd Jones (Moody's cousin), Big Maceo, Doctor (Peter) Clayton, Willie Mabon, Roosevelt Sykes, Memphis Slim, Little Brother Montgomery, Baby Face Leroy (Foster), and a host of others.[72]

Indeed, Sunnyland's joint was widely regarded as *the* place to be for fast action, firewater, and food. "Musicians was welcome," Jimmy recalled. "Yeah, when we got off workin' after a gig some place, we'd get home and we'd go to Sunnyland's house, and that's where we could eat. That's why we hung in there all the time . . . He'd give away more than he could sell sometimes."[73] Sunnyland himself was pretty smooth with a deck of cards or a pair of dice, especially since he knew how to load them both. He also knew his way around a pool table. Jimmy spent a great deal of time there, where he saw and heard "all kinds of stuff right down in that basement" as he bonded with dozens of his colleagues over the course of several mornings and evenings. He was not, however, willing to lose what little money he had to them, and Sunnyland wouldn't have let him even if he wanted to. "I wouldn't ever, *never* gamble with him [Sunnyland], but I'd bet on him," Jimmy boasted. "He didn't want me to gamble, didn't want me to get into that kind of stuff."[74]

About Sunnyland's hangout spot, Snooky Pryor said, "It was kind of rough in that neighborhood. If you won any money, you couldn't walk out of there with it. If you was kind of strange over there, you went in and come out of there, somebody be out there to stick you up, man, and take your money."[75] If there was anyone worried about whether a raid was inevitable, Sunnyland had already taken care of that: an off-duty cop had his palm comfortably greased with greenbacks, along with complimentary drinks to keep him warm as he stood guard and protected the place.

Jimmy received yet another great opportunity to play with one of his idols when he made a recording with Memphis Minnie. Minnie was one of the most popular blues artists in Chicago, and Jimmy knew her music and had been admiring her as far back as his early days in Mississippi, where he'd heard her music blasting out of the juke joints along with others like Big Bill Broonzy, Tampa Red, and the original Sonny Boy Williamson. "I cut with her back in the 40s," said Rogers, reminiscing about his longtime heroine.[76]

In much the same way as his pal Snooky Pryor described Minnie, Jimmy tried to paint a picture of the woman who was admired, feared, and loathed all at once:

> She was kind of a fussy type of a woman to get along with . . . She didn't usually have a band . . . She had a couple of her husbands [who] were guitar players, and they'd team most all of the time. But on records you'd have to take more pieces when you go to the studio, so that's why I got a chance to record with her, and on [local] gigs we'd play here. She would come and be on our set, and we introduced her on the stage . . . I guess that's how she heard me and was interested in my guitar enough to want to put it on records with her. So I was proud of that.[77]

In that same year he played harmonica with Memphis Slim and Sunnyland Slim for Harlem Records when he recorded the single "Round About Boogie."

Meanwhile, the trio of Waters, Rogers, and Smith was also playing numerous house parties and actively pursuing more gigs, including their latest score at the Purple Cat Lounge at 2119 West Madison Street.[78] Sonny Boy I was already playing there four nights a week, Thursday through Saturday. Muddy, Smitty, and Jimmy were all relying upon one another to do their part to keep things rolling smoothly on the Flame gig. Things were going just fine until Smitty got cantankerous with Sunnyland Slim during a set and got them all kicked off of not only that gig but also the one they'd recently secured at the Cotton Club.[79]

The problems didn't end there. Because Smitty worked a full-time job as an electrician from 8:00 in the morning until 4:30 in the evening, his interest in the evolution of Jimmy and Muddy's music was limited to a part-time contribution during the embryonic stages of their development. Most likely Smitty's allegiance toward his day gig led to his taking on a *laissez-faire* policy regarding his attitude toward the blues night shifts. More important, his presence couldn't always be counted on, and Jimmy and Muddy chose not to rely on anyone who wasn't as serious as they were about investing the time and energy into creating this new sound.

Jimmy had little doubt about why Smitty was being so contentious and wishy-washy when it came to committing himself to the music, citing conflicting work schedules between the band and Smitty's nine-to-five gig that always seemed to take precedence over the band's needs. Said Jimmy, "When I first met him, he didn't have no day job, he was just messin' around, playin' around here and there. After Muddy came here, Smitty got that day job. And we wasn't doin' too much—we played maybe Friday, Saturday and Sunday, and this week we wouldn't play no more, maybe the next two or three weeks or somethin' like that."[80]

While still primarily a harmonica player, Jimmy was gaining ground on the guitar as well as gaining confidence in his abilities to assume more and more control over the instrument when the opportunity arose. He'd already been chosen to pick up the slack whenever Sonny Boy I would get too drunk and pass out, rendering himself incapacitated on the gig. Now he doubled on guitar when Smitty didn't show up to rehearsals or even missed a few gigs. Jimmy and Muddy saw the writing on the wall and invested in getting affordable yet reliable equipment so that Jimmy could project his sound when they performed. Jimmy got as much volume as he could out of his little Gibson twelve-inch speaker when he cranked up his Silvertone brand electric guitar.[81]

Eventually the inevitable occurred and Smitty left the group, permanently. Jimmy was clearly disappointed, as he lamented, "I don't know why he didn't stay with it. After he got goin' he didn't show too much interest in it. He would play—we'd get there with him sometimes . . . So he was doin' his day thing, and so he just dropped out of the picture just like that—he moved, ya know."[82] Jimmy assumed even more responsibility on guitar now that Smitty was gone. He was steadily increasing his reputation as a solid guitarist. It wouldn't take long before that reputation would overshadow his brief and largely unnoticed career as a harp player in Chicago.

The Waters-Rogers duo hadn't yet established themselves as a major act on the scene, which meant they still did a fair amount of "sitting in" with other groups to make ends meet. Sometimes this meant performing certain musical styles that were more in line with whatever the particular leader of the gig wanted rather than expressing themselves as individuals with a distinct, unique sound. Fortunately for Jimmy, he had little difficulty altering his sound to fit whatever musical occasion he might encounter. Since his musical style had developed through the influence of the most popular recording artists on the airwaves and jukeboxes in the South, Jimmy was prepared to play with almost anyone. That is not to say, however, he didn't have a preferred style. Indeed, over the years he would prove to be quite consistent when it came to identifying the short list of his favorite guitarists. Among them, in no particular order, were Robert Junior Lockwood, Joe Willie Wilkins, B. B. King, T-Bone Walker, and Robert Nighthawk. These were the guitar players who continually inspired him from childhood throughout adulthood.

Luckily for Jimmy and Muddy, men like Big Bill Broonzy, Sunnyland Slim, Tampa Red, and other seasoned veterans did their best to look out for the newcomers. With the exception of only a few relatively minor setbacks, the band generally had things rolling in the right direction. There was one area, however, where Jimmy and Muddy had not yet broken through: neither of them had a major record deal. Nor did several others who were on the scene trying to make a living playing blues. This, of course, meant they weren't making hits that could be played on the radio. Still Jimmy and Muddy remained undeterred. Over the next several months, both of them, together and separately, would try to find their way to the "inside track" of the music industry as they waited for a chance to latch onto a label that might lead them and the band to fortune and fame.

Jimmy wanted to introduce Muddy to his newest running mate, Little Walter, but Walter had recently gotten into a nasty incident with a man who caught him having an affair with the man's woman. A knife was pulled, the man's face was cut severely, and Walter had to vanish from the scene; he left with Honeyboy and went to Milwaukee to cool his heels until the situation blew over.[83] Walter was well known for his hot temper and a penchant for courting danger. In the meantime Muddy and Jimmy continued to rehearse as a duo, refining the rough Delta style they both loved. Walter would be missing in action for nearly half a year, while Jimmy and Muddy slowly developed a working relationship that would be firmly established once Walter returned.

When Walter returned about six months after his sudden departure, Jimmy finally got a chance to introduce him to Muddy Waters, saying, "I was telling you about this Little Walter, such a great harmonica player." After an impromptu jam in Muddy's living room, Muddy declared, "Well, yeah, he's real good." Both Muddy and Jimmy had decided that Walter came second only to Sonny Boy II when it came to blowing a mean harp. About his ability in the early stages, Jimmy said, "His timin' was the roughest thing to get him broke down to. When we get him set in there, well then he automatically created a new style of harmonica."[84]

Within about six months of regular rehearsing, Walter started showing some significant progress in learning the musical routine that was rapidly developing between Jimmy and Muddy.[85]

Jimmy realized that Chicago didn't have a large number of harmonica players. Sure, there were Sonny Boy I, Jazz Gillum, and more recently Snooky Pryor, but the role of the harp in Chicago during the mid-1940s was downplayed, not yet elevated to the status of the piano or guitar. "They didn't really want to recognize the harmonica no way too much as an instrument during that time," Jimmy said.[86] In the beginning Snooky had more respect for Jimmy's capabilities than he did for those of Little Walter, who was, at least at the outset, rough around the edges. In 1945 Walter had a lot to learn, not so much because he wasn't gifted, but because he possessed an excessive amount of talent mixed with impatience and ego. His arrogance, combined with his incredibly quick mind for hearing musical passages and playing them back at lightning-quick speed, made him a bit careless in the beginning. He was too eager to play everything he knew.

Even though many people would eventually come to worship Walter's high level of musicianship, his skills weren't always as sharp as they ultimately became. Indeed, after Walter's first entrance to Maxwell Street, Snooky Pryor had criticized his faulty sense of musical timing during his developmental stage. By Snooky's account, his playing was "kind of sloppy . . . I'll be tellin' the truth about it. And he couldn't sing at all, but he had one song he could really sing and play a little bit, 'I Just Keep Loving Her' . . . Nobody never could play with him, hardly, but John Henry Barbee and J. T. [Brown, presumably], because Little Walter's time was bad."[87]

Years later Walter himself would admit to Billy Boy Arnold that "Sonny Boy told him that he played too fast,"[88] which mirrors the exact description by both Muddy and Jimmy when they elaborated in separate accounts how they did their best to rein Walter in just long enough to settle down. As a bluesman Walter had to learn adopt the jazzman's code, made popular by none other than Duke Ellington himself: *"It don't mean a thing if it ain't got that swing."*

Not only that, but Walter was stubborn and didn't always take advice from others very well. Whenever the veteran players like Sonny Boy or Big Walter Horton would try to help him get his licks to run smoothly, "Well, they'd argue," Jimmy quipped. "And Big Walter would try to tell him this and that, and Little Walter just throw his head back and wouldn't listen, and then go on off and what Walter would tell him then he'd practice it by himself, and then come back and it'd work. And he would say nobody's teaching him: 'nobody ever taught me nothin', see? Big Walter showed Little Walter a whole lot of cuts, but he wouldn't admit it. Rice Miller too . . . Walter got a lot of ideas from him."[89]

Walter's greatest gift was nearly becoming his greatest hindrance, and it was almost as if he couldn't tell where his thoughts began and others' ended. Still, Jimmy never denied the genius of Little Walter, saying, "He [Walter] had a good ear, he hear somethin', it's just like a tape. Once he hear it, he was tapin' it in his mind, and he'd go off by himself and get in a room and close up, and when he come out, he'd know it. He might not be playin' exactly like it's supposed to go, but he played close enough. And he'd thread it and then he got it made." Yet Jimmy knew Walter was not the sole architect of the unique approach to soloing on the harp. When describing Walter's personality, Jimmy said, "He'll say, he pat himself on the chest. 'Well, I did that,' you know . . . I heard him say it out of his own mouth that nobody helped him, everything he got he got it on his own, but he's wrong there. He had help."[90]

Evidently Jimmy noticed a significant change in Walter's style, and so did Snooky and others. "After Louis Jordan started puttin' out records . . . Little Walter picked up on [Jordan's] swing," said Snooky.[91] This element was what put Little Walter in a higher gear than anyone else around. The transformation that took place as a result of listening to the swing sax players was overwhelming. Jimmy and Muddy were already well on their way toward establishing the kind of musical bond that would allow them to read each other's minds. Now they both were trying to learn how to read Walter's as well. In turn, they wanted to teach him how to predict what they were going to be thinking once the music began. Jimmy tried to explain the *modus operandi*: "We'd find a pattern that fit what he's saying, and then I'd build and Walter would fall in, find him a pocket. Then we'd start running them patterns. It's like pushing a car—once you get it started rolling, you can't stop."[92]

Muddy took a natural liking to Walter, and the duo became a trio practically overnight. Walter's stunning harmonica technique was the final push Jimmy needed to relinquish the harmonica chair permanently. Jimmy made personal adjustments to his own future career as a harp player in the Muddy Waters band to provide the best kind of support for Muddy. History would ultimately prove that it was a wise choice. As for Jimmy, he never looked back; he relished his role as the contrapuntal guitarist and welcomed the fancy flash that Walter's harp brought to the band.

Who could compete with all that harmonica Walter was blowing? Walter blew so much, in fact, that Jimmy and Muddy actually spent time trying to decompress him, because he always appeared to be wound too tight. He played like an Olympic champion harmonica sprinter who used measures in music as if they were hurdles, and the first bar of his solo was like the sound of a starting pistol. It never ceased to amaze Jimmy, who said of Walter, "He was just wild, man. He'd get executin' and go on. He was worse than the Bird, Charlie Parker. He *gone!* You don't know when he's comin' back now . . . I would say, 'Look, I don't care how far you range on the wall, just meet me at the corner.'"[93]

Walter knew he was gifted, which meant taking orders from others wasn't what he was used to, especially when it came to music. But he was humble enough not to bite the hand that fed him. "He'd listen to me and Muddy," Jimmy admitted. "He'd never jump back and want to fight us. He never cursed us through madness. We was patient with him. We broke down songs for him and set the pace. Walter appreciated that."[94] Between the two of them, Muddy and Jimmy pushed and pulled on Walter's phrasing, tempo, and melodic structures until they fine-tuned his musicianship into a product that was crafted as a perfect fit between what was now a double helix of electric guitar lines, now that Jimmy was permanently using the Silvertone as his musical weapon of choice.

Muddy knew they had a genius on their hands. But Walter had to be dealt with very carefully. "He was a good boy," Muddy recalled, "but he had that bad, mean temper, that kind of thing, like 'you don't mess with me too much.' . . . I found out I was the only somebody that could do anything with him when he really got out of hand. He began acting like I was his daddy."[95] Jimmy agreed wholeheartedly, adding, "Walter was wild. Walter was likely to kill you or anybody that crossed him. A young buck with a lot of temper. He had more nerve than brains; he'd fuck up—and we'd have to get him out of jail, me and Muddy."[96]

As far as the music went, Muddy sized it up this way: "We learned how to play up *tight* with one another . . . It was hard work, man . . . me, Little Walter, and Jimmy. Natural from our hearts."[97] Jimmy always believed that the successful symbiosis between him and Muddy was because they were both from the Deep South. "It was very easy for me to cover for him because I was very familiar with that style of blues," Jimmy said.[98] Once Walter got his routine down, he became an unbelievable force to be reckoned with, and both Jimmy and Muddy witnessed the conversion firsthand. "His reflexes were so fast," Jimmy quipped. "Go into different channels, harmonize—anything we could do, Little Walter could stay on top of. He was a master."[99] Many are still trying to understand why one of the most gifted musicians who ever walked the streets was so constantly hounded by horrific episodes of violence that Walter either received or administered.

As time went on, Muddy and Jimmy came to rely on each other more than anyone else involved in the ensemble. They became inseparable. Clearly the two men had a connection that went well beyond the music—they seemed to be able to feel each other spiritually. Jimmy remembered it this way:

> I knew what I was listening for, what I wanted to hear. Muddy Waters felt the same way, but you could only produce so much yourself, you know? Say like a conversation—you can be talking, you can talk all day on a subject and nobody understand what you talking about but you. And then eventually somebody else come in and picks it up right away, and, man, it's a brand new ball game. Other people sitting around, they're going, "oh, wow, oh-yeah, that's what he meant." And then they'd come to you that way.[100]

Jimmy had years of experience that stretched all the way back to his teenage years in Mississippi, when he cut his teeth at the juke jam sessions. He remembered how he felt when he first brought his experience to Chicago months before, trying to get his own group started, doing his best to develop original material that might be good enough to get a serious record deal out of it. "But I was playing with different musicians," Jimmy lamented. "They didn't really know what I wanted. I would hum it to them, and I would phrase it on the guitar, run the notes on the harmonica—they still couldn't get it. Then Muddy Waters, he—I listened to him, and I said, 'I know what he need,' you know? It's like if you don't have enough salt in your food, it don't taste right. So you need a little more salt, and then it taste better."[101]

Jimmy always had an ear for the harp and was sensitive to the personality and overall demeanor that accompanied most harp players. He observed and described a particular disposition that he felt most harp players generally typified, a character type of sorts. "The average harmonica player, I don't know what it is, once he gets a few pats on the back—compliments—it goes right to his head right away," Jimmy said. "And he gets to the place where you can't tell him anything. I don't know why it's like that, but the average one is that way."[102]

While Walter wasn't exempt from this generalization, he was still rapidly earning the reputation of being the best of the best. Simply put, he had ideas about the harp that those before him wouldn't have dared even attempt, things that most thought were impossible. At the time some of his ideas weren't yet as finely tuned as they would eventually become, but he had enough of them intact that those who had ears could hear Walter execute phrases that easily made him a musician ahead of his time. About Walter's ultramodern sound, Jimmy admitted, "Well, yeah, he was swingin'. He always did have a swingin' sound with the harmonica, but he was mostly trying to play like Louis Jordan's style of saxophone on the harmonica before."[103] This was, in part, the same assertion that Snooky Pryor had made earlier about Walter's early style.

Jimmy figured it was excellent timing that Walter reappeared on the scene, because he was beginning to get frustrated with the fact that he was coming up empty when it came to finding players who could reproduce the music he heard in his head. "I could see a different type of harmony on guitar that I could play, but at the time we couldn't find anyone else who could play that way," Jimmy stated. "And then Little Walter, eventually he came to Chicago, and he was a very fantastic harmonica player at the time when he first got there. And I was playin'—I didn't even like it, really—I wanted guitar. So I just give Walter the privilege to play harmonica and I turned completely to guitar, and I been there ever since."[104]

3

CHESS MOVES

I was livin' in the Maxwell Street area durin' '45
and '46. That's where I'd see so many musicians
and things, by bein' there down in that area. And I
started joinin' in with 'em too, playin' on the street.

—Jimmy Rogers

The blues carnival atmosphere on Maxwell Street really appealed to Little Walter, so much so that he became a regular fixture there on weekends, even after he became part of an official, unionized band. Although the money-making opportunities there were well received by musicians, being part of that scene was seriously frowned upon, as Jimmy observed during an interview.

The union didn't want us to play down on Maxwell Street. The hardest job for us was to keep Walter out from down there. If they had found out about it, they would have stuck a fine on him or blackballed him—like they done to Baby Face [Leroy Foster]. But on Saturdays, maybe Sunday evenings, he'd be around there makin' him quarters and things. He could really make more money on the street than he could at a gig 'cause you'd have a thousand people durin' the day walkin' up and down Maxwell Street. When you belong to a union, they don't want you to be doin' that 'cause it's scabbin'. They can't get any money out of it. It's just like the government is about bootleggin' whiskey. They wanna have their hands in everything.[1]

Unbeknownst to many of the performers, there would even be spies strategically located on the more popular corners of Jewtown, laying low until they thought they spotted a culprit. Sometimes they'd get made by members of the blues crew, who never hesitated to send up a flare and notify all others in a coded verbal warning. Eventually Jimmy would look out for Little Walter in this way. "We'd quick run down and tell him, 'The Hawk is out,'" Rogers said.[2]

Cousins Floyd and Moody Jones also hung out with Jimmy and Snooky Pryor on Maxwell Street.[3] The atmosphere there remained attractive to musicians, both because they made substantially more money than they ever could have made in the clubs and because the club gigs were all sewn up by the leading Chicago blues stars who had been situated before the youngsters ever arrived. Out of necessity Jimmy and his boyhood pals found a different route: they hustled on the street, their egos bolstered and their pockets lined by their weekend take. Snooky, who had teamed up with Floyd Jones, said, "Man, we used to make shoeboxes of money, me and Floyd . . . We used to have to dump that shoebox about three or four times . . . I used to make so much money down there in Jewtown, I used to go home walkin' sideways!"[4]

Snooky was always down on Maxwell Street, hanging out with his buddies in pursuit of both music and money. "It was me and Floyd Jones and Stovepipe [Watson] and One-Legged Sam Norwood and a guy we used to call 'Milk Finger,' Othum Brown, who was from Marks, Mississippi." About the environment on Maxwell Street, Pryor said, "It was real nice for a beginner to learn." He described the atmosphere as "booming every day. It was like every day was Sunday . . . Just name anything in this world that you wanted, you could get it off Maxwell Street. They had fortune tellers, magicians, food, shoes . . . I think people used to steal stuff, bring it down there and sell it cheap."[5]

The musicians who entertained the throngs made less than ten dollars on average for playing all night long. With the free-spending, oversized crowds wandering up and down the streets in either direction, a few quarters here and there from several hundred patrons quickly turned into some real cash for the performers. The money served as encouragement for them to play even harder and longer in order to entice those who stood all around them to remain and drop a few more coins. In spite of the hassles, playing down on Maxwell Street was definitely worth the trouble, even if the club owners and other musicians in town frowned upon it because they thought it was "beneath them." In reality some of the greatest ideas for the lively music delivered in the blues clubs at night were born during the day on the corners along Maxwell Street. Jimmy Rogers described the musical atmosphere this way: "We were doin' [the song] 'Caldonia,' boogie woogies, all kinds of stuff. That's where I made up 'That's All Right' and all that stuff. I was building those songs up. We did that on the street. You don't worry about nobody trying to steal your stuff back then during that time. Later years they started that. Man, we'd just get some ideas and go on and do 'em."[6]

And there were dozens of other artists making their money down there too, including upright bassist Ed Newman, washboard player "Porkchop" Eddie Hines, and guitarist/singer/harp player Johnny Watson—better known as "Daddy Stovepipe." Watson, whom Jimmy described as a well-traveled "short little dude" in his forties, who wore funny striped suits, was the quintessential type of guy you'd run into on the weekend at Jewtown. He was a street-hustler type, a fast-talking entertainer who could grab your attention and hold it until both artist and observer got something out of the deal. Washboard player, jester, jokester, tap dancer, kitty collector. That's what it took to "get over" when you were laying it down on the Near West Side of town.

Since he'd arrived in 1945, Jimmy had had the fortune of placing himself at the beginning of a slowly emerging underground recording scene that took place right in the heart of Maxwell Street. By 1946 several aspiring entrepreneurs emerged to encourage the various street musicians to hitch their wagons to an independent little machine that could make them a star. These rookie producers often doubled as engineers as well, using their own rogue equipment to fashion primitive shellac recordings that, while not very not high in quality or quantity, still served as immediate feedback for local artists who wanted so badly to break through the airwaves by any means necessary. Jimmy, whether willing to admit it or not, was as eager as the rest of them to find anyone who could help further his career. Certainly to have bragging rights—to be able to say, "Hey, look at me; I have a record out!"—was of prime importance to all those blues people who aspired to someday be as big as the likes of Sonny Boy, Tampa Red, Big Maceo, Memphis Minnie, or Memphis Slim. The way Jimmy figured it, if he couldn't make it on an important label under his own steam, he'd try his best to cut sides with whatever smaller outfit he could until he could grow some funk of his own.

Jimmy got his first taste of session work in September 1946 when he managed to do a little work as a sideman. By that time J. Mayo Williams, a young entrepreneur from Pine Bluff, Arkansas (although he publicly claimed Monmouth, Illinois, as his hometown), had been in the record business for more than twenty years, serving as a producer and talent scout for "race records," or music recorded by and tailored to the black community. Williams, who worked between New York and Chicago, had started up two small labels: Chicago and Harlem (and eventually two more: Southern and Ebony Records). This former NFL pro football player (one of the first three African Americans in the history of the league) was trying to convince local blues artists like Jimmy, Muddy, Sunnyland, and several others to lay down tracks for his fledgling label, one of a small handful of independent recording companies in Chicago at the time.

Years later, when asked if he remembered recording at the label for J. Mayo Williams, Jimmy thought for a minute, then said, "Mayo Williams . . . yes, I did. I cut with Sunnyland Slim and I cut with Lee Brown," he said of his early stint with Harlem Records.[7] "We did that stuff down at 20 North Wacker Drive. Me, Sunnyland Slim, Memphis Slim, Othum Brown, Lee Brown and Leroy Foster. 'Cause I worked for that label then—Harlem Records."[8] Jimmy even recalled a few of the details regarding the circumstances surrounding how the music went down once they were in the studio: "At the time, Memphis Slim was playing the piano for Sunnyland. He could play, he could play like he do now, but he was studio-shy and he was afraid he would make a mistake. Slim was at the microphone and James Mayo Williams had to tell him to back off because they couldn't balance his voice." Jimmy tried to probe even deeper to yield more memories of the session. "I'm trying to remember the titles of the songs, it's been so long. All of us was down there. We had Big Crawford on the bass. I can't think now who was [on] drums. It was around 1946 or '47. This was around the same year that I recorded for Bernard [Abrams]. It was in the fall, maybe September or October."[9]

Jimmy's relationship with Lee Brown—a local piano player who, at the time, was working diligently at establishing his own legacy as one of the most important movers and shakers in the field—was sometimes tenuous at best. Even if Brown's musical skills met with Jimmy's approval, it wasn't by a huge margin, as Jimmy never actually gave Brown what might be called a ringing endorsement. When commenting about Lee's performance level or his personality, Jimmy mused:

> Lee Brown, he used to talk a lot. He was a little jive piano player. He couldn't play too much but he could play a little bit. And he'd run around and he'd talk a lots. He never could work with nobody too much. He's kind hard to get along with. Lee Brown was something else, man . . . He'd have to argue with himself! We'd always get along, but he had something—inferiority complex or somethin'. When you come around, he'd figure out somebody was tryin' to take advantage of him all the time or somethin'. So I just treat him nice, and we'd have a few laughs and have a few drinks and I'm gone.[10]

Jimmy, still trying to put together his own recording band while working in conjunction with Muddy Waters, had asked Brown to back him on some gigs, hoping they might create some kind of chemistry that would be worthy of capturing on tape. "Lee Brown was playing the piano with me and if I'm not mistaken, he played behind Muddy too . . ."[Bobbie Town] Boogie"—he made that before this particular date," Jimmy said. "It came out that year."[11]

"Him and Leroy Foster were playing little local gigs together. Lee Brown would run by the office and if he could catch John [J.] Mayo Williams or something, he'd give him $10.00."[12] The original recording of "Bobbie Town Boogie" that Jimmy is referring to was recorded a year earlier in 1945 by Lee Brown on Mayo's Harlem label. This time around there would be two more recordings that would confuse things exponentially.[13]

Under Mayo's leadership Jimmy recorded his first side as a leader with "Round About Boogie," recorded in Chicago, but, to his great misfortune, when the tune was released, the credit went not to Jimmy Rogers but to Memphis Slim.[14] To make matters worse, Mayo's Harlem label identified Sunnyland Slim as the lead singer and leader of the combo.[15] Essentially there was no visible trace of Jimmy Rogers on the record; one had to recognize his voice or his harp playing. Jimmy's backing band for that session had Lee Brown on piano, Alex Atkins on alto sax, probably Big Crawford on bass, and possibly Leroy Foster on drums. To complicate matters even further, the flip side listed another title that had a familiar ring, called "Bobbie Town Woogie," which featured Lee Brown, who had already recorded a tune called "Bobbie Town Boogie" just the year before![16]

Evidently Jimmy also worked on the side as a salesman, selling discs for Mayo. According to Rogers, "I was like a traveling record salesman around for different record companies like RCA, Victor, Decca. and different labels around . . . I had like a satchel and you'd pack them, those little 78s." Jimmy was obviously proud of his power of persuasion, as he told writer Norman Darwen, "If a good hit record came out and they could get ahold to it, I was on it, man, I could push it."[17]

Meanwhile, Bernard Abrams, an enterprising blues entrepreneur, owned and operated Maxwell Radio Record Company at 831 West Maxwell, a radio and TV repair store that housed Ora Nelle Records, where he managed to produce several artists over a short span and cut as many sides as he could with the limited resources he had. Abrams was a young Jewish producer who wanted to cash in on all the talent that was flowing through the Maxwell Street area on the weekends. Ultimately he succeeded in becoming the catalyst behind some of the earliest recorded works of the street musicians of the late 1940s. "These fellas that were down here, they used to come into my store," Abrams said. "I used to have a little disc recorder and a mike, they'd sit on a box or something and sing. Well, one day I thought this might sell. I took it to a pressing plant and had records made, a thousand or so."[18]

Another recording opportunity sprang up that same year when Little Walter, along with frequent Maxwell Street visitor Floyd Jones, was called in by Bernard

Abrams, who said, "Whyn't y'all come on. I want to make a dub of y'all."[19] Since none of them had contracts at the time, it didn't take much to convince Jones or many others then—Jimmy, Walter, Baby Face, Muddy, or Sunnyland—to wait for a chance to lay down some sides for the small company. Abrams briskly sold copies of the vanity discs for a dollar. Called "dubs," the early batches of recordings were eventually used to form the foundation of what became known as the Ora Nelle label.[20]

The next year, 1947, Abrams convinced Jimmy to lay down a few tracks for him. Jimmy was excited about the opportunity. He might finally have the opportunity to record songs under his own name and hoped the results would come out correctly this time. Jimmy teamed up with Little Walter and Othum Brown to record "Little Store Blues" for Ora Nelle Records.[21] "Muscadine Wine" was another tune that Jimmy and Little Walter recorded, although very few copies were pressed during this time. In the end Jimmy was a bit disappointed that the tune he'd led didn't fare very well: "I made 'Little Store Blues' for a little small label, didn't amount to very much."[22] It turned out that this performance would serve as a foreshadowing of things to come, as it represented one of the earliest cases of—for lack of a better term—"musical incest" regarding tunes connected to his career. When Jimmy and Walter recorded the sprightly jump-blues boogie tune "Little Store Blues," they used an arrangement during the Ora Nelle session that borrowed heavily from the Sleepy John Estes tune of the same key and tempo, titled "Liquor Store Blues."

About this same time period, Abrams also managed to convince singer and guitarist "Bow-Legged" Othum Brown to lay down a few tracks. Abrams had an original tune he wanted recorded that was dedicated to his wife. Brown, therefore, recorded a tune called "Ora Nelle Blues" (Ora Nelle 711), the song title chosen for the small independent label located in the heart of Maxwell Street. Little Walter first played a second guitar line with Floyd Jones behind Othum Brown's vocals. Yet again, another case of mistaken identity would rear its ugly head. Just as there was controversy surrounding "Little Store Blues," a similar situation occurred when Jimmy Rogers recorded "That's All Right," a song that had a chord progression and verse structure that were identical to Brown's version of "Ora Nelle Blues," with the exception of the hook in the lyrics identifying Ora Nelle as the woman in question.[23]

The eerily similar lyrics and arrangement created a situation that could be viewed as a "chicken or the egg" question with regard to which artist—Othum Brown or Jimmy Rogers—had the right to claim the tune as his own. It was an irrefutable fact that even though the titles were different, the lyrics were the same. Although Jimmy won out by receiving credit for the ultimate version of the tune, he did acknowledge that Brown recorded it first, even if the earlier Brown version fell on deaf ears. At one point Jimmy downplayed the significance not only of Brown's role in the tune but also of his place in the blues pantheon altogether, saying, "Othum Brown, he was a drunk, and tried to do somethin' with his 'Ora Nelle Blues.' He tried, but it didn't work."[24]

Later Jimmy's stance regarding the events surrounding the controversy softened somewhat, although he still was reluctant to give too much credit to Brown when it came to the tune he believed was rightfully his. "He [Brown] tried after we were here in Chicago . . . He cut it for some little label, couldn't get anything out of it."[25] Jimmy would say later, "Othum was a pretty good guitar player."[26] Jimmy says the song came from observing a man and a woman who got into a fight, and the guy was telling this woman that although she had mistreated him, it was all right. After he'd experienced his own personal problems, Jimmy said he developed the song from there.[27] Truth be told, the tune, which more than likely had its origins in West Memphis or Helena, Arkansas, was neither Jimmy's nor Othum's to claim. Both had probably picked up the song from Robert Junior Lockwood, who performed the tune on a regular basis as far back as the West Memphis/Helena days. Even Muddy Waters was overheard to say about the tune, "That's Robert Jr.'s song."[28]

Jimmy was clear about his affinity toward the song: "You have to feel a song. I don't think Robert or none of those guys even felt 'That's All Right.' The words that we were usin', they didn't feel it . . . I built it, put it together and lined it out with harmony and built the music around it, and then we recorded it." Still he did not deny the outside influences of a pair of artists who might claim portions of the tune for themselves. According to Rogers, "It was in between Robert Lockwood, Willie Love ideas comin' in and verses like I put some verses with it and built it that way. I built the song. Nobody wasn't doin' anything with it. We would all toss it around . . . and so I put it to work."[29]

Muddy was making his moves too, hooking up with James "Sweet Lucy" Carter, yet another performer who was mingling among the same crowd, trying to make a name for himself. Muddy and Carter both were being courted by Mayo Williams. Jimmy remembered Carter and the session, saying, "James 'Sweet Lucy' Carter—he was a friend of Lee Brown's. They all was south side boys . . . There was a joint on 31st where you could meet anybody you wanted to meet."[30] Muddy also recalled a few details about the Mayo Williams session, saying, "We got half sideman [meaning half the going rate that sidemen were entitled to under legal union rules]." None of the players who recorded that day got the full $82.50, the amount usually given to the leader of the session. Since the restricted union fee at the time was $41.25, Muddy calculated, "I musta got twenty-something dollars out of it."[31]

In a cruel twist of fate, yet another Mayo mishap occurred on the Harlem label. When the recording of "Mean Red Spider" came out, the label on the 78 disc did not identify Muddy and his boys. Instead, "Sweet Lucy" Carter's name was identified; there was no trace of Muddy's name anywhere. Jimmy knew it was another mistake made by Mayo and his careless pressing plant. According to Rogers, "I remember James Carter back in that time, he didn't record [on the session that day]. He [Muddy] had already cut when me and Lee Brown and Leroy recorded [my September '46 sides for Harlem]. James, and it was another guy—an alcoholic dude—Dr. Clayton—hooked him in there. I met a lot of guys back during that time."[32] Clayton was a man who was known as a real character. "He was just a vocal, he didn't play an instrument, but he had a pair of lungs on him there," Jimmy said. "Man, he sounded like a train blowin'. He really could holler."[33]

The botched labeling of the Mayo Williams session was a missed opportunity for Muddy and Jimmy to claim rights to one of their earliest shellac pressings. Still some good did come out of it, for on the day of their recording, Muddy was introduced to Jimmy's friend Baby Face Leroy Foster, a multitalented musician who played guitar, harp, and drums, and sang too. Baby Face was a real charismatic figure whose wealth of talent, combined with his young looks, made him popular with women and envied by men. He became a permanent fixture with Muddy and Jimmy, the group now forming a triple threat. Foster, one of the more lively characters in the band, was a first cousin to blues piano player Johnny Jones, another hopeful young artist on the Chicago scene. Jimmy remembered when Baby Face entered the picture:

> Leroy started comin' around where we was playin' with Muddy Waters and myself . . . That was [before] Little Walter came in. He started playin' with us. Played drums for a while, he was a pretty good drummer and guitarist, and he could sing good, too. And so he just got with us like that. Year in, year out, we'd be together, it'd be a lot of fun . . . He was a very fine fellow. He just liked to talk a lot and would punch your chest with his fingers when he's talkin' to you, tryin' to get his point over to you. And when you'd be talkin' to him—everybody know Leroy—they would be turnin' away from him because when he'd get down he get carried away in his conversation, so he'd punch your chest out with his fingers.[34]

The union of these four men—Jimmy, Muddy, Baby Face, and Little Walter—marked the beginning of what would become the first phase of Jimmy's participation in one of the greatest blues bands ever assembled. Their musical versatility would prove to be a great asset as they developed a routine and repertoire that represented the arrival of the next generation of young black men who wanted to propel the uniquely American art form farther than it had ever been before.

In 1948 Snooky Pryor was making his own plans for stardom on Maxwell Street, coming up with a couple of catchy tunes, one of which was strikingly similar to a tune John Lee Hooker had recently recorded. According to Snooky, "When I recorded my first record, 'Snooky and Moody Boogie' and 'Telephone Blues,' I was over on the North Side, over there playin' the harp. Hooked up out there in the street. A guy named Chester Scales heard me playin' through that amplifier." He added, "Floyd was supposed to go into the studio with me and Moody to cut the record. It was somewhere on Wacker Drive. And Floyd showed up about week later. I guess he was off somewhere 'juicin'" as we called it back then."[35]

He used the "Boogie" tune he recorded as his theme song well before Jimmy, Muddy, Big Walter, or Little Walter had arrived in town. After Muddy arrived, he and Snooky played at the 444 West Chicago Avenue at the Ebony Lounge and then talked their way into landing a gig that gave them an opportunity to play on Big Bill Hill's radio show every Sunday evening at 4:20 P.M. over the airwaves on the WOPA channel. They also had a regular gig at the Zanzibar (located at Thirteenth and Ashland Avenue), where Snooky always played his signature "Boogie" tune.

The tune obviously had some kind of impact on the local level, because a few suitors came calling once Snooky's reputation grew as a result of the song. After hearing "Snooky and Moody Boogie," Bernard Abrams managed to corner Snooky Pryor, trying to entice him with an opportunity to affiliate himself with the Ora Nelle label. "Yeah," Snooky said, "I remember when Bernard set up that thing, for he tried to get me to record on it . . . after I had done made 'Snooky and Moody Boogie' and 'Telephone Blues' . . . He was a real nice guy, but he just drank heavy. He was all the fun you want to meet. There wasn't a dull moment around him."[36]

Clearly both Jimmy and Muddy were also searching for suitable material to record in hopes that the demos would be suitable enough to get them a little play on turntables, jukeboxes, and maybe a bit of radio airplay. At the same time, they were constantly hitting the streets in search of the next gig. They could always count on one particular person to help make things happen for them: Sunnyland Slim, one of the great patriarchs and benefactors of the blues. "Sunnyland was actually in the business before any of us," said Jimmy. "He was a nice piano player but couldn't get no record out that would do anything. But he opened the door for us, man! One guy I'll always admire is Sunnyland. And he don't regret doing things for you. It's nothing he'll want you to pat him on the back for. It just makes him feel good to do things for people. He may outlive me and he may not, but he's a father of the blues."[37]

Sunnyland had already used his considerable influence to broker the deal that set up the session for Muddy for Aristocrat, a label originally owned by Charles and Evelyn Aron and Fred and Mildred Blount. About the early sessions for Leonard Chess, Jimmy told one interviewer, "We'd cut li'l records for companies that wasn't doing anything. Aristocrat wasn't big but it had big intentions. I wasn't too interested in recording at the time—wasn't any of us too interested in doing it—we just wanted to play, man! Few dollars here, few dollars there."[38]

Jimmy credits Sunnyland for connecting him with the movers and shakers in the business and encouraging them to give him a shot at a career on wax. When he and Muddy finally broke through with Leonard Chess (who was now the co-owner with Evelyn Aron), it was Sunnyland who made it happen. At the time, the company was still under the Aristocrat label, which was how Muddy's first sides were cut (the label name would change soon thereafter). Sunnyland's career was peaking then, and his reputation and word carried a lot of weight with the record executives who looked to him as an unofficial talent scout to keep the Aristocrat roster full.

On one particular day Sunnyland really promoted Muddy's talents to Leonard, who was in search of a musician who could capture the genuine Southern folk sound, something along the lines of John Lee Hooker's or Lightnin' Hopkins's style of authentic rural blues singing and guitar playing. Sunnyland told Chess he knew just the guy to fill the role, bragging that it would only take one phone call to Muddy's house and he'd be there promptly. Sunnyland first brought Muddy along with him on his own recording session when he made "Johnson Machine Gun." When the producer casually asked about Muddy's ability to sing, Sunnyland responded enthusiastically, "Like a bird!"[39]

Sunnyland proudly dialed the number and called Muddy's house to tell him the good news about his presence being required at the record company—and that it would represent his first big break. When Muddy's wife, Geneva, answered the phone to say that Muddy wasn't home, Leonard, who was not one to take no for an answer, barked, "Hell, man, go get him—tell him his mama died, anything!"[40] Leonard demanded that Sunnyland go find him immediately. Muddy was still driving a truck for Westerngrade Venetian Blind Company, the job he'd gotten through his uncle. Jimmy remembered the cushy job that Muddy had at the time: "He'd deliver them, then he'd go home, play around, then go back to the factory . . . You'd see the doggone truck sitting in front of Muddy's place a lot of the time. He'd be in there eating or something. He had a good gig like that."[41]

Muddy was out on his route at the time, and Sunnyland knew the boss at Westerngrade would be highly reluctant to let Muddy take time off for such a project. He also thought Muddy might not believe that such a big opportunity would really take place. He carried out Leonard's scheme to get Muddy's attention. Using the work number that Geneva gave him, he phoned the business office and got through to the secretary, who was then told by Sunnyland that Muddy's mother was gravely ill and that he should come home immediately. Being none the wiser, the secretary passed the message on to Muddy, who, upon receiving the cryptic message, knew immediately that something was afoot, as his mother was already dead, and the grandmother who had raised him was still living in Mississippi. Still, it sounded serious enough that it warranted attention, so some personal time off was granted. By the time Muddy made it home, Sunnyland was there to greet him, and the truth was revealed about the recording session with Aristocrat. They hopped into Muddy's Chevy and headed straight to the studio to speak with Leonard, who was eagerly waiting to meet this unknown artist whom Sunnyland just raved about.

When Leonard finally directed Muddy to record a series of sparse arrangements of country folk blues based around his voice and his guitar, Muddy was more than a bit skeptical about his ability to pull it off. Then again, Muddy thought, this was the same way guitarists Lightnin' Hopkins and John Lee Hooker performed for their respective labels, and they were scoring hits on the charts. Leonard Chess, never one to ignore a current trend in the record industry, wanted to catch the wave while it was still riding high. Muddy had his doubts, though. His interests still lay in developing the sound of the quartet he'd been building with Little Walter, Jimmy, and Baby Face Leroy. Jimmy encouraged him, saying, "Go back to the way you did it down South. Just think back . . . go on and do it!"[42]

Over the next few days they refocused their musical efforts away from the quartet format and concentrated on developing a minimalist sound that would capture what Leonard was after. They ran through several pieces they thought would be appropriate selections to accent Muddy's organic approach to singing and playing. A few songs, like Robert Johnson's "Walkin' Blues," seemed like a perfect fit for the task at hand. After sketching out a few more original arrangements, they felt they were ready. Muddy returned to the studio and delivered his best rendition of the original arrangements he and Jimmy had developed for the occasion. He laid down the superstitious fortune-telling tale of "Gypsy Woman," which went over fairly well, but not well enough to get Leonard to release it right away.

When Sunnyland added his ticklish piano phrases underneath the vocals, the tunes carried a bit more momentum, and Leonard seemed to be satisfied with the results of the session. "Gypsy Woman" (Aristocrat 1302) was recorded in 1947 with Muddy on vocals and guitar, Sunnyland Slim on piano, and Ernest "Big" Crawford on bass. "Two or three days after the session, Muddy told me he done made a tape for Chess," Jimmy said. "Muddy said, 'man, I don't know how it's gonna sound but I got my foot in the door, I think.' Finally we got hold of a disc and we played it."[43]

Still, things weren't all peaches and cream with Muddy and Leonard Chess just yet, as Muddy soon learned how hard it was to collect on the musical installment he had delivered. According to Jimmy, "Muddy couldn't pay his car note. We used to hide the old car to keep the finance company from takin' it. He'd stay in it, send somebody in the store to get what he wanted. Then he'd come back over to my house and hide it in my garage. Chess would dodge him, say he's not in or something, 'cause Chess was scufflin' himself. But Muddy had to pay rent. He'd say, 'damn! It's a wild-goose chase there with Chess.'"[44] Leonard Chess was reluctant to invest too much time and energy in Muddy because of his good, but not stellar, performance on the recent session. As far as Leonard was concerned, Sunnyland hadn't delivered on his promise. Muddy's style wouldn't fully move Chess until 1948, when he recorded two sides that put him over the top once and for all.

In the latter months of 1948 Muddy suggested to Leonard that he should sign and record Robert Nighthawk on Aristocrat. Chess took Muddy's advice and scheduled a session. Nighthawk brought along with him a robust bassist, Willie Dixon, who eventually impressed Leonard so much that he became a regular session player and producer of numerous sessions.[45] Although it is a well-known fact that Dixon eventually got the main gig as talent scout, arranger, and performer for the Aristocrat label, Jimmy provides a rare glimpse into what might have been had things fallen to Sunnyland, the one who was there first: "Sunnyland, in my opinion, about the whole deal, really was supposed to have the position Willie Dixon got. But he didn't. Dixon had a little more school trainin' than Sunny did, so he got on in there, and that knocked Sunnyland out."[46]

Still, Muddy had gotten his foot in the door, and, whether Leonard Chess wanted to admit it or not, Muddy did leave a lasting impression. How was it that Muddy got the jump on so many musicians who were already in Chicago? According to Jimmy, it was more than just talent; it was also being in the right place at the right time. "Chess was looking for a rough blues singer," Rogers recalled. "Sunnyland had tried; he couldn't make it. Eddie Boyd was playin' blues, but it was a soft, Memphis Slim–type blues, and Chess wanted a rough, Delta sound of blues. And, at the time, Johnny Shines was doin' a stretch in the pen. So Muddy was his next stop."[47] Jimmy felt that Muddy was the most logical choice, and it was the smart move for Chess to capitalize on the uniquely rural sound that Leonard was trying to capture. Muddy's unwavering dedication to the Delta style inherited from birth made him a clear front-runner, a natural. "Muddy was closer to it than Shines were," Jimmy said. "So we just pitched in and put it on the beat, really."[48]

Leonard's label—any label, for that matter—could have benefited from a sound as classic as Robert Johnson's. Jimmy understood that as well as anyone and was willing to do his part to help nurture Muddy's efforts. "If you notice in Robert Johnson's music," Jimmy pointed out, "regardless to the turnarounds and changes of his own style of playing, it had a beat . . . and Muddy was co-min' close to that. We just added the beat that Robert Johnson was lookin' for by hisself. Two can do better than one, let's put it that way. So we added to it. It wasn't too hard to just drive Muddy on across the fence, there, you know? We was groovin' together with the stuff, *communicatin'*."[49]

What Jimmy is describing here is actually profound in its simplicity: if Robert Johnson had a full band, this is what his music would have sounded like had he recorded and performed live with a quartet who understood and complemented his musical sensibilities as perfectly as Muddy's band. Rogers obviously felt that Robert Johnson was the single most important influence and ingredient to the Muddy Waters sound and to the legendary Chicago sound as a whole.

With Leonard Chess smelling a potential new star in his stable, his label produced "Good Lookin' Woman" and "Mean Disposition" with the same lineup of Muddy, Sunnyland, and Big Crawford, plus an alto saxophone added for extra measure. This same April 1948 session yielded Muddy's earliest recorded versions of "I Can't Be Satisfied" and "Feel Like Going Home," two of the choices Muddy thought would best depict rural images as he did his best to conjure up the spirits of Robert Johnson and Son House simultaneously. These were all the same tunes that Jimmy rehearsed with Muddy on a regular basis as a duo, and Muddy was none too pleased with having made his debut without his wingman. Still, Jimmy understood that business was business, and their friendship was no worse for the wear because of unexpected circumstances. "He didn't wanna play it by himself," Rogers stated. "Sunnyland kept urgin' him. At that time his bills were gettin' high, his car note and he had to pay his rent."[50]

Indeed, both men were doing their best to hang on to the money generated from the late-night gigs on the weekends. "Muddy was kind of tight with them pennies, man," Jimmy later recalled when describing the frugal manner with which the two men managed to survive during the early days. In light of that, Muddy most likely would have welcomed some form of compensation for his time and efforts for his first session, but none was forthcoming, at least for now. This was partly due to the fact that Muddy had never officially signed a contract. Leonard's brother, Phil Chess, who was in the military service at the time, recalled, "He didn't have a contract with us [Aristocrat] for a long time, it was just a mutual agreement."[51] Muddy never denied this fact, stating, "I thought Leonard Chess was the best man in the business. He did a lot for me, putting out that first record and everything, and we had a good relationship with one another. I didn't even sign no contract with him, no nothing. It was just, 'I belong to the Chess family.'"[52] In truth, Leonard was initially quite reluctant to release the material. It was his business partner, Evelyn Aron, along with talent scout Samuel Goldberg who convinced Leonard that he should support Muddy's work.[53]

Chess recording engineer Malcolm Chisholm remembered Leonard Chess's superstitious nature and how Leonard allowed his personal beliefs to dictate the proceedings of his record label, unbeknownst to the musicians who were directly affected by it: "You would find him acting irrationally in odd ways. He didn't like to record on Fridays, and he'd never record on the 13th, but the seventh and eleventh were nice."[54] Chisholm also reported, "On Muddy's first successful session, the bass player wore a red shirt. The record sold. The next session Leonard said, 'get that bass man. And have him wear a red shirt.'"[55]

"Leonard had an extraordinarily coarse outer manner," Chisholm said. "I always wanted to send him a Mother's Day card because he answered the phone that way—'Hello, Mother!'"[56] Indeed, at least one Chess Records outtake has surfaced where Leonard, speaking to Jimmy during a recording session, can be clearly identified using the "mother" phrase. Apparently it was his ultra-hip Jewish way of using black vernacular as a truncated version of "motherfucker."

After Muddy's breakthrough with the two Aristocrat sides of "I Can't Be Satisfied" and "Feel Like Going Home," his career took flight. "The little joint I was playing in doubled its business when the record came out," Muddy bragged. "Bigger joints started looking for me."[57] Meanwhile, he and his now regular crew—Jimmy, Little Walter, and Baby Face Leroy—were still hitting the late-night streets, making ends meet. They had several regular spots they'd visit, rotating from one club to another and passing the gig to the next guy when they moved on to a better one. They played at Lowell King's at 3609 South Wentworth Street, located near Comiskey Park, where the White Sox continually struggled for World Series contention. The band also had the 708 Club on Forty-seventh Street. They held court at Docie's Lounge, 5114 South Prairie Street, on the South Side. And on the West Side there was Silvio's at 2254 West Lake Street, one of the favorite blues houses among them all. Gaining popularity at an exponential rate, Jimmy and Muddy were working almost seven nights a week on a consistent basis.

The group always traveled as a unit when they roamed from club to club, and between the four of them there was little besides music, whiskey, and women that they were interested in, choosing not to spend any more time on the street than was necessary. After all, it was Chicago, a place that was about as rough as it gets. "Muddy was just a quiet type of guy, he didn't mix too much with people . . . didn't really run around too much to different clubs less'n he had us with him. We went as a group, otherwise Muddy would be someplace at home or somethin'," Jimmy revealed.[58]

They were putting in long hours, even though their pockets weren't exactly bulging with wads of bills. Every bar had a policy that restricted the amount of money a blues band could make on any given night. After all, the clubs were open to make money, and the less they spent on overhead, the more lucrative their business would be. Each club owner played by the rules of the day and paid band members under the guidelines that represented the accepted practice of an unspoken three-way agreement between all parties involved. Jimmy knew the routine all too well.

> They had a union scale but most places at that time, they would get a contract but the club would pay this union scale off for you and then they'd pay you *under* scale to have you in the place. We'd just go along with it, you know, 'cause if you'd make ten, fifteen bucks a night—for three nights, forty-five bucks—and you'd get free whiskey and he'd take care of the union tax for you, that wasn't bad . . . You gotta crawl before you walk is the old sayin'. And that's what we were doin'.[59]

By now the Waters-Rogers sound was catching on in clubs, with Muddy leading the way on live sessions. Jimmy described the telepathic relationship that he and Muddy had on the bandstand in a manner that made it sound as easy as drinking a glass of water: "We could play together so easy, I could be talkin' to somebody at the end of bandstand and playin' with the band all at the same time, 'cause it wasn't any problem, 'cause I knowed the changes and the beat. We could just do it. It was simple to us."[60]

Little Walter and John Lee Williamson (Sonny Boy I) were the undisputed kings of the harp. Everything changed on the night of June 1, 1948, however, when Sonny Boy was attacked by several men who stole his personal belongings and left him for dead with a head injury. He managed to stagger home, where he collapsed against the door. In front of his wife, gasping his last breath, he passed away. After the death of Sonny Boy I, Billy Boy Arnold, who was quickly becoming known as Williamson's disciple, would begin trying to fill his shoes, as would another youngster, Amos Blakemore, better known as Junior Wells, who had recently gotten his big break when he was allowed to sit in for Little Walter on a number with Muddy Waters at the Ebony Lounge. Wells eventually became a regular at the club where the group known as the Three Deuces (later renamed the Three Aces) performed. Two of the trio's members, Louis and David Myers, had emerged on the Chicago scene from Mississippi in 1941. Louis played lead guitar while Dave tuned his strings down and played bass on the guitar.

Meanwhile, Little Walter was still sneaking down on Maxwell Street to jam, which was really breaking the rules, because the guys were trying to go "legit" by joining the union.

> He would sneak off down there on Sunday morning. We played Saturday night, man, and somebody would come to us, said, "Hey, man, get your boy down there—go get him, man." We'd go get him, he'd get mad when he see you comin' 'cause he knows you don't want him down there, man. He's makin' more money than on the gig, but I knew about it. After you join the union they had so many rules, at that time, and we was new in the field, we was tryin' to—you know—abide by the rules, because they fine you.[61]

Jimmy, Muddy, and Little Walter were getting closer to perfecting their sound. "We'd do a lot of rehearsin' durin' that time, the three of us," Jimmy said. "And Walter wanted to learn. His ears were open, but he just didn't have nobody to sit down and really teach him. He was mostly playing between Rice Miller and that saxophone sound of Louis Jordan; after he came with us, we developed him mostly into a harder sound."[62]

Sunnyland Slim was still calling many of the shots when it came to controlling the musical events in the blues world of Chicago. He had already used his considerable influence to broker the deal for Muddy's session at Aristocrat. And he'd taken over the gig when Eddie Boyd left the Blue Flame (formerly known as the Flame). Now, in December 1948, it was Sunnyland again who had suggested that the band record a few sides for Tempo-Tone, a small, independent label run by Irving Taman, an entrepreneur who owned a bar called Irv's Boulevard Lounge located at 301 North Sacramento at Fulton Street, the urban part of the Northwest Side. Irv, a former World War II veteran, liked to record the musicians he had performing at his bar, and Sunnyland was his main man. Taman relied on him to recruit all the heavyweights for a marathon session that eventually yielded ten sides for his Tempo-Tone label. The participants included Sunnyland, Muddy Waters, Little Walter, Jimmy Rogers, Baby Face Leroy, Elga Edmonds, Floyd Jones, and Ernest "Big" Crawford.[63] According to the notes in the ledger, Jimmy took the lead vocals (and most likely guitar work) on December 22 and cut two sides: "You Don't Have to Go," and "I'm in Love with a Woman." As fate would have it, however, the X that marked the spot next to the calendar date in the recording ledger revealed that his contribution was not released, thus his music never saw the light of day.[64]

For more than a year now, Baby Face had become such a regular fixture with the Waters/Rogers/Walter trio that the band was now a quartet at their regular roster of clubs. And as they made their rounds, the foursome increased their visibility as well as their reputation as the gold standard for authentic blues from the Deep South. Their inner-city tour still included their regular stops at the 708 Club on East Forty-seventh Street, Docie's Lounge on Fifty-first Street and Prairie, and Silvio's on West Lake Street. And they added the Zanzibar on Thirteenth and Ashland Avenue, the Boogie Woogie Inn, and the Du Drop Inn on Thirty-sixth and Wentworth Street.[65]

Now that they were a well-established quartet, their assault on the public was really beginning to take hold as the band gradually worked their way across the city, spreading the blues. On an average night Jimmy and Muddy would make about eight dollars apiece, plus drinks and a few decent tips thrown in from appreciative patrons. One in particular, Bob Ross, was a serious blues fan who owned a construction firm. Serving as a benefactor of sorts, Ross would call down to whatever club Jimmy might be performing in to make sure the band had several fifths of whiskey on the table when they arrived to play.[66] This kind of special attention pleased the men and gave them encouragement as they continually pushed the envelope to get their sound across.

Sunnyland Slim had also played a vital role in pulling them in at the 708 Club, one of the more popular night hangouts in Chicago. Most nights when they finished their sets there, Muddy, Baby Face, Jimmy, and Walter paid visits to other blues clubs for the dual purpose of sizing up the competition and spreading their own name around. Soon everyone wanted them to be guest performers on the bandstand the moment they arrived. They had become blues royalty among their peers. Jimmy and Muddy would run out to the car, grab a couple of small amps, and they'd quickly launch into a few hot numbers. Walter would coolly ease into the bar, harps neatly tucked away in his pockets. Once they cranked up, they actually *moved* the audience: "When we leave, the crowd would leave too," Jimmy bragged. "So then they called us 'the Headcutters.'"[67]

This became the second and more potent version of the Muddy Waters band.[68] "There were four of us, and that's when we began hitting heavy," Muddy said.[69] "We used to call ourselves 'The Headhunters' [used synonymously and thus interchangeable with "Headcutters"]. We'd go from club to club looking for bands that are playing and cut their heads. 'Here come those boys,' they'd say." Jimmy acknowledged the band's overwhelming presence during those exciting times, saying, "Well, they called us that for a while around. We used to go around and shoot guys down like that. We never blew a gig for that particular thing, but if we were off, to keep from sitting around at home—." You knew what came next: "They'd call us on and then that's it. We could take the gig if we wanted it, but it wasn't payin' nothin' so we just drink and have some fun. That would be a bigger crowd for us on the place we were playing' on weekends, because we'd announce where we were. That's free publicity, that's the way it was. Lots of fun." When asked if others resented their headhunting approach, Jimmy said, "No. If they did, they didn't show it. They would be glad for us to come around, because they were trying to get into the beat that we had, see, and they would like to hear it."[70]

Thus was born the reputation of four of the most dangerous men who ever walked the West Side. This was the new quartet that terrorized the town with a torrential rain of fried country blues unlike anything Chicago had heard before. Indeed, the dual-guitar interaction of Jimmy and Baby Face, with Little Walter's squallin' harmonica over the top—not to mention the powerful vocal delivery of Muddy—was a unique event to witness among those who frequented the nightspots. Furthermore, any member could take the lead vocals at any point during the show. Their show had a sound and a presence that were never captured in the band's studio recordings to such an extent.

Then there was the fact that Baby Face doubled on guitar and drums, Jimmy doubled on guitar and harmonica, and Little Walter doubled on harmonica and guitar, thus adding even more depth and versatility. The band typically would casually stroll up to the stage and make themselves comfortable before firing up a tune. Jimmy explained, "We didn't stand up in those days . . . We sat down when we played. We'd have chairs lined around . . . put the mike up in front of you and you'd sing sitting down. You could keep your time that way, tappin' your foot." Jimmy observed that Baby Face had the loudest taps of all. "Oh, man, he'd click 'em both—*clap, clap, clap!*"[71]

Jimmy was still trying to shake off the disappointment of the Tempo-Tone session when Sunnyland Slim once again lent him a hand. Sunnyland was one of the main artists who recorded for Joe Brown and James Burke Oden (better known as "St. Louis Jimmy"), two entrepreneurs who co-owned the JOB label, a recent start-up in July 1949. Brown had booked a session on August 26, a sort of a variety session that featured Sunnyland, St. Louis Jimmy, Willie Mabon (vocalist, pianist, and harmonica player), and Jimmy Rogers. Under Sunnyland's auspices, Jimmy was allowed to cut two sides as a leader: "I'm in Love" (the same tune he tried to get released on the Tempo-Tone session a little more than ago in December) along with "That's All Right." Sunnyland backed him on piano.[72] Jimmy's bad luck with recording continued, as the two tracks he laid were not released at the time. In fact the six sides that were recorded by Sunnyland (including Jimmy's) would be passed around several times before eventually winding up in the hands of several labels, including Regal, Apollo, and Delmark.[73]

Leonard Chess was finally willing to give in to the pressure from Muddy to allow at least one or two of Muddy's own men to play with him. The session marked Jimmy's first official recording with Muddy for the Chess family.[74] Jimmy was on guitar (along with Muddy) and Baby Face was on drums at the September 1949 Aristocrat date, playing the role of backup band for vocalist and pianist Little Johnny Jones on two tunes, "Big Town Playboy" and "Shelby County Blues" (Aristocrat 405),[75] a tune that Jimmy would record at a later date. On "Shelby County Blues" Jimmy's second guitar part is not very prominent, but on "Big Town Playboy" his unmistakable style cuts right through, and the solo on the recording reveals his identity, with Muddy on second guitar. Muddy then took the lead as they recorded "Screamin' and Cryin'" and "Where's My Woman Been," eventually released as a single (Aristocrat 406).[76] Muddy's fifth and final tune, "Last Time I Fool Around with You," had Muddy on vocals and second guitar, Tampa Red on lead guitar, Ransom Knowling on bass, and Odie Payne on drums. (Red, Knowling, and Payne regularly performed as a unit with Jones during this time.)[77] Upon listening to the tune, one can hear the typical Tampa-style guitar riffs (unlike Muddy's "keen" sound), as well as the choice of key for this song, also common with Tampa's preference. Although this particular recording went unreleased for decades (causing much confusion about Tampa Red's presence), Jimmy confirmed to producer and friend Dick Shurman that it was indeed Tampa Red on the Aristocrat session.[78]

Jimmy began traveled with the Muddy Waters band beginning in October 1949 on a series of on-and-off gigs that would lead them out of town on an increasingly frequent basis. They went through the Southern states, covering Alabama, Louisiana, Arkansas, Tennessee, and North Carolina. Jimmy admitted that the long, late hours proved to be exhausting for some of them: "Man, we'd be sleepy. We played all till maybe 1:00 and then we'd leave out of Mississippi and take the ferry, go over to Helena and go to bed. And at 5:00 you gotta be up and gettin' ready to go to the studio, man."[79]

On Sunday, November 6, 1949, the 708 Club had a "battle of the bands" contest between Memphis Minnie and Big Bill Broonzy, with Jimmy, Muddy, and Sunnyland serving as judges.[80] In December the Headhunters traveled to Helena, Arkansas, to do the KKFA radio show, sponsored by Katz Clothing. The humorous story about Jimmy and Walter oversleeping and leaving Muddy and Baby Face to fend for themselves is now legendary. The latter two found themselves awakened to the sounds of the radio show they were supposed to be on. They were staying in a different hotel and had no way of contacting Jimmy and Walter. So they went on ahead to the radio studio and played guitars over the airwaves, and as they finished the tune, Jimmy later recounted, he heard the radio announcer say, "'Well, Jimmy Rogers and Little Walter is somewhere sleepin' it off. If they hear us, come on in.'" Jimmy and Walter frantically rushed to the station and arrived twenty minutes late (for a show that typically lasted only fifteen minutes); by then Muddy and Baby Face had performed three or four numbers. Muddy gave them both a glare that let them know how angry he was. "He was lookin' right in my face, man," Jimmy remembered. Muddy waved them in, they quickly grabbed instruments that were already set up and waiting, and, according to Jimmy, "They [the listening audience] didn't know whether we were there or not."[81]

The Chess brothers had come to appreciate the special chemistry that the Headhunters created when they performed live. Both Phil and Leonard had an acute level of business acumen that allowed them to parlay various ideas and instincts into lucrative payoffs for their enterprises, though not for their recording artists. They made the smart move, for instance, in the 1940s of buying a few bars where they could not only install the live entertainment lineup (those who happened to be on their Aristocrat label roster) but also dictate what tunes could be played on the jukebox inside in each joint. They were sometimes even smart enough to acknowledge someone else's talents in areas that lay outside of their expertise. Inevitably such acumen created an audience interested in buying the records they played and produced, resulting in expansion of their company.

The success of Chess Records was built on the shoulders of the company's top performers. Jimmy Rogers was therefore an important ingredient for Leonard, who clearly had the means to make him famous. Although it had taken awhile to achieve the bandleader status necessary to cut a deal and move out of the position of a mere sideman, Jimmy would ultimately make himself inseparable from the success of Muddy Waters. About the major impact of Jimmy's musical contribution, Dan Forte—longtime editor, author, and leading authority for *Guitar Player* magazine—once declared unequivocally, "One can't play the Chicago style without borrowing heavily from Jimmy Rogers."[82]

The significance of Jimmy's pioneering of the contrapuntal/supportive second guitar role is considered by serious musicians to be on par with the permanent, mold-shattering technique of Chuck Berry's mastery of the double-stop guitar riffs made so popular on classic R & B hits like "Carol" and "Johnny B. Goode." It's practically impossible to play old-fashioned rock 'n' roll on guitar without using Berry's technique. In similar fashion, authentic Chicago blues cannot be delivered in its pristine form without the liquid formula of harp and two guitars poured over a bed of rhythmic bass and drums. Basic to that formula is Jimmy's always steady *lumpty-lump*—the double-stop rhythmic groove he consistently applied as underpinning for Muddy's mercurial lines of slide guitar—as well as the deft melodic phrases he wove around Muddy's steady groove.

Jimmy's impact on the Muddy Waters band went far beyond his guitar technique, however. While his natural reticence and genuine affection kept him from questioning Muddy's ultimate authority, Jimmy assumed more and more responsibility in shaping the sound of the band, including having a major voice when it came to song selection, personnel, and arrangements. "I built that band," he once said matter-of-factly. "Muddy was the leader but I was leadin' the band ... I would tell him on the side what he should do, how he should work it. And it worked." Evidently Muddy wanted Jimmy to take an even greater role in the band, because according to Jimmy, "Muddy worried about me singin' all the time. He wanted me to sing. Muddy he said he didn't like his own voice. I don't know why. He sounded all right to me."[83] Jimmy apparently enjoyed his role as behind-the-scenes leader. He always felt more comfortable just seeming to fulfill the role he believed he was meant to play in the group—the ideal supplement to the musical meanderings of Muddy Waters. Over time, he learned how to fly flawlessly in tandem with Muddy to achieve an unsurpassed level of excellence. Listen to how Jimmy obviously relished his role of being the perfect foil to Muddy's every move: "I could understand where he was goin' and lay there, and get under him and ride him in them curves and things. I knew how he was gonna come up there and come down. Drive, then lay under him. You call that *feed*. I knew how to feed him real good."[84]

Even more important was the ability to master the elusive time and feel of the chord progression in Muddy's music. Developing an innate sense for the irregular pace and direction of the band was one of the elements that usually threw the average accompanist off the bucking bronco that was the blues. Jimmy had tamed the wildest aspects of the music some time ago, although he always understood how others could easily get tossed. "Peoples didn't understand the count or how we's doin' that," Jimmy remembered. "That's hard for a straight guy to learn that stuff. We done hit it and gone to something else. We wouldn't stay in one place. You got a lotta different phrases and turnovers and channels. It's like puttin' up a buildin'. You try to explain that to 'em, you disencourage 'em real quick."[85] Muddy had a more specific way of describing his music: "It may have thirteen beats in some song, and the average man, he not used to that kind of thing. He got to follow me, not himself, because I make the blues different. Do that change when I change, just the way I feel, that's the way it went . . . I got just about as good time in the blues as anyone."[86]

Rather than explain, Jimmy and Muddy simply played, and the band built up a following through the gigs they played. Money, however, was always tight. The Headhunters played with some regularity at clubs that included the Boogie Woogie Inn, Lowell King's club, Romeo's Place, the Squeeze Club, and Brown's Village. One income source they could count on was their regular gig at the Zanzibar. On one particular Friday night in 1949 they had unexpected visitors: Leonard Chess, along with a few of his business associates. "Muddy said, 'Leonard's here. He wants to hear us play some of the stuff that we do,'" Jimmy recalled.[87] Those casual words probably hid some powerful emotions—a record producer wanted to hear the band's unique brand of blues. Then and there Leonard first heard the raw effect of Muddy Waters, and he no doubt realized immediately the true potential of what Muddy could sound like back at the studio if they'd allow him to play with his own group of musicians.

Jimmy Rogers observed the natural transition from the old to the new during the late 1940s and the early 1950s, and he suddenly realized that his past, present, and future were all linked together, forming a crossroads in his musical life. Indeed, those blues heroes he worshipped in his teens were now gradually becoming relics in real time, and the future was something that Jimmy and his peers—Muddy, Little Walter, brothers Louis and Dave Myers, Baby Face, and others—held in their hands like a precious pearl that was ready to shine brighter than the gemstones of the past. "Memphis Minnie, Tampa Red and Memphis Slim and fellows of that nature, they had been real hot with the blues—but they were dying off," Jimmy recalled. "They got real common—that type of blues at that time. And we came right in at that time and grabbed the blues again and put fire behind them and started livenin' it back up again. Because all those people were playin', man, they were famous when I was a little boy, some before I was born."[88]

Part of their magic was their ability to meld the best of the old with something vibrant and new. Jimmy went on record as saying he and Little Walter dragged Muddy kicking and screaming into the modern '50s while Muddy kept both of them firmly rooted in the deep blues.[89] It deserves mentioning that the attitude toward the next generation taking over the blues was not necessarily something that the old guard was against. To the contrary, the musical impact of the blues youth had the opposite effect on most of the veterans, as Jimmy attested: "They'd come around to hear us play to see what we were doin' and every one of them gave us a good compliment. 'You're doin' somethin' for the blues. I'm glad somebody's bringin' 'em back alive.' And we livened the blues back up again, and more people decided they wanted to try to play the blues."[90]

4

HEADHUNTERS AND WOLFMEN

I told [Muddy], "We have a good sound onstage, and the
record don't sound as good." And he talked to Chess,
and they decided to let me start recording with him.

—Jimmy Rogers

Jimmy Rogers participated in a marathon recording session that took place at
Parkway Records in January and February 1950. The session was organized much
like the one held in December 1948 at Tempo-Tone Records for Irving Taman
under Sunnyland Slim's direction. At the Parkway session, Little Walter, Baby
Face Leroy, Muddy Waters, Little Rogers, Sunnyland Slim, Memphis Minnie, Big
Crawford, and Floyd and Moody Jones were all in attendance, among others. Over
time this session became famous for the unbridled enthusiasm and intense delivery of the performance on both parts of "Rollin' and Tumblin'" with Muddy, Baby
Face, and Little Walter. As it happened, this session was also indelibly marked
for what it was *not* known for: the Jimmy Rogers session with Memphis Minnie.

Parkway Records producer Monroe "Ray" Passis had two cohorts—brothers
George and Ernie Leaner, two young, assertive African Americans from Mississippi. Passis had recruited them to help influence black musicians to participate
in cutting sides for his newly founded label. When it came to knowing what was
happening on the street, musically speaking, Leonard Chess was not in the know,
but he knew who was. Sunnyland was the Chess brothers' "go-to" guy when
they needed someone to communicate effectively with the blues community. He
knew how to deal with the artists, and through his own experience as a regular
sideman for the label, he also knew how to deal with the big company men, Phil

and Leonard. He even knew what was happening at the fledgling independent studios that were much smaller and working practically underground.

Most likely Sunnyland was chosen to coordinate this significant session that, according to Muddy, took place not in a recording studio, but a warehouse.[1] Baby Face was chosen to lead a trio as vocalist and drummer, with Muddy and Walter on guitar and harp (Jimmy didn't perform on any of these Parkway versions, because he showed up a bit late). Baby Face did four songs: "Red Headed Woman" and "Boll Weevil" were two songs he'd tried, unsuccessfully, to get recorded and released earlier on Tempo-Tone (the same session in which Jimmy had his songs rejected), and then there were the two most outstanding sides, "Rollin' and Tumblin'," parts 1 and 2.

Indeed, things got rollin'—*and* tumblin'—at least for Baby Face. The lengthy all-star event would have been a total triumph were it not for a major fallout that occurred during the recording. A disagreement rose between Muddy and Baby Face over who would lead the proceedings. Even though the session was booked under Leroy Foster's name, clearly it was Muddy who was the rising star. To make matters worse, Baby Face openly challenged the King Bee on the particular details surrounding the best way to play "Rollin' and Tumblin'," one of their standard flag-wavers among a steadily growing roster of tunes in the Waters band. "'Rollin' and Tumblin',' that was a thing both Leroy *and* Muddy was doin'," Jimmy said. "One was tryin' to outdo the other one on that." Upon listening to the dynamic take, you can hear the two men battling for attention, and clearly there were two interpretations about how the tune should be laid down for posterity. "If Muddy Waters wanted to be top dog on that, Leroy figured he knew more about it than Muddy. That's where their little hang-up started," Jimmy insisted.[2] Evidently Muddy's word won out; this two-sided single had an enthusiastic version with lyrics on side 1, with an even more intense instrumental on side 2, featuring Muddy's ferocious humming of the melody.

Little Walter's turn was next to take the lead, and he led the trio of himself, Muddy, and Baby Face on "Just Keep Loving Her," "Muscadine Blues," "Moonshine Blues," and "Bad Acting Woman." Walter chose to play guitar on most of these tunes, probably to fill the void left by Jimmy, who still hadn't arrived. Memphis Minnie and Her Jumping Boys were up next, an assembled backup group that included Walter, Sunnyland, Big Crawford, and Baby Face to support Minnie and her husband, Little Son Joe (Ernest Lawlars). Minnie recorded "Down Home Girl," "Night Watchman Blues," "Why Did I Make You Cry," and "Kidman Blues." And finally we hear from Jimmy with a backing band that clearly includes Walter, Baby Face, and Sunnyland on a distant piano. Jimmy enters with an unmistakable voice on "Ludella." Inexplicably, the intro and the first verse of the tune were deleted, and Jimmy appears at the second verse, followed by a guitar solo that is not his lead work but more likely Memphis Minnie's (based on her tone and phrasing, which matches all the tunes from Minnie's portion of this marathon session featuring Sunnyland on piano).[3] Jimmy would eventually get his chance to record "Ludella" properly, but not this time around. As for the fate of Jimmy's incomplete take, his tune was coupled with the rest of Minnie's part of the session and sold to Fred Mendelsohn at Regal Records, which led to more than fifty years of confusion as to the origin and destination of Minnie's Parkway session and Jimmy's take of "Ludella."[4]

Leonard Chess caught wind of the January 1950 Parkway matter. When he actually heard the recordings, he was absolutely furious when he heard Muddy's unique slide technique and vocals on the recording. "Muddy got himself in pretty big trouble with Chess," Jimmy remembered. "I laughed myself silly about it." By now Muddy was a signed artist to Leonard's Aristocrat label but had crossed into enemy territory, so to speak, albeit temporarily. Leonard had underestimated the cumulative affect of his strict recording policy and allowing Muddy to bring in his sidemen as full-fledged members of the family label. He was not about to lose his biggest artist to Passis and Parkway without a fight.

Muddy, of course, went back to Chess; he had a contract to honor. As for Baby Face, he decided to break his bond with Muddy and go for a solo career, based on promises made by Parkway. This would be his ultimate undoing, for unbeknownst to him, Leonard Chess played ruthlessly with his record-making adversaries, with plans on systematically stripping the remnants of the session bare, including the recapture and hostile takeover of the patented sound of Muddy, Jimmy, and Little Walter. Chess's retribution toward Monroe Passis's blatant breach of etiquette resulted in severe punishment. And so it came to pass that Chess had Muddy lay down the same hellacious groove of "Rollin' and Tumblin'"—albeit without the unbridled enthusiasm that could be heard in the Parkway version—and Leonard's devilish horns were officially showing when he released it immediately to the airwaves, thus casting his irascible shadow over Parkway's efforts.[5] What Leonard still failed to realize, though, was the reason why Muddy had defected in the first place: Leonard wouldn't allow Muddy's band to record intact as a complete unit at Aristocrat.

In his second act of retribution, Leonard also bought many of the remaining tapes that Mendelsohn hadn't already sold, and he bought them at bargain-rate prices. Thus, he'd shown his intent to bring Parkway's progress to a grinding halt by first acquiring and suppressing the Parkway sides and then pushing his own Aristocrat version of the same songs and bands on the airwaves at a much faster and deeper rate than Parkway could afford to contend with. The strategy worked; Parkway lasted only four months, producing only twenty-three recordings, only fourteen of which were released. By early 1950 the original trio of Jimmy, Muddy, and Walter were again looking for a permanent fourth wheel to commit to the band. Like Blue Smitty, Baby Face was more interested in his own personal agenda; for him, Muddy's band was a second priority. Baby Face had abandoned the drum chair in favor of what he clearly thought would be greener pastures at Parkway and signed a contract to record exclusively for the company, a move he would later regret. The trio put the word out that they were looking for a reliable drummer who could lay down a solid backbeat.

Once again Sunnyland came through for Muddy when he introduced him to Elga Edmonds, who had a wide reputation as a top-notch and experienced drummer by the age of forty. Jimmy recalled it this way: "Before that, it was me, Muddy, Walter, and Baby Face. Baby Face just wasn't interested in playing too much and he just give it up and went back to Memphis. The next thing I heard he got sick and he passed. Elga joined the band 'round 1950, somewhere along in there. Elga and Baby Face was on about the same kick. They was bumpin' along about the same, but Elga was more experienced 'cause he played jazz."[6]

Elga Edmonds had one of the most often mispronounced names in the business. On records he was variously identified by the names of Elgin Evans, Elgin Edwards, Elgin Edmonds, Edward Elgin, and Elgar Edmonds. These misnomers led to several alternate incarnations, some of which Elga made use of himself. Edmonds was born in Champaign, Illinois, in 1909, one of the few major players on the Chicago scene who was not from Mississippi. He was also one of the few formally trained musicians of the blues crew, having studied jazz at a music conservatory not long after he first moved to Chicago. His dad, Bill "Speed" Edmonds, played ragtime piano and was a good dancer.[7]

Muddy picked Elga to become the final component to the Muddy Waters band, thus essentially forming the second edition of the Headhunters: Muddy on lead guitar, Jimmy on bass guitar, Elga on drums, and Little Walter on harp.[8] Elga's unique approach to drumming is evident in his patented stop-time rhythms on tunes like "I'm Ready," "(I'm Your) Hoochie Coochie Man," and "Just Make Love to Me (I Just Want to Make Love to You)." "We'd get a lot of new ideas comin' into the music," said Jimmy. "A lot of times, we'd build sounds like that, just playin' off each other. The stop time was just an idea. Break time and all that stuff. The whole band just clicked in and did it."[9]

They played at the Zanzibar and at numerous other clubs on the South and West Sides. The band rehearsed hard and sometimes made a festive party out of the event. Elga's nephew, also named Elga, remembers that they made the arduous practice sessions into something that was more like a picnic: "They'd have a big pot of chitlins, black eyed peas, collard greens, all kinds of soul food," said Elga Edmonds II. "These guys would come to my uncle's house and play and have a good time, but you could tell they were working hard."[10] Occasionally Elga would stroll with the Headhunters during their late night prowls. Unlike the others, he wasn't able to hang out at all hours and watch the sun come up; he was busy sharpening his skills on an entirely different level. During the day he'd attend classes at the Roy C. Knapp School of Percussion, where he studied vibroharp and classical drum technique.[11]

There were some people who knew that Baby Face Leroy was one of the original Headhunters and were not too pleased when they'd see the crew out prowling without him, but instead hanging out with Elga, who was nowhere near as popular a drummer as Baby Face. Just about everybody liked Baby Face; he was handsome, funny, and extremely versatile as a musician. His biggest weakness—like that of many others in the blues society—was alcohol, and when he'd had one too many, things got ugly, even when he was among his buddies, like Jimmy and Muddy. When Jimmy was asked years later what he thought happened to Baby Face, he said, "Well, they said he had tuberculosis . . . and he played with it for quite a few years and it eventually did get him, you know."[12]

Meanwhile, the band rehearsed harder than ever, still rollin' and tumblin' all night long. Jimmy concurred with Elga's nephew, saying that although they practiced long hours, the band still maintained the party environment, no matter whose house they chose as a rehearsal site. For example, whenever they practiced at Muddy's place, Jimmy said, "There wouldn't be nobody there to give you no problems, so we would suck on these little half-pints, and Muddy would cook some rice and chicken gizzards. We'd have a pot on in the kitchen and we'd get us a bowl, get us some water and get a little drink, then we'd sit back down and do it some more."[13]

Not every gig they played was glamorous. Several of the venues they played struggled to be perceived as little more than dives, according to Jimmy's assessment: "We played some pretty rough gigs, man. When somebody'd get shot or stabbed or something or die, that's a pretty rough gig. That happened a lot of times, different places."[14] They played in some of the most unlikely places, like the place that Elga's nephew remembered in later years when reminiscing about the rare opportunity to sit in with the band on drums. "You know the Blues Brothers' bar with the chicken wire fence? It was something like that," said the young Edmonds. "They had me up there playin' during the break and people broke out and started fighting and throwing bottles at the stage and stuff."[15] "The clubs were very violent," Jimmy concurred. "After we got into bigger clubs they'd fight, or some guy would get mad with his old lady and they'd fight. Somebody would get cut or get shot. Clubs had a two o'clock regular license, and if you wanted to stay open till three, you would pay extra, a patrol buy. That was a little gimmick the gangsters had going."[16]

Every now and then Little Walter would get caught up into the fracas, and Jimmy and Muddy would have to bail him out. "He'd have a misunderstanding and somebody would start pickin' at him," Jimmy recalled. "Before you knew it, Walter would crack him beside the head with a mike stand."[17] Despite those aggressive outward appearances, Walter also had a sensitive side. "He was a loner, but he loved to be petted," Jimmy remembered. "He was always over at my house or Muddy's, because he felt relaxed with us." The men developed a mutual love and respect for one another that extended well beyond the music. "We were a family. We never argued. Each of us thought of the band first," said Jimmy about Walter, Elga, and Muddy.[18]

Indeed, the four did form a family-like bond, which made the music even tighter when they hit the clubs. Walter would have a few harmonicas tucked in his pockets, ready to whip out on a moment's notice once he hit the stage. Jimmy would have his Silvertone, poised to strike, and Muddy would come in carrying two guitar cases like a gunslinger with shotguns strapped under both arms. He'd blast the audience with both barrels too. One guitar had the strings tuned to the normal pattern of E-A-D-G-B-E, and the other was tuned to an open E major chord of E-B-E-G#-B-E, which required no left-hand fingering to play the blues changes ("Open 'E' and open 'D'—we called that 'Vestapol,'" said harp ace Charlie Musselwhite[19]). "Muddy couldn't play with a slide in 'natural,'" Jimmy said. "He'd have to tune the guitar in Spanish [D-G-D-G-B-D] to play it . . . Before we'd go to these gigs he'd have one tuned 'cross.'—We called it 'Spanish' [this is actually open "G" tuning]."[20]

They played the kind of music that could be described as organic, in that they often didn't follow what could be considered a typical twelve-bar blues structure of dominant seventh chords from the first, fourth, and fifth positions that occur in a regimented, predictable form. This was Chicago blues transported from old Mississippi, and down *there*, if you were a real lowdown blues player, you moved when you *felt* like moving. Many native Mississippians—Son House, John Lee Hooker, Howlin' Wolf—enjoyed the same beautifully captivating affliction.

Like them, Muddy's music was tailor-made to his own sensibilities, and if you were going to play with him, you had to learn how to follow directly behind him. As good as Jimmy eventually became at reading Muddy's mind, it even took him awhile before he internalized the natural pulse of Muddy's music. "I knew what he was doin', but to make them turnaround changes, that's what was hard," Jimmy noted. "I didn't know how to go into those certain changes and stay with the pattern . . . we wasn't playin' like the average guy play, you know . . . that was somethin' that the average guy wouldn't understand."[21]

That irregular chord pattern combined with the relentless push of guitar, drums, and harmonica underneath the moaning vocal lines was irresistible. "Other bands would just be playin' and singin', they just made one beat," Jimmy proudly boasted, "but we had drive with what we were doin'." The razor's edge sound of the music the band produced was a direct result of Muddy's deep-cutting bass lines from the low E and A strings on his guitar, contrasted by the shimmering treble riffs culled from the rapid vibrato of his left-hand finger that was wrapped in a glass slide. Not everyone appreciated Muddy's efforts to shake the teeth of the audience. "When he'd put that guitar down and grab that other with that doggone piece of slide—oh Lord, man! That's when Walter would have a fit," Jimmy quipped. "Walter hated that. He'd say, 'he's just scratchin' on that guitar!' I wouldn't tell Muddy that."[22]

The head Chess man still wasn't willing to give Muddy what he wanted: to record with his own band. Despite having listened to the Headhunters' superior vibe at the Zanzibar, Leonard—being either superstitious or just playing it safe—stuck with what he knew, which was the successful and simple formula of Muddy on rural slide guitar and Big Crawford laying down that pumping, thunking bass underneath. "Chess wouldn't upset things—he wouldn't mess with the harp or the extra guitar," Muddy lamented. "He wanted to keep the combination that had made the hit record—just Big Crawford's bass and my guitar."[23]

Indeed, Leonard sincerely believed in rituals and sincerely feared the negative outcome that might affect the order of things if a routine was disturbed. In her seminal documentary text, *Spinning Blues into Gold*, Nadine Cohodas wrote, "Sometimes he emptied his pockets of change before going into the studio to remind himself of the times his pockets were empty."[24] Thus, Jimmy and Walter were still not allowed to come in to the studio and play; when Muddy recorded "Walkin' Blues" as a B side to the now-legendary "Tumblin'," both sides demonstrated the same stripped-down sound.

The ritual continued right through May, and then, when Leonard *finally* allowed a concession, though still not in full, he gave Muddy the green light to choose one of his homeboys to get in on the action; the lucky winner was Little Walter. On June 3 Walter played a supportive role, providing contrapuntal lines to Muddy's wicked slide, along with his chocolaty vocals dripping over the four tunes recorded that day: "You're Gonna Need My Help," "Sad Letter Blues," "Early Morning Blues," and "Appealing Blues." Leonard was pleased with the results of these sessions for his company, which no longer went under the name of Aristocrat; they were now Chess Records. With a flourish and a new logo, the Chess label was officially anointed on June 3, 1950.

In August 1950, six months after the Parkway marathon, Leonard Chess gave Jimmy his first solo break when he discovered that Rogers had also been an active participant in the sessions that had gotten Muddy into trouble. Leonard knew that Fred Mendelsohn—who bought the Sunnyland/Jimmy Rogers tapes from JOB's Joe Brown as well as the Parkway sessions from producer Monroe Passis—was on the run, taking the remaining tapes in his possession from that marathon session to any studio that would have him, including Herald, Savoy, Regal, JOB, and Apollo. It appears that Leonard wanted to sew up the competition thoroughly, so he gave Jimmy the same opportunity he gave Muddy: come in and record those same Parkway and JOB sides for Chess, and all will be forgiven.

The first time Leonard had really taken notice of Jimmy Rogers was when he paid that unannounced visit at the Zanzibar in 1949. Leonard had singled out Jimmy as the next talent he would try to cultivate and approached him about the possibilities. Jimmy, who was no novice when it came to recording, was now trying to play it close to the vest when it came to entering a long-term deal. He and other colleagues had already allowed themselves to be recorded by small independent labels that didn't have enough financial strength to record, promote, and distribute their music with any degree of impact or longevity. A record deal with Chess clearly had greater potential.

Jimmy weighed the pros and cons carefully. He knew several fellow musicians had been burned by shady deals because the artists didn't take the time to read a contract's small print. They had unwittingly locked themselves into a powerless situation where they were legally bound by contract to honor exclusive arrangements with the label's owner, thus restricting their ability to maintain control of their own musical destiny. It was a worry. However, Jimmy was encouraged by the fact that he and Muddy both trusted the status of respect that the Chess family had shown to Sunnyland Slim; it seemed, at least on the surface, to be something of value that gave Sunnyland clout in the community of blues musicians. Besides, Jimmy's main man Muddy had signed on, and he was Muddy's wingman. It just made sense. The Headhunters had a shot at eventually building a dynasty.

Even though Muddy had artistic differences with Chess, he was recording hits. Jimmy wanted hits too. He decided he'd give it a shot—he signed a contract. "That put a little pressure on me. I had a lot of songs . . . I wanted the opportunity to have somebody that meant somethin' to take it. I didn't wanna just throw it away."[25] While he didn't exactly throw his tunes away, he did practically give them away. It wouldn't take long for Jimmy to discover that the Chess organization was at least as tight with their pennies as Muddy ever was, even if they had a lot more pennies to squeeze.

When the time came for Jimmy to record his first song for Leonard Chess, he was wise enough to seek counsel with Sunnyland, the one person he knew who could steer him through the session in a way that would keep Leonard at bay. "Do what you're gonna do," Sunnyland told Jimmy.[26] In other words, *Don't let Leonard take over the entire session and turn it into something other than what you want it to be.* This was easier said than done. The Chess brothers had a routine when it came to the pecking order of musicians. It was a way to make money and to wear down a sideman's resistance: the main attraction got the lion's share of studio time on a given day, and the sidemen got whatever was left on the clock when the Chesses felt they'd gotten everything they could squeeze out of their top billing for the day. Jimmy knew their ways by now; he would be ready for them. When he'd previously recorded his first "That's All Right" on the Parkway label, he had not gotten the band to lay down the exact groove he was searching for. This time he wouldn't miss.

Thus, on August 15, 1950, the first tunes Jimmy recorded for the newly founded Chess Records were the two tunes he'd previously tried getting released by either JOB or Parkway: "Ludella" and "That's All Right." The former was a tune that Jimmy had wanted released as far back as the Tempo-Tone session with Irv Taman. With Little Walter backing him on harp and Big Crawford on bass, one take of "That's All Right" (U7269) and two takes of "Ludella" (U7270) yielded two solid tracks. When Jimmy Roger's first 78 (Chess 1435) hit the streets, with "That's All Right" on side A and "Ludella" on the flip side, it emerged at the same time as Muddy's single "Rolling Stone." Harp player Billy Boy Arnold said, "In fact, Jimmy's was the biggest hit." Blues lovers grabbed copies from local vendors for seventy-nine cents apiece.[27] Arnold elaborated on the enormous impact that a certain harmonica player had on both discs: "I heard this harmonica player, I said, *Goddam!* This wasn't no ordinary harmonica player, the harp was at least 75 percent of the success of the records . . . The harmonica player was blasting!"[28] Little Walter was clearly an important component of the triad that formed the core of the Headhunters.

"That's All Right" and "Ludella" were both recorded at the beginning of the session, giving Jimmy a rare opportunity to take top billing over Muddy Waters, when a typical session saw Jimmy serving the role of second fiddle, riding rhythm shotgun to Muddy's driving slide guitar. "Finally I got it like I wanted it when I did it for Chess," Jimmy said proudly. Once he established that perfect groove, he knew instantly that it would be the musical style he wanted to be known for. "Yeah, that was the big one. What made people recognize Jimmy Rogers was that sound . . . I won't let nobody pull me too far from there."[29]

Jimmy had quite a few songs he was itching to get down on wax, as he'd been waiting for this opportunity for some time and had built a deep backlog of lyrics and chord progressions to accompany the verses. "I build 'em from different stories of my past life and people that I've known," Jimmy said. "Quite a few people have come to me with their problems, you know, and I would give them the best advice that I could, help 'em out, because I have lived kind of rough myself."[30] The subject matter for some songs were created rather innocently, with Jimmy finding inspiration from just about anywhere. While some may have thought, for example, that "Ludella" might have been about some personal tryst with a love interest, it wasn't anything so deep as that, at least according to Jimmy's take on it: "It's no girl. In fact, I had a guitar and I called it 'Ludella.' But now I have one now, this one is 'Docie Bell,' that's my guitar."[31]

The guitar as metaphor in Jimmy's first hit resonated with the importance of the guitar in Jimmy's life as a blues artist. The music was rewarding, the bonding between the bluesmen was strengthening, but the hours were grueling. Between the sessions for Muddy and his own, newly acquired leadership role, things were getting busier for Jimmy than ever. "Man, we used to live in the studio all the time," Jimmy remembered. "Them Chess boys had us in there for days, day in and day out. We worked hard for those Chess boys." Jimmy knew the score when it came to how Phil and Leonard dealt with the musicians and why they worked for such long hours when they showed up. "They capitalizin' on what you're doin' when you're in the studio. Phil and Leonard Chess was businessmen. They was about money. We was about money too, but we was tryin' to learn to play the blues and tryin' to get on wax like we did. So I'm glad we did run up on those Chess boys."[32]

Jimmy's success in finding a unique spot on Chess's roster was due to his singular approach to the blues. He found a way to thrust forward his special brand of lyrics, and he carefully crafted stories about women who were always gentle, if not a bit wary. The words were buffed until he got it just right, even if some were borrowed from blues heroes of the past. His slow-to-medium tempos were always comfortably paced, which allowed any listener to groove right along. His solos were delivered with a clean tone; there were never any throwaway notes. He made his particular brand of the blues unique, with ideas that incorporated musical content that blended both pop and blues genres to create a highly sophisticated melodic, harmonic, and rhythmic style.

Furthermore, he had an irresistible, buttery-smooth vocal quality that totally distinguished him from anyone else on the Chess roster. His delivery of the lines was never forced, just gently and calmly executed in a manner that invited the listener to take sides with him, like putting an arm around the shoulder of the listener instead of grabbing them by the lapels. Jimmy didn't need to do any grabbing. His vocals were compelling enough in themselves to convince you of his sincerity. Neither his voice nor the words he sang ever got old, no matter how many times he sang them; they were always delivered with the same timeless passion and conviction. That was his secret: he simply loved the blues.

On October 23, 1950, both Muddy and Jimmy were called in to Universal Studios to do a triple-header recording session to follow up on the success of both their singles. Contrary to popular belief, this event did not mark the entry of drummer Elga Edmonds, who had formally taken over the drum chair when Baby Face Leroy abandoned the seat for a failed attempt at success on the Parkway label. What some listeners perceived as snare drum rim shots on that day's recordings was actually the percussive plucking sound of Big Crawford and his big bass. There is, therefore, neither drum set nor washboard present on these early sessions for either Muddy or Jimmy. Little Walter sat in on two tunes for Muddy—"Louisiana Blues" and "Evans Shuffle"—and the core trio of Muddy Waters, Little Walter Jacobs, and Big Crawford completed what would represent Muddy's next single.

Now it was Jimmy's turn to take the lead, and he wasted no time. In one take each, he and the band delivered the goods on "Going Away Baby" and "Today, Today, Blues," both of which were released as his next 78 disc (Chess 1442), under the name Jimmy Rogers and His Trio. With Little Walter on harp and Big Crawford on bass, both songs shimmered as Muddy and Jimmy intertwined their electric guitars with percolating harp and thumping bass. "Going Away Baby" sounds like a slightly sped-up version of "Louisiana Blues," with the same galloping rhythm accompaniment pinned under Crawford's click-clack bass strings. "Today, Today, Blues" is loosely borrowed from Sunnyland Slim's version, which he called "Brown Skin Woman" (sometimes on labels as "Brown Skinned Woman"). Jimmy was a great admirer of Sunnyland, and this tune no doubt had stuck in Jimmy's mind ever since he had participated in the August 26 session in 1949 for Apollo.

Jimmy joined Muddy and Walter to form the backup unit for guitarist and Southern blues vocalist Johnny Shines, an Alabama native who was becoming a seasoned artist on the Chicago scene. Born in 1915 just beyond the Memphis city limits, Shines had been playing professionally since the age of seventeen, proving his mettle while performing regularly as an imitator of Howlin' Wolf. Back then Shines was such a devout follower of Wolf that he traveled behind him everywhere, copied his repertoire, and even adopted the name of "Little Wolf."[33] And in the mid-1930s Shines had a two-year apprenticeship with none other than Robert Johnson in Mississippi, right up until a year before Johnson died. Since moving to Chicago in 1941, Shines had been trying to catch his first major breakthrough on wax, just like Jimmy and Walter. It was Jimmy who introduced Johnny to Leonard Chess and got him an audition.[34]

Chess asked the entire band—Jimmy, Muddy, Walter, and Elga—to back Shines on the October 23 session. Although things went well, his material went unreleased because Leonard said Johnny sounded too much like the music that Waters had just released and he didn't want to confuse the public. Of this decision to shelve the two sides—"Joliet Blues" and "Glad I Found You" (both eventually released on the impressive compilation, *Drop Down Mama* [Chess LP 411])—some felt as though the suspension was a ploy used by Leonard just to keep Johnny Shines on the shelf so that no one else could get him on records, thus tying him up legally.

Unbeknownst to almost everyone in the Chicago area, Chester Burnett, "The Wolf," was building his own blues dynasty down in the Memphis area. Howlin' Wolf had roots as deep as Muddy's, with similar heavy influences from Delta legends such as Charlie Patton and Son House.[35] Moreover, he was multitalented—he sang ferociously, played guitar, and blew the harp with a fat tone and simple yet fiery attack.

Like Muddy, Wolf had a sidekick guitarist who had even more of a stinging tone than Jimmy Rogers. Indeed, Willie Johnson's guitar work was practically ahead of its time, with a distorted overtone that predated rock 'n' roll. In fact, Wolf had two other guitarists waiting in the wings: Auburn "Pat" Hare had studied with Jimmy's longtime idol, Joe Willie Wilkins, and was a major threat in his own right; Matt "Guitar" Murphy was a young hotshot lead guitarist who knew enough about music to help Wolf keep his timing straight when delivering the intense vocal performances.[36] Wolf's drummer, Willie Steele, played incessant driving rhythms with a swing feel that revealed his deep knowledge of jazz history. If this weren't enough, Wolf had William Johnson, a piano player who was so intense that he was known simply as "Destruction."[37]

No one on the Chess roster in Chicago saw or heard what Howlin' Wolf was building in Memphis. But Leonard Chess, shrewd as he was, was well aware of the rising star that Wolf was to become. With his record label on the verge of becoming the biggest thing that had happened in the recent history of recorded blues, not only did Leonard have Muddy, Jimmy, and Little Walter cutting a wealth of new material, but also the latest acquisition of Howlin' Wolf's catalog would add even more depth to the legacy of Chess Records.

For the time being, however, it was Jimmy's star that was in ascendance. With his next recordings, on January 23, 1951, he was firmly established as a bona fide Chess artist under his own steam even as he continued to record and tour as part of the Muddy Waters ensemble. This session would prove to be a highly productive one for Muddy too. He and his now-routine recording sidemen of Big Crawford and Little Walter churned their way through four fresh arrangements: "Long Distance Call," "Too Young to Know," "Honey Bee," and, finally, "Howlin' Wolf." While the previous three songs propelled Muddy toward even greater success, this last tune went unreleased for several years, maybe because of the awkward inference and impending confusion over who or what the song was promoting.

Indeed, Howlin' Wolf was in the early stages of being signed to Chess Records, a logical move by Leonard after he'd acquired the masters from the Memphis studios. The tune "Howlin' Wolf" (written by "Funny Papa" Smith and recorded on Vocalion in Chicago on January 10, 1931) was a tune that Muddy was most likely already familiar with. The image of a howlin', prowlin' Wolf was more fitting for Chester Burnett than for Muddy, and in fact Muddy does a poor job of selling it; he sings it in such a shallow manner that it doesn't take much for listeners to hear that he doesn't feel the words, which might be why Leonard didn't release it. Maybe it was all for the best. Muddy's image and reputation both specifically at Chess and generally in Chicago were already firmly established, while Wolf's were yet to be on those fronts. Although Muddy and Wolf would eventually be set at such odds with each other that their impending rivalry would grow to legendary status, in the initial months after Wolf's arrival in Chicago the two were on good terms.[38]

Meanwhile, the sessions were really heating up at the Chess studio, with Jimmy laying down dozens of tracks as Muddy's wingman. But the increased number of sessions led to a greater number of clerical errors. While Jimmy Rogers has previously been identified as the second guitarist on "Honey Bee" and "Howlin' Wolf," it is in fact Little Walter on "Honey Bee" for the session on January 23, 1951. Though Walter's guitar skills were generally overlooked because of his superior harp prowess, here he demonstrates his own ability to wrap the simple yet perfect contrapuntal line around Muddy's slide work. Walter then returns to his traditional role on harp on "Howlin' Wolf," and the classic Waters-Rogers guitar melding is not present. Meanwhile, Jimmy's guitar is absent on all four of these tunes.

In typical fashion, Jimmy's turn immediately followed Muddy's on this date Interestingly, he chose a slightly different lineup for reasons that at first glance are not exactly clear. Upon closer inspection, however, one is led to surmise that Jimmy was actually not present during the Muddy Waters portion of the session, hence the need to have Little Walter play guitar on the last two Waters tunes: there would be no obvious need for that if Jimmy had been around. Add to that the idea that Muddy and Walter may have already left the building when Jimmy finally did arrive, and you have at least a plausible explanation as to why neither of them are present on Jimmy's session.

Another theory is that, based on the title of the session notes for that day, Jimmy, along with Leonard Chess, may have decided that it was time to have a band under his own name, and this was the moment to assert himself with an entirely different roster that would be identified as his own. In any event, Jimmy went with a lineup that included Eddie Ware on piano, Ernest Cotton on saxophone, and Elga Edmonds on drums. The combo recorded four tunes: "I Used to Have a Woman," "The World's in a Tangle," "She Loves Another Man," and "Give Me Another Chance." The sparkling piano riffs supplied by Eddie Ware give the first three tunes a real lift, while Ernest Cotton's honking sax sounds, although played with intensity and precision, seem somewhat out of place on "Woman" and "Tangle."

The boogie groove on "She Loves Another Man" is steady and rollin' as the second verse of the lyrics borrows a line from the first verse of "Going Away Baby." Also, we hear for the first time the simple, downbeat snare drum patterns and punchy kick drum supplied by Elga Edmonds, who is regularly identified as "Elgin Evans" in various liner notes. "The World's in a Tangle" with the flip side "She Loves Another Man" was issued as Chess 1453 and shipped to vendors almost immediately, while the last tune of Jimmy's session, "I Used to Have a Woman," was shelved. Another tune, "Give Me Another Chance," never saw the light of day. This date turned out to be a triple feature, as Jimmy's pianist, Eddie Ware, was given the opportunity to record his own session, most likely on Jimmy's recommendation. He got in five tunes under his own steam before the marathon session ended at Universal, with Little Walter reappearing as a sideman on guitar. Jimmy loved working with Eddie Ware—when he could get him, which proved to be difficult at times. "He was a pretty wild guy—he was young and whenever you would be able to catch up with him he would play," Jimmy recalled. "Maybe a week or something like that—then he was gone! He was a swift guy."[39]

The Chess date on July 11, 1951, turned out to be a full session for the members of the Muddy Waters band. It began with Muddy recording four tunes—"Country Boy," "She Moves Me," "My Fault," and "Still a Fool"—followed by four tunes that Jimmy led, and then one more tune by Muddy, "Long Distance Call." As with the previous session, they recorded all of their material at Universal Studios, a place that was known for having great facilities as well as recording engineers who were efficient at their jobs and who also had a keen sense of business, much in the same manner as Leonard did. Universal granted session time to Chess at the relatively steep rate of seventy-five dollars for only a couple of hours of studio time, according to Jimmy, which made things fairly unpleasant for musicians who were trying to handle the financial aspects of their business. The staff at Universal clearly held tightly to the belief that time is money. "Then you had to come in and rush the shit out," said Jimmy. "Box it up as quick as you can, man, and get out of there on time, 'cause he's [Universal's manager] clockin' him [Leonard]."[40]

The combination of financial and time restraints created a pressure situation that had a direct impact on Leonard's demeanor in the studio. To cut corners on expenses, he routinely instructed engineer Bill Putnam to recycle his tape reels, which were sometimes used for commercial advertisements for radio spots before they were reused for cutting sides in the studio; on some outtake material the ads can be heard bleeding through the other tracks of the tape.[41] Leonard Chess was slowly earning a reputation as quite the stubborn taskmaster and often heavy-handed in his role in the evolution of the music. He sometimes pushed his ideas to the detriment of the music itself, according to some.

It was while the band was trying to record "She Moves Me" that Elga allegedly caught hell from Leonard Chess, who must have been in some kind of a mood that day. As the story goes, Leonard supposedly got so upset with Elga that he decided he himself could play the drum part better than Elga, who had obviously spent his entire life developing his craft. This would have been an unprecedented move, since Leonard's place was usually behind the glass. Leonard had already provided a plodding, semi-steady bass drum beat for "Country Boy," "She Moves Me," and "My Fault." According to one version of the legend, Elga somehow disappointed Muddy and Leonard with his lack of ability to catch the uneven number of measures in one of the songs, thus prompting Leonard to step up to the plate. Muddy remembered it a little differently: "Leonard *was* playing the drums on that, but Leonard just wanted to play. He said that Elga wasn't beatin' loud enough or something and Elga just backed off and said, 'Well then, you go on and do it.' I mean, Elga had been playin' that number for a long time with us. Leonard just wanted to do something. He'd do things like that. Then he [Elga] went back to the drums and played on."[42]

During the recording of "Still a Fool," Muddy allowed Jimmy to assume his natural role as second-line guitarist, but Little Walter played the role of "third guitarist." "He's playin' guitar, he and I, on 'Still a Fool' because the harmonica wouldn't fit and he was in on the session," Rogers said. "And durin' the rehearsal Muddy could put more in it because it was a thing that Muddy Waters said, 'It's all right, she's all right.' He started stompin', runnin' around all over the stage. So he said, 'Well, we'll put that in there,' and therefore Walter would play the guitar and he could run around and stomp. Muddy's just only singing."[43]

Muddy's demonstrable, unrestrained stomp dance in the middle of the studio session floor during the tail end of the tune was a rare occurrence of unbridled enthusiasm that occurred as a consequence of the studio band's being able to capture a bit of what took place regularly in the nightclubs.[44] What is more interesting, though, is that you can actually hear both guitars play the exact same phrase as the introductory statement, with matching tones for added effect. This is when one realizes that, in truth, Muddy, Jimmy, and Walter could literally play musical chairs with the guitar role—they are virtually indistinguishable from one another. And, of course, there is still the ever plodding bass drum of Leonard Chess to round things out.

Soon after Muddy's delightful romp-and-stomp was brought under control, Jimmy took the leading role with four tunes of his own, including "Money, Marbles, and Chalk," "Hard Working Man," "Chance to Love," and "My Little Machine." This lineup included Jimmy on guitar; Walter, harp; Elga, drums; and Big Crawford, bass. Walter must have really been trying to develop his guitar chops over several sessions, because he yet again appears not in the role of harp player but as the guitarist on Jimmy's "Hard Working Man." What's more interesting is that Little Walter also makes his presence known on guitar on "Money, Marbles, and Chalk," supplying the same kind of strong melodic lines for Jimmy as he did for Muddy, with an impressive distorted solo that typifies his aggressive style. While "My Little Machine" and "Hard Working Man" were held back, take one of "Money, Marbles, and Chalk" was coupled with take two of "Chance to Love" and was released as Chess single 1476.

From early July to December there was a lull in the sessions recorded for Jimmy, Muddy, and Walter. Then, on December 29, 1951, the entire Headhunter group, including drummer Elga Edmonds, was finally under one roof and ready to give Leonard the classic sound they'd mastered in many nightclubs over the past few years. For the final session of the year, they laid down their patented groove on "They Call Me Muddy Waters," the only exception being that Walter was pulled off the amplified harmonica and relegated to acoustic sound, which undermined the full effect of the live Waters band sound. On "All Night Long," a tune that represents the precursor to "Rock Me Baby," the music is drenched in reverb, a result of a homemade echo chamber built by the Chess brothers.

The version that was issued had Elga removed from the take, thus sustaining the less-than-classic representation on vinyl. On "Stuff You Gotta Watch," Jimmy chants along with Little Walter on vocals for the question-and-answer groove found in the lyrics (*"should be mine, should be mine"*). Even though the full lineup delivered the goods on "Lonesome Day," all the tracks from this session (except for "Stuff You Gotta Watch") went unreleased. Once again, Leonard Chess ultimately upheld his puzzling decision to never issue a totally accurate caption of the classic Headhunter sound that patrons enjoyed on an almost nightly basis in the hole-in-the-wall clubs.

In what seems like a resigned acceptance that Leonard's will would prevail, Muddy and Elga left the studio after their duties were fulfilled for the day, while Jimmy and Little Walter—no doubt after being asked by Floyd Jones himself—chose to assist on laying down the sounds on "Dark Road," "Big World," "Overseas," and "Playhouse," the first session of Jones's career with Chess. This session served as a reunion of sorts, since several members of the Waters gang were already laying down these and other tracks alongside Floyd Jones, Snooky Pryor, and Moody Jones at the February Parkway session.

Like Muddy and Jimmy, Leonard wanted Floyd Jones to rerecord everything he'd done with Parkway. It became apparent that Chess was hell-bent on squashing any competition from the Parkway session or any other session in which his artists previously had participated. He wanted to effectively erase any musical images of the small independent labels from the minds of the masses, mainly by overlapping his own stamp and sonic seal on their brains. Leonard had bought the March 22 recordings of Floyd's "Big World" and "Dark Road" from JOB that revealed Jimmy and Walter sitting in and recut them as a Chess session on December 29, 1951. Whether the Headhunters considered their gradually increasing stockpile of material for Chess to be a blessing or a curse was yet to be determined.

Interestingly, "Dark Road" sounds eerily like the Howlin' Wolf that was to come. Maybe it was more than a coincidence that Chess had also purchased the original tapes of Howlin' Wolf's first recorded sides, the latest being two tunes recorded in Memphis after Wolf not only had signed with Sam Phillips but also was still living deep in the South. Leonard, in another one of those Chess moves that showed his acumen, talked Phillips into leasing the demos to Chess, and so Wolf's first big hits, "Moanin' at Midnight" and "How Many More Years," were already released in September 1951. This single had burned up the charts under Chess's banner (Chess 1479), as opposed to that of Sam Phillips, who had actually first discovered and recorded Wolf.[45] Leonard took no prisoners. It would take more than two years for Wolf to move to Chicago. The December 18 demos in Memphis that captured Wolf's "Howlin' Wolf Boogie" and "The Wolf Is at Your Door" were also snatched up quickly from Phillips and released as Chess 1497.[46]

Chess commissioned two more songs from Phillips with Howlin' Wolf: "Getting Old and Grey" and "Mr. Highway Man," recorded in Memphis in January 1952. It must have really felt strange—or at least ironic—for Leonard to know that it had been exactly one year before this session that he had Muddy recording a tune where he's told to sing, *"I'm a howlin' wolf . . . I been howlin' all 'round your door!"* Meanwhile, Jimmy got his first recording session for the new year under way on February 11, 1952, when he brought in what was quickly becoming his own unofficial studio band, consisting of himself and Elga Edmonds, Eddie Ware on piano, J. T. Brown on tenor saxophone, and the always present Big Crawford on bass. It had been seven months since Jimmy had been in the studio to record, and on this day they laid down only two tracks, "Back Door Friend" and "Crying Shame," which seemed like an interesting and unusual session.

What was more interesting, though, was how the first tune was paired for release not with the second, but with a title that had been recorded and shelved for more than a year (January 23, 1951). Leonard chose "I Used to Have a Woman" as the flip side. The 78 was released as Chess 1506, with the band identified as "Jimmy Rogers with his Rocking Four." "Crying Shame" was held back for years, which was probably a good thing, for it was not one of Jimmy's stronger efforts. It had the feel of a tune that was too early in its embryonic stage, resulting in a relatively weak vocal delivery, no bass player, and pallid tenor sax work from J. T. Brown, which didn't help matters.

Despite such occasional recording disappointments, the Headhunters' music remained in ascendancy. And their success meant there would be many opportunities to pull other associates in on the action over at Chess, and a good word from either Jimmy, Muddy, or Walter meant a person just might get lucky and catch a break—maybe being allowed to substitute in a pinch or perform as a guest artist on a take or two at the studio session. Toward the end of the year, the Headhunters took part in an all-star jam at Sam and Gussie's Lounge. The event marked the first time the young newcomer Billy Boy Arnold, a harp player, got inside a club to hear the live bluesmen he'd been hanging out with. He was overwhelmed at how wonderful he felt to be a part of the establishment.

Pianist Johnny Jones, the Myers brothers, and Sunnyland Slim were there as well as guitarists Jimmy Rogers and Robert Junior Lockwood. Harpists Junior Wells and Little Walter were also both in attendance. Arnold wanted to sit in with the combo that featured Louis and Dave Myers, Junior Wells, Little Walter, and Jimmy Rogers. Arnold looked at Jimmy and declared himself a harmonica player, to which Jimmy responded, "Well, *this* is *my* harmonica player," pointing to Walter. So Arnold was perplexed when they took the stage and Walters didn't play harmonica but instead picked up the guitar.[47]

Just as Muddy Waters opened the door for Jimmy and Little Walter to get their shots at stardom, Jimmy tried to help create an opportunity for his then-current pianist, Eddie Ware, to do the same. Therefore, as soon as he had completed recording the two tunes as leader, he relegated himself to a supportive role as Eddie stepped to the front with the same band roster to record four tunes as vocalist and pianist with "Give Love Another Chance," "Failure Is My Destiny," "Lonesome and Forgotten," and "Unlucky Gambler," all recorded in succession and each in one take. "Give Love Another Chance" was released as a B side to "Jealous Woman," one of the songs from the session Eddie had recorded as a leader after Jimmy's 1951 session on January 23. In both of those sessions where Eddie was the leader, Leonard Chess had chosen to take the first tune and throw away the remainder of the session.

Now that Muddy was firmly entrenched in the Chess family and Jimmy had broken through comfortably with ten singles released over the past year and a half, Leonard Chess decided to strive toward the creation of a recording dynasty within the Waters lineup. Both Jimmy and Muddy later went on record as saying that they too thought it was time to break Little Walter through and were no doubt appreciative of the great support he provided on harp to make their records a success, not to mention the high level of consistency with which he did it.

Contrary to popular belief, evidence suggests that the quartet—Muddy, Jimmy, Elga, and Walter—were brought into the newly relocated Universal Recording Studios on Ontario Street to support Little Walter on May 12, 1952, his first day as leader. Over the years there has been some speculation about the order of tunes being recorded on that day; Muddy and Jimmy both seem to remember Little Walter's first big break occurring as the last thing they recorded that day, when time was running out. But the ledger notes seem to indicate that Little Walter's first turn as leader was a *priority* for the Chess brothers, as the tape reel at Universal has identified "Juke" and "Can't Hold Out Much Longer" in the Chess archives as U7347 and U7348.[48] The band eventually did capture a Waters-led tune, "Please Have Mercy," which was labeled in the Chess logs as U7349.[49] There is real evidence, then, to support the idea that for the first time ever, Muddy—the King Bee—had a session that came in second to Little Walter's headliner.

The men routinely entered the room that day and took their usual positions. Jimmy takes up the story: "We were sitting down. They would put a mike on the amp and a mike to the vocal. Sitting in a chair, we would see each other, and we'd play off each other in the studio, like we were on the stage. We would build it and then we would give a listen to the tape. Then we'd keep it running till we get the right sound we like."[50] The band, obviously in a cheerful and relaxed mood, decided to crank up the old standby groove they had used as a closing musical statement before breaks when they were on gigs. It was a swinging instrumental arrangement of a traditional blues shuffle that featured a light but steady driving drum groove, pulsating guitar boogie bass line with countermelody, and a series of infectious, bouncing blues harmonica riffs supplied by Walter. The band had played it so many times before in the clubs, it was simply business as usual.

Unexpectedly, the groove immediately got the attention of the guys in the booth. Someone asked over the intercom, "What was that?" To the band, it was just an old thing they played for kicks, and they casually replied that it was just something they called "The Jam." Jimmy provided more details about the event: "The song was our theme song. We didn't have a name for it then but that's what we was usin' it for—comin' up and goin' down off the stage. We kept on nailin' on it 'til we got a good groove out of it. And Chess wanted it."[51]

They did, indeed. The band was asked to play it again for keeps, and when they cranked it up again for the first take, the group actually botched it, losing the internal groove at some point near the middle of the tune. The second take, a complete one, went without a hitch. The Chess brothers, in typical fashion, wanted several takes of the tune so that they could pick through them and decide which they thought was the best. Two more passes of the jump blues were recorded, and the Chesses, finally satisfied, decided that the second full take would be the one that would see daylight.

Even though the logbooks indicate the takes were recorded early on during the session, Jimmy remembers it differently. "We had about fifteen minutes left," he remembered. "One of the guys hollered up and asked [recording studio engineer] Stu Black if he would catch the sound of this tune we got. And we kicked it in and started jammin' with it . . . So finally he made about three, four takes of it. So he had enough to pick from. Then he decided to put another side, a singin' side to it. Oh, man—Walter, he wasn't singin'!" By now a bit of a panic set in with his nerves, and Walter had no idea of what to sing. Jimmy, ever on his game, called a huddle. "So he got real frightened, so I got up and we went in the bathroom."[52]

Once inside the cramped quarters, Jimmy tried to relax Walter. "Then we had to figure out somethin' to put on the back side of it," Jimmy remembered. Since they'd already nominated Little Walter as the blessed beneficiary of the tune, it was up to him to christen the back side of the 45 with some vocals. "I happen to think of an old song of Sonny Boy Williamson called 'Black Gal Blues,' but you couldn't use [the phrase] 'black gal' at that time," Jimmy said. Leonard Chess, who was always conscious of the racial climate in the country—particularly in his own demographics of urban Chicago—said, "Oh no, you can't use that 'black gal,' you gotta put somethin' else in there.'" So Jimmy came up with a simple yet clean alternative: "We was sittin' down, knee to knee, where I could nudge him when he get to that turnaround, to that black gal part, and I would say, 'no *black gal'*—baby! I'm crazy about you, *baby.'*" We kept on till we got him tightened up there and we made a big record out of it."[53]

It wasn't too difficult to get Walter's courage up for that particular tune, because, according to Jimmy, "Walter [already] knew about two, three verses of it, 'cause he would try to sing it sometimes over the night when everybody was high."[54] As it turned out, a good portion of the lyrics were stitched together from a variety of sources, including lines borrowed directly from Sonny Boy Williamson's version, a Doctor Clayton song called "I Need My Baby," and even a line borrowed from Robert Johnson's "Kind Hearted Woman."[55]

Among the members of the Headhunters, Little Walter didn't have the greatest gift of song in terms of vocal range, pitch control, or even tone quality, but, *man*, could he ever deliver a phrase, telling it like it was, like he lived every line of the lyrics (and when it comes to the blues, this quality, above all, reigns supreme). In fact it was Walter's authentic, heartfelt delivery of the lyrics that got right to the heart of listeners when it came to their positive appraisal of his vocal prowess. And then there were the gorgeous, glistening tones of that juicy, fat harmonica sound shoved right between the sets of lyrics that in reality served as only a brief respite from the wailing harp attacks.

Well after the end of the session, when Jimmy and the band had already gone home, the Chess brothers had their own bathroom huddle of sorts to decide what to do with these two sides they'd just cut with the hottest band on their roster. They still didn't have titles for either one of the songs yet. What trans-pired next represents a classic case where a few of the really great ideas by the Chess brothers were sometimes followed by really dumb ones. Case in point: the main lyric of the song Walter had just sung was clearly, "*crazy 'bout you baby*," which made obvious sense for the title—it was the first line in the hook of the tune. How could the Chesses *not* hear that? Walter sings the line no less than six times throughout the tune. But, *no*—what did the Chess brothers go for? They chose the once-stated, *least* significant phrase in the entire set of lyrics, "*can't hold out much longer*," as the song's title. Why? The phrase comes so early on in the course of the tune, the average person would totally miss it and have to dig backward through the words just to find where Walter says, "*I can't hold on much longer baby, with you treatin' me this-a-way.*" Such was and still is the nature of the music business; a significant piece of music history can be created and, unfortunately, distorted all in one fell swoop.

The same thing happened with the A side, which was the jump-blues instru-mental that ultimately led to the need for a vocal B side in the first place. Of all the things one might call a great, swinging blues shuffle, "Your Cat Will Play" is about as goofy a title as one could ever imagine. Calling it "Juke," therefore, is a major improvement over the alternative, although it is doubtful that anybody in the Water/Rogers band would have called it that. Nevertheless, the pow-ers that were, both smart and dumb, wasted little time before unveiling what would become the greatest single their label would ever have at that time: side A, "Juke"; side B, "Can't Hold Out Much Longer" (Checker 758). In only a few short weeks, life as Little Walter knew it would never be the same.

5

THE WORLD'S IN A TANGLE

The stuff that really started him, he pushed it aside.
And that happened to be Muddy Waters, myself, and
Sunnyland Slim, Wolf, Eddie Boyd, Willie Mabon . . .
a bunch of fellows. Chess, he got away from the blues.

—Jimmy Rogers

In 1952 the Muddy Waters band was the hottest thing on the Chess record label, and the group went out to promote the singles that Muddy had on the charts. On this particular tour, they went outside of their customary gig itinerary and traveled to the Deep South, into the Mississippi Delta region, covering juke joints and radio stations in various parts of Mississippi and Louisiana. Their last recording session provided a rare opportunity for Little Walter to take the lead on two tunes—one instrumental and one vocal feature. Jimmy reflected on the casual attitude that both he and Muddy had regarding the sides they had cut for Walter in the studio before they left for the tour, saying, "Now we don't know what Leonard gonna do with it. We didn't know what to name either side. So we left. We went on, and we had to hit the road in a couple of days. We went on out, down to New Orleans."[1]

From there the band traveled north through Mississippi and crossed the state line into Arkansas. The Katz Clothing radio show in Helena came on at 6:00 A.M. During that same radio show stint, the guys moonlighted at the Owl Café, where they had several guest musicians drop by and sit in, including Robert Junior Lockwood, Peck Curtis, and Houston Stackhouse. It was a raucous homecoming for the mostly Southern-born Headhunters and their old friends. The entire lot of them hung out late at night, ripping and running the streets, singing aloud in an inebriated haze of hilarity. Houston Stackhouse remembered when Jimmy,

Walter, and Muddy arrived there to do the radio show. "Cat [Katz] Clothes Store there on Cherry Street . . . They'd go over there in Mississippi and play those dances at night, and schools and different things," Stackhouse recalled. "They'd come back here and broadcast every day, and be ready to go out that evenin' to go somewhere to play. Once in a while they played there on Missouri Street at the Owl Café [in Helena]. I played there with 'em a time or two . . . They got me and Peck and them to go playin' there for 'em then."[2]

Stackhouse remembers having a direct influence on Jimmy's musical development. "Yeah, he told me I had to learn him some of them kinda chords I was makin' down there in '49," Houston said. "I think he learned 'em all right. I imagine he's a bad cat now, ain't he?" Stackhouse remembers the pleasure as well as the business: "Jimmy and I, Little Walter and Muddy Waters and Robert Jr., we drank a right smart around that town."[3]

The band had no idea what they were about to experience when they went on that first tour as hot Chess recording artists. To their credit, they had little expectations for what they'd recently recorded; there was no reason to presume any bolts of lightning would come out of the Chess Studios from their last casual session. Besides, Leonard was well known for just sitting on material, and sometimes, like in the case of the sessions for both Johnny Shines and Eddie Boyd, the recorded material might never see the light of day.[4]

The band traveled south and crossed back into Louisiana. They were in Shreveport when they decided to buy a new set of outfits, since their regular clothing items were completely soaked through with sweat from the hot, sticky humidity that clung in the air like a wet blanket over the entire region that summer. Back in the Windy City the guys would normally dress in outfits that were easy to maintain, made of material that could hold up to the nightly grind of sweating in the packed, funk-filled blues joints where they made their music come alive. Not to be taken lightly, the proper dress for a hard night's work was crucial to the band's ability to blow. Jimmy said, "We got little stuff you could wear and rinse out the shirt when you off work and come home. Hang it up for the next morning, it'd be ready to go for the next gig. We didn't have *nothin'* that thin for that part of the country where it was that hot in the summertime."[5] Taking a break from the stifling heat, the band was casually sitting at a bar when suddenly Jimmy heard the familiar strains of his own blues guitar riffs. Jimmy remembered it this way:

And I knew my playing, knew what was on it, but I didn't know what name was on it. So we went across the street to a club that was playing that number, and we still didn't know what to look for on the jukebox, see? We really didn't know. But it was playing three times to one over any other record. They'd play another number or two, then right back on it. So we're sittin' there drinkin' beer—I don't like it but anyway, it was the cheapest thing in the place . . . here comes this song, so we gets up and we runs to the jukebox 'fore the record is out, look on the rack . . . and we found it and it said *Juke*. And we kept *looking* at it—it said "Little Walter and his Jukes." We said, 'Who's them *Jukes*, man?' Wasn't no *Jukes*![6]

Still not thinking too much of it, the next day the band set out to get the appropriate band attire for the upcoming gig. Having left Walter back at the hotel, they eventually found some short-sleeved, "yellow eggshell colored" shirts to match their seersucker suit jackets and beige pants.[7] Little Walter's waist size was pretty narrow, so they took his pants to a tailor who could alter them for him. They were told to return at four to pick up the trousers.

What happened next caught them all off guard. "Muddy and me left the hotel around 3:30, goin' downtown," Jimmy recalled. "When we got back to the hotel and we had picked it up, oh, man, the girls at the desk said, 'That little guy with the checkered hat on'—that was Walter—'he said for you to take care of his amplifier. He's sick, he had a terrific nosebleed. He's goin' back to Chicago.'"[8] Muddy was suspicious all along at how Walter was acting when the tune was being repeatedly dialed up on the box. The attention clearly affected Walter's ego directly. "Every time the jukebox would ring, 'Juke . . . Juke . . . Juke,'" Muddy bemoaned. "Little Walter couldn't stand that jive. The next day, he grab a train— *pssssshhh!*—back to Chicago."[9]

A guy with the colorful name of Groove Boy was the booking agent for this part of the tour, and he found a saxophone player to replace Little Walter. The band, still reeling from this little surprise, had to go to plan B and called alternative numbers that were not in the original playbook but were easily maneuvered by their guest artist. Though they got through the gig without a hitch, they were seriously concerned about Walter, whom they knew was genuinely prone to recurring nosebleeds that were sometimes fairly intense.

They didn't find out what had really happened until they returned home from the tour. "We was looking to hear if Little Walter was in the hospital or something," Jimmy said. When he arrived home, Jimmy's wife told him that Fred Below and the Myers boys had let their harpist, Junior Wells, go from their band, the Four Aces, and that Little Walter had taken his place. Jimmy finally realized that both he and Muddy had been duped. Little Walter had pulled a fast one—a quick switch, as smooth as a pickpocket would relieve you of your wallet without your ever knowing your dough was missing. Walter had just used the nosebleed as an excuse to get out of town, and he knew Muddy and Jimmy would fall for it, at least temporarily, which was all the time he needed to make his big move and join the Four Aces.

"He had called Leonard," Jimmy remarked, "said we was making all the money and he wasn't makin' none—and he was goin' home." By the time the Muddy Waters band returned home, there were signs and banners already posted, promoting the hot new band Little Walter and the Jukes.[10] Muddy was none too happy upon seeing Little Walter after they'd been left high and dry. Waters later recalled, "When me and Jimmy got back, Walter ask me, 'Wh-Wh-where my money?'—like, for the rest of the tour. I said, 'I thought you brought it *witcha.*'"[11]

The truth was that Walter had been plotting his scheme long before the gig started. He had routinely gone over to the Flame, where the Four Aces were holding court. This cooking little band consisted of Dave Myers on lead "bass" guitar (in actuality it was the low open E-A-D-G guitar strings tuned down a fourth to get into the bass register); his brother, Louis, on lead guitar, Junior Wells on harmonica, and Fred Below on drums.[12] The group was a serious blues band, but their music had a jazz-inflected flair about it, since Fred Below had formal jazz study in his background.

This was a unique sound in blues, and Walter dug it. He regularly sat and listened to the band, throwing out compliments at regular intervals when the band took their set breaks. Walter would be sitting at the bar, saying, "Boy, you guys sure sound great tonight." In retrospect it was clear to the Aces that he had been sizing them up to see if they were interested in joining forces with him to launch his own personal assault on the music world as a front man and leader, to ride the wave of popularity of "Juke."

Many years later in an interview Dave Myers admitted that the entire harmonica player–swapping incident was not something that happened by accident. "Walter had his eye on us all the time," he said with a laugh. "He'd see me or come looking for me, and he'd always give me a good buildup. 'Hey, man, you guys really cooked. Hey, man, you guys really played, you know?' But he never would go any further. Because he knew what he had in mind, and wouldn't let these guys [Waters and Rogers] know anything. And he wouldn't let us [Four Aces] know anything . . . but he let us know his record was doing well."[13] Dave went on to describe Walter's relentless pursuits: "He'd come see us all around the city . . . he come straight to us, say, 'Hey, sure like to have you people. And it'd be real nice to have you come play with me. I already got a contract signed with Billy Shaw out of New York. For five years.' Well, we weren't aware of that!"[14]

When the switch actually took place, Dave was sitting inside the club with steam coming out of his ears from anger because of his tardy bandmates. Louis Myers and Fred Below finally arrived—but still no Junior Wells. There was a line wrapped around the corner, everyone waiting to get in to hear this hot band, and Junior was absent. More minutes passed. They chose to start without him, and before they knew it they'd performed an entire set without their front man. After they closed with their number, Dave walked to the bar, where, according to him, the conversation between him and Little Walter went something along these lines:

"Hey Walter, What are you doin' in town—y'all come back already?"
"No, I left Muddy and them out there."
"What you doin' here?"
"I just left 'em, man. They got somebody on harp."
"Well, who have they got?"
"They got Junior Wells."
"No wonder he's not at the show! He didn't even tell me he was leaving!"
"He didn't have time. Muddy sent for him."[15]

This was the birth of a new band: the Jukes. With Little Walter as the featured artist, the Jukes were about to experience an entirely unprecedented level of success. "We became the Jukes," Dave exclaimed, "and boy did we travel! Brother! Walter was the lowest and yet the very highest person. He played at all levels. And he played anywhere; he was good in the slums, he was good at the top level. That's what created so much work for us."[16] Meanwhile, the remaining Muddy Waters band knew that Little Walter had hit the jackpot and that the winning ticket was essentially handed to him uncontested. Now they were most definitely having more than a bit of remorse about their generosity toward Little Walter, especially after he abandoned them in the manner in which he did. "I could have had 'Juke' or Muddy, either one of us could've had that record—taken it," Jimmy said. "But we wanted Walter to be on a record as well. We were trying to make an all-star unit out of the deal. So we gave Little Walter the credit for 'Juke' 'cause he was the harmonica player."[17]

There seemed to be quite a bit of hullabaloo beginning to brew over a groove tune that may not have belonged to anyone particular in Muddy's band. Harmonica player Snooky Pryor had already recorded "Snooky and Moody Boogie," a tune that sounded awfully familiar to this one. About "Juke" being stolen, Snooky says, "Ask Jimmy Rogers, he'll tell you." Jimmy admitted that he and Walter both were familiar with that recording, having heard it performed by

Snooky both live and on record. He said, "We heard this thing, and Little Walter ran through the phrases of the harmonica part." Then he added, "Sunnyland Slim used to have a little thing he'd play when he's going on [stage], 'Get Up the Stairs Mademoiselle.' He'd do it on the piano. So we put the two together and kept jamming around with it. We used it, we built that for our theme song."[18]

By all accounts it was a pretty raw deal on the one hand; then again, it was an opportunity seized by someone who saw a chance and took it—damn the torpedoes. Years later there are many who still dwell on the complexities of the man who seemed to fluctuate between being possessed by both angelic and devil-like personas for his entire life. Indeed, those who knew and worked with him spent their fair share of time delving into the mysteries of Little Walter. When trying to assess Walter's mind-set and reasoning in abandoning Muddy and Jimmy for his big chance to seek fame and fortune for himself, Dave Myers attributed it to the kind of common greed that many others in Walter's position might have succumbed to under the circumstances: "To me he was an ordinary person like I think any other person. Everybody's got a fault, I guess . . . I don't think he was a bad person."[19]

Still, Walter's exit left many numb. Muddy said about losing Little Walter in the aftermath of the success of the song "Juke" in 1952, "It was like someone cutting off my oxygen—I didn't know how I was going to play without him, but I soon realized I had to put the slide back on my finger and go out and be Muddy Waters."[20]

As a direct result of the onslaught of hysteria surrounding the biggest hit Chess had ever released at the time, Little Walter was firmly established as the hottest—and the hottest-tempered—harmonica player in all of Chicago. Nobody could touch him, and the highest price was paid by those who knew him best. This included his own colleagues, who weren't shy about openly admitting that Walter had the jump on all the others. Even Sonny Boy II, from whom Walter had borrowed heavily (and whose musical ideas he had advanced to a more sophisticated art form) had to take a backseat to Walter's newly elevated status.

About Walter's influence, Jimmy mused, "Every place I go, it's harmonica players, they're trying to . . . get that sound. Certain phrases on the harmonica they can hit." Jimmy admitted that much about other harp players' success rate, but then said, "There's fundamental notes where you get your 'push' sound, they can't get it."[21] What you're hearing here is Jimmy's crude-sounding description of Walter's almost indescribable technique.

Walter was a heavyweight champion, leaving all others scrambling to try to match wits with him and create lyrical content that would allow them to at least exchange blows instead of just taking the barrage of body shots he dealt out to his contenders. In the end, however, their efforts to best him were futile. In his own time, Little Walter became the most copied harmonica player of the blues genre, a position he thoroughly enjoyed as he watched his hot new tune burn up the charts week after week. In a bizarre tale of life imitating art, West Coast harp legend Bob Corritore told a story about Little Willie Anderson, another harp player who was Little Walter's friend and personal valet (one of the numerous perks Walter received after the success of "Juke"). According to Bob, "He worshipped everything about Little Walter . . . Louis Myers told me that when Little Walter got shot in the leg, then Little Willie started limping also."[22]

Another story is also now legendary about the evolution of that first Little Walter hit. Supposedly an elderly black woman was standing at a bus stop one day, gently gyrating to the song as it was freshly recorded; the door to the recording studio was propped open and the music seeped out onto the street as the Chess brothers looked on. Evidently the woman's irresistible urge to move to the music was the tell-tale sign the Chess brothers were looking for, encouraging them to put their weight behind the tune and push it all the way.

Yet the truth was that hundreds of others had already been exposed to the tune, and on a regular basis. This hints at the notion that although the Chesses believed they made the brilliant discovery about the potency of the tune, the Muddy Waters band had already sized it up for themselves a long time ago, even if they thought very little of it at the time. After all, it was just an average blues vamp, just a way to get on and off the stage to something other than the clinking of glasses, bottles, and idle chatter. "People appeared to like it so well," Jimmy said.[23] Not even the Muddy Waters band knew how an average groove like that could soar to the top of the charts, which actually speaks positively to the issue of promotional work on the part of the Chess brothers. They seemed to be able to turn just about everything they touched into gold—if they chose to fully endorse the product. So was it the tune or was it the tune's promotion that brought on its success?

At the time of the song's conception, of course, it was no big deal among musicians to pass a tune around like a community faucet to drink from. Practically any band could have used what eventually became "Juke" to quench their thirst when things got musically dry on the bandstand. Jimmy, Muddy, and Walter weren't the least bit worried about any kind of infringement. "During that time you could get away with it—that's how we made it and didn't have nobody grab it before we recorded, because we didn't put a name to it," said Jimmy. "And they just didn't bother with it."[24]

Both Jimmy and Muddy were no doubt stunned for years to come at the accolades Little Walter reaped for the tune that, looking back, only he could have really claimed: he *was* the prime force that drove the song. The cumulative effect it had on the blues community was long-lasting. "If you couldn't play 'Juke,' you couldn't play the harmonica," Jimmy lamented. "And they'd sit there all night until we played 'Juke.' We'd have harps singin' up there on the street all the next day tryin' to do it, you know."[25] Still, Jimmy was baffled at how the song that made history had been right out there all along—it was just another song. He would repeatedly tell reporters about how "we would do the 'Juke' thing, it wasn't the title, there was no name for it then. We called it 'The Jam.' Onstage, when we opened up a set, we'd use it. Then, when we closed for the night, we'd close with that song."[26]

It is the irony of ironies that Little Walter—once shunned from the studios by the Chess brothers—became their golden cow, and now the brothers were milking it for all it was worth. "Juke" represented a perfect example of just how powerful the Chess ray of light could be when the beam was pointed at either the music or the musician. The Chess brothers could focus their full efforts on any project they chose, and—through sheer force of finances, personal favors, political influence, and good old media manipulation—would sell just about anything they wanted to the public. It was a lot easier if the product was already grooving, and "Juke" was suddenly one of the most swinging tunes on the airwaves, effectively competing with the latest jazz and R & B charts.

Some speculate that this might have been one of the reasons why both Muddy and Jimmy were more than a bit upset at the idea of Walter's abandonment as an entire career was handed to him on a silver platter, with all of those life-altering events that resulted directly from something they considered a throwaway groove. And herein lies the problem with how the story has been handed down: might there be a bit of history being rewritten because of hard feelings being held over after all these years, or did it actually happen that way? While Muddy and Jimmy's version has somewhat of a romantic tinge, they were among the few who were there when it happened. The Chess session logs, though informative, have been found to be less than accurate in various spots, no doubt due to the sudden expansion the company experienced when it outgrew the Aristocrat label and then added the Checker and Argo (later changed to Cadet) labels as a ploy to diversify their holdings in order to get more radio airplay.

Add to that the numerous and steadily increasing volume of external source recordings such as the lease purchases of Howlin' Wolf's sessions from Sam Phillips—not to mention those pillaged and plundered from smaller labels like

Parrot, JOB, Herald, and Parkway—and the odds of misnumbering, misfiling, or mislabeling any item are greatly enhanced. There would have to be some serious communication going on to make sure that all the cataloging being done was being properly coordinated. So was the legendary "Juke" session actually an afterthought, or was it the priority of the day? The real truth is, we may never know what the real truth is.

After this major shakeup had played itself out, it became clear that the run of the Headhunters was pretty much over, and the camaraderie they'd had, while not completely shattered, had dealt a great blow to the core trio of Muddy, Jimmy, and Walter. It was painfully evident in Jimmy's next recording session on August 12, which had none of the usual atmosphere he'd grown accustomed to. Neither of his wingmen, Muddy nor Walter, were flanking him on the studio floor this time as they had done for dozens of sessions. Jimmy now had a completely new lineup, with Johnny Jones on piano, Bob Woodfork as second guitarist, A. J. Gladney on drums, and Willie Dixon on bass. Jimmy cut four sides on this day, each with only one take: "Mistreated Baby," "The Last Time," "What's the Matter," and "Out on the Road." The second and fourth of these were released as Chess 1519, and the other two were shelved for the time being.

Years later, while listening to the song "The Last Time," Muddy told "Steady Rollin'" Bob Margolin (his mainstay lead guitarist since 1973) that the double-tracked voice was not Jimmy overdubbing his own voice, but was actually Jimmy and him singing the lines in almost perfect unison. "I don't know why we did that," Muddy said to Margolin. "We should have sung it in harmony."[27] Upon closer inspection, however, it doesn't sound much like Muddy's dark tone, nor does the voice reveal his typical heavy phrasing. The second voice actually sounds more like Jimmy's best attempt at a perfect duplication of the previous track's vocal phrases. So while it is unlikely that Muddy is actually singing on the tune, one wonders why Muddy would say such a thing; it would have truly been the first *and* last time they ever fooled around with that technique. History leaves a lot of gaps in understanding the past; perhaps faulty memory creates other gaping holes.

Just as in Jimmy's sessions, it was no surprise that the classic Muddy Waters lineup would not surface for the recording session on September 17, 1952, as there were a few changes on the horizon, one of which was that Muddy suddenly found himself without a piano player. Jimmy brought a friend of his, Otis Spann, into the Waters camp, after locating him on the West Side at a club where he was performing. Gigs were sporadic for Spann, and, like dozens of other blues musicians, he was, in Jimmy words, "scufflin' around, sleepin' in [his] car. He was sufferin' pretty hard at that time."[28] Still, Jimmy genuinely liked Spann, and the two grew closer as they shared experiences on the road. Jimmy remembered Spann this way:

[Spann] was my roommate when we was playing together, because you have a bunch of musicians out there, they'll steal from each other. You know, a lot of cats will, will want to borrow your shirt, or want to borrow your shorts or your socks and all that stuff. Maybe when you'd look for something, he's got it on. And it's an argument. But we didn't ever have that problem. That's the reason why he liked to share a room with me, then again I kept a buck or two. When he'd get broke, he always hit me for some money. That's another reason. So we got along real good together. All the years that we played together, we was roommates all the time.[29]

The addition of Otis Spann to the band turned out to be most auspicious, because his particular style added a depth to the music that hadn't yet been heard. "His comin' on created more power and a bigger spread on the type of music we was playin'," Jimmy said. "He could help out, a lot of cracks he could chink with that piano . . . the harp, Muddy, and myself—we played off each other all the time."[30] Spann quickly became Muddy's favorite pianist. Like Jimmy, Otis had a style that fit Muddy Waters like a glove.

Spann's response to Muddy's phrasing became almost telepathic as the rapport the two developed went well beyond the music. This mind-reading ability that stretched across band members was the primary reason why the classic Waters-Rogers-Spann-Walter studio band was considered by many to be the finest among all the incarnations of bands Muddy ever had.[31] And certainly Spann was the best pianist Muddy ever had, as they shared a musical brotherhood that brought them so close that they actually told everyone they were brothers.

There was another new addition to the Waters ensemble in the immediate wake of Little Walter's departure. Muddy recruited a worthy replacement in Junior Wells, whom he'd acquired through what amounted to a swap when Walter arrived prematurely in Chicago after he left Muddy and Jimmy back in Louisiana. While many scholars and laymen thought the howling harp present on the September 17 recording date was Little Walter's, in truth it was not. The seventeen-year-old Wells (born December 9, 1934) took full advantage of the opportunity to record with Muddy Waters, trying his best to fill Walter's shoes; he *waaaahhed* and *squaaaalled* his way right through the microphone to send "Standin' Around Cryin'," "Who's Gonna Be Your Sweet Man When I'm Gone," and "Iodine in My Coffee" beyond the limits into a beautifully distorted blues heaven. Afterward Jimmy and Junior hung around to play backup for Floyd Jones as he recorded two tunes: "You Can't Live Long" and "Early Morning."

Meanwhile, by October of that year Little Walter had already signed a five-year deal with the Shaw Agency, owned by former jazz artist manager Billy Shaw, who booked high-profile gigs for him across the country as an obvious follow-up to the success of "Juke" and "Can't Hold Out Much Longer."[32] Walter had recently brought in his new group, which consisted of former Four Aces members Louis and David Myers and Fred Below. Now officially christened as "Little Walter and His Jukes" (as they were identified on his newest 78 disc), they recorded their first band session under Walter's leadership on Chess's sister label, Checker. When they performed live, they were identified as "Little Walter and His Night Cats."

In November, Muddy's "Standin' Around Cryin'" was released at the same time as Walter's latest hit, "Mean Old World," a T-Bone Walker standard. Thinking this was as good a time as any, Jimmy followed suit approximately three months later when he too chose to mark his own independence by signing with Shaw.[33] Feeling he had garnered enough hits to establish his own musical identity, Jimmy had decided to form his own outfit. The first band he formed consisted of Henry Gray on piano, "'Po' Bob" Woodfork on bass, Big Walter Horton on harmonica, and an unidentified guy named Willie, who evidently died shortly thereafter and was replaced by S. P. Leary, on drums. Henry Gray was eventually replaced by Eddie Ware, because Henry left to join the army. At some point Jimmy also had "Good Rockin'" Charles Edwards on harp, along with guitar player Jimmy Dawkins, who worked with him for about eight or nine months. After a while Joe Young replaced Dawkins.[34] Big Walter worked off and on with Jimmy over the next two years.

Even though his attention was now fully focused on his performance career with the new group, Jimmy remained on the Chess label. Not only did he continue to record his own songs, but he also kept recording with Muddy Waters. They parted on good terms and were never cross with each other—brothers 'til the end. Rogers said of Waters, "Muddy has a whole lot of soul. Maybe it's not the words that he says so much as the way he says 'em. He has a voice that I haven't heard anybody could imitate. They can copy his style of guitar, but when the voice comes in, that's different. I know his voice anywhere I hear it."[35]

Once Jimmy put together his own band, he had shows booked under his own name, which meant that, for the first time, he would have to be absent for some of Muddy's gigs. Many times when he and his newly formed band were on the road, they crossed paths with his former bandmates Muddy and Walter. Now they were three separate entities. Even if there was no indication of a spiritual separation between the three, the physical distance was becoming obvious. "I didn't even *see* him [Muddy] for a while," said Jimmy. "I only talked to Muddy to get ready for a session or something. We'd do a session through Leonard . . . We was running in and out of town and sometimes we'd meet up in Chicago and get a chance to cut a session."[36]

Back at the Chess studio, Jimmy and Muddy were just getting used to Junior Wells when he was suddenly whisked away by military personnel to be enlisted in the army. Now they needed to break in still another new harmonica player, and Big Walter Horton was chosen to fill in the gap. Horton (also known by some as "Shakey," a nickname he earned—and detested—as a result of his nervous habit of bobbing his head) gigged with the band sporadically, even if he wasn't Muddy's first call for the studio sessions. They went into the studios somewhere between late December 1952 and early January 1953 to break Horton in, cutting "Flood," "My Life Is Ruined (Landlady)," "She's All Right," and "Sad, Sad Day."

Unfortunately, Horton's personal problems interfered with his musical output, and his tenure with the band was spotty at best; evidently, alcohol problems plagued him constantly, leaving him with an inconsistent and unreliable reputation. Things worked out for the best, though, because Little Walter was back in town, and what amounted to a band reunion took place on May 4, 1953, when Chess held a session for Muddy and Jimmy. The three reunited to make two solid tunes on that day: "Baby, Please Don't Go (Turn Your Lamp Down Low)," and "Lovin' Man."

Contrary to popular belief among blues scholars, Jimmy's two recorded tunes "Left Me with a Broken Heart" and "Act Like You Love Me" did not occur during this May 4 session. The recording of these tunes took place almost five months later, on September 24, the same session that produced Muddy's "Blow Wind Blow" and "Mad Love (I Want You to Love Me)." Since Leonard practically insisted that Muddy use Walter every chance he could, Walter showed up to play and brought his drummer, Fred Below, with him. With Otis Spann on piano, this session stands as one of the greatest of Muddy's career, as Spann was quickly cementing his position as Muddy's permanent anchorman.

Jimmy did very little recording in 1954, which must have come as a surprise to him. The first session, on January 7, produced two songs led by Muddy: "(I'm Your) Hoochie Coochie Man" and "She's So Pretty," released as Chess 1560. As was routine, Jimmy followed with a couple of tunes for his session: "Blues All Day Long" and "Chicago Bound." Interestingly, in the Chess logs the songs were originally labeled under Muddy's name as "Blues Leave Me Alone" and "Memphis Blues."[37] Some ledger notes on Jimmy's session also indicate that either

Johnny Jones or Henry Gray played piano, while Odie Payne played drums, but upon repeated listenings, it seems more likely that Jimmy kept the Waters band intact after wrapping Muddy's session and used the familiar backup team of Little Walter, Muddy Waters, and Elga Edmonds on his tunes.

There's good reason to believe this: it took *thirteen* takes to get "Blues All Day Long" laid down, and Jimmy and his regular crew never needed that kind of time to put in work, especially since they knew better than anyone that time was money. More than likely Jimmy was trying to work his new band members in, and for whatever reason, it wasn't working, so he had to resort to Muddy's first team. Whatever the case, it doesn't sound like they were on the released take. On "Blues All Day Long," Below's wicked shuffle is used to drive the band, while Spann's rollicking finger work shimmers in the background, urging Little Walter to squall even more. After requiring three takes to get "Chicago Bound," the long ordeal was over. Tasty though they were, both "Blues All Day Long" and "Chicago Bound" were shelved.

On April 13, 1954, the classic Waters lineup was back in full force, and, in typical fashion, they laid down Muddy's tracks first, followed by Jimmy's cuts. "I Just Want to Make Love to You" is delivered with forceful vocals from Muddy, with the band simmering and percolating underneath, while "Oh Yeah" features an overjoyed Muddy shouting to the rooftops about "whuppin' and cuttin'" some woman who done him wrong; on this tune the band is so deep in the groove that it almost hurts. Jimmy followed Muddy's session with "Sloppy Drunk," a Lucille Bogan original from 1931 that was covered by many blues musicians, including the original Sonny Boy Williamson (upon which Jimmy's version is based). This particular take has an aggressive, driving rhythm; it shows off Fred Below's tasty brushwork, perfectly accenting Willie Dixon's thumping bass lines, while Jimmy's fingerpicking intertwines beautifully through Spann's thick piano chords. Little Walter's consistently strong harp work takes the tune out on a high note. "Sloppy Drunk" and the previously shelved "Chicago Bound" were released as Chess 1574.

Toward the beginning of his association with Chess back in 1950, Jimmy was recording under his own name, with four tunes or more per session. Later, as he got his turn at bat—only after Muddy completed his cuts—Jimmy's allotment dropped below an average of three tunes per session. Now in 1954 he was being relegated first to two tunes and then downsized to only one. Jimmy's recorded output as a leader was vanishing before his very eyes, and he wasn't too pleased about it. He was also starting to notice that the songs being shelved on his behalf were starting to pile up. Actually, Muddy's output was also starting to decrease in frequency. In fact, after April 13, 1954, neither he nor Jimmy had another session until September—a full five months with no activity at Universal. And when the long-awaited session finally did take place, Jimmy—in a rare instance of either unavailable material or unwillingness on his part—recorded nothing at all under his name. It was becoming apparent that he and Leonard Chess were at some kind of impasse.

Jimmy and Muddy both realized that the steadily rising popularity and success of Little Walter meant there would be fewer opportunities to use him in the studio, because he was constantly on the road. Meanwhile, in his live performances Muddy replaced Walter with Henry Strong, who earned the nickname of "Pot" as a consequence of his constant possession and consumption of marijuana. Strong was making serious progress on learning the repertoire of the Waters band, and he was beginning to attract attention as the band performed weekly at the 708 Club.

A well-known photo taken in 1953 shows the entire group in a classic pose, sitting down in their respective positions, at the Zanzibar. From left to right there was Muddy, pianist Otis Spann, Henry Strong, drummer Elga Edmonds, and Jimmy. In between Muddy and Otis stands an unknown man holding the maracas. Eventually, after what long stood as a mystery, it was determined that the man's name was Henry Armstrong (not to be confused with the harp player Henry Strong), who was essentially a hanger-on, a band mascot of sorts, who just wanted to find a way to bond with the group during the after-hours shows. Since he was not known as a highly skilled blues artist, he chose the simplest way to be involved musically: he shook the maracas. "He wasn't getting paid to do that," Jimmy recalled. "He'd just—every night he was just like a member of the band. He was there on time and he would be there until we closed. On each number he'd shake his maracas and he'd make a lot of girlfriends . . . but he would paint signs for us for free just to be with the group."[38]

On one particular night in early June 1954, after the band had finished a particularly good set, Henry Strong got off the bandstand and went over to a table and began making moves on a woman in the club. Unbeknownst to him, he was being watched. "His old lady was in the club, too, watchin' what was goin' on—and she was angry," Jimmy said later. Once the final set was over, Strong caught a ride home with Jimmy and Muddy, who dropped him off at the building where he lived, which was managed by Leonard Chess's father, Joseph. Jimmy and Muddy were waiting downstairs in the car. Guitarist Jody Williams, who lived in the same apartment building along with Henry and an uncle of Little Walter named Louis, witnessed the macabre scene. Jimmy came upstairs after hearing the commotion. "Henry was in the lobby on the marble floor. He was bleedin' like hell, didn't have no shirt on. Muddy got a sheet and wrapped him in it and carried him out there and put him in his car. Didn't have no time to wait for no ambulance to come and get him 'cause he was bleeding like hell, man. Muddy was trying to get him to the hospital but he died on the way there."[39]

Henry Strong never got to record or tour with the Muddy Waters band. Jimmy next suggested George "Harmonica" Smith as a replacement. Smith joined, and the band put together a tour of the West Coast, where Smith developed such a fondness for the California lifestyle that he decided to stay. Before Muddy knew it, he'd gone through three harmonica players within only a few months and was once more without a regular harp player in his band. He again went to his old standby, Big Walter Horton.

On September 1, Jimmy, Muddy, and Little Walter joined Otis Spann, Fred Below, and Willie Dixon to lay down four tunes: "I'm Ready," "Smokestack Lightning," "I Don't Know Why," and "Shake It Baby." It was becoming clearer by then that as Leonard was seemingly trying to conquer the world with his ever expanding operation, his allegiance was shifting further away from Jimmy and Muddy. Indeed, the Chess label was recording more and more artists, so many that it was hard to imagine how anyone on the roster could get the special attention that the likes of Muddy and Jimmy had once enjoyed. Names like Al Hibbler, Slim Saunders, Willie Mabon, Jimmy Witherspoon, Eddie Boyd, and Lowell Fulson stretched the Chess coffers; the list of names on the label's roster seemed endless. The outside acquisitions list on Checker was even lengthier, ranging from gospel music to doo-wop.

Meanwhile, Leonard continued to grow closer to Howlin' Wolf, and even Muddy had to succumb to the pressure of doing songs that Willie Dixon would try out on either Muddy or Wolf. Depending on which one delivered the best rendition, they'd have their next big hit, with Leonard putting his full weight behind the tune. Jimmy's tunes, however, were steadily collecting dust; consequently, he grew less and less enthusiastic about offering Leonard Chess fresh material. This was getting to be a poisonous situation, and Jimmy was losing confidence in Leonard's faith and trust in him to deliver as a solo artist. Still, he showed up for recording sessions. Jimmy knew he had always been the only guitarist that Muddy ever wanted or needed. Walter too showed up, giving his old friends his best. Near the end of the year, the Waters band laid down two more tunes: "I'm a Natural Born Lover" and "Ooh, Wee." Both tunes were relatively weak in content, delivery, and performance, despite Little Walter's heroic efforts.

The next year saw relatively little change to the downward spiral in the group's track record, and more trouble was on the horizon. The session on February 3, 1955, yielded four songs that seemed to indicate that Muddy was out of material, out of step, and maybe even out of steam. "This Pain," "Young Fashioned Ways," "I Want to Be Loved," and the March 9 recording of "My Eyes Keep Me in Trouble" made very little impact. In fact, it was some of the weakest material Muddy ever recorded and maybe should have been left on the shelf. As for Jimmy, he managed to get off one tune, "You're the One," which had a strong, driving beat but also a vocal delivery that came across sounding forced; maybe the tempo was too brisk, or the long lyrics were being forced into too short a space. In what was becoming an old routine, Leonard chose to shelve the day's take. Totally frustrated, Jimmy had had enough. He began his own retaliation, deliberately refusing to offer any new material to Chess. He would not record again for almost the entire year.

On both Jimmy's and Muddy's tunes, Chess rookie Francis Clay played the drums; Fred Below had abandoned the chair after Little Walter's band fell apart over money problems. Below, along with Louis and Dave Myers, went back to being the Four Aces and got a regular gig alternating shows with Muddy at the 708 Club. Little Walter, always volatile, appears to have fallen apart with his band by then. Even worse, he was constantly getting into fights with street thugs or racist policemen, which often led to his receiving brutal beatings. He would sometimes be found unconscious or bleeding profusely after being left in his car or on the curb somewhere.[40] Walter lived hard and fast, and it looked as if his musical dominance was coming to a violent end.

With every passing month, the picture was getting clearer: Muddy's style was rapidly becoming dated. In a sign of things to come, that same month Bo Diddley had his first session for Chess, bringing with him a more upbeat, edgier sound with guitars bathed in tremolo and echo. "I'm a Man" and "Bo Diddley" emerged as huge hits for Bo Diddley, and the changing of the guard was officially taking place. Even Little Walter was losing steam; his latest releases lacked their earlier punch, although in March he recovered nicely with a big hit, "My Babe," which made it all the way to the top of the charts.[41] Muddy too did his best to fight back, even recording his own version of Bo Diddley's "I'm a Man," calling it "Mannish Boy." Jimmy was in on this May 24 session, but as it turned out, it would be the last song he would record with Muddy for the next five years.

Jimmy was beginning to look toward his future in other places and somehow found himself in the studio with legendary Texas guitarist T-Bone Walker, who had recently spent some time in Chicago. They must have struck up a friendship at some point—more than likely it was in one of the after-hours joints like the

Zanzibar—and ended up recording together on a session that took place on April 21. "I went in the studio with T-Bone Walker," said Jimmy, "[and] cut with him . . . He made 'Why Not,' and he made several more . . . Junior Wells and myself was with him."[42]

Indeed, Jimmy's smooth *lumpty-lump* rhythm pattern and Junior's hard-edged harp attack can be heard on "T-Bone Blues Special," while T-Bone put his special brand of vocals and lead guitar over the top. "Play On Little Girl" has a stop-time feel that is slightly similar to Muddy's "I Just Want to Make Love to You." Jimmy lays down the staccato riff while Junior howls a tasty solo after the second verse. Walker laid down five songs that day, with Jimmy and Junior on just the two selections. What was more significant than the recordings, though, was the medium-tempo swing tune of T-Bone's "Why Not," which had a "walking" feel to it. Jimmy picked up on the tune's strolling groove and stored it in his memory; the tune and its inherent shuffle had made a lasting impression.

The winds of change were blowing mighty cold and fast, and both Muddy and Jimmy were feeling unprotected from the stinging Hawk. Instead of sitting and listening attentively on the more laid-back songs, allowing the blues to wash over them as they bathed in the groove, club-goers these days felt compelled to get up and gyrate more than ever, writhing back and forth until they worked themselves into a tizzy. Muddy noticed it too: "Rock 'n' roll—it hurt the blues pretty bad. People wanted to 'bug' all the time and we couldn't play slow blues anymore. But we still hustled around and kept going. We survived."[43] The surge toward a heavier, more aggressive sound went well beyond Chess—it was becoming a national obsession among teenagers. Fats Domino, Elvis Presley's "That's All Right," Bill Haley's "Rock Around the Clock"—they were all overtaking the airwaves, squeezing the blues into the corner to make room for what was now being called "rhythm and blues," a phrase first coined by Jerry Wexler while he was working for *Billboard* magazine during the latter half of the decade. By 1949 the magazine had officially adopted the catchphrase as a replacement for their "race music" category. Now another new term had cropped up, started by the leading radio disc jockey in the country, Alan Freed, who coined "rock and roll" as a descriptor for the exciting new music that had the young white crowds ecstatic about the latest dance fads that were beginning to get paired with some of the music.

Leonard was now looking for the next big thing after his success with Bo Diddley had caused such a stir. It didn't take long for an even bigger wave to come crashing right through Leonard's door. Charles "Chuck" Berry, born October 18, 1926, wasn't exactly unfamiliar with the artist roster on the Chess label, having played regularly at the Cosmopolitan club in the nearby city of East St. Louis and encountering several of them there, including Jimmy and Muddy. When Chuck Berry suddenly popped up in May 1955, he did so upon the recommendation of none other than Muddy himself. Berry had sought Leonard out to see if he could get a record deal. Jimmy remembered Berry's arrival on the scene: "He came to Chicago, and he'd play around where we'd be in Chicago there, different clubs, and trying to get to meet Leonard Chess. And he met Leonard Chess through Muddy Waters and myself. Otherwise, Chess didn't like no rock 'n' roll for himself—he was hung up on blues, because that was his meal ticket at the time."[44]

But Leonard *was* interested in turning a fast and steady buck. Within days Berry entered the studio to record "Maybelline" and "Wee Wee Hours," the former making a humongous impact upon its release. In fact, by September "Maybelline" had struck number one on three different *Billboard* charts.[45] In Jimmy's words, "He put Chuck Berry on [the airwaves], and it just went like wildfire." After that, it seemed like people were coming out of the woodwork just to be affiliated with Chess. Jimmy always felt that too many people on Chess's roster would ruin things: "Man, they'd come in there and they'd say, 'how much would I have to put up for you to record me?' I said, 'Oh, man, this cat is desperate!' And he made a few bucks fast on rock 'n' roll, and that's what he was in the whole thing for, anyway. And he just lightened up off of pushin' the blues and went pushin' more rock."[46]

Jimmy had picked a bad time to take his act on the road and leave the comfort and familiarity of Muddy's band, even if it was totally understandable that he felt he was able to carry the load on his own, which by then he clearly was. What he had not anticipated was the onslaught of an entire genre of music that seemingly came out of nowhere yet gripped the public as if they had been waiting for it all along. Jimmy expressed a real distress about the way he and other Chess artists felt about the neglect Leonard showed them: "He really got behind Chuck on that stuff, and I think he kind of turned away—he really didn't turn from the blues, but he was putting more into this rock thing than he was the blues, because it was a big fast turnover for him at the time."[47]

Toward the end of the year, Jimmy saw the writing on the wall and tried to write and produce material that reflected a more modern approach to the blues. The first thing he did was to rerecord his last tune that he'd offered Leonard, "You're the One," which had resulted in what was now becoming an old routine: being shelved. This time the tune boasted a medium-mellow groove established by Willie Dixon; tasty single-note licks splashed across the top by Robert Junior Lockwood; simmering harmonica riffs from Little Walter; and supportive, steady propulsion from Fred Below that joyously exploded under Walter's second-chorus solo. And beneath it all, Jimmy, as always, provided the perfect "*lump*."

Jimmy laid the tune down in December 1955, but, based on Leonard's track record with him, he had every reason not to be optimistic about the tune's fate. Still, it was one of the tightest grooves he'd ever recorded, with the firm and steady backbeat that was becoming all the rage on the latest recordings; it seemed to be the thing that made the people move, and Fred Below was fast becoming a master at delivering the infectious rhythm. Leonard heard the tune, liked it, and reached back almost two years and grabbed a tune off the shelf to serve as the B side. "Blues All Day Long," recorded in early January 1954, was paired with "You're the One" and released as Chess 1616 early the following year. (During its reign it would be difficult to ascertain the exact figures related to the amount of sales generated by artists on the label roster, because the Chess brothers routinely kept their numbers close to the vest.)

Meanwhile, harmonica player Rice Miller, better known as Sonny Boy Williamson II, had recently joined the Chess stable, recording his first session for Checker back in August. Sonny Boy II was already established as a legend in West Helena and had just come up to Chicago. Ever since he was a teenager, Jimmy Rogers had been following Sonny Boy's career. The session booked on August 12, 1955, yielded five tunes that captured the essence of Sonny Boy's unique style, including the classic "Don't Start Me to Talkin'." Contrary to popular belief, Jimmy was not on the session as second guitarist in the rhythm section that included Waters, Spann, and Below. It was in fact Jody Williams, whose versatility as a guitarist made him one of the most sought-after players among the Chess roster. It seemed that for a brief spell Leonard was willing to at least preserve the classic blues sound for a while longer.

On November 3 Muddy went in to lay down four tracks. Little Walter was replaced by Big Walter; the fact that drummer Francis Clay was also there hints that Little Walter was probably out gigging and took Below (Muddy's favorite drummer) with him. And then there was something else different this time: no follow-up session for Jimmy; in fact, Jimmy wasn't in attendance at all. Previous blues researchers, somewhat unsure about who exactly was sitting in the guitar chair that day, have listed Jimmy as the session player. Alas, it was not; the playing heard on the tracks doesn't reflect Jimmy's style. Certainly Jimmy never demonstrated those thick dominant ninth chords on "Clouds in My Heart" or the single-note riffs interspersed among the chords as part of his arsenal.

Jimmy had already left the Waters outfit as a regularly performing sideman for local and touring gigs when he started his own band in 1952. Now he'd effectively removed himself from the other half of the winning combination, leaving Muddy's studio band after May 1955. He left the vacancy for the next wave of Chess studio guitarists—either Pat Hare, Jody Williams, Robert Junior Lockwood, or Luther Tucker—to fill in his absence. Williams had already been mistaken once for Jimmy Rogers on the Sonny Boy Williamson session, and the Chess logs were continually listing Jimmy as the session guitarist, even though his legendary complementary lines no longer reverberated from within the studio walls. The classic guitar tandem would not resurface for another five years, effectively bringing to a close one of the most successful runs in music history.

6

BLUES LEAVE ME ALONE

You supposed to go in the studio happy and
come out happy, man. You don't supposed to
go in there like you're goin' in a steel mill.

—Jimmy Rogers

What led to Jimmy's distancing himself from Leonard Chess? Maybe it was his mounting frustration with the pressure from the label to follow the beat of acts who were brought in to lead the way toward the emergence of the new rock 'n' roll groove. Maybe it was the ever expanding gulf that lay between himself and Leonard, with Chess constantly holding back almost every tune Jimmy put in the can. Maybe the harrowing thirteen-take session when he recorded "Blues All Day Long" was the final straw. Or maybe he was just fed up with the fact that several others, including Muddy, Wolf, Chuck Berry, Bo Diddley, and Little Walter, had charted hits—seemingly everybody but him. On the other hand, maybe Leonard was similarly disappointed in Jimmy's lack of hits, or maybe he thought the Rogers sound was too outdated.

There was only one sure thing: Jimmy held Leonard totally responsible, and the slow dissolution of their relationship affected him so profoundly that finally he felt he needed to take a proactive stance, no longer able to endure the way Leonard had forced him into being reactive all the time. This decision was no doubt a troubling one for Jimmy. He was never into confrontations or show-downs; his habit of avoiding the scuffles in the juke joints and clubs he'd played throughout his career was a character trait that reflected a major component of his basic philosophy of life.

Everyone who knew Jimmy knew he was all about having a good time, being easygoing about handling situations, and avoiding complications—both physical and verbal—at every turn. He was a relatively quiet man who kept to himself, was known for his ability to get along with just about anyone, and always had a decent sense of humor. Where most people got bent out of shape over the little things, Jimmy was the one who was able to let them just roll right off his back, saying, "Well . . . *that's all right.*" This approach was further reflected in the music itself, which might shed some light as to why Leonard may have felt that Jimmy's music was, relatively speaking, not as aggressive as a few of his contemporaries, whose musical output may have been yielding better results at the time.

Leonard Chess's high-handed treatment of what Jimmy cared about most—his music—began to feel distinctly disrespectful to Jimmy. By 1955 he was holding in a quite a bit of anger and resentment toward Leonard and the entire situation he found himself in, and it would take years before he publicly admitted just how bitter he was about it all. Leonard Chess was undoubtedly aware of Jimmy's frustrations. Still, he let Jimmy record only a few numbers to keep him under obligation, just as he had with Johnny Shines a few years earlier. Many years later the dam did burst. In a series of exclusive interviews for *Living Blues* magazine, Jimmy revealed to interviewer Jim O'Neal exactly how he felt about numerous issues regarding his relationship with Leonard Chess and his entire recording operation.

Jimmy admitted to O'Neal that from the beginning he had never liked the fact that he wasn't allowed to use his own band members on his Chess recording sessions, even though he was trying to establish his unique identity during the crucial phase of his independence from Muddy. As Jimmy explained: "See, Leonard didn't like the sound of nobody together but Muddy Waters, myself, and Little Walter. Now he liked that sound for recording. We played with other musicians on gigs, but when we'd go to the studio, we would be together. But the way I feel about it, the band that I played with, I think that if they're good enough to play a gig with me, they're good enough to record with me."[1]

At least Leonard's treatment of Jimmy on this issue was consistent. When Walter tried to establish his independence in the studio and incorporate his backing band (the Jukes), he was soundly rejected as well. Leonard didn't want to record Walter's hand-picked musicians, consisting of Louis and Dave Myers, Robert Junior Lockwood, and Fred Below. "Leonard Chess didn't like them, [and] wanted to pick who he wanted," Jimmy commented. "Willie Dixon played bass on practically all of Little Walter's numbers. And Otis Spann played piano on a lot of his numbers. And then a few he cut with Louis and Dave, but Below was on just about all of 'em for drums. He [Chess] liked Below's drummin'."[2]

Jimmy was also quite bothered about the way Leonard would interfere with Jimmy's proceedings when he was trying to get the music right for sessions scheduled by Leonard. Being a man who liked having his act together, Jimmy was proud of the fact that his musicians were well rehearsed. His disciplined approach to getting the music right went all the way back to when he and Muddy first met. In the beginning, when he first recorded with Chess in 1950, they had a system that worked well for everyone, as the three forces were slowly building their dynasty. "So we'd go in and just Muddy first, I'm second and then Walter would be third," Jimmy elaborated.[3] The guys were comfortable with that, and when things were unfettered, all was well and everyone went home happy.

Jimmy was always quite irritated with the interference coming from the booth. When it came to recording songs, he had a hands-off attitude toward Leonard that said, "You do your job, and let us do ours." But things were never as simple as that at Chess Studios. Leonard was a hands-on kind of guy, and he crossed the line between producer and artist many times when he shouldn't have. His reputation for barking instructions from behind the glass—or even worse, jumping into the middle of the floor to dictate directions (as was the case with the legendary story about taking the drums from Elga Edmonds)—was a bit much for Jimmy to take. He described in detail how hard the musicians would work to prepare their music, yet things would fall apart so badly under Leonard's orders that they didn't want to work anymore. Jimmy remembered it this way:

> You can rehearse a number and you get 'em timed, and get your lyrics right and get the arrangement right the way you want it. Then go on in the studio. When you get there the man said, "*Ho-hold it.*" Say, "come *back* here. What'd ya *do* with this thing? Let's change this and do such-and-such a thing." He gonna turn me around, and when he turn me around he automatically turn the *band* around and I get disgusted. And what he's telling me to do, I don't like it, see, I don't feel it and I really don't like it, so that gets you to the place you don't care then whether you record or not.[4]

It wasn't just Jimmy—Muddy got frustrated a lot too. One such incident happened when Leonard was trying to get Muddy to record a Charles Brown–like version of "Merry Christmas Baby." Leonard wouldn't stop meddling, and he pushed Muddy's buttons. "We had a hell of a time tryin' to cut that thing down there," Jimmy recalled. "Muddy couldn't get it right. Muddy said, 'goddammit! If it's this hard, I'm takin' my goddam contract and go on back to Mississippi! Got to work this goddam hard.' I know what he was goin' through, man. We didn't cut it. All that time we spent for nothin'. He [Leonard] got Chuck Berry to cut it later. He kept on, he was determined to get that damn song, man. He got it out of Chuck Berry."[5] (Indeed, Berry did get it right after two takes in a session on November 19, 1958.) And there was Little Walter's frustration too, and he had the hottest head of them all. "Oh yeah," Jimmy said. "He was another guy, man. He'd get mad and just walk out of the studio. Get in his car and go on home and stay for two or three days. The band wouldn't know what to do . . . it was rough, I tell you. And he [Leonard] wasn't getting any better, he was getting worse."[6]

It didn't take long for Leonard to ruffle the feathers of even the newest member of the Chess family, Sonny Boy Williamson, who at the time was trying to record a song he wanted to call "Little Village." Leonard cussed him out for it, saying the song had nothing to do with a little village, which sent Sonny Boy into a blind rage. The ensuing back-and-forth cussing and shouting match became legendary, as it was captured on tape. "Yeah, well, that was the real thing," Jimmy quipped. "That's what went on at Leonard's studio quite a bit. That same thing that Sonny Boy did, that happened every day with the blues. You should have heard some sessions down there with Muddy Waters and Leonard that I [was] on. I'd sit and get my kicks, man. Sit back there. I know that I was gonna get paid anyway. I just sit back there and drink and listen at this rap, you know. *Whoo*, they be fightin' mad. One would be thinkin' the other one would knock him in the head, man."[7]

Clearly most of the guys did not appreciate Leonard's unsolicited help. Jimmy observed that Chess's idea about what would make the song better was usually counterintuitive to the original architect's vision of the music. According to Rogers, "The numbers they were changin', tryin' to get all jazzy with us . . . That take all the soul out of the blues. That's for sure. And it was really Leonard's fault."[8] For Jimmy, Leonard's constant tampering with the music meant the situation was getting personal. Judging by the way things fell apart during that marathon thirteen-take session for "Blues All Day Long," toxic fumes had infiltrated Jimmy's system, and Leonard was the poison. "Only time it'd be a rerun would be somethin' Chess would want to change, and that would be the end of a good record," Jimmy said. "When he changed it, he'd take all the soul and everything from it. And that happened quite a few times."[9] Things were seriously getting off track, and the potential for a train wreck was ever present. Consider this daily dichotomy: The musicians are there to make music, which usually cannot be rushed if it is to be done right. The artists want little or no interference, because they know exactly what they're going after; the studio owner, on the other hand, is trying to save a buck at every turn, wanting to squeeze out as much product in as little time possible, and sometimes he tries too hard to help it along. It was a recipe for disaster.

Musicians were forced to record at a fast pace because, according to Jimmy, if you took too long, you'd end up owing the studio quite a bit of money. "When we'd start takin' a lot of time, you know, sometimes it'll take you two or three days to record; you'd come up there owin' the studio $4,000 and the record would sell about 100 copies," Jimmy recalled."[10] This is exactly what he knew he would be faced with when the "Blues All Day Long" session occurred. For the first time in his career, he showed his frustration. He also changed his strategy—if for no other reason than to stay out of debt—even though he knew he was sacrificing quality for quantity. "So I figure the best way to do a blues tune [is to] catch it as you play 'em, as you feel it. Whatever you feel, play it that way and forget it, you know. Because you keep turnin' it around, you's gonna start findin' fault, and once you start findin' faults, it's dead."[11]

The musical consequences are painfully obvious when you listen to the steady decline in both the performance level and sound quality on many of the sides that were issued during one particularly tumultuous stretch of sessions around 1955. Stressful conditions became aurally evident when Jimmy recorded the horribly hurried version of "You're the One," where the tempo for the song is set so fast that he could barely get the lyrics out (in hindsight it seems apparent that he was simply trying to beat the clock). For Muddy, the decline began even earlier, starting around November 1954 and lasting beyond January 1958. For both great artists, these years include some of the worst tunes of their storied canons. Jimmy knew it himself, leading him to say when it was all over, "I made a lot of stuff, I hope they don't ever release it . . . Some of it is terrible . . . I hear some of the stuff they released on Muddy Waters, it's terrible, man."[12]

Even though Jimmy had left the Deep South, certain aspects of working at Chess reminded him of the bad old days down in the Delta. Take, for example, the payout system that Leonard Chess used for recording sessions. Although everything started out fine, Jimmy became thoroughly disgusted with the grueling working hours down at Chess, and he felt as if he and his musicians were not adequately compensated for their efforts: "Man, you'd be down there sometimes two or three days . . . Now, he wouldn't pay you for all those hours that you had put down there. He'd just pay you for the session. It'd take you three days to do a session which you've supposed to have done in two hours or three hours. Well, you get the same money that you was gonna get if you'd have done it in an hour. So, I didn't like his setup at all . . . So I got out of it."[13]

The worst part, though, was that even after all that blood and sweat in the studio, Leonard routinely exercised the most ruthless power of all: he wouldn't press copies of the song to release to the public. This ultimate veto power was what finally sent Jimmy over the edge.

So after [a while] I see I'm just stackin' my stuff on the shelf . . . I cut four songs on a session each time we'd record, [and] he'd release one and put one on the shelf. That one would go. The next time you'd get a release, you'd record again, see, and he'd release one more. See, now he got four songs on the shelf and four on the street. That's the way he would do. He was just tyin' you up. Stead[il]y tyin' your material up there. I told him I didn't have anything to record once, and I said, "What about the stuff that's up there?" [Leonard says,] "Well, it's not too good. I would like for you to do something new, you know what I mean?" Well, I just fold up on him, said, "Well, I ain't got nothin'." That's the way it happened.[14]

But how was he able to escape Leonard's clutches? The truth was, Jimmy had been plotting his escape for several years. He'd cooked up a plan of retreat that went all the way back to 1951, and it worked for him. Listen to how he describes his strategy: "I hadn't signed a contract with Chess but once, and that was in 1951." When asked how long the contract was for, Jimmy provided a detailed response:

Five years. And in 1956 I was automatically free. He would tell me, "Well, I got some contracts here. Your contract[s] is back, you know. You can sign 'em when you stop in." And I'd say, "okay." Well, when I would come in his office, I'd call the office, and if he were there, I wouldn't go in. So I would go in when he wasn't there, see. They'd say, "Mr. Chess left some contracts here." So I'd say, "Oh, yeah, okay then, I'll check 'em out." I'd take the contracts and look at 'em, and be talkin' and then fold 'em up and then lay 'em on the desk and get out! So I kept doin' that and he got the message: "Hey, this guy don't want to sign." So that's the way I worked."[15]

To be fair, Leonard had no legal obligation whatsoever to release the music just because his constituents were upset over his timing or his choices. Although Jimmy chose to get out, he had to resign himself to the idea that he couldn't take his music with him. "But he still had my material there, see," Rogers woefully lamented. "That's what I was worried about. What he had, I knew he had all that. So that's why eventually he'd release one. And I was doin' some other things too then. I wasn't gettin' no money out of the records, no way, so what's the use of me steady pilin' up material there for him, you know what I mean? So I just stopped."[16]

Although being on a major label like Chess Records looked glamorous on the surface, just below that surface lay a world of turmoil. For Jimmy, the agony he endured wasn't worth the trouble, and if anybody thought the average Chess recording artist was rolling in the dough, they had another thing coming. According to Jimmy's recollection, "A [leader] session was $90.00, sideman was $45.00. Well, you'd get that money in 14 days. That's all the money you would get until the record sells so many. He wasn't goin' by the rule of what's supposed to cover the front money. You didn't get no money out of Chess. You think you get front money, man, you don't know what you're talking about."[17]

Jimmy had logged countless hours of session time and had no less than sixteen songs that had made it to the airwaves by 1955. But as it turned out, all he had to show for it were a few skimpy royalty statements, which were basically turned right back over to Leonard as a result of the record company's sharecropper-like system. This was the technique that the average record label executive used to keep his artists indebted to him, recalling the famous lines of the song "Sixteen Tons," *"I owe my soul to the company store."* Jimmy explained it this way: "I owed Leonard maybe a thousand dollars and my royalty check was supposed to be like maybe twelve hundred, and I'd pay him his thousand and I'd get two hundred. And that would go on for another six months and, like, it wasn't nothin'. He was just gyppin' everybody. But one thing: *I didn't ever let him buy me no car.*"[18]

This last statement was delivered as a source of immense pride from Jimmy, as he was clearly dismayed by the fact that other artists fell for Leonard's trick of luring them into submission with the candy of a Cadillac dangling like a sugar-coated carrot in front of their faces, a luxury item that could placate them even further and for a greater length of time. Jimmy never fell for it, though, because he knew from those who had that the supposed "owner" never saw car payments or statements of any kind and therefore never knew exactly what the terms were (Howlin' Wolf was also never lured by this particular bait). "They didn't pay no car note, man, didn't know how much money they was making, they just ridin'. And Chess takin' all the money, man. He might just go in and pay for the car and be through with it, instead of givin' it all to them . . . You get sick, or if anything happen, man, you were walkin', and everything else was messed up."[19]

Jimmy would have rather had the control over his own fate and had no problem turning down the falsely generous gesture—an offer of a prepaid monthly car note that he knew was coming straight off the top of the royalty statement checks anyway, which meant those who accepted the "gift" weren't riding for free by any means: "I said 'you give me the money, I'll buy my own car.'"[20] It was well known that whenever Muddy and Little Walter were upset with the company for not being compensated appropriately when their tunes shot up the charts and brought in a huge windfall of cash for Chess, they'd be pacified in almost the exact same way every time—with a shiny, new Cadillac. This seemed to work well for Leonard with those two, but Jimmy never allowed himself to be bamboozled.

When he first signed in 1951, the terms he agreed to were under informal conditions, and Jimmy didn't worry about holding up his end of the deal at the time, saying, "We had one of those little do-it-yourself contracts back then . . . I'm a fellow that I'm not hard to get along with, with nobody, you know. I try to do what I say I'll do." Now he felt that since Leonard was repeatedly opting not to release the bulk of his recordings in a timely fashion, Chess had reneged on his word. "He promised one thing, and he did something else," Jimmy said. "And I got tired of it, I paid the dues."[21]

The matter was further complicated when Jimmy realized that his means of recourse were fairly limited when it came to forcing Chess to capitulate and give him what he thought he deserved. "Chess was heavy and he was holdin' all the sticks," Rogers said. "So, I had to go through a lot of trouble and it's not too good to have lawyers comin' involved in these record companies, because they get afraid of you, and they fold up on you. That was what happened to Willie Mabon. Willie Mabon was with Chess, and about this 'I Don't Know' number, he tried to sue Chess and Chess bought the lawyer and froze him out everywhere he turned to. So he messed hisself around." In Jimmy's mind, refusing to offer any new material was the only card he had left to play: "I knew about all those tricks before, so I would just rather go on and say, 'Well, I don't have anything,' you know. Which he gotta—he'll take it."[22]

Jimmy kept his eyes open as his dissatisfaction with Chess grew. He realized that several artists who were affiliated with other labels may have been working in a somewhat healthier environment and with better contracts. "I think Vee-Jay [run by Vivian Carter and James Bracken] treated [their] artists better than Leonard did. Jimmy Reed's made a lot of money. He *blew* it, but he made a lot."[23] The degree to which Jimmy's suspicions about a better atmosphere at Vee-Jay was accurate or not is a matter of conjecture; the truth was, no matter how much he thought about jumping over to another label, the possibility was nearly nonexistent. Jimmy alluded to Leonard as a powerful force to be reckoned with, acknowledging the terrifying grip that Chess had not only on the artists on the roster but also on the rival companies that jockeyed for the attention of the Chess artists who might have entertained the idea of leaving. "Man, if I'd have been with any company, they couldn't touch Chess, see. That's the problem," said Rogers. "During that time if you was tied up with Chess, wouldn't no other company fool with you. So, man, I had a couple of guys hit on me about it, and they was ready to challenge him, but man, he was too heavy . . . Chess was heavy. You couldn't get no place unless'n you come through him, see. Everything they got, it was through Chess, because he had the whole thing sewed up."[24]

Jimmy had his own theory about where Leonard's hard-line stance originated: "Leonard's daddy, old man Chess—I knew him too—Leonard was much like his daddy, see. Phil was most like his mother, see. You know, the *good* guy. And Leonard, he was like the old man. That's the reason why he [Phil] dropped everything in Leonard's hands, you know. Leonard was the big boss . . . he was a hard nut to crack, man. He was out to get you."[25]

Leonard was also determined to keep his company on top. When the popularity of the blues began to wane, so did his interest in it. Early in the 1950s, Jimmy observed the change: "I didn't ever hear none of 'em *say* it, but their reaction I could tell, they weren't approvin' the blues at all, and I'm thinkin' that they were about tired of tryin' to push the blues anyway."[26] Chess had recently signed the Flamingos, a black vocal group. The forward-looking Leonard was keeping abreast of the steadily rising trend of doo-wop groups and had expanded his conglomerate even further by adding a new branch, Argo Records, to his stable in order to accommodate the Flamingos and other upcoming acquisitions. The Moonglows and the Ravens were of a similar vein, and Chess signed them as well that same year.[27]

In his revelatory interviews Jimmy tried to put it all in perspective: "He started off good but after a while there, after he got a-hold to the Moonglows and Chuck Berry, Bo Diddley, and they was makin' that rock-type stuff, see. And it was sellin' pretty fast then. And so he just forgot about the blues completely . . . As soon as he'd get his money, well, the heck with it. He didn't do nothin' for no blues."[28] Still, Rogers was wise enough to see the writing on the wall and realized the fickleness of it all: "It was just like the wind—it blow hard, then it cease, then it's gone. But the blues was steady rolling: it's a steady thing. Chess made Chuck a pretty big man, and I really appreciate what he did for him. I didn't make any money from Chess. In fact, nobody did make too much money from Chess."[29]

Hubert Sumlin, Howlin' Wolf's ace guitarist, alludes to the fact that Wolf, Muddy, and Jimmy might have been relegated to a backseat not only on the airwaves and jukeboxes but maybe even in the Chess studio too. "We'd record about three or four in the morning," Sumlin recalled. "After we did the gig, we had to leave the job and come to the studio. That was the only available time that they had at the studio then. Chuck Berry and the Moonglows would be cutting a record in there—and sometimes it would take days for them to do it. By the time they were through, it would be nearly two in the morning."[30]

In the field of rhythm and blues, Muddy had posted on the R & B charts in January 1956 with "Sugar Sweet" and "Trouble No More." Howlin' Wolf was on in February with "Smokestack Lightning." Chuck Berry struck again in June with "Roll Over Beethoven." By February, Muddy and Wolf were still challenging each other on who was king of the blues. In a serious game of one-upmanship, Muddy took advantage of a falling out that occurred between Wolf and Hubert Sumlin, who maintained a love-hate relationship—mostly love—off and on for several years. Sumlin dealt Wolf the cruelest blow of all when he decided to join forces with Muddy, well known as Wolf's primary adversary. On February 2, Sumlin, along with Pat Hare, tag-teamed to make one of Muddy's strongest vocal efforts of his career, "Forty Days and Forty Nights."

In a stark contrast, Jimmy had no chart positions to speak of and no sessions booked; the last time he'd been in the studio was in December 1955. During the following summer he held a regular Tuesday night gig under his own steam with his "rocking four" combo at the 708 Club, while Muddy had Mondays and Thursdays.[31] Although Jimmy held on to his gig throughout September and beyond, it was not until October 1956, when the ten-month recording drought ended, that he finally got another shot to lay down tracks. He cooked up one of his best tunes in some time, a tune called "If It Ain't Me (Who Are You Thinking Of)." The band really found the pocket on that track; the music is swinging deep and wide, with lyrics aimed at a woman who is being told emphatically, "That ain't it!"

Then Jimmy remembered the strolling T-Bone Walker groove he heard when they recorded "Why Not" together in April 1955 and decided to slightly revamp the lyrics and layer it with a hard-edged South Side blues shuffle. Jimmy retitled the tune "Walkin' by Myself," and it swung even harder than the previous tune, primarily because of Fred Below's incredibly rocking bass drum and pumping snare, which fit perfectly with Jimmy's always steady *lump*. To kick it into high gear, the "Big" Walter took an absolutely howling solo that stands as one of his absolute best—one that would have made the "Little" one (Marion Jacobs) proud. In a surprise move, Leonard didn't shelve all the music or reach back to pair the tunes with older material. He released the two sides (as Chess 1643) in November 1956.

The harmonica role for that session was supposed to be played by "Good Rockin'" Charles Edwards. The only problem was, Edwards was nervous about performing in recording studios. Jimmy showed up at the session ready to cut. After he learned that Charles had chickened out, Jimmy sent someone to go find Big Walter, who was busy doing a plastering job.[32] Jimmy talked him into coming to the recording session, and, as usual, time was of the essence, which meant Horton had no time to change out of his worker's garb. He was somewhat embarrassed, though, when he entered the studio. "He was covered head-to-toe in plaster dust—he looked like a ghost," Jimmy told Scott Dirks one night when Dirks was sitting in at Lilly's.[33] It is a real testament to Horton's harmonica prowess when one considers the fact that he went from being totally focused on doing a stellar plaster job to delivering a blistering solo with no preparation time whatsoever. "On 'Walkin' By Myself' Walter did a *good* job of it," Jimmy said emphatically. "He got so mad about that, didn't want anybody in the studio to look at him."[34]

The next month Jimmy was back in the studio, laying down more tracks. Maybe Chess was trying to capitalize on the good vibes that accompanied the previous session, which had clearly yielded the best results in months. On December 1, Jimmy recorded three songs in rapid succession: "I Can't Believe," "One Kiss," and "Can't Keep from Worrying," each in only one take. The band was stellar and firing on all cylinders, with Jimmy on guitar, Otis Spann on piano, Willie Dixon on bass, Fred Below on drums, Big Walter Horton on harp, and Jody Williams as hot lead guitarist, brought in for added firepower. "I Can't Believe" and "One Kiss" were both mellow rockers that swung like mad, propelled by the patented Below backbeat. Leonard pushed it immediately out into the market (Chess 1659). As for the fate of "Can't Keep from Worrying," the tune somehow got lost and was never heard from again. Still, Jimmy was satisfied—at least for the time being—with the release of the other two.

Around this same time period, Muddy was traveling on the road with his band, which had recently experienced some personnel changes. A relatively young harmonica player, James Cotton, was introduced to the band when Junior Wells unexpectedly had to quit, leaving Muddy's group stranded in Florida. Junior had known the tour would be heading near Cotton's hometown and seized the opportunity to abandon Muddy. The gig was at the Hippodrome Ballroom in Memphis.

With the advent of the rock 'n' roll era, Muddy had decided that he wanted a more aggressive sound than what Elga Edmonds was supplying, and he went with the heavier backbeat of newcomer Francis Clay. About Elga, Muddy complained, "He was straight right down—*bop, bop, bop, bop*. I had to part from him 'cause he just couldn't hit the backbeat."[35] Muddy was trying to keep up with the changing times, and he knew that drums were the essential ingredient in getting people to pay attention. He said, "I had to find me a drummer that would *drive . . .*

the blues *do* have a backbeat to it, you know, *today*."[36] Cotton missed Edmonds immediately, saying, "Elga was the onliest one in the band who ever didn't drink . . . Elga would just go for a walk and then he'd just want to go to sleep."[37]

As for Rogers, he also used a different drummer than Elga on his own sessions, opting for A. J. Gladney because, according to Jimmy, "he had more of a blues drive than Elga did."[38] Jimmy would have preferred to have Fred Below, who was now the hottest session drummer at the Chess studio. Fred's mean backbeat is the driving force behind practically all of Chuck Berry's biggest hits, including "Roll Over Beethoven," "Johnny B. Goode," and "Sweet Little Sixteen." Ironically, it was Elga Edmonds who steered Fred Below in the direction of blues, because at that time, according to what Edmonds told Below, he could make more money playing blues than jazz.

Because Jimmy looked at both Edmonds and Below as struggling jazz enthusiasts trying to cross over to the world of blues in order to make money, he viewed them as sinking in the same boat: "He and Elga both was learnin', but Elga caught on a little quicker than he [Below] did."[39] In the end, however, it would be Below's musical imprint that would stick deeper and longer than Elga's, and, even more significantly, it would be because of Below's sense of jazz and the hard swinging backbeat that he employed in everything he played. This ultimately would be the sound that most modern jazz drummers of the 1950s would move toward, indicating that perhaps Fred Below's style was ahead of its time.

After several years of working together as a core unit, Jimmy's opportunities to record great music with Muddy had ceased to exist, and, beyond the quick flurry of action he saw in November and December, his sessions as a leader were now few and far between. He shifted his focus, therefore, toward his working band and tried his best to find gigs to support himself and his bandmates. It was not an easy thing to do; the entire country's attention had already shifted toward the hard-hitting rhythm and blues, which, in turn, spawned a dance craze that fueled songwriters to create songs that were tailor-made for the youth.

One of the sidemen Jimmy chose was Big Leon Brooks, a harp player who had been on the scene in Chicago for a few years and had made a name for himself, primarily as an exceptionally good imitator of Little Walter and Sonny Boy Williamson II. "Little Walter was the hottest thing on the scene," Brooks said, "and so everyone was sounding like [him]." One of the things Brooks had correctly assessed was Walter's ability to incorporate ideas borrowed from jazz saxophonists of their day. Indeed, Leon noted, "If a musician was playin' harmonica, he had to swing his harmonica . . . something like a saxophone was [doing], and I think Walter, he was the tops on doing that."[40] Brooks, however, did not last long in

Jimmy's band, due to personal problems with drugs. Jimmy, reluctantly, had to let him go: "He was heavy. When he was with me he was goin' real hot. If it hadn't been tied up in that stuff, we probably coulda' made it way up on the road."[41]

On a national level the youth were not all that interested in the Chicago blues style that emanated from on the South and West Sides. This had a direct impact on Jimmy when he sought out club owners who might be interested in hiring him and his band for out-of-town engagements, especially since local owners were paying paltry sums for a full night's work. By 1957 times were getting tight, and Jimmy was genuinely concerned about how long he could hold out under the current conditions. At the end of January of this new year, he was one of the featured headliners scheduled to perform at the Leaders Cleaners twenty-sixth anniversary party, held at the Trianon Ballroom, located on Sixty-second and Cottage Grove Avenue. The advertisement in the *Chicago Daily Defender* provided a Chess press kit photo of Jimmy, with a subheading that identified him as being "socko on the T-Bone Walker and Elvis Presley kick," a clear indicator that Jimmy was trying his best to change with the times.[42] "The blues went into a slump," he said. "Nobody was makin' any money to amount to anything. Gigs was pretty hard to get around '55, '56, '57. It was hard to get good gigs here in Chicago. And a bunch of musicians that I had, they were workin'; they had day jobs. And to go out of town for a week, and then when he come back he done blew his job, see, and I couldn't guarantee when we'd have another gig. So therefore I had to turn down a lot of gigs like that. So that didn't do me any good."[43]

Jimmy's money wasn't flowing like Muddy's, who, by that time, had a national reputation along with rapid music sales. Because of his newly attained status, Muddy was starting to relax a bit, making more money for each outing while performing fewer engagements. It didn't work for Jimmy. "He wasn't gettin' gigs too good . . . He didn't work too hard," said Jimmy. "He'd get a gig once in a while that was small and he couldn't afford to pay me, see. Otherwise, I mean, we was alright [*sic*]."[44] Muddy's sidemen were making the kind of money that allowed them to afford the idle time in between big paydays, but not Jimmy's: "If they didn't work, they would just sit around until somethin' jump off. And I couldn't handle it like that."[45]

The main reason why Jimmy couldn't survive under those conditions was that he was no longer thinking only of himself. He and his common-law wife, Mattie, had a growing family that by this time had expanded to include six children: Robert, Vera, Michael, Larry, Deborah, and Jacquelyn.[46] "My family was too big," said Jimmy, "and I always was a man that tried to provide for my family. So I had to cut it a-loose."[47] There was some good news, however. "Walkin' by Myself" turned out to be the biggest hit of Jimmy's career—the first and only tune to appear on the national *Billboard* R & B charts, reaching number fourteen in February 1957. That gave him some hope, so he continued to make a few remaining sides for Chess, even though he steadfastly resisted signing a new contract. In June he performed with Sonny Boy Williamson II for more than seven hundred inmates at the Cook County Jail, with Dinah Washington headlining the event.[48]

Jimmy saw no action in the studio, which was a strange way to celebrate the success of his last two singles. His dry spell lasted throughout most of the year, finally ending on September 18 when he was brought into the studio to lay down three tunes—"What Have I Done," "My Baby Don't Love Me No More," and "Trace of You"—each with two takes. On "Trace of You," Jimmy has a guest female vocalist, Margaret Whitfield, who, according to author Scott Dirks, was the owner of a nightclub where Jimmy was working when the session took place. Whitfield sang on Freddie King's first single, a tune called "Country Boy."[49] Whitfield and Little Walter shared the unison vocals throughout the tune, as they intersperse the phrases *"not a trace of you,"* and *"try me one more time"* between Jimmy's vocal lines. Wayne Bennett, then guitarist for Bobby Blue Bland, made a guest appearance to handle the lead work.

There are several unique aspects about this recording session. For starters, it was clear that Willie Dixon had a hand in the writing credits, as he was the arranger-composer in residence (although some believe he did a lot more arranging than composing). Dixon was clearly trying to write some kind of pop hit for Jimmy, but he fell flat on "My Baby Don't Love Me No More," which has a New Orleans "second line" groove to it that would have sounded more typical of world-renowned piano legend Professor Longhair (one of the pioneers of the uniquely New Orleans piano style). At the other end of the spectrum was "What Have I Done," which has a groove that sounds like an ultramodern version of the pop vocal tune "Fever."

The lame chorus lyrics of "What Have I Done"—*"You got me koo-koo, baby / koo-koo in my head / you got me koo-koo, baby / I wish I was dead"*—sound absolutely dreadful coming from someone of Jimmy's stature. The entire batch of tunes, which clearly fall out of bounds from the blues category, represent a feeble attempt to channel some of the latest popular sounds on the airwaves. While "Trace of You" and "What Have I Done" are almost identical in tempo and key, Little Walter does his best to save the tunes with sparse yet tasty solos. Leonard took the best of the worst and released "Trace of You" and "What Have I Done" (Chess 1687) and spared the public the ridiculous "My Baby Don't Love Me No More," at least for the time being.

By the end of September, Jimmy held a regular four-night engagement at Rickey's Show Lounge, located at 3839 South Indiana Avenue. On Thursday and Friday nights blues lovers could catch Jimmy's act, with Thursday being an "all-request" night for those who wanted to hear his hits.[50] The year came to an end with little recording activity. In late January 1958 he played a repeat performance at the Leaders Cleaners annual anniversary party.[51] Almost exactly eight months after Jimmy's last session, they were at it again, with equally dismal results. The band this time consisted of Jimmy, Otis Spann, Willie Dixon, Joe Young on guitar, and Odie Payne on drums. Four tunes were recorded at the session on May 20, 1958: "Don't You Know My Baby," "Don't Turn Me Down," "Looka Here," and "This Has Never Been." All of these tunes required more than one take each except one—"Looka Here." "Don't You Know My Baby" has a medium up-tempo groove reminiscent of Fats Domino's "Blueberry Hill," with rockabilly guitar licks thrown in by Young, complete with Domino riffs supplied by Spann. "Don't Turn Me Down" is an absolutely dismal tune that sounds like a watered-down version of "Rock Around the Clock," with syrupy lyrics and an atrocious, honking tenor sax solo that was evidently so bad the engineers didn't even identify the culprit in the credits. "Looka Here" is somewhat better, if only for the fact that it actually was a blues shuffle, with Jimmy's official stamp of groovy *lumpty-lump* to give the tune some drive.

On "This Has Never Been" the band develops a groove that sounds almost identical to Muddy's acoustic version of "Country Boy" from the album *Folk Singer* (released years later in 1964). Before the second take begins, Leonard can be heard telling Jimmy, in an obvious attempt to motivate him to play something of substance, "Look, man—this is a *blues*, daddy, you gotta *cry* that shit!" Obviously having a good time, he says to the drummer, "Odie, a straight beat—a lotta high shit on there . . . all right, let's cut . . . take one, 'The *Hand* Has Never Been Told!'"[52] There is some laughter from a couple of the band members, sniggling at the obvious masturbatory reference. Jimmy, clearly irritated at the distraction taking place while he's trying to be serious, immediately snaps back at Leonard, "Hey, *cool* it, man!" Leonard, who apparently is not too happy with Jimmy's retort, shoots a barbed comment back toward him and stops the proceedings, saying, "Hold it—hold it. Hey Jimmy—stay on mike, *will ya*, mother? I know you gotta be told the words, but stay on mike, you got off." Jimmy simply responds, "Okay," and cranks up the slow blues again, doing his best to ignore the comment. Of all eight takes captured that session, nothing was released that year, which was a direct reflection of Leonard's impression of the entire proceedings.

And just like the time before, another eight months passed before Jimmy got the chance to record again. In February 1959 he went in to record two tunes: "Rock This House," and "My Last Meal." "Rock This House" featured some serious Bill Haley–type guitar work by Reggie Boyd, and the jump-blues tune really swung hard. Arguably one of Jimmy's best tunes, he had made his final concessions toward the rock 'n' roll movement and in one swift motion succumbed to the "if you can't beat 'em, join 'em" ideology. Ironically, his white flag was raised near the end of the actual R & B movement, which had started almost five years earlier and wouldn't last five years longer before running out of gas and giving up the ghost to white American pop, black soul music, and British rock.

"My Last Meal" was not a Rogers original, but a tune written three years earlier by Jack Hammer (also known as "Hurricane Harry"), which Jimmy adopted to his own tastes by pulling the tempo back and adding a heavier blues feel.[53] Whose idea it was to have Jimmy record the parody is anybody's guess, but the selection had Willie Dixon's fingerprints all over it. The novelty song is about a man who has one final meal before he's off to prison, and chooses to order a sumptuous soul food meal of gigantic proportions. The unreal menu items he requests include dinosaur eggs, mosquito knees, butter bebop beans, zebra tooth, tiger steak, and well-baked hippopotamus. Two complete takes of each tune were recorded, and Leonard released the first takes of "Rock This House" and "My Last Meal" (Chess 1721) the following month.

Just as Jimmy had come to expect, another long recording drought followed. Unbelievably, an entire nine months later, in November 1959, Jimmy went in to record what would be his last session for Chess. "You Don't Know" and "Can't Keep from Worrying" were captured with Little Walter, Otis Spann, Luther Tucker on guitar, Freddie Robinson on bass, and George Hunter on drums. "You Don't Know" has the second-line feel of a New Orleans street party (and also has traces of the groove in Cow Cow Davenport's "Cow Cow Boogie"), while "Can't Keep from Worrying (derived from Chuck Willis's "I've Been Treated Wrong So Long") is, refreshingly, a straight blues tune that does not masquerade as anything other than what it is. Little Walter, as usual, offers his special brand of overdrive harp hysteria, while Jimmy, for some strange reason, has his guitar tuned way down and plays a drone-like pitch throughout Walter's solo. Though two takes each were recorded, nothing was issued from this session at that time.

The payday for bands in 1960 was considerably less than what one might consider acceptable in today's world. According to Jimmy's recollection, the average local gig paid "about twelve dollars a night. Then you'd buy whiskey out of that twelve dollars, you'd get home with six, five, sometimes nothin'. That's no good."[54] As the leader Jimmy was responsible for negotiating the best deals possible for the entire group, which wasn't always easy: "The top money I could get out of a gig was $350 a night, and I got five fellows to pay out of that, you know. Plus transportation—you gotta buy gas, wear out the tires. Couldn't make no money like that." The band had tough road schedules, playing the South, back and forth, in Florida, Georgia, Louisiana, and Texas, and on the East Coast in New York and Pennsylvania. Jimmy's booking agent, the Shaw Agency, did not help matters much, as they booked the band in a wild, seemingly unorganized route that exhausted the band members. According to Jimmy, "He would have me booked here in Chicago tonight and then I gotta leave here and maybe my next gig where I'll be in Texas, and that's no good, see. Stretchin' me too far, runnin' me to death, and I didn't like it. We had a car, a station wagon. That's the way we traveled."[55] There were some good times, some hard ones too. Jimmy kept the morale up as best he could, paid his band members as well as he could, and treated his men with dignity. Indeed, he could always get along with anyone, primarily because he used mutual respect as the basis for any relationship he chose to maintain. "You don't really go around doggin' musicians," said Jimmy. "I never tries to control no man, but I'll tell him the way I feel about how things is supposed to be goin'. I respects them and they respects me. We gets along like that."[56] It was a philosophy he would carry throughout the entirety of his life, and it would prove to serve him well, with nary a person to speak ill of him at any point during or after his career.

Every now and then there would be a gig where Jimmy couldn't afford to take his entire band, so he might take just one or two members along for the trip. Quite naturally this would upset the remaining members of the band, which would, in turn, upset Jimmy. "I'm not happy, they're not happy, so I said, the heck with it," he said dejectedly. Then, Jimmy's drummer, S. P. Leary, began having problems with alcohol. "S. P. starting drinking pretty heavy . . . , when he's drinking, you couldn't tell him anything," Jimmy recalled.[57] That's when he decided to break up the entire outfit. Thus came the abrupt end of Jimmy Rogers's solo career, as he quietly disbanded the group and went into an isolation that would last for the next eight years.[58] According to Scott Dirks, "Bob Koester of Delmark was ready to record an LP on Jimmy with his regular band, but Jimmy ultimately declined because Bob didn't intend to issue a single—Delmark has always been an LP-only company. Without a single, Jimmy couldn't get anything on jukeboxes or the radio, so he apparently didn't see the point in it."[59] In other words, with Jimmy assuming he'd be giving up the recording and publishing rights—because "that's the way it's done" at that time—why give up twelve songs if they're not even going to get a single out of it that could get jukebox and radio play that could result in some gigs?

Now Jimmy *really* had the blues. His band had fallen apart. He needed some real money very soon to take care of his family. His beloved blues music was dying in popularity. And he missed the good old days with his friend Muddy, a time when things were much simpler. His tumultuous relationship with Leonard Chess still left a bitter taste. In the end Jimmy was philosophical about the entire situation and just chalked it up to experience. *That's all right,* he thought to himself.

PART II

RISING FROM THE ASHES
(1970–1989)

7

WALKIN' BY MYSELF

I got inactive in music in the '60s because the blues
players wasn't really makin' too much money, wasn't
doin' too much movin' around and tourin'. We weren't
doin' that much strong giggin' . . . even in Chicago.

—Jimmy Rogers

When asked whether there were any extenuating circumstances beyond money
that drove Jimmy Rogers away from the music business, he replied, "No, the
financial reasons, that's all. It wasn't enough in it for me with the family I had.
So I had to do something to make some heavy money, that's what I'd need. With
a family like I had, you can't be playin' around."[1] He knew that his change in direction would have an immediate impact on those around him, including the
sidemen he used for the nucleus of his band. Jimmy added, "I wasn't doin' any
gigging because everybody was cryin' the blues, you know: 'Man, if I could, I
would.' And I couldn't handle that, you know, so I said, 'forget it.' I had Joe Young,
I told him to try to get him a better gig. He had a family too. I understood how
it was. I didn't try to hold him down. 'Cause I know what I was goin' through
myself. So he started with Otis Rush."[2]

Although Jimmy had effectively ended his working relationship with Chess,
the respect given to him from his colleagues never wavered, and he remained
one of the most sought-after musicians in Chicago—especially when someone needed a solid guitarist who was reliable and could be expected to deliver
the goods on the bandstand. Therefore, although he no longer maintained an
active recording schedule, and had also disbanded the group he'd struggled so
long to maintain, he was still on the scene, operating as a freelance artist on
an independent work-for-hire basis. He wasn't out of the limelight long when

Muddy's old adversary—none other than the Wolf himself—came howlin' 'round his door. "He and his guitar player had had some trouble, and he called me up to go out of town on a gig with him," Jimmy recalled. At the time, Howlin' Wolf had a touring group that routinely had Hubert Sumlin on guitar, Henry Gray on piano, Cassell Burrow on drums, and eventually Sam Lay on drums.

In a surprise move, Jimmy said yes to Wolf's request—after all, in Jimmy's eyes, Wolf had never had any real *personal* beef with Muddy; it was the bosses who always had issues as to who could best sustain the *image* of who was the true King of the Blues in Chicago. Besides, Jimmy already had a relationship going with Wolf, one that reached as far back as his early days roaming around West Memphis toward the end of the 1930s, which was also when he first bumped into Little Walter. "Yeah, we'd take the bus—or ride in a car with somebody we knew—[We'd go] from Memphis that had a curfew to West Memphis that was wide open. Me and Joe Willie Wilkins and Howlin' Wolf would play at this roller rink in Memphis and the Baby Grand in West Memphis. We used to jam. Not too many places, but I remember those two. Sometimes we'd get three dollars a night, five at most," or, Jimmy added humorously, "a drink of whiskey and *two* dollars. But this was something I wanted to do."[3]

Back at the Chess studio, Willie Dixon was the main recruiting force for the recording sessions as well as the prime mover when it came to arranging the tunes. Leonard Chess trusted Dixon's instincts and allowed Willie carte blanche when it came to dictating directions on the session floor. In fact, his first session serving as arranger and bassist for the freshly minted Chess label in 1952 was the Jimmy Rogers session for "Back Door Friend."[4] Even before that, Jimmy had watched as Dixon laid his hands on Muddy while they were on the set. According to Jimmy, "This 'Hoochie Coochie Man' thing, Dixon came to the [Zanzibar] club and he would hum it to Muddy and wrote the lyrics out. Muddy would work them around for a while until he got it down where he could understand it and fool around with it. He would be onstage and try it out, do a few licks of it. We were building the arrangement, that's what we were doing."[5]

Almost ten years later, things were definitely being done Big Willie–style. "After we would get through with a session, Dixon would be one of the men who had a little say-so—like, 'this should be this way,' or 'take this out,' overdubbing things like that," Jimmy recalled. "Dixon had a big hand there because he was working around the studio just about all the time. He didn't do any performing at all when he got his foot in the door."[6] With regard to Dixon's prowess as a bassist, Jimmy always appreciated the fact that Dixon understood his role in the studio when it came to laying the bass in just the right place. "It wasn't hard at all to work with Dixon," Rogers stated, "because he never would really stay in the way. He knows how to lay in the background. An upright bass is not very loud anyway and in the studio he wasn't really coming through to interfere with our sound. He really tried to play what we was playing."

At the very least Dixon knew not to make the same mistake that Leonard frequently made, which was to go too far when trying to tell Jimmy or Muddy what to do. Indeed, these were men who had very specific ideas about how they wanted their music to be perceived, and no matter how much Leonard or Willie wanted to be a part of the building process, they needed to first show respect to the architects who held the blueprints. Jimmy and Muddy were extremely sensitive with regard to how much input they were willing to allow. "The only thing we listened to him for was when he would be arranging a song," Jimmy said. "We would stop playing and listen to the way he would phrase the lyrics and changes; we'd get that down and practice on it until we got it straightened out."[7]

Jimmy was an artist who knew when to listen and how to respond to even difficult personalities. His experiences with Leonard and Willie in the recording studio kept him in good standing on his out-of-town gig with Wolf in 1961. Jimmy never had the kind of problems some other artists did with Wolf, because he had a pretty clear understanding about Wolf's nature. In Jimmy's opinion, "Wolf, he was all right. A lot of people didn't understand Wolf. He was a man that let you know that he knew what he knew and you gotta deal with that or you weren't gonna deal with him at all. I liked Wolf."[8] All those musicians who didn't really grasp that concept of Wolf's temperament were inevitably faced with a confrontation, and Jimmy—not one for such interactions—usually stood back and watched it unfold.

"Wolf was pretty hard to get along with, anyway, and in the studio he was *very* hard to get along with. He was slow to catch on, he'd take the stuff off, play around with it with the band or by himself and mold it into his head. He would never really get it right but he'd get it close enough to record with it," Jimmy recalled. "He and Dixon had a few misunderstandings there in the studio because Wolf was set in his own ways. They were big guys, both of them. Dixon was pushing 300 and Wolf was well over 250, these big freight car boxes, and we just laid back and tried to back them up. We wouldn't hardly get into the conversation."[9]

Jimmy had gotten to know Wolf over the years, because both Muddy and Wolf were constantly traveling in the same circles and interacting with the same group of players, who were often used by both bandleaders like interchangeable parts of an engine. This put Jimmy in the position of knowing both men really well. As Jimmy explained:

Muddy wanted to be the big bear, Wolf wanted to be big—nobody was getting too close to Chess but they was thinking one would outdo the other one. Chess would get Muddy cars every two years, and take it off his royalties. Wolf would get his own car, wouldn't let Chess buy one for him. Really, Wolf was better managing a bunch of people than Muddy was. Muddy would go along with the company, Wolf would speak up for himself. And when you speak up for [your] self, you automatically gonna speak up for the band, because if you don't agree to record, there's no recording. It was more of a business thing with Wolf.[10]

Before they embarked upon their tour of the South, a recording session took place in May. The band included Wolf on guitar and vocals, Jimmy and Hubert Sumlin on guitars, Henry Gray on piano, Sam Lay on drums, and Willie Dixon on bass. This resulted in the release of two tunes—"Down in the Bottom" and "Little Baby" (Chess 1793)—and the single reportedly has Jimmy supplying background rhythm to what is clearly Wolf's well-executed slide work. In addition, according to the Chess logs, Jimmy lent his musical support on two other sessions: the June session that yielded "Shake for Me" and "The Red Rooster," as well as the December session that produced "Just Like I Treat You," "I Ain't Superstitious," "Goin' Down Slow," and "You'll Be Mine." Although it is widely accepted that Jimmy participated in both of these sessions, it is difficult—*impossible*—to find even a trace of Jimmy's playing on any of these tunes for which he is credited.

Jimmy toured "for about a year" with Howlin' Wolf, including a few stops in the South. One of their performances was at a fund-raiser in Memphis at the WDIA Goodwill Revue at Ellis Auditorium, where Jimmy ran into his old boss Muddy Waters, who was also on the bill, along with B. B. King and Ivory Joe Hunter. Jimmy was playing backup in the Wolf band when they launched into "Spoonful," Wolf's latest hit. When Wolf went into sexually charged gesticula- tions using an enlarged wooden spoon as a prop, the sponsors closed the curtain on the band. Such visuals were totally inappropriate for the young children who were in attendance that day, as the purpose for the entire day's event was to raise funds for the black Little League.[11]

Things went better in October at an event at the Grand Terrace Club in Bir- mingham, Alabama, and the Delta Kappa Epsilon fraternity homecoming party on the University of Mississippi campus. This was during the height of racial tension in the South, yet the all-white fraternity, led by David Hervey, was fer- vently awaiting the arrival of the Wolf and his band, who regularly played at the campus frat house because of Hervey's love of the blues. On October 27 Wolf gave his patented "Spoonful" performance—prop and all—that shocked yet another crowd: the older white female alumni who were there in attendance.[12]

The group later played shows in Greenville, Mississippi, and Tallulah, Louisiana. In Bastrop, Louisiana, Sam Lay remembered they were so deep into the backwoods that some of the patrons "come up on mules. And I had never been in a place where you go in there to use the washroom and there's a lady on the commode, and here's two or three guys rollin' dice on the floor by the stool and the lady sittin' [right] there on the toilet."[13] Jimmy remembered his yearlong tenure with Wolf, saying: "He got rid of [drummer] Cassell durin' the time I was with him and he got Sam Lay. When I quit, Sam Lay was with him . . . We worked out so well, and the way he was talkin' with me, I wasn't giggin', and he asked me if I would stay and back him some. 'You can stay as long as you want to,' you know, so I did. I stayed with him until I got tired."[14]

As the new decade—the 1960s—continued to roll on, more and more of the local Chicago work dried up. Dozens of talented musicians were just scraping by, including Jimmy, who could no longer afford to play the music he loved because of the meager income that most blues players in Chicago had been forced to grow accustomed to. Consequently, he shifted his attention further and further away from being viewed as a musician and instead chose to focus his efforts on being a family man, which meant he had more issues to be concerned about beyond himself. "We weren't doin' that much strong giggin' even in Chicago. But I had little Jimmy [Jimmy's first son, James, known as J. D.] here and his sisters and brothers, kids comin' in. And I had to do somethin' I could depend on for my family."[15]

Indeed, he did make the radical move of walking away from the lifestyle that he'd so thoroughly enjoyed for the better part of his life. "In the early '60s I stopped playing for a while," Jimmy recalled. "I didn't *stop*—but gigs were poor back then. Even Muddy Waters was having trouble making a buck."[16] Jimmy went into relative seclusion from the music scene, not only because he was having trouble making ends meet but also because other musicians were pressuring him for work—not just as leaders but also as sidemen. Too many hungry men and not enough food to go around created a stressful environment, one in which Jimmy was no longer willing to participate, even as his comrades were seeking him out to either offer him a job or to ask for one. "They was wondering why I didn't come back to the field," Rogers said. "And so I could explain to them, the average musician, they'll crawl on their knees and hands to get 'em on a gig, and then they jump up and they want to demand more money than you can make for yourself, you know, to back you up on these gigs. So that's not where it's at."[17]

Jimmy always thought of himself as a person who would try to do right by people, even if they sometimes didn't do right by him. He knew firsthand what it felt like to be given the short end of the stick after a few encounters with Leonard regarding what he thought was a fair shake. There were many stories about how even though both Little Walter and Muddy were paid handsomely as bandleaders, they still paid their sidemen nothing more than the standard rate set by the local union. Was this legal? Yes. Was it exactly fair? It depends upon whom you ask.

Several band members in Little Walter's band quit over money-related issues such as these. Undoubtedly Jimmy would have liked to have had a larger cut for his contribution. However, he tried to be generous with his band members, even when the earnings were meager, "because I would give a musician a fair shake, of money, anyway. I don't want to make every quarter for myself, and starve him, you know. I don't want it like that. The more money I make, the more I can afford to pay him. So I just rather not be worried with all that stuff."[18]

And so there he was, faced with the prospect of no regular income from the work he had dedicated his life to. The blues business had taken a turn for the worse, and he needed to somehow ride out the storm. Not knowing just how long the hiatus would be made it tough on him and his family. "I had growin' children and couldn't support 'em off what I was making," Jimmy stated, "so I got in with a cab company on the West Side and I did that for a couple of years."[19] In the interest of doing everything he could to provide for his expanding family, Jimmy also explored a few other possibilities. From about 1964 through 1966, he used his own personal vehicle as a taxicab to earn income for his family. His son Jimmy D. remembered the spot where Jimmy worked as a driver. "The cab stand was a livery service. It was a craphouse; they'd shoot dice in the back. They'd call for a cab when they wanted to go somewhere from there. He was using his own car, a '59 Cadillac, blue-green with fins on the back. I remember once when I was little, riding with my dad. I was standing on the floorboard in that car looking out the window and he hit the brakes, and I busted my mouth."[20]

Jimmy didn't work that job for very long before the winds of change blew once again. Indeed, a bit of good fortune had come their way when Jimmy's wife, Dorothy (who, by this time, he had married in Chicago), came into some money when a relative of hers passed away. Jimmy fully supported his wife's lifelong dream to run her own business. "I tried the livery cab business and then my wife's daddy died," Jimmy remembered. "There were three children and they split the settlement between the three of them. She wanted to invest [her third] in women's and children's clothing."[21] The small lump sum made them entrepreneurs. They used her inheritance to purchase a building located on the West Side so that they could set up her clothing shop. "That was the thing she wanted to do so I stood behind her," he said. But Jimmy did more than just that: he put his heart and soul into the new store, like everything else he did. "I liked the business. I was like, plumber, carpenter, different things like that, around that store," he remembered with pride. Most of the time, the income was enough to get by. "That's the way I put my kids through school," he once explained.[22]

Jimmy discovered that his street sense served him well in the world of retail sales. Even so, he sometimes needed to make a little extra hustle to keep things moving. "I had a clothing store on the West Side, and my family was growing," he said. "I was doin' odds and ends."[23] It would not be an absurd notion to say that at this point in his life the "odds and ends" may have included a few areas of specialty that were, one might say, off the menu. His son J. D. Mosley remembered the survival credo that was passed from Jimmy to him and still remains a part of his education to this day: "A man's gotta do what a man's gotta do."

Even though the official word on the street was that Jimmy had dropped out of the Chicago scene and no one knew where he was, this wasn't entirely true; some of his closest friends knew the score and chose to protect Jimmy's anonymity while simultaneously supporting his cause. "Sunnyland used to come over, [to the store] and Luther Tucker, Willie Dixon, bunch of guys would come over," Jimmy recalled fondly. "Sunnyland—the only thing that would fit him were socks! He tall, and has big feet. He['d] say, 'this the first store I been in, in a long time, has socks'll fit me!'—and he bought 'em all!"[24] Meanwhile, his former boss, Muddy, was deliberately vague about the where and why regarding Jimmy's departure. It was a subject that he seemed a bit reluctant to discuss in detail, and maybe he was somewhat disappointed in Jimmy's decision to take himself out of the game.

Maybe Muddy felt like he was being abandoned. "Why [did] he quit? I don't know, this is a hard thing for me to answer," Muddy said. "He just didn't have the willpower, I guess, you know it take willpower to stay out there, man. Because if things get hard, you know sometimes it ain't all kick out there, some people can't wait on it." Eventually Muddy showed his hand, however, revealing that he'd always known where Jimmy was while also revealing that he was indeed disappointed in Jimmy's decision. "Last I heard he was working in a second-hand clothes store," Waters said."[25] The tone of his admission kind of hung, clung, and stung—the same way as when he had delivered that barbed response to Little Walter over a decade ago when after abandoning the band on the road Walter had asked Muddy for "his money."

In 1961 Bob Dylan had made his first mark; his performance in New York City at Gerde's Folk City (located at 11 West Fourth Street in the West Village) led to an unexpected record deal with legendary Columbia Records producer John Hammond. Hammond's discerning ear turned out to be quite profitable in the case of Dylan; he was fortunate to have caught the new wave early. Folk music was practically the new pop music now. Along with this movement came a surge of renewed interest in people like Howlin' Wolf and Lightnin' Hopkins. Chess Records was trying to figure out a way to cash in on the movement, launching a series of albums with the catchphrase "Real Folk Blues" embedded in each LP title.

The heads of the Chess studios had already read the writing on the wall: the once-mighty Chuck Berry had pretty much exhausted his cache of ideas related to hot dates, hot rods, and high school dances. The songs about hanging 'round the jukebox and drinking malts were passé by now. Berry resurfaced briefly with well-delivered performances of "Nadine," "You Never Can Tell," "The Promised Land," and "No Particular Place to Go," all of which had been written from behind bars while he spent nearly two years in a Springfield, Missouri, prison (since the spring of 1962). With the exception of these tunes, there was relatively little activity from Berry; he was playing it low key after he was released on October 18, 1963, and was no longer a lightning rod for attention of any kind.[26] He'd had a tremendous run, but he too—just like Jimmy and Muddy—realized that their golden era was over and all good things must come to an end.

Leonard Chess and company didn't really know what to do with Muddy at this pivotal time, so they did what they did best: they tapped in to what was moving and shaking in the biz, which was folk music. They quickly released an all-acoustic album with a bare-bones, stripped-down approach that worked astonishingly well from a sonic standpoint. The LP *Folk Singer* was released in 1964 with Buddy Guy on rhythm guitar and Willie Dixon on bass. Undoubtedly Jimmy would have been given the nod had he still been on the Chess studio scene—nobody backed Muddy like Jimmy. Still, Buddy sounded like the perfect match under the circumstances, and when his time came to step up to the plate, he damn sure hit a home run.

About the only Delta blues–based Chess artist who was still surging forward in the blues world was Howlin' Wolf, and it might have had a lot to do with the fact that he put on a show—every single outing—that was totally captivating to the public. He was almost a freak of nature: huge hands, a ferocious scowl, and a thunderous, guttural growl that seemed to shake the rafters when he groaned into the mike, *"Wooo-ooahh, smokestack lightnin'!"* He cupped those humongous hands around the mike and fell to his knees, rolled and crawled, the entire time emitting that anguished voice that sounded at times as if he were squeezing the very last stream of air out of his lungs. And he had that burning stare that seared a hole right through the collective heart of his audience, who sat, trance-like, in simultaneous ecstasy, fear, and wonder.

"And then the madness began," wrote British music scholar Mike Rowe. "It seemed as if every British teenager was an avid Blues fan, either listening to, attempting to play, or researching the music in a great explosion of activity." Rowe went on to describe how tunes such as "Smokestack Lightning" by the Wolf, "Shame, Shame, Shame" by Jimmy Reed, and "Dimples" by John Lee Hooker entered the charts over in London. Not the blues charts this time—the *pop* charts. It was reported that even Princess Margaret listened to the blues and had named Muddy Waters as one of her favorite singers.[27]

Within the same year, the American Folk Blues and Gospel Caravan (April–May) along with the American Folk Blues Festival (October) represented two incredible and rare opportunities for the British cognoscenti to receive an imported product viewed as one of the most valuable overseas commodities in Europe: authentic American blues, with the original artists being exported from major U.S. cities delivered directly to the cobblestone streets of Manchester. Muddy had made his first trip across the Atlantic in 1958 with Otis Spann in tow, and Memphis Slim and Champion Jack Dupree arrived the following year, enjoying themselves so much they made permanent moves to Europe.[28]

There was an underground movement bubbling deep beneath the surface of the proper English tradition, and an upstart magazine, *Blues Unlimited,* had recently been born (in May 1963), within a year after the first American Folk Blues Festival took place. The following year provided even more thrills, including Big Joe Williams and Muddy Waters appearing on the BBC television channel, as the caravan of stars traveled throughout Great Britain, delivering stunning performances in seventeen cities.[29] In 1964 Wolf's band joined the overseas movement, spurred annually by Horst Lippmann and Fritz Rau, two Germans who would visit Chicago each year for the sole purpose of raiding the bandstands in a recruitment effort to build the lineup for the annual festival tour. That year it was Wolf, Sonny Boy Williamson, John Lee Hooker, Lightnin' Hopkins, Sunnyland Slim, Willie Dixon, and others.[30]

Sonny Boy himself, like others before him, fell in love with the lifestyle that he'd fully embraced once he first visited Europe in 1963, and he decided to stay. In fact, Sonny Boy went so far as to apply for citizenship to prove how serious he was about not coming back to America, where he'd received lifelong scars from racism. He adapted himself in short order and within a year had made recordings with two of the biggest groups in England, the Animals and the Yardbirds. Sonny

Boy became known instantly for sporting the new British look: a bowler hat, a walking cane, gloves, and two-toned suits. He even adopted a clipped British accent. He made it clear to everyone that he had no intentions of coming back to the States. However, gradually debilitating health issues prompted him to rethink this decision. After long deliberation Sonny Boy realized he would have to return to America, at least for the time being. After the 1964 British tour was over, Sonny Boy returned to Helena, where he told several close to him, including Sonny Payne, he had returned to die.[31]

By this time the Beatles were planning their U.S. invasion after burning up their own British charts with "Twist and Shout," a tune lifted from the black R & B group the Isley Brothers. In June the Rolling Stones had made their first visit to the States, and one of their priorities was to come to the relatively new Chess Studios, now located at 2120 South Michigan Avenue, to try to capture the magic that their heroes had created.

By 1965 there was a visible change in the complexion of the Chicago blues scene. Attendance was dropping in the blues clubs as many regular black patrons began to move away from blues, in large part due to the slow but steady surge in social protests that would soon become a full-blown civil rights movement against the country's unbalanced agendas and unfair policies. Blues music was a genre that many blacks felt did not best reflect the progressive black mind-set of the moment. Those leaders who preached for equal rights, better treatment, better working conditions, and better schools were busy listening to the Motown sound of "Baby Love" by the Supremes from Detroit and the Memphis sound of "In the Midnight Hour" by Wilson Pickett on Atlantic Records.

In early 1966 there was yet another sound becoming more prominent within the blues community, although its roots had been planted years before. Several members of what amounted to the "new vanguard" were making strides that eventually would be identified by critics and historians as a subculture within the genre: the "West Side" sound. For the moment, though, guitarists like Magic Sam, Buddy Guy, Syl Johnson, Luther Johnson Jr., Otis Rush, Eddy Clearwater, and Freddie King were not at all (if ever) concerned with what labels were used to describe the shared elements of their music that created an identifiable sound.

These upcoming artists were not immune to the current styles of the day, and allowed the R & B, pop, and jazz trends to seep into their blues genre. Their pervasive style was generally marked by a dripping-tempo minor-chord tonality; dominant-ninth chord riffs that simulated big band horn sections; B. B. King–based string bending; and a pleading, swooping vocal style sung in the upper register—not a falsetto, but an all-natural, full-throated technique. Underneath the gospel-inflected vocals was a shimmering, trebly tone, typically delivered on a Fender Stratocaster—the preferred instrument of choice for Magic Sam, Buddy Guy, and Otis Rush, three of the leading proponents of the sound.

Culturally speaking, on the other end of the color spectrum lay an entirely different movement, one that originated with a handful of blues-starved teens who couldn't get enough of the music they'd come to love. So they decided to go where it flowed. They came from various parts of the country, and they all came for the same purpose: to be bathed in the music they loved, and to experience firsthand the sights and sounds of the living blues they previously had only imagined through vinyl grooves. Some were already there waiting. Harp player Paul Butterfield, a native Chicagoan, emerged along with another guitar neophyte named Elvin Bishop. The two were serious enough that they managed to snatch veteran drummer Sam Lay at an opportune moment, when Lay had experienced one of his many fallouts with Wolf. Then they hired bassist Jerome Arnold away from Wolf's band. The Paul Butterfield Blues Band was born, and they held court at Big John's, a blues club situated on the North Side. The heat was turned up even higher when guitarist Mike Bloomfield joined the fray.

Meanwhile, harp enthusiast Charlie Musselwhite had arrived on the Chicago scene by 1962, at the tender age of eighteen, and had already paid his dues after logging countless hours with South Side musicians who ultimately embraced him as one of the members of the blues fraternity. Like Bloomfield and Butterfield, Musselwhite was fearless when pursuing his passion. "I didn't give a damn about being white," Charlie said. "I was brazen—I didn't give a damn about nothing . . . I was just there to have a good time, and people sense that about you. I was just in the swing of life, having a *hell* of a good time."[32] Still, he knew he couldn't be too careless with his free-wheeling attitude. "I lived at the dead-end of Blackstone Avenue on 61st Place between the IC [Illinois Central train] tracks, and the Blackstone Rangers were in full force all the time I was there," Musselwhite recalled. "West of that neighborhood was the Disciples. Both of these gangs had lots of smaller gangs under their wings. It was wild times for me around there, but we worked out all right—haha!!"[33]

Charlie was getting used to people getting him mixed up with Paul Butterfield, which he simply filed under the "all white people look alike" generalization that he suspected some blacks possessed. Musselwhite was living with guitarist Big Joe Williams at the time, and after Williams got offered a regular gig at Big John's tavern on the North Side, he offered Charlie a chance to ride shotgun. "We were living behind the 'Old Wells Records' record store on Wells & Schiller. Big John's hired Joe to play on a holiday—could have been the 4th of July. Joe asked me to play with him. Business was so good they asked Joe to come back the next night and play some more. It turned into a regular gig!"[34] Soon after, Mike Bloomfield came around to sit in as the pianist, then switched over to guitar when Big Joe moved away from Chicago. "We looked around and got a drummer and a bass player," Bloomfield said. "In a matter of months Big John's turned into, like, *the* place to go."[35] It was only after the Bloomfield band left for another gig that Butterfield entered the scene and took over at Big John's.[36]

To some it may have appeared as if there might have been some deliberate attempt to usurp the power and control of the blues scene from the blacks to the slowly but steadily growing white contingency. Indeed, blues vocalist Bobby Rush confessed, "Some guys say that the blues was taken from us," and then quickly countered, "There ain't nobody taking anything from us. You *gave* it away. You stopped doing it, you stopped appreciating it. I saw the white guys trying to learn how to play the blues as well as the black guys—and they learned it well."[37] Bob Koester, the founder and owner of Delmark Records, the oldest independent record label in the United States, agreed: "Kids were coming around to see kids their own age. The folk thing was taken over by white kids. Dylan using Butterfield's band cracked the whole thing open."[38]

In late 1966 Jimmy's longtime musician friend Elga Edmonds finally succumbed to the illnesses he'd suffered from for many years.[39] "You name it, he had it," Rogers lamented. "High blood pressure, heart trouble, kidney ailment. Elgin was somewhere around 70 years old when he died. He wasn't playin' then. The last work he was doin' was drivin' a cab."[40]

In June 1967 Chess Studios moved to an even larger building on 320 East Twenty-first Street, with a new label, Cadet Concept. This label would chart the company's new direction by December of that year.[41] One of its former musicians, Little Walter Jacobs, wasn't doing so well. The cumulative effect of the changing times, lack of self-control over his violent temper, and no longer having a regular band led to his inevitable fall from grace in the eyes of the public.[42] And then in early 1968, after yet another physical confrontation with a stranger, the feisty harp man Little Walter died on February 15 after receiving a blow to the head from a combatant. His death deeply affected Muddy Waters, who had already lost Otis Spann. Upon his wife's advice, Otis had become the leader of his own group when he left Muddy to help his wife, Lucille, pursue a career as a vocalist—a family affair, as it were.

When asked about the practicality of Spann's career choice, Muddy, again with unshakable cool—at least on the surface—said, "Well, if he feel like that. If you feel like that, you go." Muddy went on to philosophize further, choosing to summarize the totality of his experience of losing the three best men he ever had—Little Walter, Jimmy Rogers, and Otis Spann—in what must have felt like one body blow after another. "See, everybody looking for a name in this business," Muddy confessed. "Everybody looking for a star name. He may be playing sideman, but in his mind he wish he was the star . . . when that comes, well, let him go . . . of course a real good man like Little Walter, Jimmy, Otis, them was extra to me."[43] It was more than a bit ironic, however, that Otis Spann, sometime before his death, had told an English reporter that Jimmy wasn't playing with Muddy anymore because he'd gotten kicked out of the group for "lack of discipline" and "drinking and smoking on stage." According to the writer's report, when asked why Muddy took the hard line with Jimmy and enforced the local musicians union guidelines, Otis simply said, "Rules are rules."[44]

On April 4, 1968, the evening that Dr. Martin Luther King Jr. was assassinated, untold numbers of black folk practically lost their minds. They were angry, and they became violent immediately after the announcement was made through the newspapers, radios, television sets, and the lightning-speed "word on the street." The city of Chicago caught fire, both literally and figuratively, and hundreds of shops began to burn on the South and West Sides.

The Rogers family business took a direct hit as a result of the riots. "Martin Luther King got killed and the fires got me," Jimmy said. "Lost pretty good money, and by pretty good money I mean just about every dime me and my wife had! And that was a pretty good business."[45] Thus came an abrupt end to the dreams of his wife, Dorothy, and the modest but meaningful income that the family relied upon heavily to keep food on the table. "I lost quite a bit of money in that," he reflected in later years.[46] It would take years before Jimmy's family received a settlement from the city for their personal losses.

Bob Riedy, a blues pianist and founder of the Chicago Blues Foundation, was a struggling musician at the time, trying to book gigs to make a living. He unwittingly found himself in the midst of what rapidly escalated into a dangerous racial situation. According to Riedy:

> The riots lasted for about a week. I was in the area of Ma Bea's Club (Sacramento and Madison) and Big Duke's Blue Flame Lounge (Madison and California) when the riots started. Whole blocks of the city were burned down to the ground, debris in the streets prevented vehicle traffic. Gang members were prominently showing themselves by walking down the middle of the streets they owned with handguns and shotguns. They used this lawless time to settle old scores by shooting at personal enemies and torching any store that was either white owned or they thought disrespected them some time in the past.[47]

Riedy first arrived in Chicago in the early to mid-1960s, right in the middle of one of the worst periods of Chicago's history. "I moved to Chicago to go and have an apprenticeship with the architects of urban Chicago blues," Bob said. "There wasn't anybody I didn't play with."[48] Six days after King's murder, Riedy and his new band, Graham Paper Press, signed a five-year deal with Chess Records and received an advance of one thousand dollars to deliver twelve sides under the direction of Willie Dixon. By now Leonard had redirected his efforts away from blues and toward other causes. Phil, along with Leonard's son, Marshall, were running things now and had their offices side by side. They did their best to maintain business as usual, even if they didn't always get along. "I remember Marshall barking at Phil, and Phil threw a giant telephone book that hit Marshall on the side of the head," Riedy said.[49]

Riedy and his band had been handpicked by the latest generation of Chess A & R (artist and repertoire) men. He worked alongside engineer Freddie Breitberg, a producer who for some reason went by the name of "Eddie B. Flick." According to Riedy, "Marshall signed us, gave us an advance, and he assigned Willie Dixon to write songs for us, and it was our job to record them. He would show up every day, come in with his briefcase, pull out a set of lyrics and would beat out the beat on his briefcase, and we tried to interpret what he was hearing, and we would then try to work out what he wanted, and if he liked it then he'd take us into the studio and that's where Freddie would take over, to arrange and record us."[50]

Riedy took stock of the situation inside the legendary studio, which was still trying to keep its eye on the next hot thing and develop their own version of it. The Chess brothers had recently acquired the entire eight-story, 172,000-square-foot building at 320 East Twenty-first Street and begun moving in September 1966, with the move completed by the spring of 1967.[51] Riedy painted a picture of what it was like on the inside of their new location: "You could see the deejay working for WVON, you could see through the clear glass window that showed the guy mastering the discs, you could see the rehearsal rooms, the studio room. It was like a Hollywood studio system, where it was all self-contained."[52]

By now Leonard was spending more time with his radio station, WVON (Voice of the Negro), than he did with the record label. He was showing his devotion to the black cause and sensibility, especially in light of the King assassination. He went on to say his music on WVON was programmed "for the lower-to-middle-class Negro. We want a 'Top 40' format with Negro music, not the Uncle Tom . . . Stepin' Fetchit." He said of his radio station (purchased in 1963), "I made money on the Negro, and I want to spend it on him."[53]

By the end of 1968 Phil and Leonard had decided to sell Chess Records—a shocking move that even Leonard's son, Marshall, wasn't prepared for.[54] When Allen Arrow, legal representative for Chess Records and its related Arc Music Publishing Company, negotiated a deal with the Chess brothers and Alan Bayley, who represented General Recorded Tape (GRT), Chess Records would ultimately pay for the unreliable method of chasing the trendy, fickle tastes of the public that dominated the late 1960s.[55] GRT promptly began dismantling the entire Chess operation, thus immediately sending the message that the new owners had no real interest in the business, only in whatever monies they could squeeze out of what was largely considered leftovers. Before he knew it, Riedy's deal had collapsed, and he was living on the street after the label folded.

In January 1969 Marshall Chess released a psychedelic album, simply titled *Howlin' Wolf.* Wolf said the album was a "piece of shit." This kind of "psychedeli-crap" had flowed downstream once before, when Muddy Waters's *Electric Mud* was released back in October 1968, and he, like Wolf, admitted publicly in *Rolling Stone* magazine that it was "a piece of dogshit."[56] By November the writing was clearly on the wall: blues was out, and soul music was in. The Stax sound from Memphis, the Motown sound from Detroit, and the Southern soul of Muscle Shoals coming from Atlantic Records were now all the rage. The soul music coming from Chicago prominently featured several emerging local artists, including Jerry Butler, Denise LaSalle, the Dells, Curtis Mayfield, Gene Chandler, and others. Urban blues appeared to have taken a relatively less significant role in the collective hearts and minds of many.

Early in 1969 the men who were now considered veterans of the blues figured out what a potent punch it would be if they joined forces. Led by Willie Dixon, a newly formed collective called the Chicago Blues All-Stars were taking the show on the road and made it all the way to the East Coast, with an entire week's showcase in Boston. The band consisted of Johnny Shines on guitar, Sunnyland Slim on piano, Big Walter on harp, Willie Dixon on bass, and Clifton James on drums.[57] Later that year, in Ann Arbor, Michigan, Muddy and the Wolf continued to play out their drama in front of the world at the first annual Ann Arbor Blues Festival, with Wolf taking an extra-long turn at the microphone in an obvious attempt to simultaneously upstage Muddy and keep him at bay while he pulled out all the stops.

Things were not going so well back in Chicago, however. Nearly a year after the King riots, the urban gang wars had resurfaced among the black neighborhoods in Chicago, a nasty situation that had to be dealt with before things got even further out of control. To make matters worse, there was an entirely new level of drugs, a much more potent, uncut form of heroin coming out of New York and Los Angeles and into Chicago that was literally causing terminal heart attacks all across the city. The beloved blues club Silvio's (then located at 3200 West Lake Street at Lake and Kedzie Avenue) had burned down during the riots (to be reopened as the Riviera more than a year later).[58] The outlook regarding the future for blues musicians and viable performing opportunities was looking bleaker than ever.

Living Blues magazine founder, Jim O'Neal, was just arriving on the scene to document the entire proceedings. Jim was a young student attending Northwestern University at the time, and he and about ten other blues fans had immersed themselves wholly into the Chicago blues fabric. "I would always tell my white friends that I would go, and they thought I was crazy or that I would get killed," Jim said. "But I never got accosted or robbed or beaten or anything. Once in a while someone might get held up or something, but the blues clubs seemed pretty safe. The biggest problem we had was the white police. They would ask, 'What are you doing here? You don't belong here.' They were in one way trying to be protective and in another keeping the city segregated." Ironically, O'Neal was catching it from both sides, even to the point of being suspected of operating undercover for the CIA, FBI, or maybe even the IRS. "Then there were the questions that black people had. 'Why are you here?' 'What is your motive?'"[59]

O'Neal also noticed the effect that the cops had on the blues scene and how the long arm of the law tried to influence which music went down and which didn't. The police were getting pretty antsy those days. Trouble was on the horizon, and they had been alerted months before about how to deal with a major event that would take place in the near future: the Democratic National Convention. The whole world would be watching.

The riots that accompanied the death of Reverend Dr. Martin Luther King Jr. and the Democratic National Convention changed the way people in Chicago felt about one another, their politics, their country, and their music. On Wells Street, near North Avenue in Old Town, was Mother Blues, one of the most popular blues clubs during the late 1960s. It was, according to Bob Riedy, "a place where all the big blues artists played—Muddy, Odetta, Otis Rush, James Cotton." A woman named Lorraine Blue owned it and did her best to run a respectable joint, at a time when there was getting to be less and less respect for the blues. "Lorraine allowed me to sleep there under the pool table," Riedy said, "and take care of things during the business hours." Bob heard them all there.

During the convention, "The city went around and shut down places where they thought hippies and yippies would hang out," Bob recalled. Mother Blues had conveniently been shut down by the cops for some unspecified violation, thus forcing the owner and all of the patrons to evacuate immediately. According to Riedy, "They couldn't go in the club and pull them out, but if they were on the streets, they could gather 'em up and arrest them, which was essentially what they did in Lincoln Park on North and Wells."[60] Naturally this meant they were now exposed and vulnerable to being rounded up by the local cops. Riedy and his guitarist Jim Proffitt went back to their usual routine of sleeping in the park, totally unaware of what awaited them.

The Vietnam War created an us-against-them attitude between antiwar demonstrators and the government. President Johnson was backing the war, and the hippies were adamant on making their presence felt. But Chicago mayor Richard Daley was proud to host the convention; therefore he gave the order to "kill arsonists and maim looters" to stop any further disruption. Grant Park was the site where most of the clashing took place. "The whole world is watching" became the battle cry of the protesters, many of whom were beaten down with nightsticks.[61] In Riedy's opinion the entire city was in meltdown mode. It was a nightmare for all involved. "Police formed a straight line on the eastern end of the park on Lake Shore Drive with tear gas and light trucks," Bob said, "with gas masks and bayonets sticking out, and hoses that would distribute tear gas, pushing everyone out of the park onto Lincoln Avenue . . . As you go west, you go over to Clark Street; from Clark they pushed them into Wells—a north-south street—and from Wells was North Avenue, and they just backed up the paddy wagon and loaded them up as they forced them into that circle."[62]

Bob was trying to escape the park and get to Lorraine Blue's house for shelter, so he and Proffitt ran as they were chased with billy clubs. "We thought, that was it," Bob said. "They'd read about us in the paper the next day: 'two unknown persons beat to death in the alley.'" A third guy was running with Riedy and Proffitt. As it turned out, he was a newspaper photographer. In mid-stride he spun around, dropped to one knee, and got off a quick snap. The flash of his cameras hit the pursuers squarely in their eyes, which not only temporarily blinded them but also gave them permanent pause, allowing their quarry to get away. "We got over to Piper's Alley, made it to Mother Blues," Riedy related. "We got up to Lorraine's apartment on the second floor, and we sat in the window and watched the rest of the war from her second floor."[63]

While the world was going mad, Jimmy Rogers was quietly plotting his return. He'd had plenty of time to reflect on his contribution to blues history, and now it was time to write a new chapter. The interviewers had been asking him the same old questions lately. Looking to put it all behind him, Jimmy summed up the entire episode of retiring and resurging in a few succinct phrases: "It was around '61 when I got out. And I came back, I'd say, the last of '69. It was about eight years."[64]

For Jimmy, the new decade couldn't come soon enough. The smell of smoke still stung his nostrils, hanging in the air, and the dust from cold ashes clouded his view as he tried to see the point of burning down one's own neighborhood as an appropriate retaliation for rage brought about by a senseless assassination. The neighborhoods he frequented—on both the West and South Sides—were shells of their former selves, with only the outer frames of shops and homes still standing where a thriving community once was. Now, as helicopters and airplanes flew over and hovered above Chicago, every other building stood blackened and gaping, forming what looked like a decaying, soot-stained mouth full of cavities—living and dying monuments to both black and white hatred. As in a living nightmare, the black folk of the inner city had awakened to a sight that made them sure that on the previous night it must have rained glass. It would take a thousand more nights to overcome such a travesty.

8

SHELTER FROM THE STORM

Things had changed in some ways, and in others they
hadn't. "Everything was small then, it wasn't big like it
is now, you know. Get a gig now, you ask the guy for five
thousand dollars, and he just smiles. 'Ok, that's all? We'll
pay you, you can go ahead.' But durin' that time, if you
ask them for five hundred, they'd holler."

—Jimmy Rogers

When word hit the streets that Jimmy was back on the scene and ready to hit
the road, musicians and promoters rallied around him, offering him work from
all directions. They'd missed him, and not just his playing. Jimmy had always
maintained good relations with his comrades and was widely regarded as a man
with integrity. And people were always fond of that huge smile of his. "They was
all worryin' me about hittin' the road again, Sunnyland Slim, Dixon, all these
guys," Jimmy said shyly.

> They said, " Man, come on back out here and help us," you know. They just kept
> on like that, and so my wife, she said, "Well, you want to try it?" And I said,
> "Well, I'll try it for a while." So it wasn't hard for me to get back into because
> I was well acquainted with playin' with bands anyway. They wanted me to
> come back because I was pretty well liked [by] blues musicians. I carry myself
> in that way, see. So it's no trouble, I could get just about any blues musician I
> want to play with me if I have a gig and need him."[1]

As it turned out, his old friends had never abandoned him; they were anxiously awaiting his return. According to Jimmy, he picked up his guitar even

earlier than most had assumed—he just wasn't ready to show his hand. "I started back playin' music then in '68, '69," he said. But wouldn't Jimmy's chops be a bit out of shape after such a long layover? "No, I'd still [have] rehearsal. Magic Sam was livin' pretty close to me and I started Sam out on the blues. And he'd come over and rehearse. We'd jam like that. And he would invite me over to the club that he was giggin' at, and I'd say, 'okay,' and I wouldn't show up. I wasn't interested in playin'. I wanted to keep myself kind of in shape, see, but as far as playin' around these local gigs, I wasn't interested in that at all." There was, however, another guitarist who figured prominently in Jimmy's life at this point in his career, one who would eventually play a leading role in drawing Jimmy out of the shadows. He told a reporter, "There was a boy, [guitarist] Johnny Littlejohn, he was having a rough time getting off the ground so he and I started messing around like me and Muddy had did. We kept on, got a little band together with a piano player."[2]

Apparently while Jimmy stayed under the radar screen, he kept in shape by sparring regularly with Littlejohn. He and Jimmy had become close-knit buddies and musical partners during the latter part of Jimmy's "retirement" phase. They were such close friends now, in fact, that they lived as next-floor neighbors in a two-story apartment near the clubs they played. Jimmy lived upstairs; John lived just below him. They made great music together every day and even raised their children together. Jimmy's son Jimmy D. Lane—known then as "Little Jimmy"—remembers this as a happy time period.

There were other motivational factors at work too, according to Jimmy Sr., who was beginning to think all the signs were pointing at him, hinting that he should be getting back to doing what he did best. He recalled, "My store had burned down and I had some business people approach from a different area, you understand, where I could see my way out. And that's the only reason why I came back was to see my way out. Otherwise I would have still been doing something [else]."[3] When asked about the time he spent away from the music scene, Jimmy replied in a manner that left no doubt about his views regarding what was most important to him: "I don't regret leavin' music for a *minute*. I don't have gray hair for mistreatin' my family. I sacrificed for them instead of them sacrificin' for me. They love me for that."[4]

Bob Riedy deserves the most credit for helping resurrect Jimmy's career. He almost single-handedly developed the blues scene on the North Side of Chicago. It was extremely difficult at first. "All those guys were out of work. I finally got to Muddy, Wolf and all these guys—I had no trouble getting them to play with me; but they all said the same thing: *'You can play with me any time you want, but what I need is jobs.'"* According to Bob, white-owned establishments on that side of town wanted no part of the blues scene. "Before, the blues was just dying, but after the riots, blues was a *bad* word."[5] Later he elaborated, saying, "Clubs' owners on the North Side looked at blues like it was trashy music—they pictured out-of-tune guitars, kicking over drinks, singin' out of key, showin' up late, and being too drunk to finish the sessions."[6]

But it wasn't just white people who were turned off from the blues; the African American culture was shifting. "I had a helluva time getting bass players and drummers who were young and black who liked blues," Riedy said. "It was like how my generation feels about polkas and folk music like that. They looked at it as old-fashioned music of their parents. *Soul* music was the next thing . . . The Supremes. They weren't into blues at all."[7] Riedy was happy when harp king Big Walter Horton moved to the North Side: "We started playing together, then Johnny Young came too. We started playing together in our apartment."[8] Riedy caught a lucky break when Peter Ghast, the owner of an Irish bar, let him use part of the bar to bring in entertainment. "We built a little stage, and we got Muddy Waters, Howlin' Wolf, then Jimmy Reed and Johnny Young."

Meanwhile, good news was coming in Jimmy's direction. After more than a decade of inactivity on Chess Records, with a backlog of songs that were essentially out of print, Jimmy's association with the label was rekindled when the company released an album under his name, titled *Chicago Bound*, a "greatest hits" compilation unveiled as an installment in the company's Vintage series that first appeared in 1969. Having already released similar collections for the reissue series on Sonny Boy Williamson, along with "two-for-one combo packaging" (as in the Otis Rush/Albert King and Elmore James/John Brim releases), the Jimmy Rogers album was the first Chess Records LP to debut in 1970. By the end of the summer, T. T. Swan, the producer of the series, had left the company, with no one named as a replacement.[9] Serendipitously, he'd compiled and released Jimmy's album just before he made his unexpected exit.

Although it may have begun as nothing more than a blind, last-ditch effort to milk as much money as possible out of the best material that had been collected and shelved for years, the Chess family had inadvertently launched the comeback of a star. No one at the company could have guessed what kind of enormous impact the Jimmy Rogers compilation LP would have on the new generation of hard-core blues fans among the white teen population. Until then most of them had been largely unaware of Jimmy's contribution to the canon, for three primary reasons: first, his music wasn't played on the radio much at all; second, he was barely visible on the Chicago scene and had no local gigging or touring band under his own name; finally, the record stores no longer carried his 45s that were once in circulation and on the jukeboxes during the songs' heyday, going as far back as twenty years before. For the most part Jimmy Rogers was a forgotten bluesman. That was all about to change.

Chicago Bound (Chess LP 407), a stunning collection that was nearly perfect in content, could easily be regarded as one of the only significant acts that GRT executed during its tumultuous tenure at the helm of the Chess empire. Released as a monaural recording under the newly designed banner "The Original Chess Masters," the album is expertly balanced with regard to the sequence of songs, and the pacing of the disc truly captures both Jimmy's musical style and his smooth, laid-back persona. The relaxed facial expression depicted in the close-up shot used for the black-and-white album cover served as an open invitation for many blues guitar fans who wanted to hear what was on the vinyl between the cardboard, even if they didn't know exactly who the guy was on the cover.

With his tilted head sporting a neatly cropped mustache, a curled lower lip with barely protruding tongue, and eyes shifted downward toward his guitar neck, Jimmy just looked like he was busy takin' care of business. His left-hand thumb leaning over the edge of the seventh fret—the bluesman's embouchure, so to speak—completed the perfect pose. Between the grooves lay his best work: fourteen gems, covering six years of music, so smartly arranged that they form a *tour de force* that still stands today as his finest and most popular album among blues aficionados. Side A offered an impressive lineup: "You're the One"; "Money, Marbles, and Chalk"; "Ludella"; "Act Like You Love Me"; "Back Door Friend"; "Last Time"; and "I Used to Have a Woman." Side B contained more gems: "Sloppy Drunk; "Blues Leave Me Alone"; "Out on the Road"; "Going Away Baby"; "That's All Right"; "Chicago Bound"; and "Walkin' by Myself."

The album was not an overnight sensation. But once the record hit the shelves, a steadily building legion of fans grew, and the impression left upon them after hearing the songs on *Chicago Bound* got people talking. Across the country, the disc spurred such often-repeated inquiries as "Who is Jimmy Rogers?" "Where did he come from?" and "Is he still alive?" Those questions would soon be answered. Jimmy's self-imposed exile was gradually reversing its course. He was like a Chicago phoenix rising up from the ashes of the riots and the ruins of his home city.

Things just kept getting better for Jimmy. Not only did the Chess release represent a positive sign for his career, but the album was also about to get a healthy dose of publicity. Chicago blues fans saw the very first issue of *Living Blues*, a fledgling little magazine that was published at 917 West Dakin Street, located on the North Side. The magazine grew by leaps and bounds in very short order. Jimmy Rogers received a glowing review of his music when Chess released *Chicago Bound*. It was incredible luck for him. While having no influence whatsoever on the timing of the release (when did he ever have influence over such matters with Leonard?), the emergence of the recording could not have come at a better time for him and the album to receive free publicity in the pages of *Living Blues*.

The reviewer for the magazine was ecstatic about the musical content and penned a lengthy and thorough send-up about the virtues of the LP: "Don't be fooled; this isn't an album by Muddy Waters' former second guitarist with a bunch of studio musicians," the writer warned. "The total effort is an amazingly solid blues sound, uninfluenced by rock, soul, or commercially oriented A & R men . . . the approach is relaxed, confident, and unpretentiously funky."[10] The article describes Jimmy's contribution to the Waters sound as "extremely important." Both Little Walter and Big Walter receive high praise for delivering "almost flawless" performances. The three pianists on the album received honorable mentions, although Spann was singled out as slightly less mature musically than Henry Gray or Eddie Ware. "Honestly, there isn't a bad track on this LP," the article continues. "Perhaps its only weaknesses are the rather monotonous drumming of Elgin Evans on some tracks, and the unnecessary bits of studio talk." The second tune on side A, "Money, Marbles, and Chalk," was identified by the reviewer as the most outstanding track, with the comment that the band sounds generally more confident on those slow tunes, as opposed to the jump-blues arrangements like the title track, "Chicago Bound," where things "occasionally get a little frantic and jumbled, but never seriously."[11]

The perfect timing between the release of *Chicago Bound* and the launching of *Living Blues* was followed by another fortunate event. In August, Frank Scott, an English record producer who co-owned Advent Records with Dave Sax, spent time seeking out Chicago musicians for a special album project. Scott had the unique idea to record various Chicago bluesmen in their natural habitat—their own homes—because he felt that the familiar environment might keep them loose and allow the creative juices to flow. Scott's intentions were to give the audience "a rare chance to hear some of Chicago's finest blues artists captured in informal settings playing the kind of music they enjoyed when on their own or with friends and family. Absent are the pressures of the recording studio or live club date."[12] Participants in the project included Louis Myers, Bob Myers, Eddie Taylor, Johnny Shines, and Homesick James (the album received a Grammy nomination). Upon his discovery that Jimmy and John lived as neighbors in the same apartment building, Scott knew it was a natural thing to ask Jimmy and

John to participate in the project. The two men readily agreed; they jammed with each other practically every day anyway, so the idea was a no-brainer.

On August 21, 1970, Jimmy and John went through their normal routine of setting up two amps in the living room, grabbed a couple of chairs, and just played the blues. All Scott needed to do was set up his recording equipment and a few microphones for the guitar amps and vocals. John Littlejohn went first with "Mean Old World," delivering the lyrical phrases in a style very much reminiscent of Little Walter. Jimmy laid down a solid rhythm as a backdrop as Littlejohn took a brief but tasty solo, trilling the strings in the same fashion Little Walter might have executed his patented warble on the harp. Littlejohn then sang "The Moon Is Rising" with gusto, and Jimmy took a solo that opened first with a stumble but after a quick recovery successfully high-stepped through the chord changes for the remainder of the chorus. Littlejohn ends his portion of the session with a slide guitar instrumental, appropriately titled "Slidin'." The tune had changes that were similar to those found in Elmore James's "It Hurts Me Too," and John did his best Elmore impression as he joyfully slipped and slid his way through the shuffle.

When Jimmy's turn at bat came, he launched into the beautiful ringing chord tones for the opening phrase of "Ludella." Littlejohn laid down the perfect backdrop for Jimmy's winding lead lines, with a steady double-stop shuffle pattern and contrapuntal line each time they approached the turnaround to get to the next verse. "Back Door Friend" was next, with similar excellent results. Jimmy obviously was quite satisfied with the proceedings, as he can be heard exclaiming "Well, all right!" on his tunes right before he launches into the solo. His single-note phrases on "What Have I Done" are superb in their simplicity.

Even better was Jimmy's voice, which was in excellent form that day; his pitch was dead-center and his tone crystal-clear. His lyrical phrases totally captured the mood Scott was going after: a laid-back affair where the two guitarists strummed the chord changes in a medium-slow gallop, with lots of space between the two to shape their phrases. No bass and drums to clutter up the sound this time, just two guitars wrapping their lines around each other. For Jimmy, it must have felt like the good old days when he first met Muddy and they sat together all night, mastering the musical rapport that would serve as the new standard for electric blues. It was the first time Jimmy had recorded anything for a record label since 1959 when he walked away from Chess Studios.

The lucky combination of *Chicago Bound*'s release, the positive *Living Blues* magazine review, and the renewed appreciation for Jimmy's brand of Chicago blues among white audiences signaled that it was time for Jimmy Rogers's star to shine again. He was gaining momentum, and it was time to strike while things were hot. Bob Riedy had a regular extended engagement at the Wise Fools Pub. The band included Johnny Young on mandolin, John Littlejohn on guitar, Sam Lay on drums, and Dave Myers on bass. Louis Myers came in as a substitute when Littlejohn wasn't able to be there. When Jimmy called Riedy on September 26 and expressed an interest in joining his house band full-time, Riedy was more than happy to accommodate his request. "We agreed on thirty-five dollars a night—he was the highest paid in the band," Riedy said. " I said he could start [a week later] Saturday night, on October 2."[13]

Riedy and his passion for the blues had an enormous impact on the musical culture of Chicago's North Side. He regularly booked gigs for Jimmy Rogers, Koko Taylor, Muddy Waters, Johnny Young, Jimmy Reed, John Littlejohn, Otis Rush, and the individual members of the Three Aces (Dave and Louis Myers and Fred Below) at Alice's and Wise Fools Pub. "I had Fred Below, Louis Myers, and Dave Myers, but I had them all separately," Riedy said. "I never had them as the Aces—I didn't even know about that." Riedy set high standards for his performances, and if you were going to play with him, you'd better be organized about it—he'd see to it personally. His job was to make sure the featured artist was happy. He had the regular band members paid by payroll and even had their taxes withheld for legal purposes.[14]

Armed with the latest compilation of Rogers songs just recently released on *Chicago Bound*, Riedy was ready. "At Wise Fools Pub I kept a binder of all the tunes that worked well for every artist," he reported. "When Jimmy stepped up to the mike, I called out to the band what the tune was, and Jimmy took off from there after we started. Between songs lots of artists would tune their guitars, take a drink . . . I looked at a set the same way you put together a song. You have a certain amount of time between. My purpose was to make the set seamless, with little time wasted in between."[15]

Still, there were certain circumstances that Bob had a hard time controlling, such as featured guest artists wanting to play a set from their most recently released album. Unlike Jimmy, many of them didn't have a compilation album of all their hits conveniently organized on one disc. "The thing that was toughest for us," Riedy said, "is that they would never have copies of the recordings. They would play a new song and start singing, and we'd have to feel what was right for that song and put it in." But Riedy showed the artists respect: "I'd name the bands for whoever we were featuring. I didn't feel right, because with the caliber of headlining musicians I was choosing, I didn't feel right about using my own name." Indeed, when Jimmy joined the group, within a week Riedy had changed the name on the marquee from the "Johnny Young Blues Band" to the "Jimmy Rogers Blues Band." It was hard to keep up with for some of the blues faithful. "Finally the club owner told me, 'Look, Bob, everybody's calling asking who's playing, and I don't know what the name of the band is tonight! You need to name the band the Bob Riedy Blues Band.'"[16]

Blues fans appreciated Riedy's efforts to bring in big names like Jimmy, Muddy, and Wolf. Riedy reflected with glee: "Howlin' Wolf was such a big guy—he was huge. He would come in and do one of those howls, and he'd pop his eyes out and would scare everybody in the front row."[17] Then there was the King Bee, Muddy.

> We had Muddy at Wise Fools. DePaul University was just down the alley. I kept putting these posters up and the DePaul kids kept asking me, "I thought he was dead! Are you sure he's alive?" The night we booked him, the street was lined all the way around the corner. The place was packed; we brought Muddy up from the dressing room, he walked in and said nothing; the people just stared in shock to see him. He gets up on the stage and he pulls the mike up. Everything came to a hush; it was so quiet you could hear a pin drop. And the first thing out of his mouth was . . ."*Forrrty Daayys*!" And the hair went up on the back of your neck. They just screamed for the first whole chorus—they couldn't believe it—it was like somebody came to life right before their eyes.[18]

The good news of Jimmy's regular engagement with Riedy brought joy to many who had missed him in his absence. Jimmy's old pal Muddy was scheduled to play Wise Fools Pub on October 18. It would be a grand reunion of sorts. It had been years now since they had played together on a regular basis during the golden era of Chess. But things had changed so much for both Jimmy and Muddy, especially now that Leonard was gone. Almost exactly a year earlier, on October 16, 1969, Leonard Chess had died of a sudden heart attack while driving his car from the office building. Jimmy had mourned along with the rest of the artists on the Chess roster. Among them none was more visibly shaken by the loss than Muddy, who had built a bond with Leonard that was almost like father and son, or maybe even brothers. About Chess, Jimmy said later, "Chess was about as up front with me as it was any of its artists."[19]

Then his words turned a bit darker. "Len Chess would take any buck he could get off anybody. I didn't get too much money out of my records, but him getting the money and pushing the record, I guess that's what got me surviving now. He got me a pretty good name out there in the blues field. He made the money, but he's gone and I'm still going. That's the way I feel about that!"[20] Jimmy's disdain for the Chess organization did not extend across the entire family. In fact, he had high regard for Leonard's brother, Phil:

> He got a wonderful brother, man, Phil is a sweet guy. That man, after I got burned out, I called and told him what had happened, and he told me to leave a number and he'd call me back. And I was thinking that maybe he's gonna give $100 or $50 or somethin'. The man wrote me a check for $800. And I said, "Man I'll pay you this money back." He said, "Man, you pay me when you can. To hell with it, M. F. Take it. [You] got that wife and them kids to care of." He calls me right now and asks me how things are going. If I need anything, he said, let him know. Maybe I'm wrong for saying this, but my opinion about it in a business way, the way everybody I've talked with about this says, I think Leonard should have let Phil been the head man, and he was in the background all the time. It would have been better because that man . . . he knows how to treat people. He *feel* people, you understand? He's a smart man. I think Phil should have been the big wheel.[21]

At some point, inevitably, issues with Jimmy became less about music and more about money—not because he was interested in money for money's sake, but because of his new situation with his family, whom he loved and clearly put above all else, including his obvious love for being a bluesman. Of the two Chess brothers, Phil demonstrated more of a genuine concern about Jimmy's financial well-being than Leonard ever did. About Phil, Jimmy said, "Any [time] he can pull some strings for you to get what you deserve from that Chess bank, he's right on the case, man. Gettin' you your money. I got more money out of Chess since Leonard died than I did the whole time I was recordin'! That's right. Phil hooked me up with [music publishing firm] BMI, since Leonard died. And all my back money's comin' in."[22]

In the end Jimmy was philosophical about the entire ordeal: "I got exactly what I deserved. What counts, I was fortunate enough to pay a good price for it and now I know. Chess had trouble out of quite a few of his artists down through the years on that same account, you know. I never tried to give him any trouble, like to sue him or go through all those changes. Best thing I know to do in a case like that is what I did do, is cut out. Then I'm clear with him, and everybody's happy."[23]

Jimmy was becoming more and more visible on the local scene, and he was enjoying the lifestyle. On Sunday, March 19, 1971, with Bob Riedy's band performing as backup, Muddy, James Cotton, and Jimmy Rogers gave a seven o'clock evening concert at Wise Fools Pub, the proceedings billed as the group being "Back Together Again." Admission was three dollars. In the summer of 1971

Jimmy was seen performing with Good Rockin' Charles as the two backed Sam Lay at the Milwaukee Summerfest on July 26. Also on the bill were Sonny Terry and Brownie McGhee, Jim Brewer, Hound Dog Taylor, and Blind John Davis.[24]

Jimmy was starting to receive several offers from guitarists who wanted to play second guitar for him, the way he did with Muddy. There were several young white guitarists making the rounds during this time, and they all knew Jimmy played with Bob, so they might have access to him through Riedy's band. Jim Kahr was from the South Side of Chicago and was considered a good lead player. "Frank Capek was my first lead guitarist, then Bill Flood, and Jim was next," Riedy remembered. One after another they were gravitating toward Jimmy as his stock slowly climbed in the eyes of fellow musicians, promoters, managers, and record executives who were interested in his return to the scene. He was on a roll.

But one particular day in late August 1971 would seriously dampen Jimmy's spirits. "We were living on Albany Street on the West Side of Chicago," Jimmy D. Lane (Little Jimmy) recalled somberly, "right across the street from Our Lady of Sorrows Church. The old man got back from a tour of the West Coast. They had to play at a place called Ma Bea's on Madison—him and Johnny Littlejohn, who was living downstairs. Johnny had two kids; the daughter's name was Valerie, and Little Johnny was the son—they were underage. The wife didn't fix them anything to eat, because she wanted to go to the club. My mother stayed home, she was next door. There was a house full of kids, because we had cousins over visiting."[25]

Indeed, the gig down at Ma Bea's was running smoothly until Jimmy's other son, known as J. D., rushed into the club and exclaimed, "The house is on fire!" Both Jimmy and John leapt off the stage simultaneously, rushed to their cars, and sped down the street and around the corner, where both of their families lived close by. Little Jimmy explained what happened:

> It was a Friday night. Valerie got hungry; she wanted to fix something to eat for her and Little Johnny. She put a steak in the broiler. When she opened it up to check on it, the greases jumped out, and instead of using salt to put the flame out she threw water on it. She was a child, about twelve years old; she didn't know any better. The water spread the oil, carried it behind the stove onto the curtains, catching the walls and the wood. Next thing we know, there's a banging on the door, and screaming. We heard, "Where's Mrs. Lane? The house is on fire!"[26]

The boys, who were in the back room playing board games at the time, sprang into action. "My oldest cousin got all of us together, and before we could go outside, I looked up, and there were flames everywhere," said Little Jimmy. "J. D. and Ludia Turner, my cousin, were throwing water on it using a water basin. How can you put out a fire with that? So we got outside. It was chaos. The house burned down. It was a very devastating time."[27] By the time Jimmy and Johnny got there, the entire building was engulfed in flames, and it was too late to save much of anything in Jimmy's upper-story apartment.[28]

After a thorough head count, everyone appeared to have emerged from the building safely. Since his family had long been his first priority, Jimmy no doubt thought to himself, *Thank goodness, no one was hurt*. Nevertheless, it was a major setback to Jimmy's family; the personal and financial damage was almost overwhelming. And there was still something left in the ruins that Jimmy absolutely had to retrieve. Little Jimmy picks up the story again:

> The next day the fire chief came to find out the cause. My dad had just come in off the road, so he had his money at the house; the money was all we had at the time. He'd put it in a Bible under the mattress. I was right there with him the next day . . . He told the fire chief, "Hey, look, I got something in that house I need to get out of there, I don't know if it's there, but I need to get into that house." I'm standing right next to him when it happened.[29]

Strict policies usually prohibit fire inspectors from allowing tenants to return inside a burned-out building before it has been officially cleared of the possibility of further damage, but the inspector knew how serious the situation was. He allowed Jimmy to enter. "He followed him inside the building," Little Jimmy said. "He went back there and he came out of the house. The money he had was still in the Bible." It was a miracle. "The pages were singed. The bed had fallen from the second floor down to the first floor. The mattress was pretty badly burned. But all the money was still intact. I saw that with my own eyes."[30]

Bob Riedy sprang into action to do what he could to help out his bandmates and organized an all-out tribute show to raise relief funds for the victims of the house fire. The Big Blues Benefit concert was held on Sunday, October 3, 1971, at Alice's, from 6:00 in the evening until 12:00 A.M. The lineup of guest performers planned to serve up some of the best music that Chicago had to offer: Otis Rush, Buddy Guy, Johnny Young, Junior Wells, Big Walter, Jimmy Dawkins, Billy Boy Arnold, Howlin' Wolf, Mighty Joe Young, Alvin "Youngblood" Nichols, and disc jockey Gene Clay from WOPA radio were scheduled to appear. Noticeably absent from the promotional flyer for the concert was the name Muddy Waters (who'd recently recorded a new album, *Live at Mister Kelly's*). "Muddy wasn't 'allowed' to perform at the local clubs anymore in Chicago, because his management now thought it would hurt his national image at that time," Riedy surmised. And he was right. According to Waters biographer Robert Gordon, Mister Kelly's was, in his words, both a beginning and an end. *Living Blues* magazine founder, Jim O'Neal, agreed, saying, "I think I saw the last real regularly booked black Chicago club that he [Muddy] played; it was New Year's night, 1971."[31]

Most of the other blues artists were there to support the Riedy benefit, including some whose names were not on the flyer, like Little Brother Montgomery, Big Voice Odom, and Carey Bell. They took donations at the door of one dollar and raised one thousand for the cause. "We did a full night with everybody playing," Bob said, "and because there were so many stars there, we just turned all the money over to Jimmy and John."[32] Little Jimmy remembered a few more details: "At the end of the night, the man was splitting the money, and instead of giving them half each, he just gave it to Johnny. [Littlejohn] gave my old man a very small portion and pocketed the rest. My old man found out about it. He didn't hold a grudge."[33]

The story didn't end there. Jimmy D. continued his story by adding, "We were onstage years later, at the club B.L.U.E.S. Johnny came in and was looking very down and out. My old man looked at Johnny. He shook his hand, and he had a hundred-dollar bill, and said, 'Man, I'm not mad about what happened.' Johnny looked at him with a tear in his eye and said, 'Thank you, I'm sorry.' My old man patted him on the back, said, 'Don't worry about it; take care of yourself.'" Jimmy D. couldn't have been prouder of his dad: "Johnny helped me see something in my old man, a characteristic that I already knew, but this reinforced that."[34]

In early January 1972, Jimmy got a call from a representative of legendary pianist/vocalist Leon Russell (involved with Shelter Records), who found out that Jimmy was back on the scene and wanted him to do a West Coast tour. After they called him at home, Jimmy called Bob Riedy immediately to ask if he could put a road band together. Riedy recruited Jim Kahr on guitar; Bill Lupkin on harmonica; his brother, Steve Lupkin, on bass; and Richard "Hubcap" Robinson on drums to serve as the backing band for Jimmy. Bill Lupkin's very first Chicago gig had been with guitarist and mandolin player Johnny Young, after Riedy arranged an audition for him. Lupkin played at Ma Bea's and Wise Fools Pub and eventually got a chance to join the band.

"I remember when I was with Jimmy Rogers, I was just a kid," Bill said. "I was trying to play [like] Little Walter—like every other person that was tryin' to back in the late '60s and '70s—and Jimmy said, 'No, baby, you just got to try to be yourself. Try to say what you want to say.' And in the last four or five years it's really started to sink in."[35] Lupkin was doing his research on learning Jimmy's music when he stumbled into Bernard Abrams's shop on Maxwell Street. He was amazed at what he found. "Even through the early '70s there were still a few copies of the old Jimmy and Little Walter sides recorded on Ora Nelle available for sale . . ., and I bought one for ninety-seven cents," Lupkin boasted proudly.[36]

Richard "Hubcap" Robinson was a friend of John Littlejohn's, which was how Jimmy met him. Once they got acquainted, Jimmy found that Hubcap's laid-back style meshed perfectly with his own. Riedy said of Hubcap, "He was happy-go-lucky. All he wanted out of life was to get a seafood shop. And he liked wine. He turned out to be a great emcee. He would sometimes show up with a number of his drums missing. He would hock them when he saw something else that he wanted to buy or trade. He didn't take any of this very seriously."[37] About Jimmy, Bob said, "He was a soft-spoken, polite, intellectual musician, unlike any other." But on the other end of the spectrum, there was this comment: "John Littlejohn described himself as a redneck."[38] According to Riedy, Littlejohn's self-assessment fit perfectly with his reputation; he came complete with all kinds of off-color jokes befitting his self-described persona.

In late January, Jimmy, along with Bob Riedy's band, left Chicago to do a series of shows on the West Coast. Bob Riedy had a great thing going with his revolving gigs between Ma Bea's, Alice's, and Wise Fools, and he didn't necessarily want to lose that when he took time off to travel west with Jimmy for this tour. "We were playing at the Wise Fools, and after the fourteen-month solid booking, I put Otis Rush in," Bob recalled. "The promoters reached in and took us all, but they did the business through Jimmy Rogers. So I had the unfortunate job of getting in a station wagon with no rear windows and driving across the desert with oil leaking and dust coming in the back. We went through Washington and back to Oklahoma." The trip was long and grueling, with the usual number of breakdowns, rest stops, and long stretches of silence from boredom. Finally, they arrived. "We drove across the desert on Route 66, with just a car and a trailer," Riedy recalled.[39]

When Jimmy arrived on the California shores, he was met by supportive friends who wanted him to do well on the West Coast. Bob Hite, who was a member of the blues-rock band Canned Heat, wrote a promotional flyer that extolled the virtues of Jimmy and his band: "Jimmy Rogers, one of Chicago's legends, is coming to your town. If you want to hear it played the way it should be, boogie on down and dig the real shit . . . Take my word for it, they're the finest Chicago band around." The letter was signed under the caption, "Don't forget to boogie."[40] Jimmy appreciated Hite's gesture, and said of him, "Bob Hite—now he's a nice fellow, Bob Hite. He's a wonderful fellow. When I hit Los Angeles, he heard that I was in town at [the] Ash Grove, he came to the Ash Grove the first night, on my opening night there, and he gave me a crisp $100 bill to party with. He had maybe twelve or fifteen hundred dollars in his pocket."[41]

The band played their first gigs at the Ash Grove from January 20 to 23. The opening act, an all-female group called Revolutionary Change, was described by local *College Times* staff writer David J. Russell as a band that was "at times repetitive to the point of boredom."[42] Jimmy's band performed superbly and even had a few surprise guests. Riedy was amazed at what he saw that day:

> I remember Mick Jagger, who came to the club after a concert they'd done in Los Angeles and brought all his band members to see Jimmy Rogers. I took them up to the dressing room. Mick and Keith [Richards] told me that when they first started playing guitar in Liverpool they used to get the sailors from the merchant marine ships that would dock at Navy Pier in Chicago. When they got off the ships, they'd go to Bob Koester's Jazz Record Mart, and they'd buy these blues records from Chess and take them back to Liverpool—and that's how the Stones first got to hear Howlin' Wolf, Muddy Waters, and Jimmy Rogers.[43]

The gigs went well for Jimmy and his crew. The entire band was praised on their performance, with Jimmy receiving high marks. "His singing is actually as much of a strong point as his guitar playing," Russell commented in his review. Bill Lupkin's reputation was in good standing as well: "Bill Leskin [sic] turned out some of the tastiest harp licks I've heard since seeing Charlie Musselwhite two months ago." Lupkin also got praise for his vocals on the tune "Popcorn Man," while Jim Kahr—whose name was also innocently misspelled—was complimented on his dexterity: "His riffs were clean and crisp, even when double-stringing his way down the neck."[44]

They were enjoying some time off between gigs when Jimmy received a phone call that would have a significant impact on his career. "I was playing in [the] Ash Grove for one week and Freddie [King] called me," Jimmy recalled. "He come over from Glendale to pick me up and take me to Shelter [Records]. He introduced me to Dennis Cordell and this is the way I got with Shelter."[45] They offered Jimmy an exclusive recording contract, and he happily agreed. Once the deal was secured, he was elated with the terms he'd arranged with the team of executives. He was also quite relieved: he had finally landed a deal that he thought would allow him the kind of musical freedom he'd always wanted at Chess.

On January 28 Jimmy and his band went to the Paramount recording studio in Hollywood, California, to record his new album, produced by his longtime apprentice Freddie King, who still remembered the good old days when he had snuck into the club Zanzibar just to see Jimmy with Muddy on Thirteenth Street and Ashland Avenue in Chicago. Freddie, who had moved to the West Coast, had made a huge splash since he'd joined the Shelter label and was literally the only blues artist on the roster. Never forgetting the generosity Jimmy showed him in earlier days, he decided to do a good turn toward Jimmy, who obviously had mutual respect for King. "I remember Freddie, he was a youngster back when Muddy Waters and I were together, over on the West Side," Jimmy reminisced. "He was livin' right behind the Zanzibar. His mother still lives there, and he would slip in the side door of the Zanzibar and came back there where I [was]. The boss knew he was big and husky but he was nothin' but a boy, about 17 or 18 years old. And he'd come back there and sit right there at the bar, right next to me, watch every move I make on the guitar."[46]

The entire staff at Shelter Records treated Jimmy with respect. This wasn't lost on Jimmy, who showed his elation during every interview he sat for. "Leon Russell's a beautiful guy, and they doin' some wonderful things for me," Jimmy said. "The whole Shelter staff, they were wonderful, man. Dennis Cordell, Arlene and the secretary Sue, Leon Russell, and J. J. Cale. All the guys there, that whole Shelter staff, is wonderful people. And Fredd[ie] King, I can't leave him out ... he's a wonderful guy."[47]

Early reports indicated that the album was supposed to be called *Walkin'*, after Jimmy's hit single. Freddie King's album, ultimately titled *Getting Ready*, had a version of Jimmy's classic "Walkin' by Myself."[48] Jim Kahr, whom Jimmy once referred to publicly as his favorite guitarist, recalled, "Our *Gold Tailed Bird* recording in Hollywood Paramount studio was followed by a tour out West, including Seattle for five nights. [In Los Angeles] Freddie King often joined in, too, since he co-produced the album."[49] The Rogers band took the stage and gave an impressive showing that delighted the West Coast crowd, who were always glad to have a taste of Chicago in their own backyard. "Then we went to play at the Whiskey-A-Go-Go in Hollywood, where B. B. King played with us, and Edgar Winter jammed with us, Paul Butterfield, Freddie King, too," Riedy said.[50] About that *Bird* session, Riedy remembered, "It was tough for the three guitars—Freddie, Jimmy, and Jim—because Freddie was not a regular with us. Anybody in Chicago could step on our stage and play with us; we'd know exactly where to pause and what to do—they knew how we played. But Freddie wasn't from there, and he knew Jimmy at an earlier time, so there was some conflict there."[51] (Although technically correct about Freddie's birthplace, Freddie spent a substantial amount of time playing on the West Side of Chicago, which is how he and Jimmy met and established an early bond.)

While on the West Coast tour laying down tracks for the *Gold Tailed Bird* sessions, Jimmy gave an interview in January 1972 to Frank Voce of *Blues Unlimited*, a magazine that was now serving as the European counterpart to *Living Blues*. When Voce asked Jimmy what had brought him out to the West Coast, he responded, "Let's say the album did, through Willie Dixon," a somewhat cryptic reference to Dixon's connection in the music world to either Freddie King or the Shelter record label. Jimmy told Voce that for the past couple of years he'd been playing not only in hometown Chicago but also in Philadelphia, Cleveland, Nashville, and Memphis. After asking several questions about the early Chess days, the conversation shifted to Jimmy's current recording project and band roster. The interview is quite revealing as to Jimmy's state of mind during the beginning of 1972:

FV: What brought you out here to the West Coast? Was it the album you're doing here in L.A.?

JR: Well, let's just say the album did, through Willie Dixon.

FV: You're recording for Shelter now?

JR: I'm going for Shelter now.

FV: How long have you been playing with the band you have now?

JR: We've been working together for about a year and a half now. My piano player is Bob Riedy, the harmonica player is a fellow named Bill Lupkin and his brother Steve is on the bass. Richard Robinson, I call him the "Hubcap," is on drums, and my new guitar player is Jim Kahr.

FV: Were you playing with anyone before then?

JR: Yes, a fellow back in Chicago when I started back in the field, a cat named John Littlejohn.

FV: So you started up again about three years ago?

JR: That's right.

FV: Did you play at all between the time you were with Muddy Waters and John Littlejohn?

JR: Yes. I played with Howlin' Wolf from about 1959 to 1961.

FV: What are the chances, if any, of you and Muddy getting together again?

JR: You know it'd be a great thing for us to maybe cut an album or something. We worked at a place called Alice's Revue on the North Side and we had a wonderful set over there. It was some time in December [1971].

FV: What do you think of the band you're playing with now?

JR: I think they're great. I think they're about the greatest band I've played with since the Muddy Waters group. Coming out here to the Coast and recording looks like the break we needed, and I wouldn't leave 'em for nothin'. They are great.[52]

Unfortunately, this session had a bad ending, because, according to several accounts, no one got paid for it; evidently, some strange dealings went down between Jimmy and an unidentified promoter. Although Riedy could not (or would not) say exactly what happened, he certainly felt the sting when he got back from the long road trip. "I had a basement apartment at the time," Riedy said, "and I was out of a place to stay, because I didn't get any money and couldn't pay any of my bills when I got back."[53] Needless to say, the majority of the band members were upset, and the entire group folded shortly after their return. When asked about just how it happened that they weren't compensated for their efforts, Bob wasn't bitter—just philosophical: "I can't tell you why we didn't get paid. That's why I had to form my own band, because the band members had to get paid. Back then there was *always* some story about why we couldn't get paid—no matter who you played with or who you played for. There was even one guy who told me we couldn't get paid because there was a fire and all the money got burned up."[54] Still, it wasn't all bad news for Riedy, who got something out of the deal. As a result of his close association with Riedy, yet another opportunity for Jimmy to record surfaced unexpectedly. While relaxing during a stop on the West Coast tour, "a guy knocked on my motel door and said he was Bruce Kaplan from Rounder Records. He asked if we could do something once we got back to Chicago."[55]

When they returned, Jimmy immediately formed a new band, and by the following month, the Three Aces—Louis and Dave Myers, along with Fred Below—joined Bob Riedy and Jimmy Rogers. Jimmy and Bob went into a studio on Michigan Avenue in February 1972 to lay down six tracks. The producer was J. J. Cale. "Act Like You Love Me," "Broken Hearted Blues," "Information Please," "Bad Luck Blues," "Gold Tailed Bird," and "Lonesome Blues" were the tunes that were used as side A of the album that would be released on Shelter Records. The spring 1972 issue of *Living Blues* magazine posted a write-up in their "Blues News" column that read, "The long-awaited Shelter album by Jimmy Rogers should be available within weeks . . . Jimmy has already recorded a second album at Chicago's Sound Studio, produced by Denny Cordell."[56] In truth it would take another year before the album was completed.

In the early months of 1972, Bob Riedy brought in the first band in a series of groups to kick off what would be a long-standing engagement at Ma Bea's. His regularly revolving guest artist series featured John Littlejohn first. Then came Jimmy Rogers, followed by Mighty Joe Young, Jimmy Dawkins, and a host of others beyond them.[57] Bob immediately set up a local studio date at Sound Studio and brought the band in to lay down several tracks. "I put together all the music

. . . Everything was done in one day," Riedy remembered.[58] The recording band included the regulars who played at Wise Fools: Sam Lay, Jim Wydra, Bob Riedy, Johnny Young, and Frank Capek. Indeed, the album flows like an extensive jam session as the band burns their way through fifteen tunes.

Conceptually, the LP *Lake Michigan Ain't No River* was a true collaborative effort, with Riedy putting his best foot forward in the wisest way: he took a handful of the best performances from a handful of his best front men who played regularly at Wise Fools Pub and Alice's Revisited. Guitarists Jimmy Rogers and Johnny Littlejohn, along with mandolinist Johnny Young, are presented as the three headlining artists on the album, with guest turns on vocals by the second team, drummer Richard Hubcap Robinson and harpist Carey Bell. The band sounds well rehearsed here, mainly because the song list for the recording session was extracted directly from the set list, thus ensuring that the time in the studio would deliver maximum results with minimum rehearsal.

The album starts with "My Eyes (Keep Me in Trouble)," a tune that features vocals by a young Carey Bell, who has a plaintive yet direct approach to delivering the lines, even as he goes beyond his natural upper range a few times during the verses. The tune has the same feel as Chuck Willis's "Feel So Bad." Frank Capek's sparse guitar solo, combined with Bob Riedy's rollicking piano solo, maintains the forward motion. "House Rocker" is a jump-blues tune that is almost identical to the version recorded only months earlier and eventually issued on Jimmy's comeback album, *Gold Tailed Bird*. The version heard here has a rougher edge, which gives it a slightly leaner, rawer groove.

The next tune begins with an unexpected spoken introduction by Jimmy, and it comes as a rare treat to hear him speak on tape. "Thank you, ladies and gentlemen," he begins politely. "I am Jimmy Rogers and I have the privilege to be in the Sound Studio today—feelin' good and everything." He pauses slightly, then declares humbly, "I'm going to try and attempt to record one of my records that was recorded back in the early fifties along with the Muddy Waters group and the late Little Walter. The title of this tune happens to be, 'I'm Walking by Myself.'"[59]

"Walkin'" is promptly delivered crisply, with a hard-driving bass and deep drum shuffle. Carey Bell demonstrates respect and deference to Big Walter in his straightforward approach to the original version—he doesn't try to improve on perfection. "Slick Chick" (a tune based on John Lee Williamson's "Mellow Chick Swing") is essentially "Looka Here," and for some odd reason Jimmy doesn't begin with the phrase "Looka here'; instead he starts with a line from the second verse: "She's kinda fine, stays on my mind." While "Sloppy Drunk" has an up-tempo pace that is a step quicker than the standard, Jimmy offers his lyrics with the typical relaxed manner one has come to expect. The band holds the tune together quite well.

Jimmy had turned down several offers in the past that reminded him of the bad old days when he fought with Leonard to treat his music the way he wanted it to be treated. "Bob Koester, he wanted to record me," Jimmy recalled. "And Muddy was talking to me about Chess. And Stax [Records] sent a fellow here to talk with me. And Stax was still on me out there on the West Coast. I had about ten different companies that I had a chance to record with since I been back out in the field."[60] For Jimmy, it was an easy decision to go with his new employers at Shelter Records and refuse the other advances that came his way. "They don't touch Shelter," Rogers bragged. "A couple of 'em, in money line, they did. But a lot of these companies they'll give you a big money in front, then lock you up, see. They'll tie you up and hold you. But Shelter does not deal that way. And Dennis Cordell, he's short [looking] for blues artists. And they push the blues, they interested in blues, see. I felt that I would get a better deal with Shelter for advertisement push and records than I would have with the other companies."[61]

One of the advantages of being with Shelter was that Jimmy no longer had to compete with the long list of names on the artists roster, which was so typical of Chess. Jimmy discovered very quickly the perks that come with being on the short list. "Definitely it's better," he said. "So now Shelter only have two, that's me and Freddie, to worry about. So it's a pretty good thing. Yeah, let 'em go on ahead and play rock, and let me sell their blues. They don't bother me that way."[62] During the first quarter of the year, Jimmy played as a featured guest at the Wabash Street YMCA. *Gold Tailed Bird* was doing fairly well. Jimmy sat in with drummer Richie Robbins (who was known for Alvin Cash and the Crawlers' hit "Twine Time"), and Tim Schuller and drummer Mot Dutko came to visit him. Jimmy introduced them to the audience from the stage, referring to them as "two buddies of his who came all the way from Cleveland to see him," says Schuller.[63]

In the spring 1973 issue of *Living Blues*, a special section that listed the current recording studios included both large and small operations throughout the city of Chicago. In a somewhat shocking revelation, the announcement about Chess Records read like an obituary notice: "When Chess deserted Chicago for the confines of its new parent corporation GRT in New York, it left behind only a studio, Ralph Bass and a few vestiges of its once-bustling Chicago operation. Nowadays the New York Chessmen seem content with occasional re-packaging of old material and infrequent sessions with their established blues stars."[64] By mid-April, Marshall Chess had quit the company that his father and uncle had built, one he should have owned. By the summer of 1972, GRT had turned Chess into a shell of its former self.

Jimmy was not concerned about either the success or demise of Chess Records; he was busy getting busy again. There were several places to play in Chicago, and the blues scene was beginning to show some renewed signs of life, although, like Chess Records, it would never quite return to its former self. Still, several locations were opening up on every side of town for musicians to play, even if most didn't pay that well. On the South Side, the Burning Spear at 5523 South State Street was the place where the highest profile artists, like B. B. King and his fabulous band, performed when visiting Chicago. The new Checkerboard Lounge (formerly the Sackadelic Shack), located at 423 East Forty-third Street, was a local hangout for artists like Buddy Guy and Junior Wells to play, and Buddy eventually bought the place. The Blue Monday sets were among the best in town. The Sweet Queen Bee Lounge (named for the hostess/owner Bee Taylor) at 7401 South Chicago was always jumping.

Carl Jones (who briefly had Jimmy Rogers on his C. J. label during this period) could be counted upon to tend bar at Theresa's at 4801 South Indiana Avenue; Junior Wells, Muddy Waters Jr., Otis Rush, and Pee Wee Madison were frequent visitors who'd sit in regularly. There was Florence's at 5443 South Shields Street, where Hound Dog Taylor, Lefty Dizz, Magic Slim, Carey Bell, and "Left Hand Frank" Craig held court. And ever since Pepper's Lounge got a new look and location at 1321 South Michigan Avenue, Howlin' Wolf, Johnny "Big Moose" Walker, and James Cotton all had turns headlining there. Even the Sutherland Hotel at 4659 South Drexel Avenue had the Hotsy Totsy Club, where you could catch either Howlin' Wolf, Junior Wells, or maybe Lucille Spann—Otis's beloved wife, a recent widow. And then there was Porter's at 5944 South Halsted Street, where Ted Porter tended bar while wearing a .45 on his hip and a six-gallon hat on his head.[65]

On the West Side, Duke Rogers owned two spots: Big Duke's Lounge, located at 2755 West Madison Avenue, and Big Duke's Blue Flame at 2657 West Roosevelt Road. Jimmy Rogers could be found in the 1815 Club at 1815 West Roosevelt, performing with the Bob Riedy Band (although this spot would be firmly established over the next four years as the home base for Howlin' Wolf and his bandleader, superb tenor saxophonist Eddie Shaw). Ma Bea's at 3001 West Madison was home to Jimmy Dawkins, who claimed to have seen no fights in the bar beyond those that were initiated between him and his own band members.[66] Mister Kelly's was reserved for artists of such caliber and distinction as Muddy Waters and B. B. King, who were both considered among the blues royalty, a cut above the rest during this time period.[67]

And on the North Side there was, of course, Alice's Revisited at 950 West Wrightwood Avenue, the home base of Bob Riedy's band. Wise Fools Pub at 2270 North Lincoln Avenue had blues four nights a week, and—beyond the entire Riedy showcase, which revolved around artists like Jimmy, John Littlejohn, and Johnny Young—it also featured others like Otis Rush, J. B. Hutto, and Sam Lay. Riedy talked about how rough-and-tumble it was to play in one particular place they frequented. "John Littlejohn was friends with the owner of Ma Bea's on Madison and Sacramento, located in a rough area," he said. "It was not a job that anybody really went after. You always wondered whether your van would still be there when you walked out of the place. We'd start at ten in the morning and then we'd play until about four, on Friday, Saturday, and Sunday. There were so few people there; the patrons were people who would come in and cash their government checks and hang around and socialize. The people who played there was anybody who was out of work. Carey Bell, Magic Slim, they played there."[68]

In fact, that was the reason Jimmy eventually lost a modicum of respect for Littlejohn: he liked playing at Ma Bea's much more than Jimmy ever did. "Johnny Littlejohn, myself, and we had a bass player, Dave Matthews, and we had Jesse Green on drums," Jimmy recalled. "And Bob Riedy, he was with me when I was gettin' back—he was my piano player. So Johnny Littlejohn and I, we had a little difference, and he left."[69] Clearly the rift affected Jimmy; after all, they'd literally been through fire together. Still, he couldn't seem to get over the fact that John would subject himself to situations that Jimmy felt were beneath both of them. "When I came in, John didn't have any band. He would go over there and just stop off where he could to play his gig. Because Bob and I, we wouldn't go in there [anymore] with him. So John, he would play with us, and then he'd go over here in these cut-throat joints to play. He just was like that. He likes to be around that stuff. I've heard Johnny say he would give up a gig for $25 and go play where somebody else is playin', cut their head."[70]

Jimmy always had a sense of duty to himself. But he also expressed a sincere sense of duty to his audience as well. He never wanted to short-change the people who came out to see him. Nor did he want to undermine the quality of the atmosphere in whatever club he might be playing. He clearly spent a lot of time thinking about the ramifications of what might happen if things got out of hand while performing for paying customers.

I don't let just anybody come on my bandstand because you got a public audience out there, and they wants to hear somethin'. If it's not you, they want to hear somethin' sound pretty good, you know. Don't let just any old drunk come up there on your bandstand and kick over your amp, break a wire or something or start cursing or maybe start a fight in the place. He don't care. It's not his gig anyway. He don't have nothing to lose, 'less he get his head busted or somethin', that's all. But the best thing, I just turn 'em off nice, you know, and tell 'em we have a system. But Johnny, he would do those things. He let anybody on his bandstand, and the way I picture him, he let them make a fool of himself. But it's burnin' him that way. He don't see that.[71]

Jimmy's anger was not directed specifically at his friend John; rather, it was aimed at anyone who would allow such things to happen. Jimmy remembered when another well-known musician was dogging it by letting anyone and everyone who said they could play a little come up on stage, as if they belonged there. "Little Walter, he was bad about lettin' anybody on his bandstand," Rogers lamented. "Throw 'em on the bandstand with the band, and that really mix your musicians up. Little Walter'd come down and get in his car and go drive and get him some whiskey or somethin'. When he come back it's closin' time and he's drunk, the man's mad, people done walked out."[72]

Bob Riedy did his best to avoid those kinds of situations by establishing some kind of consistency in personnel for the clubs where he played, although it was nearly impossible at times. Even Jimmy was vulnerable and was often tempted by promoters to earn decent money by going overseas. "Every time the European producers realized that these people were still alive and active and playing well at the Wise Fools, they would come in, sign them up on a break and try to take them on a European tour, and then we'd end up missing two or three guys," Riedy complained.[73]

Horst Lippmann (the partner of Fritz Rau) was one such promoter who arrived almost like clockwork from Germany to see what talent he could pluck from the Chicago blues bands to build a tour package for an overseas festival. The concert agency and record label called L + R (Lippmann and Rau) had a good reputation among American musicians, built from several blues and gospel tours in years past. The shows were produced by Willy Leiser, who hailed from Geneva, Switzerland. The organization offered some serious work to anyone who would cross the pond for an extended period. Now they were after Jimmy, who realized that this was just the opportunity he'd been looking for: a way to make some real money on a consistent basis in order to deal with his real priority, his family. According to Jimmy, "I didn't go [before] because the money they were talking about, if I'd stay in the store for an hour and a half I could make what he'd have paid me for a whole night in Europe. But after I got burned out, I didn't have no choice." Indeed, he finally relented. "I did decide to go over to Europe and I went over for [producer] Horst Lippmann, that was my first trip . . . that kind of got things movin' again."[74]

Jimmy was always thinking of his family and how much it could benefit them financially. Lippmann's offer served as a great motivator. It was the final push Jimmy needed to fully rekindle his musical fire to the intense heat that it had once reached—not that the flames had ever really died. "Europe was somethin' I was wanting to see anyway," he said, convincing himself that he shouldn't miss the opportunity.[75] He accepted the deal and officially joined the tour package—with one caveat: "I don't mind travelin' just as long as I got my train fare home." Jimmy knew Riedy wouldn't be thrilled. Riedy had seen it all before. "I would have to learn how to do without Jimmy Rogers for a month," Bob said, "because they were going off to Europe. I'd get John Littlejohn to take his place; then he'd go and I'd get Jimmy back. They never called for the whole band—just the artist."[76]

In October 1972 Jimmy performed as one of the main attractions on Lippmann and Rau's eleventh annual American Folk Blues Festival, which went through Frankfurt, Berlin, and Bonn, Germany, as well as other countries on the tour—Sweden, France, and Switzerland (little did Jimmy realize he would be participating in what turned out to be the last Lippmann and Rau festival for the next eight years). On October 25 the entire entourage arrived in Munich, Germany. Lippmann and Rau made sure that the event was star-studded: T-Bone Walker, Big Mama Thornton, Memphis Slim, Roosevelt Sykes, Bukka White, Jimmy Dawkins, and several others were scheduled on the bill. The next night Jimmy performed several tunes with his backing band that consisted of Jimmy on guitar, Moses "Whispering" Smith on harp, Jimmy Davenport on drums, and Willie Kent on bass. Jimmy played on several tunes, including his classic hits "Chicago Bound" and "Walkin' by Myself."

Another tune on the song list, "Tricky Woman," was calibrated to a deliberately slow-dripping Rogers pace, purposely contrasted with a juicy, razor-edged harmonica solo by Smith. While Jimmy did his usual laid-back, smooth delivery, others on the tour seized the opportunity to entertain with more outward demonstrations, such as Bukka White, Roosevelt Sykes, and Johnny Young, who enticed the crowd with his "ass-shaking," according to Living Blues writer Norbert Hess. Not giving in to such antics, Jimmy maintained his typical demeanor, content to just stand there and deliver the steady, solid blues he was known for, even if it left some puzzled as to why the foreign audiences didn't appreciate his efforts when compared to some others on the tour package. "I wonder why they didn't like Chicago's old-time Jimmy Rogers as much as the country cats," Hess grumbled. "And 'Walkin by Myself' was *soooo* nice!"[77] A live double album of a portion of the proceedings—eighteen tracks—was soon to follow, scheduled for release on Atlantic Records (G60036) sometime in 1973.

While in Europe, Jimmy was interviewed by three gentlemen for *Blues Unlimited* magazine: David Walters, Laurence Garman, and John Matthews. Jimmy was in a cordial mood. As the three reporters approached him with a copy of the *Chicago Bound* LP in hand, they asked him about the vintage Chess years. "I was playing this guitar for about three years," he said as he pointed to the photo on the back of the LP cover. "I kept that guitar about ten years." More questions followed. "This amp . . . wasn't worth a damn," he responded, pointing to one of the amps a band member was sitting on in the photo. "This boy here, Henry Strong . . . his wife killed him. He had the same suit on that he has in this picture and she killed him before morning." When asked about the chemistry between the band members back then, he pointed to the group photo and stated firmly, "A group like this . . . we [could] close our eyes and almost hear each other thinking, when we're playing the blues. You can't do that with other musicians." Then the subject of Leonard Chess came up, to which he responded with his usual mixed emotions about that topic: "Leonard mostly confused me by changing the beat, but he would never change my lyrics." Eventually the interview worked its way toward the current lineup of artists, songs, and concerts Jimmy was involved in. "Today I play rock clubs mostly, colleges and those coffee shops and things like that." After being asked about the new forthcoming album, Jimmy was asked to comment about his musical preferences. "Well, I play a little jazz, but I don't like it myself," Rogers informed the interviewers. "I like it as music—it's good to hear—but to play, my tastes is the blues."[78]

9

GOLD TAILED BIRD

Now I'm not interested in local gigs too much.
'Course I'm wanted in a lot of places, but the price
that they're paying for this local stuff just don't
interest me, so I just don't fool with it.

—Jimmy Rogers

Jimmy's simple tastes were reflected in how he lived and how he played. While the latest rage of the 1970s seemed to involve cranking the amps up and blasting away at the guitar while "squeezing the strings," Jimmy stuck to the basic approach he had consistently maintained throughout his performing career: his style was embedded in the interplay that lay between either two guitars, guitar and piano, or guitar and harmonica. Simply put, he liked to play off the other guy. "I always would use a second guitar when I had my own group," Jimmy said. "It's pretty hard to fill in the harmony with a small group and play your own lead and sing at the same time."[1]

Jimmy knew his limitations. An artist like B. B. King would have been a perfect example of what Jimmy was depicting when he explained his technique, and B. B. could have easily been the person Jimmy had in mind when he made the earlier comment about not singing and playing simultaneously, especially when one considers the huge impact King was having on lead guitarists everywhere who were copying his style at the time. "A lot of musicians plays lead guitar and sings, but he's only cuttin' in and out. He'll sing, you don't hear his guitar until he stops singin'. The other part of the band carries on. So you need a second guitar man to hit those spots," Jimmy noted.[2] Indeed it is a rare chance to hear B. B.'s wonderful stinging guitar work overlapping his vocals. On the other hand, the tag-team work he orchestrates is what pulls the listeners in closer to both his guitar and his powerful voice. Still, B. B.'s overall band sound had a different set of dynamics, because he rarely used a harp player, while Jimmy's guitar style was largely designed to allow for a space for the harmonica to breathe.

In the winter 1972 issue of *Living Blues*, the Biograph album *Love Changin' Blues* was reviewed by Kip Lornell, who was correctly suspicious about the odd inclusion of Jimmy Rogers's version of "Ludella" showing up as one of the highlights of the album. "It seems out of place here just being thrown in as a filler," Lornell wrote. "The story behind this [from Arnie Caplin] is that, for some reason, Jimmy Rogers owed Fred Mendelsohn a favor. Jimmy said that, as payment, he would record for Fred. The results of which is this version of 'Ludella,' which was supposedly recorded a few days after Jimmy did it for Chess. They are similar when you compare the two." Clearly Lornell wasn't buying into what Caplin was selling as he made the skeptic-laden final comment, "At least it makes for an interesting story!"[3]

Meanwhile, Jimmy and his band were planning a new recording, scheduled to take place on the return trip from a short West Coast tour. The new album was to be recorded in Oklahoma, not in Leon Russell's home, but at a converted church located nearby.[4] The route they took to get to Russell's Tulsa town was a bit out of the way, but the band tried to make the best of it. They caught up with Russell at his Grand Lake home, which had a studio called Paradise Recording Studio located inside the summer house near the water's edge. By the time they arrived, however, things went from bad to worse. "The situation was strained," Bob Riedy recalled. "The money was a problem. The police were not happy to see these long-haired guys showing up. We were staying in a house next to the church, which was actually the studio. The control board was up in the altar, and the musicians were down on the floor, where the benches used to be. If we ventured outside the house, the police were right on us, jumping out of their cars, wondering who we were."[5]

If nothing else, they were confident that the music would be tight. Even so, they encountered a few obstacles once they got there. According to Bob, "At that point, we had been playing together so long, it didn't matter where we were—sometimes you'd be in a place where you couldn't hear each other. In those days you didn't have the nice monitors where you could hear. That's where all those many nights and days of playing made a difference." Leon Russell was supposed to be the producer of the session, but evidently he took the role lightly. When asked how Russell interacted with them on both a musical and personal level, Riedy's blunt answer was, "He didn't. We only saw him at a distance. I'm not sure he was there all the time."[6]

On September 21 and 30 of 1972, Jimmy sat at his home at 6340 South Ellis Avenue on the South Side of Chicago for an extensive feature story for *Living Blues* magazine. Jim O'Neal did the interview, along with Bill Greensmith, who tagged along as a writer for *Blues Unlimited* (the magazine's UK counterpart), which also published a story on Jimmy. Early in 1973 Jimmy's name was mentioned along with a host of other artists on a compilation album under the Barrelhouse Records label, located locally at 6512 South Talman Avenue. The owner, George Paulus, had issued only two albums before this one—the first recorded by John Wrencher, and the other by Washboard Willie.[7] The third launch, *Chicago Boogie!* was a project that took all the masters from the 1947 Ora Nelle sessions and put them into album format, with incredibly ornate cover art designed by Paulus that presented the record in an attractive package. The LP contained four previously issued sides and ten unissued sides (including extra takes of the formerly released tunes) for six dollars plus postage.[8]

The year 1973 would turn out to be the most productive of Jimmy's entire career. He could not have known what was on the horizon, but the upcoming months would yield more musical rewards than he could have ever imagined. In fact, it would not be too much of a stretch to say that this specific year single-handedly made up for the short shrift that Leonard Chess had dealt to him. Jimmy was now finding all the energy and motivation he needed to carry him throughout the remainder of his career. In many ways 1973 was poetic justice for the self-imposed musical silence of the previous decade. Bob Riedy's band featuring Jimmy Rogers returned to their regular gig at Dave Ungerleider's Wise Fools Pub at 2270 North Lincoln, performing Wednesday through Sunday nights.[9] Riedy's *Lake Michigan Ain't No River* was now in stores, and the band recorded a follow-up album for Bruce Kaplan's Flying Fish label.[10] In the early summer, Jean-Marie Monestier, owner of the French Black & Blue label, decided he would put together his own tour as an answer to the absence of the American Folk Blues Festival that year. Called the Chicago Blues Festival Tour, it would feature Jimmy Rogers, Koko Taylor, and Willie Mabon.[11] The tour took the artists through southern Germany, Switzerland, and France.[12]

Meanwhile, *Living Blues* announced that Jimmy had recorded a second album for Shelter on June 4–5 in Tulsa, Oklahoma. This second album, the magazine reported, featured a new Jimmy Rogers band. The dissolution of that first January 1972 West Coast touring band—Bob Riedy, Steve and Bill Lupkin, Jim Kahr, and Richard Hubcap Robinson—had been a direct result of the money mix-up that had left the musicians unpaid and, at least in Riedy's case, in serious need of rent money. Financially that trip had been a wash, but professionally it helped them to make their names. By June 1973 Kahr and Bill Lupkin had decided they would try their luck and return to the West Coast to launch solo careers of their own. "Bill, Steve, and myself eventually left the band and relocated in LA to promote our own band, Slamhammer," recalled Kahr. "We opened for many major artists around Los Angeles and launched our career out there."[13]

The separation was by no means bitter. Jim Kahr remembered Jimmy fondly, even years after the band broke up: "I held the highest respect for Jimmy over the years. He set a high respectable standard for the blues scene, as a composer, artist, and gentleman." Kahr went on to pursue his career, eventually backing, recording, and touring with legendary artists such as John Lee Hooker, Bobby Blue Bland, Charlie Musselwhite, and others. Kahr acknowledged Jimmy as a great role model who had a definite impact on the way he conducted himself, saying, "Jimmy was a calm and collected bluesman, paying extra attention to events around him. His awareness was acute."[14]

In Jimmy's new band, Jim Kahr and Steve Lupkin were replaced by Frank Capek on guitar and Jim Wydra on bass. Jimmy was now harpless. Of the new band roster, Jimmy told one reporter, "Well, the best group that I've had since I've been in the music business here was Little Walter, Muddy Waters, Elgin [Elga] Edmonds and myself. But the unit that I have now is the next best group. We have a very young bass player and guitar player. Frank [Capek] the guitar and Jim [Wydra] the bass. They're young. They're tryin' hard to play, and they're doin' a wonderful job."[15] It was a solid group of musicians. Yet Jimmy still felt it was lacking something, later saying, "I just wish[ed] that I could find a good harmonica player . . . I wouldn't be able to find one that could top Little Walter. But if I could find one that could just compete with him pretty close and would stick, that would strengthen the unit, see."[16]

Even though Jimmy was dealing well with present situations, he couldn't help making comparisons to the hard-core blues veterans of the past and wishing out loud that he could have his old colleagues right beside him again, or at least a reasonable facsimile. Finding that kind of talent in someone interested in the blues was not an easy task in the 1970s. In Jimmy's opinion at the time, "Big Walter is one of the best now that's living . . . in all the harps that I've heard, even Bill Lupkin, the boy that's in California that was with me for a while—now he's good—he can't play with Big Walter if Walter would settle down and play. James Cotton is good. Carey Bell is good. But Big Walter is the boss. He knows more, he's got more experience, he can settle down and he can bring some notes out of that harmonica that's out of sight."[17]

On August 29, 1973, as the third in a series of interviews by O'Neal and Greensmith, Jimmy was asked about the new band and how the songs for the second album were coming along. In the article Jimmy went out of his way to express how much he valued keeping the band together so that it would allow them to gel as a unit, and how detrimental it was to continually retool the group. He even went so far as to compare his philosophy with that of other greats such as Louis Armstrong and Duke Ellington, his point being that his chosen formula to success was not unprecedented. Jimmy also shared Ellington's attitude about having talented musicians of all races, creeds, or colors. When asked why he had a mixed bag of blacks and white in the group, he responded:

> No particular reason. Just good musicians, that's all. When I recorded I had part of my group with me and I had Below, Dave, and Louis [Myers]. It doesn't make no difference, I go on stage with anybody just so they can play. Color doesn't mean nothin'. Just understand it as a musician, that's all. I don't care who can play it. If I was to walk up outside, if you hear a sound comin' through the wall, you don't know what color it is. You can't see it, you just hear it. That's the way I see it.[18]

When the feature article was published, it included a picture, a live-action shot taken at the 1815 Club, with Jimmy on guitar, Riedy on piano, Frank Capek on rhythm guitar, and Sam Lay on drums. (Jim Wydra, most likely on bass, was out of the frame.)

Living Blues released the untimely announcement that Alice's Revisited had closed during the early summer of 1973. The good news was that two album projects that Jimmy had worked on were finally out: *Gold Tailed Bird* on Shelter Records and the Bob Riedy Blues Band's *Lake Michigan Ain't No River* produced by Bruce Kaplan for Rounder Records.[19] In the magazine's review of Riedy's album, Jim DeKoster wrote, "Not surprisingly, these fall short of the originals, but are by no means bad. Jimmy still has the same straight-ahead vocal style, and 'Slick Chick' makes for a good 50s-period piece." Riedy gets a good evaluation, with DeKoster assessing his performance as "rock-solid," and the band was deemed to be "more solid than flashy. In fact, that pretty well describes the LP itself."[20]

However, the bigger news was that *Gold Tailed Bird* had finally hit the record store shelves. As the first official album to announce Jimmy Rogers's resurgence on the blues scene, this LP was released with high expectations and to great anticipation. The album of mostly original tunes unfortunately contained liner notes with incorrect information regarding the round-robin lineup of players, which caused considerable confusion over the upcoming years to blues aficionados. In the process of identifying who did what during the trifecta of groups recording albums, their names got tangled up.

For example, the liner notes indicate that the February session was produced by J. J. Cale, although on the LP the producer was identified as Stu Black, who was probably the engineer of this Chicago Sound Studio date. Fortunately there were no such mistakes about the music. For side A, "You're the One" was given a total makeover, with the old hard and deep shuffle replaced by a good-time boogie groove and a fatback drumbeat supplied by Hubcap. "Brown Skin Woman" showed the first sign of Freddie King, with his angular melodic guitar lines. "That's All Right" was a bit quicker, with a busier yet less potent harmonica than the original. "You're Sweet" has a greater of a sense of urgency, with Bill Lupkin providing a clean yet soft-edged harp solo that fit quite well with the groove established by Riedy and Robinson. Freddie's short guitar solo is bathed in treble and reverb, which was the way he preferred it during this period.

"Sloppy Drunk" has a laid-back, straight-four funky feel as opposed to the two-beat jump groove of the original. Jim Kahr takes a perfunctory solo while Bill Lupkin percolates underneath, keeping the groove hustling down the track. "Live at Ma Bea's" (which is based on "Sonny Moon for Two" by Sonny Rollins) is straight-ahead jazz jump blues, with some deft harp work from Lupkin and driving bass from Steve Lupkin—Bill's brother—who is not even listed on the original album's credit nor on the CD reissue compilation. "Rock This House" has tons of drive, a perfect vehicle for Jimmy's rich and relaxed vocals, which always come across as more refreshing when superimposed over a hot and heavy groove. "Pretty Baby" is given the classic 6/8 medium shuffle feel that settles the tune into a comfortable groove for Jimmy to ease into each verse. Finally, "You're the One" has the most drastic overhaul, with a boogie shuffle from Hubcap, spicy interspersed jabs from Lupkin, and a typical high-and-tight guitar vibrato from Freddie King.

The B side of the album contained tunes from the second recording session produced by J. J. Cale in February, when Jimmy had used Bob Riedy and the Aces. An up-tempo jump-blues version of "Act Like You Love Me" has a lot more spunk than the original Chess version and is peppered with jazzy riffs from Louis. Jimmy's first recorded version of "Broken Hearted Blues" is heard here, with Jimmy singing in the patented *lemme take my time* slow-drip tempo. The slightly faster "Information Please" demonstrates that Jimmy had lost nothing in his vocal delivery. "Bad Luck Blues" has a mojo-workin' feel to it, with a tight backbeat and a clean, economic guitar solo. The title track, "Gold Tailed Bird," was named as a result of a reference to one of the popular commercials for

Continental Airlines, according to Jimmy's son J. D. Mosley. "Lonesome Blues" has a lazy, country feel that would make Muddy Waters feel right at home.

John Kally wrote up a review of the album for *Living Blues* magazine, and his notes chronicling the musical content contained within the vinyl grooves did not exactly equate with a ringing endorsement. "His first release in 14 years has its moments," Kally wrote, "but *Gold Tailed Bird* is a bit of a disappointment . . . The record is uneven mainly because the tracks come from different sessions." Kally went on to find a few kind words for Jimmy's better-known tunes, saying "Versions of 'That's All Right' and 'You're the One,' while hardly equaling the original recordings, are still fine examples of solid Chicago Blues . . . Jimmy's voice hasn't been too affected by age; the major difference between these and earlier sessions appears to be the sidemen, who are hardly a match for Little Walter, Otis Spann, and others who played on his first sides."[21] Indeed it would be near impossible for anyone besides the original architects to measure up to such high standards, which was what made those sides so legendary. Kally continues to complain, correctly observing, "Lupkin's harp wasn't properly recorded, and as a result loses the heavy tone that is a trademark of Chicago-styled harp." Kally does eventually manage to find something nice to say about the sidemen: "Still, he [Lupkin] gets in some good licks." He adds that there are "fine solos throughout the band on the jazz-flavored 'Live at Ma Bea's,' and 'Houserocker.'"[22]

After a bit more complaining about Jimmy's voice becoming somewhat stiffer in the remaining material—which, Kally decides, has a negative affect on the band—he compliments the title cut by calling the Aces an "able backing band." He concludes the review with a backhanded compliment in his final statement, "Even with its weaknesses, *Gold Tailed Bird* is probably still worth having," but recommends the latest Chess release from Jimmy Rogers, *Chicago Bound*, as the preferable choice to investing time and money in the Shelter sides.[23]

Though in many ways the release of *Gold Tailed Bird* did not represent the high reentry point of Jimmy Rogers onto the music scene, in other ways it did serve as notice that his recording career was back in full swing. After the album hit the shelves, the word was out that Jimmy was officially open for business. Meanwhile, Bob Riedy had already adjusted to the fact that the European market was chomping at the bit for as much authentic American blues as they could get their hands on, and promoters from many different tour packages were continually circling around the North Side Chicago clubs like buzzards, ready to pick the meatiest parts out from the blues bars, leaving Riedy's bands bone-dry at times.

GRT, the new landlords of Chess, now had a new slogan: "Chess: The Mother of It All"—no doubt an insider's joke on Leonard's widely known slang term for the artists who worked for and beside him. GRT had released what was called the Genesis series, a four-volume LP box set, which now contained Jimmy's complete 1970 Chess album as its fourth disc. Disc 1 was a compilation of a few tunes from several artists, including Sunnyland Slim, Muddy, "Baby Face" Leroy Foster, Forrest City Joe (Joe Bennie Pugh), Robert Nighthawk, and Little Johnny Jones. Disc 2 was fourteen Muddy Waters tunes that had Jimmy on most of them. Disc 3 had music from Memphis Minnie, Robert Nighthawk, Big Bill Broonzy, and Washboard Sam.[24] It was quite perplexing programming to be sure, and one wonders not only who was behind the entire concept to begin with but why. The Genesis set adequately represented a harbinger of things to come, as it became clearer by the day that those who ran GRT had no intelligent producer at the helm, nor did their choices reflect any interest in maintaining the best reputation or image of the artists who had made the Chess label what it once was.

Nevertheless, by 1973 things had clearly gotten better for Jimmy. After he recorded the *Gold Tailed Bird* session, he felt like he didn't need to bother with the local scene as much as before, and he usually opted out of participating in offers to come out and play on gigs for what he considered an inferior payday. He was taking it easy, not working too hard, just playing mainly for the sheer joy of it. On his gigs he even resorted to the routine he had developed when he'd played with Muddy. "Jimmy started sitting in a chair in the latter days at Wise Fools Pub," Riedy recalled. "On other songs he stood up when he wanted to belt out a song."[25]

In December 1973 Atlantic Records released a double-album set that was a compilation of the music captured in March and October at the tenth annual American Folk Blues Festival, the first overseas festival that Jimmy had participated in since his "return." The crowds in Europe loved Jimmy's performances, and the promoters found him to be easygoing and a pleasure to work with. As a result, he was repeatedly asked to return across the waters to perform as one of the main attractions for the tours. Eager to capitalize on appearances in countries throughout the Continent, Horst Lippmann and Siegfried Loch had recorded the proceedings from 1972 as the bands made their stop in Germany.

Meanwhile, the European Folk Festival came to a grinding halt for the next ten years. French record producer Jacques Morgantini seized the opportunity to start his own tour and recruited several Chicago artists for his own purposes. He recorded several of the artists as leaders and as sidemen, in both live and studio settings. To maximize the output, he wisely placed the array of artists in different combinations to create marathon recording stretches that yielded dozens of sides per session. It reminded Jimmy of the early Chess days, when they would go for hours laying down tracks as they rotated the featured artist to be spotlighted for designated songs.

It was under these circumstances that Jimmy laid down fourteen tracks in Toulouse, France, at the Concordet Studio for the Black & Blue label on December 13, 1973. The event marked another opportunity for Jimmy to record with the Aces—Fred Below and the Myers brothers, along with Willie Mabon, who'd moved to Paris permanently in 1972. Jimmy recorded eleven individual songs that fell into two different categories: first, his biggest Chess hits; second, a few songs from *Gold Tailed Bird*. In addition to the eleven initial studio takes, he recorded extra takes of three tunes: "I Can't Sleep for Worrying," "Pretty Baby," and "Sloppy Drunk." Several of the "greatest hits" cuts are live performances from a December 8 concert delivered in the Biarritz Casino, in the legendary gambling city. These tunes feature Jimmy with a backing trio of the Aces, whereas the others are studio takes with the addition of Willie Mabon on piano. The album, titled *That's All Right*, was released in France in 1974, but the LP never made it to American shores.

The first side of the album reads like a "greatest hits" showcase: "Sloppy Drunk," "Gold Tailed Bird," "Walkin' by Myself," "That's All Right," and "Ludella" are all live from the December 8 Biarritz concert. "Gold Tailed Bird" and "Walkin' by Myself" both possess the kind of power that only a live atmosphere can capture, and this entire live side would have been an absolute masterpiece if only Little or Big Walter had been there to add the extra firepower to kick it into overdrive. Still, the audience signals its approval with healthy applause. Jimmy follows quickly with "That's All Right," which is pleasantly delivered in a more laid-back pocket than the original, with Below laying down that supple 6/8 feel underneath Myers's 4/4 beat shuffle. "Ludella," the last song on side A, presents Jimmy's vocals slightly dabbed with a touch of natural reverb from the room, which gives the tracks a bit more depth and creates a nice balance between his natural tone and the band's ambiance.

The second side of the album shifts to five songs taken from the December 13 studio session that was booked five days after the concert, including recorded versions of familiar tunes, even though some of them have slightly altered titles: "I Lost the Good Woman," "You're So Sweet," "The Last Time," "Shelby County," and "Tricky Woman." "I Lost the Good Woman" and "You're So Sweet" both have classic Jimmy Reed shuffles that give them a leisurely bounce that was unprecedented for this particular tune. "The Last Time" has a heavier groove than the Chess version, with Louis Myers playing an edgy solo that provides bite in all the right places, and Willie Mabon flashes an Otis Spann–flavored solo that pushes the tune into an even deeper groove. Jimmy obviously was feeling the spirit—he even sings an extra verse that wasn't on the Chess version. "Shelby County," another rare Jimmy gem, drips with Southern flavor. In a moment that creates sheer bewilderment, Jimmy sings one of the strangest verses ever. What he meant in the first two lines is anybody's guess, until upon closer observation you realize that he was improvising on the lyrics to "Kidman Blues," penned by Big Maceo Merriweather. Jimmy probably got the idea to sing it from either remembering the recording of Little Johnny Jones at the Aristocrat Records session in 1950, or he might have sung it as a result of being so close to Memphis Minnie, who also recorded a stellar version of it when she and Jimmy did their famed "lost" 1950 session together at Parkway:

I had a gal on my gal
a kid gal on my doggone kid
I've had so many doggone women
Boys, I can hardly keep it hid

On the final track, "Tricky Woman," the band percolates smooth and slow as Jimmy avoids a fast-talking woman's deceitful ways just in time to make his getaway.

On the same day as Jimmy's recording session, Jacques Morgantini maximized his opportunity and minimized his expenses by using the same backing band to record Willie Dixon's protégé, gritty blues vocalist Koko Taylor, for ten tracks. Taylor (whose real name is Cora Walton) had left Chess just as the label was making its final descent. As in Jimmy's recordings, the music captured between stops on the 1973 Chicago Blues Festival tour served to complement the five live tracks that were captured in a previous all-star concert on December 8. Koko's live set was recorded on December 1, at Casmir Hall in Amstelveen, Netherlands. All fifteen selections were eventually released as *South Side Lady*, her first solo outing after leaving Chess and just before embarking on her long and prosperous career with Bruce Iglauer's newly formed Alligator Records.

Jimmy once told a story about meeting the great big-band leader Louis Jordan in Paris while they were recording the music for Black & Blue. Jordan had dropped by to say hello and to see what was going on in the studio. At some point he decided he wanted to sit in on sax. Jimmy recalled the following events:

> Louis Jordan didn't like the electric bass. He never did like it. And when we was getting ready to record, he said he wouldn't record unless they could find an upright bass player. They looked for hours and couldn't find one. And [Dave] Myers, who was with me, he could play a bass and get the sound. So we went

in the studio and did our thing, and then we started a jam, you know—we were baitin' Louis, that's what we were really doing. And the sound came in and Louis started lookin' around, and he could hear. The old man got up there and worked—Worked out! First time in his life he played with an electric bass! He said, "man, you—that thing sounds like an upright." He say, "How do you do that, how do you get . . . ?" We had fun that day down there . . . so we really did a good album.[26]

Jimmy said he listened to the music for relaxation when he was at home. He never specified whether Jordan actually laid down tracks with them for posterity that day. There would be no other opportunities to play with Jordan, because almost a year and a half after the French session, Jordan died, on February 4, 1975. (Some of the material from this session eventually did get released, on the Aces CD of Louis Jordan, called *I Believe in Music*.)

The musical successes were not tragic for Jimmy in the 1970s, but strange twists of fate also befell a few other blues musicians. Blues mandolinist/guitarist Johnny Young unexpectedly died on April 18 from a heart attack. Bob Riedy once again stepped forward for the cause and held an all-star benefit at the Attic on May 7.[27] Jimmy was not in attendance, and one can only assume that he was out of town on another engagement. In late 1974 drummer Kansas City Red (real name Arthur Stevenson) was blinded in one eye, the result of a senseless brawl in a club called the Rat Trap Inn; Buddy Guy took a tumble and broke his arm while performing a stunt at the Checkerboard Lounge. Magic Slim's drummer, Steve Cushing (later to become a famed disc jockey for the award-winning radio show *Blues Before Sunrise*), was shot somewhere on Chicago's South Side. One of Otis Rush's sons was murdered, and Tampa Red had to be hospitalized after he lost his psychological balance as a result of his wife's death.[28]

Jimmy did have somewhat of a setback: he had ended his relationship with Shelter Records, a relatively premature separation that evidently arose over issues related to management. In summarizing the situation, Jimmy said, "It was all right. Leon Russell and I got along good. But he was stickin' too many irons in the fire. Fast as the money came in—well, he was investing it but things seemed to go sour on him. Freddie [King] made a few things for him and that was a pretty nice LP I cut for him. But I got a fairly decent buck out of *Gold Tailed Bird*. I got more out of that than any one record I did for Chess. He [Russell] gave me a fair shake on that one."[29]

By early 1975 Fritz Rau was spreading the rumor that there might be another American Folk Blues Festival in October of that year.[30] The last Lippmann and Rau festival tour had been in October 1972, and rumors about another upcoming festival were received with excitement. *Living Blues* ran an announcement that Jimmy Rogers was one of several artists being recorded by Dick Shurman for Advent Records.[31] This written statement more than likely was in reference to the *Chicago Blues at Home* project under the direction of Frank Scott, which had not yet been released. Although Jimmy and John Littlejohn had recorded their six songs for the album, Scott wanted more material from a wider variety of artists and was still setting up sessions with the Myers family. Although guitarist Louis and harp player Bob participated in this project, bassist brother Dave was absent. Meanwhile, Jimmy was preparing to launch his own new band with "Good Rockin'" Charles on harp and Sam Lay on drums.[32]

C. J. Records was an extremely small, independent label run by Carl Jones, located at 4827 South Prairie Avenue on Chicago's Southwest Side. Evidently Jimmy Rogers really wanted to have a single out on the air and in the streets, because his "Blues Falling" and "Broken Heart" (CJ 666) was released in early 1975 to try to garner interest some of the material found on the latest Shelter release. In actuality this was music taken straight from *Gold Tailed Bird:* "Broken Heart" was a thinly disguised "Broken Hearted Blues," and "Blues Falling" was "Bad Luck Blues." It didn't take long for record reviewers to figure out that the songs had been recycled from two years earlier. "Jimmy Rogers'[s] first single since 1959 would have made more exciting news if both sides hadn't already somehow appeared on his recent Shelter LP . . . still, this is good Chicago blues not in the same class as Rogers'[s] '50s classics, but a fair representation of his current music. Straightforward, unadorned blues vocals and guitar with support from Bob Riedy and the Aces."[33] Carl Jones later released a compilation album of songs culled from the small roster of artists on his label titled *C. J. Roots of Chicago Blues, Vol. 2.*[34] And of course, Jimmy's two sides, "borrowed" from *Gold Tailed Bird,* were on the LP, shining stars among the lesser lights of little-known artists.

Living Blues wrote the following about his status and whereabouts in early 1975: "Jimmy Rogers, whose comeback career has been less than spectacular, turned up playing second guitar in Sam Lay's band at a recent gig."[35] In the May-June issue of that same year, the latest Koko Taylor album by French label Black & Blue was given a not-so-great review. The album, *South Side Lady,* had been captured during the blues tour that Koko and Jimmy attended as featured artists. Like Jimmy's French album, it contained nine tracks, some live and others studio. "I'm sorry to say that this isn't the blues album everyone involved intended it to be," the reviewer wrote. "Jimmy Rogers'[s] rhythm can barely be heard . . . Aside from the fact that *South Side Lady* was poorly engineered and produced, I feel that although the musicians did their best . . . that just isn't enough to make this an essential purchase."[36] The writer then goes on to extol the virtues of Koko's first album for Bruce Iglauer's Alligator label, titled *I Got What It Takes*, released during this same period.

Although he had made a few successful moves, things weren't developing as quickly in Chicago as Jimmy had hoped since his reemergence. He decided to investigate the buzz on the street about some serious blues activity happening in a different city—Austin, Texas. Most of the talk focused on a man who, like Bob Riedy, was on a personal crusade to keep the blues alive and kicking. His name was Clifford Antone, and he was the owner of a new blues club in Austin, a city that traditionally had very little blues activity to speak of. He hoped his little blues joint would change all that.

Clifford Antone, born October 27, 1949, grew up in the eastern corner of Texas, in the coastal city of Port Arthur. As a youth he often crossed the border into Louisiana to hear a wide variety of gospel, blues, and Cajun groups perform in juke joints like Lou Ann's and the Big Oaks Club.[37] At those venues he got large doses of his favorite acts, first heard when he was a child. Clarence "Gatemouth" Brown, the Fabulous Boogie Kings, and Lazy Lester were just a few of the artists he dreamed of someday meeting and having a chance to work with.

In 1969, when Antone was twenty-one, he moved to Austin. Six years later, on July 15, 1975, in a rundown section of downtown Austin, he opened Antone's nightclub with his good friend, blues singer Angela Strehli. The former furniture warehouse, located at Sixth and Brazos Street, slowly earned the reputation as the place to be to hear blues at a time when the blues wasn't at all popular in Austin. Zydeco king Clifton Chenier, along with his Red Hot Louisiana Band, played the grand opening, which netted a crowd so large they ran out of ice, air conditioning, and just about everything else.[38]

What would be next? Clifford and Angela hadn't even given a thought about how to follow up the opening act, but after their unexpectedly huge success with Chenier, it was critical that they follow up big. Clifford realized that the 1970s was a dry period for bluesmen, not just in Austin but all across the country. Blues wasn't the "in" thing at the time; instead, disco was all the rage. Thinking quickly, he decided to offer extra special treatment to any Chicago blues legend who would come to his club, and he'd book them for an entire week each time they visited. "We were just blues nuts and that was all there was to it," Antone said. "We weren't trying to be shrewd businessmen. We just loved blues. It was simple."[39] His first offers went out to veterans like pianist Sunnyland Slim and guitarist Eddie Taylor, both of whom readily welcomed the opportunity to play.

When Sunnyland and Taylor went back to Chicago bragging about how well they were treated, other Chicago blues kings followed, a list that read like a who's-who in Chicago blues: Jimmy Rogers, Muddy Waters, John Lee Hooker, Big Walter, Pinetop Perkins, Jimmy Reed, Buddy Guy, Otis Rush, and Junior Wells. They also tried early on to book Howlin' Wolf as their biggest payday act, offering him five thousand dollars, but he died before the gig took place.[40] When a Fourth of July concert the following year, 1976, featured B. B. King and Bobby Blue Bland and drew large numbers, Clifford Antone knew he was onto something special.[41]

Within just a few months it became difficult to tell which city was Austin and which was Chicago. The heaviest hitters from the Windy City reveled in the opportunity to recreate the magic of the 1950s, when gigs were plentiful, money was flowing, and musicians were throwing down hot and heavy blues. It had been a long time since Jimmy had seen days like that, and he was leading the trek to Austin.

Harp ace Kim Wilson, co-founder of the Fabulous Thunderbirds, was on the scene when Jimmy Rogers did his first gigs there. Kim said, "The first time I met him in Antone's was in '75; I told everybody, 'I gotta be the guy to play with him.'"[42] Wilson knew how lucky he was for not having to travel all the way to Chicago to see his heroes; they were coming straight to him instead. He evidently wasn't too surprised at their arrival. "Back then there was no way that was happening in Chicago," he said. "Those veteran guys couldn't get work in Chicago. He [Jimmy] didn't have those kind of people behind him. That's why they were down there all the time. It didn't happen anywhere else."[43] Wilson also recalls that Jimmy wasn't alone when he arrived: "At first in the mid-seventies, Jimmy would bring down Richard 'Hubcap' Robinson when he came down for a few weeks at a time to do gigs at Antone's."[44]

Each time one of the legends would visit, Wilson somehow found a way to be on that stage with them. "It was like being in heaven," Kim boasted. "You sit back and pinch yourself—'goddam, I can't believe it.' After you pinch yourself, you gotta bear down. Because you got to be able to do it."[45] And he was able to do it—to run with the big dogs. It didn't take long for the word to spread about the hot new harp man who came not out of Chicago, but from Austin. Suddenly Wilson found himself in the throes of a mutual admiration society. As he recalled, "I was only twenty-four years old when those guys were raving about me; you gotta be really careful or that stuff would go to your head. Jimmy and Muddy said a lot of unbelievably good stuff about me to the press, which allowed me to work. It kept me going. It gave me inspiration."[46]

In August 1975, GRT, then based out of New Jersey, sold all that was left of their Chess holdings to All Platinum Records. Without enough money to produce new albums, GRT had been stalled for years and was reduced to recycling extant material. Meanwhile, back in Chicago, the old Chess building was sold, and more than 250,000 albums were completely destroyed (not to mention countless 45s, cassettes, and whatever else), signaling the end of an era.[47] After GRT sold Chess to All Platinum Records, the new owners moved fairly quickly to release Muddy Waters from his contract. Only three months after their purchase, on November 20 Muddy experienced—for the first time in his career—being dropped as an artist.[48] He was clearly rattled by the move but recovered quite nicely once the word got out that he was a free agent. It didn't take long for him to get picked up by Blue Sky Records.

In 1976 one of the first orders of business for All Platinum was to repackage the *already* repackaged Chess material they'd acquired from GRT. The company released their own version of Jimmy Rogers material, titled *Jimmy Rogers: Chess Blues Masters*. Located on the inside cover of the double album were liner notes written by Pete Welding, who had the task of summarizing the Chess Records' legacy of Jimmy Rogers: "[His] recordings were always characterized by a well-ordered simplicity and directness of expression. Spare, logical and free of gimmicks, they were carried forward by the solid, traditional-rooted intelligence of his songs, the effortless pulsation of his guitar lines and, above all, by the suave, emphatic yet unforced power and immediacy of his vocals. These virtues animate every one of the performances."[49]

Seven previously unreleased performances—as well as nine others heard only on the British Genesis collection—were included in this 1976 double-disc set, alongside nine other classic Rogers sides, making for a refreshing majority of new material among the twenty-five tunes.[50] By any standard this was an impressive package, and scores of fans were either reacquainted with or finally introduced to the fuller musical legacy of Jimmy Rogers.

Meanwhile, the French Black & Blue label also released a new Jimmy Rogers album in 1976. His songs from the 1974 album *That's All Right* were rereleased as volume 5 in a series of LPs called *The Blues Singers & Players Collection*. The music was similar to their previous release, except they added five tunes from both live and studio sessions on December 8 and 13 for side A: "I Can't Sleep for Worrying," "Mistreated Baby," "Slick Chick," "Pretty Baby," and "Left Me with a Broken Heart" were new contributions. The side B studio set from the previous album was kept intact for this 1976 issue.

Muddy's star was also rising again. His January recording of *Hard Again* was released in August 1977 and was highly successful. He and his band had just finished touring to promote the album when Bob Margolin, the guitarist in Muddy's band, caught Jimmy as he was sitting in with harp man Keith Dunn in

Providence, Rhode Island. When Margolin asked Jimmy if he had any greetings for Muddy, Jimmy responded by saying, "Anytime he wants to get together and play those old blues like we used to, I'd love to do that again."[51] Margolin said he got chills hearing that because, "Muddy and Jimmy's parts meshed like very creative lovers . . . 'lead' and 'rhythm' guitar designations didn't apply."[52] When Muddy got the news from Margolin, he too was open to the opportunity. Producer Johnny Winter made arrangements for the historic reunion to take place.

With Jimmy joining in on the fun, Bob Margolin would be moving over to the role of bass player, which he didn't mind in the least. Jimmy's fishing buddy and Muddy's longtime sideman Pinetop Perkins was already slated to play piano, and Willie "Big Eyes" Smith was holding down the drum chair. One of the biggest surprises in this reunion, though, was that Big Walter was also scheduled to join in. Muddy and Jimmy both knew Walter's penchant for drinking binges, so harp man Jerry Portnoy was installed as a backup in case Walter's proclivities got the best of him.

And so it was that Muddy, Jimmy, Pinetop, and Big Walter played the blues together the way blues were meant to be played. The album reunited the men in a way that a recording project had not done for twenty years. They started sessions in August at a studio in Westport, Connecticut. Bob Margolin, the one primarily responsible for putting the wheels in motion, said, "Watching what Jimmy played with Muddy was an amazing education for me."[53] He complimented Jimmy's generosity toward him when it came to explaining his simpatico technique that created the classic "old school" sound of the '50s.

Bob watched as Jimmy dropped his guitar from the key of E down to D for the title track, "I'm Ready," and effortlessly unleashed the patented licks heard on the original recordings of the '50s. Jimmy shared even more secrets when he told Bob he had first developed the contrapuntal lines on the tune "Good Morning Little School Girl" when he played with Memphis Minnie in the late 1940s.[54] (Muddy's arrangement was taken directly from Memphis Minnie's "Me and My Chauffeur Blues," a tune that Jimmy most likely played when he performed with Minnie in his early Chicago days.) On the tune "Rock Me" they stripped the band down to a quartet plus harp, with just Muddy and Jimmy intertwining their lines, just like old times, while Bob and Willie supplied rhythmic support.

Unfortunately, the most intimate moment of the entire session did not make the final cut to get on the album. Right before the tape rolls, Muddy exclaims, enthusiastically, "We gonna get this one, now take your time, take your time, we gonna *make it*!" Then Jimmy kicks off the tune with his classic three-note cluster. You can definitely hear the love and happiness in Jimmy's voice when he launches into the words of the first verse. And when he sings the line, "But that's all right," Muddy, who clearly couldn't resist himself, jumps in and says, "I *know* it's all right!"[55] This unexpected, unscripted comment apparently was the cue that Jimmy was looking for. It told him that everything really was all right between him and Muddy after all these years.

From that point on, the song became a vocal embrace between the two men, a musical confirmation of their love for each other captured permanently on wax. When Jimmy says he wonders who's loving his woman tonight, Muddy counters gleefully with, "You will never find that out, boy!" One can practically hear them smiling from ear to ear as the music swings in time.

As if providing a gift to Muddy, Jimmy suddenly decided to add a previously unrecorded verse, perfectly delivered in the throes of the moment:

You left me baby
you left me in a strain
you know you put me down
just to go with some outside man
but that's all right . . .

Things just kept getting juicier: Jimmy plays a beautiful single-note solo, and Muddy supplies a delicate counter-line that weaves above and below Jimmy's arpeggios. After Jimmy's solo, Muddy countered by singing the well-known second verse of the Rogers tune with such gusto, you'd think he'd written the tune himself. He calls Jimmy by name near the end of the verse as he wonders who's making love to his old lady, and Jimmy responds by saying, "I hear ya, Muddy!"

The back-and-forth banter between the two was priceless, with Muddy shouting, "Well, all right!" over Johnny Winter's solo. As if things couldn't get any better, Jimmy sings yet another original fourth verse, which sounded like it should have been there all along:

I love you baby,
I don't know why I should ["You should love her!" inserts Muddy]
You know you're going with every man
living in your neighborhood
but that's all right . . .

By the time the tune was over, the joy in the room was palpable, with congratulatory hugs and pats on the back all around. Sadly, this incredible rendition of "That's All Right" would not surface for almost thirty years, when Bob Margolin would finally unearth the tapes for a reissue album.[56]

Pinetop Perkins reflected on the rare recordings that he and Jimmy shared at a reunion with Muddy in the late '70s, and he reminisced with glee: "One of the best times I had was when me and Jimmy was in the studio. He [Muddy] had that boy Johnny Winter in there and Big Walter was there too. We had fun cutting that day. We also played with all those rock stars, the Rolling Stones, Eric Clapton, Bonnie Raitt, and Jeff Beck." Pinetop, in one simple phrase, summed up the reverence that the new breed of musicians had for Jimmy's legacy. "Them rock stars like Jimmy a lot."[57]

The rock stars were not the only ones who liked Jimmy. When Muddy was on the road, he'd sometimes travel with the band, as opposed to driving his own car or traveling by plane. On those occasions, if someone had music playing on the stereo cassette player in the vehicle, he'd announce, "Give me MY shit!"[58] Bob Margolin, Muddy's understudy, reminisced about those trips, explaining that Muddy's "shit" was one lone cassette. Side A was all Robert Johnson songs; side B was music from the entire *Chicago Bound* LP by Jimmy Rogers.[59] A single gesture like this by Muddy made mere words seem shallow—it said everything. When Jimmy heard about that, he was humbled.

Muddy knew good guitar playing when he heard it. Jimmy provided all he needed, and everyone else was second best. Muddy once told Margolin, "Don't ever play that again; it makes my dick sore." On another occasion, he also told Margolin that he played his guitar in a manner that was so annoying it sounded like someone stepped on a cat. Muddy said there were only two types of players: those who are born talented and those you can build with a hammer and nails.[60] He clearly felt assured that Margolin was talented; you don't offer gems like that to anyone except those that you love. This was why Buddy Guy and Junior Wells got slapped, literally, when they showed up at Muddy's surprise birthday party. It was Muddy's way of showing love, and you had to be closer than family to understand a gesture like that.

In 1978 Jimmy was performing regularly with drummer Sam Lay in a band called the All-Stars. In what might be described as a musical medicine show, Sam Lay had several different bands within the band. He allowed certain artists, like guitarist Willie Richard—better known as "Hip Linkchain"—to front his own band, as well as Jimmy. Richard was born near Jackson, Mississippi, on November 10, 1936. His father, a logger, was nicknamed "Long Linkchain" and Hip was originally called "Hipstick." His dad, along with his brother, Jug, played guitar. Hip began playing too after he moved to Chicago and bought his first guitar. By 1959 he had his own band, the Chicago Twisters, which included

Jug and the soul singer Tyrone Davis. Hip was also part of the house band at the Silver Dollar Lounge, backing Howlin' Wolf, Sonny Boy Williamson, and Muddy Waters in the early '60s.[61]

During this period Lay liked to travel with multiple rhythm section players. At times there were as many as three guitarists, two bassists, and two or three piano players, which obviously made the money pot smaller when payday came. Jimmy gradually found this kind of atmosphere a bit stifling and began seeking ways to establish his own band—at first locally, and then for the road. This is a description of one of the earliest incarnations of that particular Jimmy Rogers band as it was presented through the Sam Lay All-Stars tour package:

Guitar—Jimmy Rogers
Harp—Big Walter, then Joe Berson, harp (locally only)
Piano—Johnny "Big Moose" Walker or Pinetop Perkins
Guitar—"Left Hand Frank" Craig
Bass, vocals—Hayes Ware
Drums—S. P. Leary

Moose Walker, born June 27, 1927, was a multitalented musician who played guitar, tuba, vibes, and piano. He had played with Ike Turner's Kings of Rhythm in Clarkdale, Mississippi, as well as the King Biscuit Boys in Helena, Arkansas. He paid further dues touring with Lowell Fulson, Elmore James, and Sonny Boy Williamson as he made his way to Chicago at the urging of Sunnyland Slim. Once there, he connected with Earl Hooker.[62] It didn't take long for Jimmy and Moose to find each other and discover their musical compatibility (Walker had become a permanent teammate of Jimmy's once the two of them made their exit from this Sam Lay All-Star band).

Over the years there would be a high level of turnover in the Sam Lay All-Star lineup, which Jimmy never cared for; he would have preferred to have one group that played and stayed together like a family. On the lack of longevity among working bands, Jimmy said, "Those guys, they don't stick. Muddy Waters and myself, we stuck together better for all those long years together—Little Walter, Muddy, Elgin and myself—we stuck together better than any group that I know in Chicago . . . through thick and thin."[63] After all those years had passed, the original lineup still stood as his crowning achievement. "That's where we organized a good different sound on Muddy Waters from what he had been doing back when he was playing with Son House and others of that nature," Jimmy said. "We created him a fantastic style, and the old man is still kicking with it!"[64]

Jimmy was trying to recreate this fantastic sound with his current lineup during the early months of 1978, which included Left Hand Frank on guitar, Big Walter on harp, Fred Below on drums, and Rich Molina on bass.[65]

Molina, known to Jimmy as "Rick," played an instrumental role in booking a few gigs for the band during this time. According to Molina, "Big Walter introduced me to Jimmy one winter night, and I had been playing with Jimmy and Walter in and around Chicago. He [Jimmy] wanted to talk and see if we could get some gigs together and we did. I had a P.A., and a van to get the band to the gigs if needed." Jimmy's instincts were right on—Molina did have some outside sources that proved to be lucrative for the group. "In the late 1970s and early 1980s, I booked many gigs at a club in Springfield, Illinois, called Crows Mill School House," he remembered. "Jimmy said he would find us a drummer for that evening. I lived in Champaign-Urbana, so I drove to Chicago to pick the 'fellas' up, as Jimmy would call his stage lineup. I was surprised and I absolutely *flipped* when we pulled up to Fred Below's apartment to pick him up!"[66]

The band headed to the gig, located at Rural Route 3 on Toronto Road. "We were wearing light jackets—it wasn't very cold, it wasn't yet winter," Molina said. He also remembered that their setup was Left Hand Frank on the left, then Jimmy to his left. Next was Fred Below's drum set, in front of which sat Big Walter. Molina was to Walter's left, standing next to the P.A. system. At the start of the gig, Fred Below leaned over to Molina and told him with a wink and a nod of approval, "Hey, kid—get up right next to me and we will hold it down!" Molina just loved that. He even recalled the nicknames Jimmy gave to the band members: "He called Frank 'Lefty Frank,' Big Walter was 'The Old Man' or 'The Maestro of the Blues Harp,' and he called Fred Below 'The Best Blues Drummer.'" As for Rich, he humbly added, "Well . . . it was just 'Rick Molina on the bass.'" Molina had only positive things to say about the impact Jimmy made on him that evening. "Jimmy was a real gentleman and a real pro," Rich said fondly. "He wrote some great songs—his lyrics, his guitar licks and the way he sang was his own style—that was a great night of music."[67]

Jimmy was in Manchester and London, England, in the fall of 1978, performing gigs as a last-minute replacement for John Stedman, the owner of JSP Records. While there, he gave a revealing interview to Elaine Melish, a British newspaper reporter, about a wide range of topics. She was lucky to catch Jimmy in an extroverted moment, and he talked about the changes in the blues scene. "You have more white kids—22, 20, it goes up from there to maybe 50 sometimes," Jimmy quipped. "You see 'em, black and white, but it's mostly white be there." Melish also asked about why Jimmy was so suddenly popular on the East

Coast, particularly in the New England area. "The blues is coming alive again," Jimmy announced. "It dies off, then something else'll come in, and come right back to the old standard: it'll come back to jazz and blues."[68]

Jimmy continued dispensing his philosophy about the evolution of American music, declaring, "Rock 'n' roll came in, swept the country, and provided a different sound. But you have to make a record every week to get it goin', 'cause kids—their mind is just like the rock 'n' roll, it's movin'. Disco and what have you—their minds is travelin' so fast. You make a record this week, if you don't make another one before the end of the week," Jimmy humorously elucidated.[69]

Jimmy even spoke to Melish about the sensitive issue of racism, and although during the interview she never actually identified the topic as such, it didn't take much reading between the lines to know what he was getting at. In print the shift in conversation appears to come out of nowhere, go nowhere, and disappear into nothingness. But in actuality it was one of the rarest moments out of hundreds of interviews. Rogers expressed his personal views this way:

> They try all they can to shun it, really, try to sweep it under the rug, and then it hits them and they say, "there it is," you know, there's no way out. But I was facing reality at the time. I could see it going through my grandmother and my uncles, and other people that I know that were older. I could see what they were going through, you know, and they would talk to me. They had the feeling that maybe I understood, what they be talking about—but I did, I could SEE it. I didn't like it . . . I never liked the South. I like the weather okay, as far that goes, but I never did like it. And I always said, "as soon as I get big, I'm GONE. That's it."[70]

During the fall of 1978, *Living Blues* founder Jim O'Neal was responsible for organizing a band and convincing Jimmy to do a series of performances in Mexico City. Billed as the Jimmy Rogers Blues Band, the group featured Jimmy and Left Hand Frank Craig on guitars, Big Walter Horton on harp, and S. P. Leary on drums. The series of gigs were performed on behalf of CREA, an institute to help young people in Mexico.

Consequently, in October Jimmy got reacquainted with O'Neal, the man who'd given him his first exclusive and extended interview. O'Neal had somehow found himself in a unique situation where he would serve as an ambassador of sorts for a first annual blues festival. According to O'Neal:

> They had a blues festival in Mexico; I booked him on that. Blues Festival en Mexico was sponsored by a government youth organization. They sent some resident blues aficionados from Mexico City up to Chicago to meet with us—

this was when Amy [van Singel] and I were running the magazine—and we helped them. I took them around to all the blues clubs and made contacts with a lot of the bands. We ended up being the liaison for booking a lot of the acts—they would go through us. I got Muddy Waters, Willie Dixon, Lightnin' Hopkins, John Lee Hooker; I got all the good guys during that time. Walter Horton, Otis Rush.[71]

The Chicago legends played on October 12, 14, and 15.

In 1979 John Stedman, for whom Jimmy had filled in at the festival during the previous year, convinced Jimmy and Left Hand Frank to go into a studio facility as a duo to lay down a few fun tracks for his London-based record label, JSP. They recorded four tunes, three of which Jimmy contributed as originals—something Jimmy hadn't offered to a producer in years. On "Fishin' in My Pond" (recorded by Lee Jackson for Cobra Records), Jimmy used lyrics that could either be taken literally or viewed as a sizzling sexual metaphor, particularly when he refers to an intruder who's trespassing on his favorite pastime:

Oh yeah
somebody's fishing in my pond
catchin' all my fish
they must be burnin' up the barn[72]

When Jimmy sings the T-Bone Walker–inspired "Crazy Woman Blues," one can almost see the furrowed brows of every man who just can't believe the audacity of a woman who assumes too much of him. The snappy lyrics are delivered with some serious attitude as Jimmy boasts a couple of delicious little lines:

you can read my letters baby
but you sho' can't read my mind
someday you may look for me baby
I'll be somewhere way down the line[73]

Jimmy also used the recording opportunity to revive his original "Information Please," first recorded in a February 1972 Chicago studio session with the Bob Riedy Blues Band. The sparse, pared-down version really shows the dexterity of Jimmy's right hand, and you can actually hear his fingernails coaxing the rich tones from the strings, perfectly complementing his clear voice, unfettered by bass, drums, or harmonica in this rare setting. "Baby Please," on the other hand, was delivered in a relatively timid fashion by Left Hand Frank, although the vocals on his live set were far more rambunctious.

Later that same year, Stedman brought Jimmy and Left Hand Frank over on a European tour. Together with bassist Bob Brunning and drummer Ray Weston, they gave live shows at the 100 Club in London on September 22 and 23. "Take a Little Walk with Me" and "You're Sweet" simmered at medium-slow tempos. The quartet was buoyed by an enthusiastic and seemingly well-lubricated audience. It appears that the two guitarists, sensing the jovial mood of the crowd, were up to the task of going toe-to-toe with their constituents as the entire proceeding evolved (or devolved) and took on the feel of a loose jam session.

While the live version of "Rock This House" doesn't start out nearly as rockin' as his studio version, the tune picks up considerable steam as it moves along, even as Jimmy seems to be gradually losing his voice as the song progresses. It didn't help that Brunning and Weston failed to stick the landing at the end of the tune. Left Hand Frank clearly hadn't rehearsed the pickup band members on drums and bass when he delivered the raunchy lyrics contained in "Dirty Dozens," which features the highly repetitive phrase "mutha-fo'ya," used as the vulgar punch line at the end of each X-rated line. Frank belts out "Mean Red Spider" and "Oh Baby" with unabashed vocal technique, nearly causing him to surpass Jimmy's raspiness.

Sensing that they both needed to give their pipes a rest, Jimmy and Left Hand Frank launched into Frank's good-old standby, "Honky Tonk," although the liner notes identify the tune as "You Don't Have to Go," an understandable mistake made because of the patented Jimmy Reed shuffle and the tenor sax quote in "Honky Tonk" from the Reed melody. Jimmy dug deeper into his past glory as he dusted off "Chicago Bound" with relish, and the crowd showed their apprecia-tion with rapturous applause when the song was done. Meanwhile, the solo on "Blue and Lonesome" demonstrates how well the aggressive approach of Left Hand Frank works against Jimmy's laid-back vocal approach to the blues. From that material, combined with the four previous Chicago studio tracks, Stedman produced *Chicago Blues* (JSP 1008), releasing the disc in late 1979.

Back at home in Chicago, Jimmy was busy refining his band with the Sam Lay All-Stars. As in almost every blues band during this period, the person-nel was subject to change, depending on the availability—or lack thereof—of musicians. On harp was Little Joe Berson, and on piano was either Big Moose Walker or Pinetop Perkins, depending upon whoever was available. On guitar was Left Hand Frank, and the drummer was S. P. Leary. Bassist Frank Bandy joined the band in June 1979. Bandy's entrance to the Jimmy Rogers group was quite exciting for the newcomer. According to Frank, "Joe Berson and I were friends at that time; we'd played together in a band back in Florida called the Tampa Fred Blues Band. He had come up here [to Chicago] about a year and a half earlier. Little Joe was looking out for Big Walter—Walter was his mentor; Joe was his protégé. Joe told me if I came up here, he'd get me an audition with Jimmy. I came specifically to join the band."[74] Because Left Hand Frank was already in the band at the time, Frank Bandy became "Right Hand Frank," just to keep both heads from turning whenever someone yelled "Hey, Frank!"

Even though his purpose was clear, Bandy had no idea what awaited him when he arrived. What he originally thought would be a routine audition in a private setting turned out to be much more. "I drove up here on Memorial Day weekend in June of '79," Frank said. "It turned out that Big Walter needed a bass player with a van to drive him to a gig in Ann Arbor, Michigan, to play at the Blind Pig. I was supposed to play with Jimmy Rogers, and S. P. Leary on drums. I would be the bass player for the weekend, and this would serve as my audition for the Jimmy Rogers Band. We played the gig and it was absolutely fantastic."[75] Even after the gig was over, Bandy—still stunned—wasn't exactly sure whether or not he'd passed inspection. No one had yet confirmed or denied his membership, so he patiently waited for a signal. Bandy said, "I dropped Jimmy off—he lived at Ida B. Wells [an urban housing project on the South Side] at the time—he said he was looking for a bass player, and asked me if I would stick. I said, 'Absolutely, Jimmy, that's why I came to Chicago!' He said, 'Okay, little brother—you got the job.'"[76]

Bandy went right to work with the Jimmy Rogers All-Stars, playing in town at two of the best local blues clubs as well as making the out-of-town engagements. "We had a regular gig in Matteson, Illinois, on Tuesday nights," he recalled.[77] He enjoyed the thrill of playing with his idol, watching his every move and supplying the supportive bass lines as Jimmy swapped licks with Frank Craig. Bandy commented, "Although he [Jimmy] played lead on every song, he would alternate on every song—he liked to have a fiery lead on songs, and Left Hand Frank was a really good guitarist."[78] Bandy's relationship with Jimmy blossomed in short order as they spent time talking during some of the longer road trips.

These were the times when Rogers—if he was in the mood—shared bits and pieces of his personal life with members of the band. Bandy was one of the people Jimmy felt comfortable with, because Bandy showed genuine interest in getting to know him as a man, not just as a musician. "I used to ask him what he liked for music; he said he liked Big Bill Broonzy," Frank said. When Bandy asked about when and how Jimmy began playing guitar, "he said he got his first guitar selling seeds. His grandmother helped him get the seeds, and helped him buy his first guitar. I think it was a Kay."[79]

Then Bandy asked about the good old days with the Muddy Waters band: "I asked Jimmy about Otis Spann once. He told me they would pick up Spann, and he [Spann] would cry and cry because he didn't want to leave his wife [Lucille]." Bandy also mentioned a rarely told story about an onstage incident that happened one particular night when Otis was on the gig: "S. P. Leary told me once that he got mad at Spann because he thought Spann took his drink, and he got up and punched Spann right off the piano stool. They sent him [Spann] home for that." Bandy was enjoying the high-profile performances he played with Jimmy as the band got more and more exposure in front of the hometown crowd. "The ChicagoFest on Navy Pier was one of the first gigs we did that year," Bandy recalled. "I remember they had several stages, a blues stage, a rock stage. It was sponsored by Olympia Beer. The festival would go on for about a week. Jimmy told me, 'Hey, take "Little Jimmy" [his son] down there to hear some of those rock bands, that's what he likes.'"[80]

For the piano chair Jimmy used Big Moose Walker. "At B.L.U.E.S. [located at 2519 North Halsted Street] and Lilly's [2513 North Lincoln Avenue]—both places had pianos," Bandy said.[81] "Pinetop had recently left the Muddy Waters band, and most of those guys had come home to Chicago. So he alternated between Pinetop Perkins and Moose."[82] Jimmy's roster was undergoing a few other changes as well. "S. P. Leary was starting to slow down a bit in '79, so Jimmy replaced him with Dean Haas, [who'd been] around Chicago for many years. Dean didn't like to travel. When we traveled, Fred Grady did some gigs, then Jimmy settled in on Ted Harvey. He became the drummer 'til the end."[83]

Bandy has some great stories that came along with riding shotgun with Rogers. Several of them involved short excursions to indulge Jimmy in his favorite pastime. "This guy booked Jimmy in '79 at a place called Littlejohn's in McHenry, Illinois," Bandy remembered. "The guy's name is Elmer, nicknamed 'Grubb.' The five-piece band was me, S. P. Leary, Little Joe, Left Hand Frank, no piano player. We went up early in the day because Jimmy and Left Hand wanted to fish. They had these five-gallon buckets. Me, Jimmy, and Left Hand went together. They both caught a bunch of fish and brought them back with them; they were good at it."[84]

During the third quarter of 1979, in the late summer days of August, Jimmy traveled to the West Coast to participate in the annual San Francisco Blues Festival, a yearly event that had begun in 1973; it now served as the West Coast counterpart to that highly successful Midwestern gathering, the Chicago Blues Festival. Back in the 1960s, blues in the Bay Area was so popular that it had become the foundation for the burgeoning rock movement that was rapidly spreading up and down the California coast. "Prior to the '60s, the band shell in Golden Gate Park was the location for classical and brass bands to perform on Sunday afternoons. Needless to say, the '60s changed all that!" recalled Jerry Haussler, photographer for the '79 festival.[85]

Festival producer Tom Mazzolini boasted in his liner notes to the album that chronicled the festivities, "The audience was unbelievable. We had to turn away thousands of people from the packed little theatre on the edge of lower Haight Street . . . They wanted to hear the blues!"[86] Jimmy, as it turned out, was the very first Chicago blues musician to grace the festival's stage, and Mazzolini was both proud and honored to have secured the arrangement, bringing the real deal to his crowd, many of whom had never witnessed an authentic Chicago blues performance. The fans got a double dose, as Jimmy brought along his longtime homeboy Louis Myers to accompany him on guitar. With local artists Mark Naftalin on piano, Byron Sutton on bass, and Lee Hildebrand on drums serving as the backing rhythm section, the band took the stage on August 12 to enthusiastic applause.

It was immediately apparent that Jimmy was in a good mood, as he acknowledged the crowd with thanks and appreciation for the chance to be in San Francisco, "swingin' and singin' the blues." Jimmy then hit the audience with what eventually became his most famous declaration: "If you can't dig the blues, you must have a hole in your soul!" He quickly kicked off the set by introducing "House Rocker" as a tune "in the key of G—as in 'girl!'" During the course of the tune, Louis Myers laid down some juicy jazz riffs underneath Jimmy's boogie shuffle. "Ludella" was next, delivered at a slow, sensual pace that allowed Mark Naftalin to insert some tasty piano riffs à la Pinetop as Jimmy crowed the lyrics with gusto.

He was now flirting with the audience as he introduced his next number. "You're so sweet—hahaaaa! Sweet, sweet, sweet . . . each and every one of you, I love ya." For the introduction to his biggest hit, "That's All Right," Jimmy entertained the audience with a short story about falling for a woman who hurt him with lies, concluding, "She put another star in my crown, but now I can make it." They hung on his every word. He had them in the palm of his hand, and he knew it. During Jimmy's announcement of his final tune, "Walkin' by Myself," he was pleasantly interrupted by unrestrained applause, prompting him to preface the song with the personalized comment, "I been walkin' by myself a long time . . . I gotta have somebody to walk with me." The audience's response clearly indicated they were most happy to accompany him. Not only was Louis Myers onstage with him, but also Chicago guitar flash Luther Tucker was there as a guest, invited by festival producer Tom Mazzolini. "If I recall correctly, he was called out about half way through Jimmy & Louis' set," said photographer Jerry Haussler.[87] After the set was over, Jimmy relaxed backstage behind the Golden Gate Park band shell, sitting comfortably between his two pals Louis Myers and Luther Tucker. With his white patent leather shoes planted squarely in front of him and a beer placed at his feet, Jimmy sported a huge grin on his face as Myers and Tucker draped their arms around his broad shoulders. Jimmy was never really walkin' by himself, anyway—he had his homeboys with him.

As successful as the festival appeared on the surface, Haussler put it all in perspective: "1979 was the beginning of the end for the free San Francisco Blues Festival. It was initially paid for—over an eight-year run—on grant money. That all ran out after Proposition 13—a property tax overhaul."[88] Jimmy definitely sent them out on a high note.

10

FEELIN' GOOD

The blues goes in cycles. Sometimes they're red
hot. Then they about to die. But somebody's
always out there strugglin' to keep them goin'.
Now they're comin' back.

—Jimmy Rogers

In Chicago, Jimmy Rogers held court in local clubs with his usual lineup of musicians, which included Joe Berson on harp, Big Moose Walker on piano, Left Hand Frank Craig on guitar, Right Hand Frank Bandy on bass, and S. P. Leary on drums. The band took a few short tours throughout the Midwest during the late 1970s, but by the time the '80s arrived, the East Coast fully embraced the music they'd largely ignored during the '50s. "There was a huge interest in blues for a while here in this area," said bassist Michael "Mudcat" Ward, a well-known musician from the Boston area who played with the also locally popular blues guitarist Ronnie Earl. As for himself, Mudcat's reputation was about as large as Earl's when it came to rubbing shoulders with the legends. "I played with Buddy Guy and Junior Wells, Otis Rush, J. B. Hutto, Big Walter—they'd be coming from Chicago constantly," Ward recalled.[1]

Jimmy was another Chicago musician who had been known to venture into the yet unconquered East Coast territory. With only Richard Hubcap Robinson as his sidekick, he had gone up to scout out a few venues that he might have a chance at performing in at a later date. Now his legwork was beginning to pay off. The hot spots included clubs like the Bottom Line in New York City, the Speakeasy in Cambridge, the Tam in Boston, Lupo's in Providence, and the Knickerbocker in Westerly, Rhode Island. From a practical standpoint it was financially cost-prohibitive to bring along the entire Chicago band with him when he lined up his first series of East Coast gigs. It would be easier to just ride the new wave of fascination with blues among the young lions already there waiting for him, hungry for an opportunity to get an authentic taste of playing the Chicago blues.

Consequently, Jimmy kicked off his mini-tour using musicians who were familiar with the East Coast as home turf. Through a New England area promoter he'd made very strong connections with several players who introduced him to the movers and shakers of the club scene in several major cities like Boston; Providence; Portland, Maine; and New York City. Jimmy's East Coast band was comprised of members from two local blues bands who knew his music well, the Excellos and the Bluetones.[2] The Excellos were led by Philly-born harp player Steve Guyger, while members of the Bluetones included harp player Sugar Ray Norcia and Mudcat Ward.

Mudcat remembered the days when he first encountered Rogers:

> I met Jimmy Rogers in late '78 or early '79. He came up to New England by himself to play with East Coast guys. I met him when I was playing with Ronnie Earl at a club called the Met Café in Providence, Rhode Island. He was traveling with his drummer, Hubcap. Jimmy didn't have a band at that time, and hadn't for a while; he was just looking to make a little money. I think Hubcap had a girlfriend up here at the time. The two of them came in, and about a month later we had some gigs. So me, Ronnie, and our piano player hooked up with Jimmy and Hubcap. We played about two weeks' worth of gigs, at the Speakeasy in Cambridge and Lupo's in Providence. He came back with Hubcap again later, then again without him.[3]

The two bands had specifically asked for Jimmy to come to the East Coast and allow them to play with him. And when they hit the stage, they motivated him to "take the music to its highest levels," according to a local Boston paper, as he in turn motivated them to play the blues in the classic '50s style: "Good drive, moderate volume, hesitating the second and fourth beats, and short, rhythmic soloing in keeping true to Rogers'[s] earlier style . . . a refreshing compliment to him and a nod to a simpler, more relaxed musical era."[4]

On Friday and Saturday, February 22–23, Jimmy performed at Tramps, one of the most popular venues in New York City. So popular was this trendy nightclub that it attracted the legendary leader of the Rolling Stones, who, according to the Weekly *Soho News*, was in attendance that night: "The house was packed and the audience, which included blues enthusiast Mick Jagger, were surprisingly familiar with much of Rogers'[s] material."[5] Jimmy made an extra effort not only to deliver the tunes that the audience expected night after night but also to offer them a variety of lesser-known tunes that had been shelved by Leonard Chess at the height of his run during the Chess years.

In addition, Jimmy augmented his sets with a carefully selected roster of blues standards that, although not penned by himself, meshed perfectly within the format of his set. Performing other people's music came quite naturally to him, and yet he was always able to put his unique touch on a tune to deliver it in his own inimitable style. Robert Palmer, author of *Deep Blues*, acknowledging Jimmy's efforts, wrote the following comments the following Monday for the *New York Times*: "He was always a thoughtful lyricist and an expressive but understated singer, and his late show on Saturday night spotlighted both these qualities. It was refreshing to hear a set that included little-known originals and intelligently selected blues standards along with a few of the artists' better-known tunes, instead of the predictable programming of warhorses and greatest hits one gets at too many blues performances."[6]

Palmer went on to describe Jimmy's overall demeanor on the bandstand as an artist who "isn't the sort of intense blues artist who wears his heart on his sleeve," insinuating that Jimmy's vocal delivery was smooth rather than rough-edged like some other bluesmen. About his guitar skills and his singing, Palmer summed up by conceding that Jimmy's "punchy guitar playing made up in rhythmic acumen and blues feeling what it lacked in virtuosity, and his slightly sweet, slightly pungent, full-toned vocal quality was a constant delight."[7]

During an intermission in this strong performance in front of a blues-thirsty crowd with pleasantly discriminating tastes, Jimmy, dripping with sweat, retreated from the stage for a brief but welcome rest. Backstage he was more chatty than usual, providing fodder for Palmer on a wide range of topics. He reminisced about finally playing with his Mississippi childhood heroes in Chicago; the rough clubs he'd frequented to make a living; the "Juke" saga with Little Walter; the rock 'n'roll push that Chuck Berry received from Leonard Chess ("When he cut [recorded] him, *bango!*"); the reason for his withdrawal from the music scene ("my kids was growing and it was getting more and more expensive"); and, finally, the cab driver and clothing store manager roles he pursued upon his retirement. After a final statement announcing the upcoming release of the JSP recording of the 1979 collaboration with Left Hand Frank, Jimmy ended the bull session with the somber statement, "Time keeps marching on," as he led the procession back toward the stage.[8]

At some point during that week, Jimmy found time to play at the Bottom Line with Tracy Nelson, who was also on the bill. Jimmy was actually the opening act, which "didn't seem right to me," said Steve Guyger, an experienced Philadelphia-bred harp player. Bassist Mudcat Ward agreed: "That was backwards—*she* even said it wasn't right."[9] In any event, they performed two shows a night, starting at 9:00 and midnight, with admission set at $7.50.[10] On February 27, Jimmy played at Jonathan Swift's in Cambridge, Massachusetts, and later at the Kearsarge Hotel in Portsmouth, New Hampshire. Guyger remembered the impact Jimmy's music had on his playing, ten years before he'd joined the East Coast tour and a number of years before he'd met Jimmy. "Man, I was so far into the blues it was ridiculous," Steve said. "I had gotten *Chicago Bound* and I had the *Gold Tailed Bird* album. When I first heard Jimmy, I thought, 'This is the guy I want to be with!'" Since he lived in North Philadelphia, Guyger found a unique way to get in touch with Jimmy in Chicago. "I wrote Jimmy a letter," said Steve. "I had read that article about him in *Living Blues* in 1973. I was in love with Jimmy's playing, so I thought what the hell, why not take a chance! His wife, Dorothy, wrote me back. I wind up seven years later finally playing with him."[11]

Steve was making regular visits to Chicago in the late 1970s, which was when he first met Jimmy. "I had a friend of mine who didn't live far from me back in Philly, [bass, guitar, and harmonica player] Richie Yescalis," Guyger recalled. Yescalis spent the summer of '73 in Chicago, because he'd turned twenty-one and was old enough to go into bars. He found and followed Big Walter around like a shadow. When Yescalis returned to Philly, Steve asked his friend about his experience in the blues city. Then in '76, they went together to Chicago, and Richie got a job as a cook at a club called Kingston Mines. The first time Steve saw Jimmy perform, he recalled, "had to be at Elsewhere's in Chicago in 1978. Joe Berson was on harp. Big Walter used to come in and sit in a lot."[12]

Guyger wasn't an official member of the Rogers group just yet, but he was close, and he could tell that Jimmy had already taken a liking to him; it was just a matter of timing now. "We started hanging out, and in early 1980 he was playing in New York," Steve said. "I hadn't joined the band yet. He had another harmonica player from Boston playing with him named Barbecue Bob [Maglinte]."[13] Barbecue Bob Maglinte was another East Coast harp player who'd mastered the Chicago style. Jimmy hadn't actually hired him as a full-fledged member, either, but he'd been doing gigs with Jimmy on and off since the '70's.

The opportunity for Steve to play with Jimmy came when Barbecue Bob quit the band. East Coast drummer Ola Dixon recommended Steve, who sometimes came up from Philly to watch her play with former Muddy Waters harp player Paul Oscher, and they had become very good friends. "Hey, *that's* your man," Ola told Jimmy, referring to Guyger as a replacement for Barbecue Bob.

"I wanted a good harp player for Jimmy, and Jimmy needed one," she said.[14] Jimmy, remembering Guyger from the letter, took Ola's advice and hired him. For Guyger it was a lifelong dream, and it didn't take long for the bond to grow strong between him and Jimmy. "By the time we hooked up in 1980, we were like father and son," Guyger recalled. "I just had such a great time with him. It was the first time I was on the road, and I was already 27!"[15]

Jimmy's band now consisted of Ola Dixon on drums, Michael "Mudcat" Ward on bass, George Lewis on guitar, and Steve Guyger on harp. "We would do three-week tours with Jimmy. George Lewis would book these gigs; he'd get Ola Dixon and Steve Guyger from Philly," said Mudcat, who remembered how it all started. "Anthony Geraci played with Jimmy, who called him 'Ant.' Ant was playing with Ronnie Earl and Sugar Ray at the time."[16] Boston guitarist George Lewis was a well-connected East Coast mover and shaker—a character who was able to "make things happen"—and was well known for maintaining personal relationships with some key New York club owners. Ola Dixon credited him for giving Jimmy the opportunity to play at Tramps, a premier club. According to several accounts by members of the band, Lewis wasn't much of a guitarist, but he knew quite a few people. Mudcat said, "George . . . he had money and means; he would take this attitude like he was the biggest, baddest musician out there. He wanted a gig at the Bottom Line. He figured if he got Jimmy Rogers, he'd get in there. George was the one that was paying everybody, so we did it."[17]

Mudcat was designated as the driver. "I had a Chevy van with three rows of seats, the whole band was in it, and I'd drive . . . we drove all over. We would travel from club to club." Mudcat remembers one particular event when he saw a different side of Jimmy. "One of those trips he brought his wife. We'd ride around in the van. He said he wanted martinis! I got a cooler with ice, and plastic martini glasses; he was mixing drinks. He could drink out of a bottle at any time, but there was this 'elegant' side to him when his wife was around, which was funny."[18]

By the time summer rolled around, Jimmy had established a strong foothold in New England. He did it with the help of concert promoter Paul Kahn, who booked Jimmy on a two-week tour up the coast.[19] Jimmy even canceled his European tour that year, preferring to bolster his reputation with the East Coast clientele for future bookings that extended throughout the summer and into the fall. The tour started with the two nights of June 27 and 28 at Mr. Kite's in Camden, Maine. The band was scheduled to perform two days later on the *Good Day Show*, a local morning television show on Channel 5 in Boston.

From July 2 through 5 the band performed at Sandy's Jazz-Blues Revival in Beverly, Massachusetts; Two Mattoon in Springfield, Massachusetts; and Café

Northern Lights in White River Junction, Vermont, for two nights. They then hit Portsmouth, New Hampshire, for two nights at the Kearsarge House on July 8–9, and on July 10 the Tam, a popular club in the Boston suburb of Brookline, Massachusetts. There, before a packed house, Jimmy threw down in front of blues diva Koko Taylor and her entourage. John Hubner wrote for the *Boston Phoenix* the following week: "Rogers pulled out all the stops. When he sang blues ballads like 'That's All Right,' his voice was soft, clear, and full of pain. People listened carefully. On up-tempo numbers like 'Rock This House' . . . Rogers performed dazzling guitar runs with ease. The dance floor was mobbed, and when the song ended, the dancers faced the bandstand and applauded, holding their hands above their heads."[20]

Later, in a kitchen apartment in Cambridge, Jimmy sat for an interview for the *Boston Phoenix*, where he again relaxed and reflected upon his storied past. He also revealed that he was enjoying the present, saying, "Things are comin' together real good. The band is a happy family, just like the old Muddy band. I got some ideas for new songs, and I will explore them." He was gaining momentum, and he could feel it. His popularity was at an all-time high, and his band was working more than ever. Fully realizing that he was in the midst of a triumphant tour, he coolly deflected any notions of slowing down, saying, "There may be snow on the mountain, but there's a fire inside."[21]

Jimmy became philosophical when asked to summarize why his popularity was so overwhelming during this stretch. "The blues goes in cycles," he said. "Sometimes they're red hot. Then they about to die. But somebody's always out there strugglin' to keep them goin'. Now they're comin' back." He seemed proud to be one of the last men standing. "Me and Muddy are the only ones from the first band still playin' . . . I'm so pleased to be feelin' good and playin' the blues for so many nice people."[22]

Indeed, Jimmy played night after night for the appreciative East Coast crowds. It was Harpo's on Friday, July 11, in Newport, Rhode Island, from 10 'til closing;[23] Tramps in New York City; then on to the Knickerbocker in Westerly on Sunday, July 13. In Maine they hit Jetty's in Bar Harbor from July 15 to July 17, followed by two nights at the Cellar Door in Auburn. On Wednesday, July 23, Jimmy and his four-piece backing band of Guyger, Dixon, Lewis, and Ward opened in Washington, D.C., at Desperado's, again to a packed house. After Guyger led a few tunes, including Little Walter's "Last Night" to open the set, Jimmy strolled onto the stage and used the clarion bell tones of the opening phrase of "That's All Right" to kick off his portion of the show. The band went on to deliver gems like "Ludella" and "You're the One" with fire.

Columnist Michael Joyce of the *Washington Post* praised Jimmy's work, saying, "Compared to younger blues guitarists entranced by speed and volume, Rogers'[s] subtle embellishments are genuinely refreshing." He ended his article by complimenting Jimmy's "discriminating technique," which, according to Joyce, "reflected his long-held philosophy that for some guitarists, less really is more."[24] The group ended the busy tour with a gig at the Hideaway in Front Royal, Virginia. The band members worked hard and, according to a few accounts, played hard too. They all admired Jimmy's ability to consistently make good music while simultaneously maintaining a comfortable and casual atmosphere on and off the bandstand. "I couldn't ask for such a nicer person to be on the road with," Guyger said. "He was just a regular, down-to-earth person—*very* intelligent."[25]

Two years earlier Jimmy had played the San Francisco Blues Festival. When the live album that captured the music of Golden Gate Park was released in 1981, Jimmy was given the entire first side of the LP on volume 2 of the series. Frank Bandy made a quick observation about the performance on one particular tune: "On 'Walkin' by Myself,' when Jimmy played it at the San Francisco Blues Festival, they had a different chord progression; Gary Moore's [version of "Walkin' by Myself"] went up to the V chord. I asked Jimmy, 'Which way should we do it?' 'Always play my stuff the way we did it in the Chess days. If you're playing with some influential guy, do it however they want to, but if you're with *me*, do it the way it is on the record.'"[26]

In 1981 Jimmy still had the following lineup as his primary band: Joe Berson, harp; Big Moose Walker, piano; Left Hand Frank Craig, guitar; Right Hand Frank Bandy, bass; and S. P. Leary, drums. Bandy was impressed with the lineup, particularly the harp player. "In the early '80s we played at the Zoo Bar in Lincoln, Nebraska," Bandy recalled. "Joe [Berson] had a huge tone." Bandy also reported that Left Hand Frank had then left the band and moved to Massachusetts. "For a short time after that Jimmy used Brewer Phillips from Hound Dog Taylor's band," Bandy remembered. "We went from Chicago, to Minneapolis, to Kansas City, two to three nights in Omaha, then Lincoln, Nebraska, then back to Chicago. Carey Bell played harmonica on this tour with us. After that tour Jimmy let Brewer go and hired Hip Linkchain after we got back."[27]

According to Bandy, Jimmy had a regular routine whenever he returned home from his successful tours—two specific clubs that he preferred. "He played one to three nights at B.L.U.E.S in Chicago at 2519 North Halsted, either weeknights or weekends, Friday through Saturday," said Bandy. "Bill Gilmore owned B.L.U.E.S., and Jimmy had me handling the bookings for him for that club. The other—Lilly's—was a weekend gig. Both places had a piano, so he used Pinetop and Big

Moose Walker; Sunnyland did a few nights at Lilly's, but we did an extraordinary amount of gigs with Pinetop and Moose."[28]

Things were going well for Jimmy when he was hit with two personal losses. His longtime friend and part-time bandmate Big Walter Horton died on December 8, 1981, at the age of sixty-four. It was a major blow to Jimmy, who loved Big Walter's playing, saying often that when Walter was on, absolutely no one could touch him, not even Little Walter Jacobs. Jimmy had played alongside Horton on Big Walter's last European performance (and one of the very last performances of his life) at the Blues Estafette Festival in Utrecht, Holland, in December 1981, less than a week before Horton passed away.

Then another personal friend passed—Fred Jones, the brother of Floyd Jones. At a tribute concert at B.L.U.E.S., Jimmy and Floyd performed and reminisced about Fred. Jimmy recollected, "Yeah, me and Floyd and Eddie Taylor, we used to go to Fred's house . . . and cook and eat up all his food!" Floyd then leaned over to whisper something in Jimmy's ear. Jimmy cleared his throat and somberly announced, "I've got this special request, and I've got to do this for him."[29] With all the passion he could muster, he launched into "Walkin' by Myself" as a tribute to Fred Jones.

By early to mid-1982, Jimmy Rogers—for the second time—was also officially a part of the Sam Lay All-Star Revue. Sam Lay still maintained his time-honored tradition of featuring several members of the ensemble within his main group, but he also allowed them to front their own bands within the All-Star entourage. According to several sources, Lay's band was set up in sort of a pyramid, with Sam Lay as the leader at the top and two generals underneath him. Jimmy Rogers was second in command, and either parallel to or slightly underneath Jimmy was George "Wild Child" Butler. Born on a plantation in Autaugaville, Alabama, in 1936, Butler grew up playing a harp he made out of a Prince Albert tobacco can, since he couldn't afford a real one that cost $1.36. He returned to Chicago in 1969, where he joined Mercury Records. (He would also go on to record for the Roots label in the late 1970s, under the direction of former Chess producer Ralph Bass.) Butler and Jimmy had been playing together informally for a few years as part of the Sam Lay tour package. While performing as part of Jimmy's band, Butler had his own spot in the show to front his own group. To complicate matters even further, guitarist Hip Linkchain also had the ability to take the lead role when he wasn't serving as backup to Jimmy's band.

There were, then, somewhere between two and three configurations functioning as separate entities. From what can be ascertained by some who were present during the round-robin roster of musicians, the 1982 installment of the

Sam Lay All-Stars included the following lineup: Sam Lay, drums; Joe Kelly, guitar; Dave Clark, bass; and a tall, lean German guy named Chris Rannenberg on piano, who was recruited somewhere along the tour. Jimmy Rogers, who played with Sam at various points during the tour, also used his own band by late in 1982: Hip Linkchain, guitar; Mark "Madison Slim" Koenig, harp; and Johnny "Big Moose" Walker, piano.[30]

The large traveling ensemble had the feel of a blues caravan, medicine show, and carnival all rolled into one. But make no mistake—the music was no laughing matter; the blues revue was serious business, and Sam Lay was hell on wheels when it came to demonstrating his talent for successfully barnstorming across the country. The interchangeable personnel, however, made it a bit complicated to decipher who was playing with whom, since at different points a few of them—like Lay, Rogers, Clark, or Walker—might have played with every group, while others played with only one or two. What made it even more difficult to sort out was how different players revolved in and out of the Lay band over the years, while others simply switched allegiances with the band over time, playing exclusively for a time with either Lay, Rogers, Butler, or Linkchain.

Chuck Goering, better known as "Barrelhouse Chuck," was born July 10, 1958, in Columbus, Ohio. He grew up fast when he moved to Florida, playing piano there with Bo Diddley. At the time, Chicago piano kings Little Brother Montgomery and Sunnyland Slim were his idols. "I started listening to Muddy Waters since I was nine years old," Chuck said. He had a couple of connections to the Windy City, the strongest being Little Joe Berson, a friend he'd made back in Florida. According to Chuck, "I met him when I was sixteen, when I was in Gainesville, playing for $10 a night in juke joints. Joe was from Brooklyn. He was just like Little Walter: he would fight in a minute."[31]

Chuck dreamed of doing something big with his life, and Chicago represented a chance to meet the heroes he had grown up admiring. "I heard that Sunnyland Slim was playing in Chicago," Chuck recalled, "and Little Joe Berson would play as Big Walter's apprentice." Joe had a huge impact on Chuck, who wanted to run with the big boys in the big city like Berson did. "He was like my big brother," Chuck stated. "He went there in '75. He told me he was going to Chicago. I said, 'Can I go with you?' He said, 'Hell, no!' He came back a coupla years later and said, 'I'm playin' with Jimmy Rogers—Do you know how cool that is?'"[32]

Coincidently, Right Hand Frank Bandy also knew Chuck from back in Florida during the early part of the '70s, before he himself had made the move to Chi-Town. "Chuck and I were playing in a band called Red House," Bandy said. After repeated requests, Berson gave Barrelhouse the green light and told him to make the trek, even though he wasn't going to be playing in the Rogers band. The invitation came with a huge caveat. According to Chuck, "He told me, 'When you come here, people are going to hate you.' I said 'Why?' He said, ''cause you're with *me*!'"[33]

Goering gave further details, saying, "I came down to Chicago in '77, and I moved in the same place as he was when I first came to Chicago to play with Joe while he was playing with Jimmy. I stayed at the Tokyo Hotel, $24 a week, room 1106; Joe was in 1117 down the hall. I was working at B.L.U.E.S. on Halsted since 1979." Chuck's reputation spread quickly, and before he knew it he was a regular at Lilly's too. It was there that he saw firsthand the power of the great Big Walter. "Big Walter was playing the most wickedest shit ever," Chuck declared.; "He made the top of my head go numb, I swear." Chuck also saw just how dangerous his mentor, Joe, could be, as he watched Berson deliberately provoke the legend just to get a rise out of him. Chuck said, "He'd get up and play all of Walter's stuff—'Hard Hearted Woman,' 'Walter's Boogie,' everything—note for note. He'd say, 'Check it out, man—I'm gonna make the muthafucka *play* tonite!' He'd piss Walter off, and then Walter would grab the mike and say, '*This* is how it's done, mutha*fucka*!' He would get up and blow the most amazing shit *ever*."[34]

Barrelhouse was back at the hotel cooling his heels on an off night when he received an unexpected phone call from Sam Lay. "In 1982 he called me up," Chuck recalled, "and said, 'I'd like for you to go on the road with me for a month.' I asked, 'Who do you have in the band with you?' He said, 'I got Jimmy Rogers . . .' I said, 'That's good enough for me!'"[35] Thus, Barrelhouse Chuck was added to the equation, taking the place of Big Moose Walker, who had recently suffered a stroke and was physically hampered by the lingering effects. Barrelhouse recounted his impressions of the band members. Sam Lay, for starters, was an outgoing personality with a physicality that definitely left an impression. Lay, a truly soulful brother of the '70s, had a look that reflected the psychedelic era that typified the decade. Along with some pretty hip and funky clothing, "Sam had this huge, wild Afro," according to Chuck, who later came to realize that the look was eerily similar to the legendary rock 'n' roller Little Richard's hairstyle—and so were some of Lay's band-leading techniques.

Chuck had never seen characters like the ones he was about to join. Much of what he experienced in the upcoming years he would find hilarious; some of it he wouldn't. For example, one time Dave Clark and Barrelhouse Chuck were standing outside as they were loading the car for an upcoming road trip. A small group of black guys—apparently thinking these two "white dudes" had maybe wandered onto the wrong side of town—decided to send a message and lobbed a wine bottle directly across the street, which shattered violently at Dave and Chuck's feet. They told Sam about it, and Sam immediately took up for his blues brothers and went to get reinforcements to deal with the culprits. "He went and got a Thompson Machine gun, and said, 'I hope those goddamn sonsabitches come back! I got grenades, too. These bullets cost me a lot of money.' And this was the very first time I met him!"[36]

Sam Lay and the All-Stars, a relatively large ensemble, traveled north through the mountains several times on various Canadian tours, through Saskatchewan, Calgary, and Alberta. At some point there were two completely separate bands that hit the same venues, only they were a week apart in arrival times. There were many occasions when one band would be leaving their hotel, only to cross paths with the arriving band as they were arriving. "Tom [Radai] booked the Hip Linkchain band, and we would be one week behind those guys," Bandy said. "In the early to mid-eighties, in those days in Canada you worked six days a week and traveled on Sunday, so we would be arriving as they were leaving, so we would hang out together in the hotels as we were passing each other."[37]

Radai had first been bitten by the blues bug when as a fanatic he met and hung out with blues musicians down on Maxwell Street. It didn't take long before he decided to take a more proactive approach to mingling with his heroes and try his hand at becoming a personal business manager of the artists. His first client was pianist Otis Spann (from the Muddy Waters band), followed over the next two years by the likes of mandolin/guitar/vocalist Johnny Young, guitarist/vocalist Johnny Littlejohn, and harp/vocalist Charlie Musselwhite. By the relatively young age of nineteen, Radai had already booked his first European tour, and by twenty he broadened his horizons. He further extended his services to his clients by performing the role of road manager, public relations point man, valet, and musical technician. Sam Lay was one of his biggest clients during this period.

At some point at least one member expressed a bit of frustration with the idea of Lay, the ringleader, traveling with such a large entourage in a multiple-instrumental ensemble. Barrelhouse Chuck was unhappy with having to split up his share of the money with so many people. "When we were in Sam Lay's band, he'd bring all these extra pieces—two of everything," he said. Between 1979 and 1982 the Sam Lay All-Stars did hundreds of performances with Jimmy Rogers as part of the traveling road show (as Tom Radai remained Jimmy's manager/agent for over twenty-five years until his death). The Jimmy Rogers band featured Sam Lay on drums, Bob Anderson on bass, Eddie Taylor on second guitar, "Detroit Junior" Williams on keyboards, Wild Child Butler on harp, and Otis Spann's wife, Lucille, as guest vocalist.

In 1982 John Stedman released *Jimmy Rogers & Left Hand Frank—Live* (JSP 1043), an album that combined a cadre of Jimmy's biggest hits with a few lengthy instrumentals served up as padding to round out the evening's festivities for inclusion on this live LP, captured on September 22 and 23 of 1979. Having already released a Rogers/Craig collaboration with a combination of studio and live performances three years before this outing, Stedman had depleted his in-house material and instead chose to dig deeper in the repository and pull out Jimmy's guaranteed flag-wavers that would no doubt grab the attention of Rogers fans everywhere.

"Sloppy Drunk," "That's All Right," "Brown Skin Woman," "Ludella," and "Walkin' by Myself" were included in the performance, while "I Can't Keep from Worrying," "Frank's Blues," "Linda Lu," and "Blues for Freddy" adequately dilute the proceedings and keep it from becoming a pure Rogers production. With "Frank's Blues" clocking in at over eight minutes—a bit much, relatively speaking—there were a few too many ballads included on the album, which potentially pulled the momentum down a few notches.

By 1982 Jimmy was playing regularly in cities across Texas, including Dallas, Fort Worth, and Austin, at the most popular blues club in the South—Antone's. Jimmy was such a frequent visitor at Antone's, he was essentially accepted as an honorary Texan at the club and was given the red carpet treatment every time he arrived. Harp blower Kim Wilson clearly relished the time he spent with Rogers, and he took every advantage of the opportunity to fill the role of Little Walter when it came to providing the intense, howling harmonica that was so organic to the Chicago sound.

The entire operation down in Austin was so refreshing to Jimmy. "Jimmie Vaughan and Kim Wilson, those guys down there [at] Antone's, [Clifford] is a man that loves the blues, and he's doin' all he can to help the blues," Jimmy recalled with glee. "I wish we had more in power like he is—we wouldn't need but five in the whole United States like that, and all blues players . . . well, you'd have something to do; you'd live comfortable."[38] Jimmy was speaking directly to the fact that Clifford Antone really knew how to take care of the musicians when they came to play down in Austin. He gave them constant attention, almost pampering the musicians, which was the main reason why, once the place opened, he always had the best in the business as its entertainment. Kim Wilson raves about how many greats were there on an around-the-clock basis, and he was a permanent fixture there.

By the early 1980s, Right Hand Frank Bandy had formed his own small independent label, Tear Drop Records. In October 1982 he got the idea to place

Jimmy and Hip Linkchain together in the studio to perform a totally acoustic set, similar to the approach Leonard Chess and Ralph Bass had come up with on the concept album *Folk Singer* for Muddy Waters in 1963. "I borrowed a couple of Martin guitars from a local music store, Chicago Music," Bandy said. "John Shaw was the manager. The album was recorded at Soto Sound, the engineer was Jerry Soto."[39]

Pianist and bandmate Barrelhouse Chuck was in attendance at the session, but Bandy chose not to let him play on it, because he had a very specific concept in mind. "I produced the album *Stickshift*, a totally acoustic album with just Jimmy and Hip," Bandy recalled. "They called the album that because in the cotton fields the acoustic guitar was the 'stickshift,' and the electric was the 'automatic,' so to speak."[40] The album is a rare treat—an opportunity to hear what Jimmy might have sounded like before he ever arrived in Chicago, and when listening to the tracks, it's not hard to imagine the two of them sitting on a front porch in Mississippi just tearing through the songs for nothing more than the sheer fun of it. The album would go on to be nominated for the W. C. Handy Award for "Best Traditional Blues Album of the Year."[41]

Hip takes the entire first side, beginning the proceedings with "Somebody Stole My Mule," a galloping shuffle that surges forward with verve until the end, when the two strummers turn the beat backward, eventually coasting to safety. Hip then sings the old 1941 Yank Rachell tune "Mellow Peaches Blues" (listed as "Don't Your Peaches Look Mellow"). St. Louis Jimmy Oden's classic tune "Goin' Down Slow" is next, followed by "Blow Wind Blow," where it becomes nearly impossible to tell which guitarist is actually taking the solo.

Hip closes his set with the humorous "I Don't Know" as he passes the baton to Jimmy, who offers an original, "Find Myself," as the opener for the flip side. While this tune is just a routine twelve-bar blues vehicle about waking up and finding a woman gone, the next tune serves as the real treat on the album. "Floating Bridge," the Sleepy John Estes tune, is sung with deep emotion. "Jimmy sang one of the most incredible versions of 'Floating Bridge.' They had a really intense groove going on that one," Bandy recalled.[42] The tune lasts less than two minutes, but it is the only recording that exists of Jimmy performing the tune. Playing to his strengths, Jimmy slows things down and takes a beautiful single-string solo on two more originals, "Dorcie Bell" and "Cold Chills," and closes the set with the classic "Rock Me Baby." Because the music was recorded, in Bandy's words, on a "boutique label," the album had minimal circulation and as yet is still unreleased on CD. Still, "The sales that were generated led to the LP being nominated for a W. C. Handy Award," Bandy said proudly, "although it didn't win."[43] On October 20, 1982, Jimmy was doing a weeklong stint in Edmonton, Alberta, while on his Canadian tour. He dropped by his old friend Holger Peterson's radio station, CKUA, where he gave a thirty-minute radio interview for Peterson's show, *Natch'l Blues*. Peterson was invited to attend the evening performance. "The live show was fantastic," he remarked.[44]

By February 1983 Sam Lay's band had changed slightly. Dave Clark was still in the band but had moved to guitar, Richie " Little Rich" Yescalis was added as a newcomer on bass, and Pinetop Perkins was playing piano. This group also took weeklong Canadian tours. Meanwhile, Wild Child Butler still played his own set, with Jimmy Rogers on guitar, either Walker or Perkins on piano, and Rich Yescalis on bass performing with both Rogers and Butler, who took turns as the leader of their own sets. Barrelhouse remembers the whirlwind tours. "Wild Child Butler, Jimmy, Sam, and myself," Chuck said. "We toured around for about two years, constantly. We'd be gone for a month, come back for a week, be gone again . . . I worked with Sam for a good while. At the time he had 'Barking Bill' Smith as a vocalist, who always carried a pistol, like when we went through Georgia."[45]

Sam Lay had one of the most unique and successful runs with the All-Stars of anyone in American music history—a track record that was hard enough to achieve then and even harder to pull off in today's world. As a drummer, bandleader, and showman, he was one of a kind. The band's exploits are the stuff of legend, and there are scores of "you-had-to-be-there" stories that are connected to the glory days of the late '70s and early '80s. For Barrelhouse Chuck, the fabulous run was nearing its end: "With Sam we went to Colorado, Texas, Niagara Falls, Canada, California. Jimmy said, 'Why don't you come and play with me?' He stole me from Sam after about a year and a half."[46] Although they were still on the same tour package, Barrelhouse switched teams and worked in the Rogers band.

Chuck was honored to have the opportunity to play with such a soulful group and for the remainder of his life wore it as badge of honor. "When I was in the band, it was all 'brothers'—Wild Child, on harp, Ted Harvey on drums, Jimmy on lead, and Hip Linkchain playing second guitar. We did forty-two states and six countries, probably a thousand gigs. Wild Child was nothing but fun, Ted was hilarious, Hip was outrageous, and Jimmy was a blast. It was always an adventure!" Once he was in the Rogers band, he got to know Jimmy better and began to observe a few of his personal traits. Chuck noticed that "Jimmy always seemed to be a quiet person; he smoked his More brand cigarettes. We'd be drivin' down the road, and he'd be up front in the passenger seat. He'd have salted peanuts and drop them into his orange soda—he loved that."[47]

He also observed the habits of a few others of his bandmates. In particular, he found the drummer to be hysterically humorous, even when it wasn't intentional. According to Chuck, "Ted Harvey was the funniest guy there ever was . . . he'd bring his own food all the time to save money. He would bring a whole chicken to fry up and a dozen eggs. He'd leave eggshells and chicken bones all over the countertop!"[48] Chuck knew that Harvey was being seriously entertaining out of sheer boredom. It was a great way to break the monotony of seeing in every town the same motels and highway signs and the same truck stops serving the same greasy eggs, toast, and bacon. Ted Harvey was the unrivaled king when it came to finding ways to pass away the hours on the road. "He'd do crossword puzzles all the time," Chuck said. "He'd ask Jimmy in this funny voice, 'Hey, Jimmy . . . what's a four letter word for *muthafucka*?' Jimmy would laugh this great wheezing laugh—like that cartoon dog Smedley? Jimmy would hold his head down, his shoulders shaking; he'd adjust his glasses with one hand, laughing hysterically, and just go, "*god-damn!*"[49]

Chuck also recalled yet another humorous incident, this time with Sam Lay, so Barrelhouse shared this story: "I went by his room one night, I heard this *clankety-clank, clankety-clank* . . . I walk past his room one night, it's like four in the morning, I'm gettin' some ice; the machine's right next to his door. It's Sam. He's playing drums and singing along to a record, '*Dang me—dang me . . . They oughta take a rope and hang me . . .*' He's singin' 'Dang Me' at four in the morning. Next day I told Jimmy. He just goes, laughing with that laugh of his, you know, '*god-damn. . . . god-damn!*'"[50]

On April 30, 1983, Muddy Waters died. Jimmy told Tamara Chapman of the *El Paso Times* that he'd talked with him only a week and a half before he passed. "He told me to keep on," Jimmy lamented. "He said, 'I'm plannin' to come back and play.' I was just talking to him to keep him in spirits, but I knew he wouldn't come back."[51] Jimmy was unable to attend the funeral, which hurt him deeply. He and his band were on the road when Muddy died, and harp player Madison Slim said that when Jimmy heard the news from his wife, Dorothy, he broke down and wept inconsolably. He kept his mind occupied over the next few weeks by doing what he did best—playing his guitar. The Sam Lay band was booked for another series of gigs in the late summer.

From mid-June to early July 1983, under Lay's "double band" configuration, they trekked across Canada and into Alaska. Bandy recalled the usual length of a road tour for the group: "We were out for a total of about three weeks." According to Richie Yescalis, in the first week of the Canadian leg they toured Canada, dipping down into Minnesota, Niagara Falls, and New York, then back up to Rouyn-Noranda in Quebec. Early on during this trip, they picked up pianist David Hart in Saskatchewan (for some reason Barrelhouse Chuck had refused to go into Canada for this trip). The next segment of the tour took the band into Calgary, Edmonton, Banff, and Vancouver. The third leg brought them up into Alaska, where they performed in Fairbanks, Valdez, and Kenai. Yescalis remembers one particular gig in Whitehorse, Yukon, where they played at a joint called the Sluice Box. "The club was named after a device that separates the gold from the dirt," said Ritchie. "We played there for two weeks on the way up, and one on the way back. Whenever the people danced, you could see the dust rise right up off the floor and into the air, where it just floated."

The tour lasted three and a half months. When they returned, a few members of the band were none too pleased with Lay for having paid them in Canadian dollars instead of American currency, which left them on the short end. As Dave Clark and Richie Yescalis made their exit from the tour, Jimmy decided this would be an opportune time for him to step out of Lay's shadow and form his own band again. Jimmy promptly picked up both Yescalis and Clark for bass and rhythm guitar, respectively. Now, along with Madison Slim on harp, Barrelhouse Chuck on piano, and the recent addition of Ted Harvey on drums, Jimmy had finally formed his own "all-star" band of the '80s.

Once he joined Jimmy's tour, the traveling accommodations shifted from Sam Lay's truck to Jimmy's van, which had a contraption sitting squarely in the center of the floor, unattached. "Jimmy Rogers had a kerosene heater in his van, driving down the road," Chuck recalled. Bassist Bob Stroger, who played with Jimmy on and off over the years, reflected on the circumstances surrounding the van with both trepidation and wonder:

I remember when I was on the road with Jimmy Rogers and we almost froze to death. I never will forget that. We had an oil heater in that thing . . . and boy oh boy, when we'd get to clubs, we were lucky that thing didn't just blow up. We used to get to the clubs and all of us'd be smelling like fuel oil. We were in Wyoming or some doggone where. At the Savannah Dream, beautiful club. We got out the van and started unloading the van and looked around and here come a fire truck with a siren and there was all that smoke coming out from that damn oil heater. Those were some days. Almost froze.

Evidently this badly rigged van provided little relief to Jimmy's sidemen. "Man, you could put a [soda] pop in that van and 20 minutes it would have almost froze," Stroger lamented. "Man, those were some tough gigs."[52]

Chuck didn't think that was too funny. He also wasn't too keen on the tour schedule, which was prepared in advanced by Tom Radai, the booking agent for both Sam Lay and Jimmy Rogers. "Radai was booking us—he'd book a gig that was miles away in between gigs; we'd be sittin' in the van after drivin' for two and a half days," Chuck said. "We'd drive from one gig, then five states to the next gig, and the hotels were always closed when we got there. He was so untogether."[53]

Barrelhouse Chuck was in the band that Jimmy took on tour during this time in late August. They had a gig on Sunday, August 28. According to Chuck, "We were playing at John Denver's club in Snow Mass, Colorado, and there was no snow, and that night Jimmy got drunk after nobody showed up. He said, 'I just need someone to talk to.'" But it wasn't the lack of an audience that was the source of his sorrow. It was that he was still grieving the death of Muddy. "We sat up until five in the morning, talking about Muddy, Otis Spann, how the 'Juke' song went down," Chuck said. "He told me, 'We recorded it on a Wednesday, and left on Thursday. Friday, in Kentwood, Louisiana, we heard the song blaring out a club jukebox on a 78.' He said they couldn't believe it. He said Little Walter grabbed his hat and hauled ass out of the bar."[54] Indeed, those were the days.

The next Sunday, September 4, Jimmy took his band to the first annual Border Blues Festival, a one-day event in El Paso, Texas. Featured on the bill were Brownie McGhee and a series of lesser-known regional artists: Long John Hunter, the Hard Knocks Blues Band, Dan Lambert, and Mario Otero. With Wild Child Butler on harp, Barrelhouse Chuck on piano, Hip Linkchain on guitar, Ted Harvey on drums, and Frank Bandy on bass, Jimmy was the festival headliner, and his group was chosen as an authentic blues band to come and deliver the "lowdown blues," as Jimmy referred to it. Of his current lineup, Jimmy said, "We're just four guys playing the blues and we are happy." By the time Jimmy came onstage it was late, and the crowd had thinned considerably after having grown tired from the heat and beer. Still, according to Dan Lambert of *Guitar Player* magazine, those who did stay were "in for something really special." He called Rogers "the true gentleman of the blues with his sincere smiling presence." Lambert went on to compliment Jimmy, saying, "He frequently shares the spotlight with band members, putting himself in the accompanist's role, then watching like a proud father."[55]

The day before, Jimmy and Hip were scheduled to perform on Saturday afternoon for the guitar workshop at the Señor Blues club. Apparently they made a misstep when they were noticeably absent, and everyone went searching for them, only to find them relaxing back at the hotel across town, unaware that anyone was looking for them. Once they realized that the show was being put on hold pending their arrival, they rushed to the stage and ripped into two acoustic numbers on their Martin guitars, performing tunes from the recently recorded *Stickshift* album. "Jimmy and Hip made their guitars sound as one, weaving lines in and out and using a type of musical ESP to know where the other is going," Lambert boasted in his article.[56]

When asked before the performance about what it means and what it takes to live the blues life, Jimmy told a local writer, "Lots of musicians think they understand the blues . . . you gotta live it to understand." When asked to elaborate, he said solemnly, "I don't have no guys with me who lived on the bed of ease." As if to further elucidate on the importance of this role of the bluesman from an artistic standpoint, he made the following comparison as he went on to describe the important role of the underdog: "The man who pushes a wheelchair, his life is just as important as the man who flies a plane."[57]

On Friday, September 9, and Saturday, September 10, Jimmy brought his band to Danbi's Pub in Albuquerque for a two-night stand. The group, which Jimmy now called the Chicago All-Stars Blues Revue, had Jimmy and Hip Linkchain on guitars, Wild Child Butler on harp, Ted Harvey on drums, Barrelhouse Chuck on piano, and Right Hand Frank on bass. Jimmy exuded confidence in this lineup. "I've got faith that these guys have it," he said. "I know I've got a future playing the blues. I know what I want and I know what type of musicians I need to support me."[58] He went on to explain his relationship with the public and his perspective regarding his role in the pantheon of blues legends. He tried to clarify his position regarding the pressures to succumb to the heavier rock music as opposed to the more subtle art form of blues: "The public is mine to a certain degree—I know that. All I need is the tunes to appeal to that following I have. I know I can step in front of this rock and roll and make some real good blues."[59]

Before the tour came to an end, Jimmy had one last obligation to fulfill. Early on he had decided to make a date with Rob and Hugh Murray, who owned the Murray Brothers record label on the West Coast. Heavily influenced by their dad, known as "Blackie," Rob and his brother grew up listening constantly to boogie-woogie and blues music in the home of their parents. Harp player Rod Piazza, leader of a band called the Mighty Flyers, reminisced about how the idea of forming the Murray Brothers label came about: "One day me and Rob were riding in the car after I took him to see George 'Harmonica' Smith. We talked and Rob wondered why he wasn't doing albums. He put up the bread to do the first record; *Boogie'n with George* was the first album. We didn't really know what we were doing. Other albums we did were with Shakey Jake, Johnny Dyer, and Pee Wee Crayton."[60]

Rod was well aware of the music of Jimmy Rogers. "Like every other cat that came up, I had his records," Rod continued. "He was being booked by Tom Radai, who was also booking the Mighty Flyers. Tom came to us and said, 'I know you guys are recording those others, why don't you do one on Jimmy?' I said, 'We'd love to do that.'"[61] The Mighty Flyers was a band that knew quite a bit about how Chicago blues was played. Piazza, born December 18, 1947, was a chromatic and diatonic harp player who was at the front of this red-hot quintet, backed by Honey Alexander on piano (a dead-on Otis Spann disciple), Bill Schwartz on drums, Bill Stuve on bass, and Michael "Junior" Watson, an incredibly talented musician who played guitar so stylistically on point that it was as if he had been born in an earlier generation, alongside Waters and Rogers. Watson, born in 1949, grew up in San Jose, California, and had joined Rod in January of '77. When asked about Jimmy's music, Junior said, "I'd been listening to his music as a kid."[62]

Piazza had specially requested that Jimmy make an appearance, and Jimmy seemed quite pleased and honored with the idea of playing with the band he'd never worked with prior to this occasion. Jimmy said, "Well, Rob Murray has a friend there who's a fantastic harmonica player, Rod Piazza. He was taught by a good fellow . . . George Smith." After listening to Piazza's band perform, Jimmy concluded that they were artists who knew how to play the blues, saying "Rod [had] taken it seriously, man. So did Honey [Alexander], that's Rod's wife. She got that Otis Spann style down pretty well. She got just about every record Spann played on."[63]

The recording session was scheduled, and Jimmy committed to swinging the tour toward the West Coast. "Hip, Chuck, Wild Child, me, and Ted were on the road when the *Feelin' Good* album happened," said Right Hand Frank. "We started in Chicago, we played Albuquerque, San Diego, then they put us in Riverside while he was making the album."[64] Barrelhouse Chuck remembered how it happened: "We drove a day and a half from a gig in Texas to get to California." After checking into a hotel, Jimmy "left us for about three days," which disconcerted some of the band members. According to Barrelhouse, Jimmy had left him under the impression that he would be included in the making of the album. Evidently, Jimmy had given him the word confidentially. "He said 'I'm not goin' to use everybody, just you, Chuck.' The band was Bandy, Hip, Ted, Jimmy, Wild Child and me."[65]

Bandy remembered how the event occurred in a slightly different manner. "About the *Feelin' Good* album, here's what happened," he said. "There was always an 'anything-can-happen' situation. This particular album, I didn't feel like we were going to be on it. We knew that Jimmy was going to make an album, but we really didn't know any details. I never thought we were supposed to be on it." The band finally arrived, and Jimmy instructed Bandy to make connections with their greeting party. "When we eventually got out to California, Shakey Jake was our liaison, and we got in town at six o'clock in the morning. We go to a Denny's restaurant, and Jimmy gives me Shakey Jake's phone number and says, 'Call him; he's going to tell us what we're supposed to do.' So he shows up an hour later, takes us over to a Travelodge motel in Hollywood; we stayed there a coupla days."[66]

The session was slated to take place at a studio in Los Angeles, but things got complicated and somehow the original plan of action collapsed. "The studio they'd booked, they couldn't get in there," Bandy said. "So we hung around in Hollywood for about two or three days; we didn't really have anything to do. We were just bumming around in L.A., looking at used record stores and stuff." Jimmy and the band took the layover in stride and shifted their attention to the next performance, which had already been set up in advance by a local blues society. "We went down and played in San Diego for one night, Wednesday, at the Mandolin Wind," recalled Bandy.[67]

Meanwhile, Rod Piazza and the Murray Brothers still could not work out the details of the original studio location in Hollywood, so they found an alternative site to record the album. They contacted engineer and studio owner Wayne Vinnick, who finally cleared the way for the sessions to begin. After a successful San Diego gig on Wednesday night, the band then drove to Riverside the next morning and got a hotel room. Bandy remembers the details of that day vividly "because I was born on September 15th and that Thursday was my birthday."[68] Barrelhouse Chuck, a close friend, said, "I wanted to create a special occasion for him, so I took him out to dinner . . . We ate a delicious barbecue dinner at a really nice restaurant."[69]

Rod Piazza and Rob Murray arrived at the hotel early Friday morning to pick Jimmy up for the session. "We hit at about eleven in the morning," said Piazza. "Jimmy brought in his guitar—we had an early Fender amp waiting for him; we wanted the authentic, traditional sound. He just sat calmly in the chair. There wasn't a lot of rehearsal; it was just spontaneous."[70] Junior agreed, adding, "I remember how relaxed he was. I was curious to see how these guys explain how their music goes. There was no talking whatsoever. He never said a key, tempo, anything. He'd just start playing, then when we heard where he was, we'd stop him, then go, 'Okay, we got it, let's go.'"[71]

Rod originally thought he might need to take on more of a leadership role, since Jimmy hadn't worked with his band. Now he knew it wasn't necessary. Piazza recalled it this way:

> I didn't have a whole lot to do. He'd set the time, he'd give the key, so I could just play as a sideman and try to point him in a particular direction that we wanted to achieve. At one point, he pulled out a little book he had in his pocket. He looked at it a minute, and closed it back up. It looked like a little address book, maybe three inches in size. Maybe he went in there to check his notation, or song list, to give him an idea of where he was going next . . . that's when we did either "Tricky Woman" or "Slick Chick."[72]

Jimmy had called an audible from his playbook, and it caught Junior a bit off guard. According to Rod, "By the time we did 'Slick Chick'—I think it was the second to last tune, or the last one—he didn't want to play anymore—he had a pretty good buzz going by that time. So I asked him, 'How does it go?' So he said, 'It goes, kinda like, 'Ain't No Need to Go No Further'—you know, the Little Walter tune?' I play the groove, then he goes, 'Yeah!' So we did it, and he was smilin' like a Cheshire cat!" Piazza had his own special request for the project: "I told Tom [Radai] that I wanted to do 'You Don't Know.'"[73]

Piazza's band was well prepared for the session and nailed the tunes in quick succession. "We did almost every one of them in one take," he boasted. Jimmy, always appreciative of the fact that those who wanted to play with him took the time to learn the music correctly, was getting more and more relaxed as the session progressed. If he had any initial reservations about being in unfamiliar surroundings with a band he hadn't been with before, they had vanished by now. "The musicians were familiar with that groove. We fell in behind him and made the record," said Piazza. Especially tasty was Junior Watson's guitar work with Jimmy. "Junior knew what to put with Jimmy's music without him having to say a thing," Piazza boasted, "and he loved Honey's playing, too." Indeed, Rod was overjoyed about what had taken place. "Listening to his voice—when he would sing the songs, they sounded exactly like the records I heard twenty years earlier. It really inspired you to play. Just to hear him singing in that natural voice."[74]

The juices were flowing, and, unlike some of the marathon sessions Jimmy had had during the Chess years, he breezed through nine tunes in a relatively short time. Before they knew it, it was over. Rod was ecstatic, later saying, "We had a good time making it—doin' a little drinkin' . . . feelin' good. We had a ball. I'll bet we did that whole record in about five or six hours."[75] Based on the photo that graced the back cover of the LP, taken at the session after the last track was laid, the title, *Feelin' Good*, worked on several levels. There Jimmy sits smiling, cradling his beloved red Gibson 335 with his slightly glassy eyes sailing at half-mast, surrounded by the Mighty Flyers, each of them also with prideful smiles that seem to say, *We've just done something really special with a legend.*

The respect and admiration they had for Jimmy went beyond the music, as Junior indicated: "The guy just exudes relaxedness. He was so easygoing; that's the way his personality was, his singing was, and his guitar playing was. I don't think there's any greater example of Chicago blues than Muddy and Jimmy Rogers intertwining those guitar parts." Junior made his mind up about Jimmy Rogers that night, concluding, "He was the gentlest, kindest guy ever."[76]

After the session was over, they were all ready to let their hair down. A good meal would serve as the perfect ending to a stellar event. They went to a popular restaurant at a nearby hotel. "After that," Junior said, "me and Rob, Honey, and Jimmy went to a little restaurant over here on the East Side—in the lounge of the Ramada Inn, I think." Now that they were officially off the clock, they decided to seize the opportunity to ask Jimmy a few questions about the legendary Chess days. One of the questions Junior asked was about the picture that graced the back cover of *Chicago Bound*, Jimmy's first Chess album. Junior wanted to know why all the men looked so nattily dressed. According to Watson, "He said about his Chicago days, 'You had to have a suit on. If you played blues, you were a man. You had to have a suit and tie on.'"[77]

Junior continued sharing his memories of Jimmy, saying, "We had some food and we were sitting there drinking, and Jimmy was talking about how he didn't want to go back to Japan." Jimmy, who by now was totally relaxed and enjoying the adulation, hammed it up for his new friends. "He just kept saying it over and over again," Watson recalled, "and we were just sitting there laughing as he said it over and over again."[78] Meanwhile, back at the Travelodge, the Chicago All-Star Blues Revue waited patiently for Jimmy's return. "They brought him back that night," says Frank Bandy. "I asked if we were going to hang out in the hotel that night, and Jimmy said, 'Naaaww, Little Brother, we're *outta here!*' We left Riverside about seven that evening," Bandy recalled. Jimmy, obviously pleased with the results, waved a thick wad of money in the air, his take-home pay for a hard day's play. "Those guys sure know how to back me up!" he declared as they pulled out of the hotel parking lot and onto the highway.[79]

There was good reason for Jimmy to express such joy about the session with Piazza and his crew. Soon after the album was released, it received high praise in *Guitar Player* magazine, with Dan Forte commenting that the reason Jimmy sounded in the best form since his peak years of the '50s was because of the "killer backup work provided by the Mighty Flyers . . . they swing as hard or harder than any blues band in this country." Forte went on to compliment Jimmy on his solos and vocals but tossed the ultimate tribute to the backup guitarist, saying, "Most of the picking is handled by Watson, who sounds more like the Rogers of old than does Jimmy himself." Forte clearly felt that the pairing of Jimmy with Piazza's band fit like a glove, calling it "a marriage made in heaven."[80]

The album is nothing short of spectacular. On "Rock This House," Watson opens the proceedings with a classic rockabilly guitar blast—a biting tone drenched in reverb—perfectly bouncing off of Bill Stuve's thumping, driving bass as Jimmy later yells one of his late '40s pet phrases with glee: *Play a long time!* The second track, "You're So Sweet," has a purely vicious drive and introduces Piazza's fat "Walter" tone, with Honey's ivory-tickling touches underneath on piano. The ballad "Blue and Lonesome" is actually "Lonesome Blues," first introduced on 1973's *Gold Tailed Bird* session. Jimmy takes a more subdued solo as a contrast to Junior's stinging lines while Rod swoops lines à la Little Walter. To close the first side of the LP, Jimmy brushed the dust off a longtime Leonard-shelved tune, "You Don't Know," recorded in November 1959 on the very last session as a leader for Chess.

On the flip side "Tricky Woman" has a harder medium-tempo shuffle than even the original, and one wonders why this approach wasn't used in the first place. It truly has the deep pocket that "You're the One" possessed, and Piazza promptly conjured up the spirit of Big Walter for this one. "Angel Child" is the ultimate showcase of both Honey's ability to possess the spirit of Spann and Rod's similar strength in channeling Little Walter Jacobs. Jimmy sang the tune with a kind of happiness in his voice that couldn't hide his pleasure with the band's performance. "Slick Chick," originally known as "Looka' Here," had quite the verve and gained energy as the band drove in a mad dash toward the finish line, inciting Jimmy to make his famous "hole in your soul" declaration.

"St. Louis" has the patented, slow Muddy Waters feel, and it is the one tune that captures the intertwining guitar duo with stunning precision. It had to have sent chills down Jimmy's back. Without question, no recording previous to this one got so close to the real thing in the '50s. Refreshingly, "Chicago Bound" has the same passion and drive as the original Chess recording. Honey takes a short but passionate solo, and Rod provides hard, choppy harp lines. It was an absolutely superb effort.

The Jimmy Rogers band returned to Chicago toward the end of September. At that point Barrelhouse Chuck quit the band, furious about the circumstances surrounding the recording session that he felt he should have been a part of.

Regardless of how Jimmy might have felt about the departure, his own mu-sic-making remained a constant. In late October 1983 he was asked to join the American Folk Blues Festival concerts, another European tour promoted by Horst Lippmann and Fritz Rau. The concerts on the tour were dedicated to Muddy Waters, whose recent passing still had an overwhelming effect on most blues musicians. As the tour wound its way to Frankfurt, Germany, the festivities were held at the historic Volksbildungsheim on October 30. Jimmy performed not with his own band, but with a "supergroup" that included Louisiana Red on vocals and guitar, Queen Sylvia Embry on bass, Lovie Lee on piano, Carey Bell on harp, and Charles "Honey Boy" Otis on drums.

After the group, billed as Louisiana Red and His Chicago Blues Friends, per-formed "Tribute to Muddy Waters," "Louisiana Hot Sauce," and "Future Blues," Jimmy Rogers stepped in front to lead his portion of the show as he performed "Gold Tailed Bird." Then Carey Bell led the band with "She Is Worse." Later in the tour, on November 11 at Music Hall in Würzburg, Jimmy joined Lovie Lee's band as Honey Boy Otis led the crowd to a short and sweet, slow-percolating groove on the traditional New Orleans classic "Iko Iko." Immediately following Lee's set, "Blues Queen Sylvia" Embry stepped up front and delivered a groov-ing rendition of "I Love You," with a passionate harp solo by Carey Bell. Jimmy churned out his patented blues shuffle to drive the band, then opened the next tune, "Baby What Do I Do," with the perfected triad cluster of notes he always used as the clarion call to announce a slow blues. Sylvia belted out hard-hitting vocals with a sass on par with Koko Taylor's as she enticed the crowd.

Once Jimmy returned home in late 1983, he settled back into his regular routine of playing at his favorite haunts: Lilly's and B.L.U.E.S. His local band lineup reflected some recent changes. The new drummer, Tony Mangiullo, was an Italian immigrant who had recently come to America with his mother. Hip Linkchain and Wild Child Butler were still in the band, with Big Moose and Pinetop alternating piano spots according to whomever was available. Long-time member Rich Yescalis had now returned to the bass chair.[81] According to Jimmy D. Lane's count, this was only the second official band that his dad had formed in his career (a slightly confusing comment on the surface, but maybe he was referring to the length of the current band's stability—Jimmy D. may have viewed the other previous groups as pickup bands).

In January 1984 a talented pianist named Sumito Ariyoshi—better known as simply "Ariyo"—joined the band too as the regular pianist in the Jimmy Rogers Blues Band. He was roommates with Mangiullo, who was already in the band. It didn't take long for Ariyo to work his way toward the Windy City, intent on implanting himself squarely in the middle of the blues scene. He found a job working as a waiter and kitchen helper at the Ginza restaurant near O'Hare Airport and booked a room at the Tokyo Motel, located directly behind the restaurant. It was the same place where Barrelhouse Chuck and Little Joe Berson had stayed when they first arrived.[82]

On Sunday nights Ariyo made it down to B.L.U.E.S., where Jimmy performed on Sunnyland Slim's gig throughout the remainder of 1983. According to writer Elizabeth Winkowski, when Ariyo arrived, "The doorman often mistook him for a tourist. Ariyo always took out money to pay the cover charge until other blues musicians yelled, 'Hey, stop it! He's with us!'"[83] It was there that Jimmy first heard Ariyo, and he was impressed. The young Japanese player was still in his twenties when Jimmy invited him to join the band for the upcoming tour. Ariyo gladly accepted. "They treated me right," said Ariyo "They didn't treat me like a guest, like a tourist. They treated me like their own people. I didn't think, 'I'm Japanese.' I'm just a piano player."[84]

Ariyo learned quickly by observing. He soon realized that Jimmy had given him an incredible opportunity to launch a long-lasting career. "After Jimmy Rogers got me, I erased any planning," Ariyo says. "I thought 'Hey man, I could make a living.'"[85] Upon their return to Chicago, Jimmy moved Ariyo out of the Tokyo Motel and into a three-bedroom house in Summit, an area on the Southwest Side of town near Midway Airport. Jimmy had the rest of band staying there, and all the rooms were occupied, so Ariyo shared a room with Rogers's drummer, Tony Mangiullo.[86]

Richie Yescalis affectionately referred to Jimmy's lineup as the "International Blues Band," because the performers just happened to include a wide array of nationalities: African American (Wild Child Butler and Hip Linkchain); Caucasian (Rich Yescalis); Japanese (Ariyo); and Italian (Tony Mangiullo). According to Yescalis, this rare group made only one short tour through the States—a trip to the West Coast, with stops that included Seattle, Montana, and Salt Lake City.

Mangiullo and Ariyo hit it off immediately and got along really well. Tony taught Ariyo "Italian English." Eventually Mangiullo would go on to start his own blues club, naming it Rosa's Lounge after his mother. Ariyo took a room in the upstairs apartment on the second floor of the same building. "After Tony opened Rosa's," Winkowski reported, "he [Ariyo] tried to learn English from homeless people who lived on the streets, offering them cigarettes or beer in exchange for rudimentary English lessons."[87]

In early 1984 Jimmy's popularity was soaring on the tour circuit, his recorded output was steadily increasing, and his visibility had increased in his hometown, which was a conscientious act on his part, as opposed to his deliberate withdrawal from the club scene during the early 1970s. These days he wanted to get out and play—he was catching his second wind. "I did a lot of the driving," recalls Bandy, who had been in the band nearly five solid years at this point. Bandy also did some of the recruiting for new members and suggested to Jimmy that he bring in Rich Kirch as second guitarist. "Hip eventually went out on his own, and that's when Jimmy hired Rich Kirch," Bandy said.[88]

"Jimmy had always encouraged us to make bands within his bands," Bandy said. "Since he actually played in Chicago, he did from two to seven nights a month, so he encouraged us to play with other people, but to be available when he needed us." Rich Kirch had been around the Chicago scene for years before he was invited to join the group. "The first time I met Jimmy Rogers, I think, was at a club in New Town called On Broadway," Rich said. "He was being featured with the Bob Riedy Blues Band, along with Sam Lay on drums."[89]

Before joining Jimmy's band, Kirch had been playing with Delmark recording artist Jimmy Dawkins. Back then Kirch and Barrelhouse Chuck shared a rented apartment. Now Kirch and Frank Bandy were roommates as they worked the North Side gigs. Similar in height and hairstyle, they looked like pillars as they stood towering over the other band members—sporting long manes and thin frames, giving Jimmy's band a more contemporary look and sound. They were responsible for setting up Jimmy's equipment for the shows—a pretty straightforward task, since Jimmy's requirements were minimal. During this period, by Kirch's account, "He played a red Gibson 335 and an old Fender Tweed Twin Reverb."[90]

Beyond the twin towers, "the band had Ted Harvey on drums, Little Joe Berson on harp, either Johnny Big Moose Walker or Pinetop Perkins on piano, and sometimes Sunnyland Slim would drop by and play," said Kirch.[91] They had a high degree of visibility in Chicago during this stretch of Jimmy's career. The band continued to hold down regular gigs at Lilly's on Lincoln Avenue and B.L.U.E.S on North Halsted, the two designated areas Jimmy chose specifically as the spots where one could catch him. By choice, he wasn't necessarily making the rounds.

Bandy understood Jimmy's logic, and said, "He loved to play Lilly's and B.L.U.E.S., because his name would be in the paper, and if anyone was looking for him, they could find him, anybody who wanted access to him. He didn't make a lot of money there. It really wasn't a big deal for him, but you could find him at either place."[92] Kirch agreed with Bandy's assessment, adding, "I don't remember him sitting in much. He seemed to be happy, but he didn't really hang out."[93] Kirch's description fit perfectly with what just about everyone else said about Jimmy's general demeanor. He was content to just relax and enjoy his surroundings, as he was a creature of comfort and had his own routine. A good cigarette, a good drink, some good food, and some good blues were all he required to be at peace. "Jimmy smoked 'More' brand cigarettes and drank V.O.," recalls Kirch.[94]

Jimmy also continued making road trips with the band, taking the blues to nearby states fairly often. On one particular out-of-town gig Jimmy and his entire group found themselves questioning whether they were actually in their proper surroundings. "We were hired to play a club in Milwaukee, Wisconsin," Kirch said. "When we entered the club we were surprised to see a crowd of people sporting multicolored Mohawks, slamming into one another. I guess that it was called 'slam-dancing,' but we wondered if we were in the right club. The group that was playing before us was called the Exploited. We did follow them and they turned out to be quite congenial." Jimmy, in his typical cool, didn't let it rattle him; he just kicked off the first tune and stuck to his regular set the entire night. He casually strolled onstage and launched into his routine, which the band executed to perfection. "Our usual playlist included 'Walkin' by Myself,' 'Gold Tailed Bird,' 'That's All Right,' 'Sloppy Drunk,' and 'Mojo,' 'Ludella,' and 'Blow Wind Blow,'" Kirch recalled.[95]

That year they gave a relatively brief tour in Canada and the United States. One particular show was captured for posterity. "Our performance at the Mississippi Valley Blues Festival in Davenport, Iowa, was filmed and recorded live," Kirch said.[96] His story was confirmed by Tony Mangiullo, who said that he saw a bootleg tape of the show.

From mid-1984 on, Jimmy's work schedule increased steadily, with performances that fell roughly into four categories: local gigs; regional mini-tours (lasting roughly a week or so); two- to three-week regional tours across several states; and overseas tours that lasted three or four weeks. He needed to "deepen the bench," so to speak, with regard to having a specific set of players available to travel with him on shorter two- to three-week furloughs, as well as those who would be willing to go on some of the lengthier European tours that were now becoming a yearly ritual. Then there were those promoters, both stateside and abroad, who put together tour packages where they formed their own all-star bands; on these Jimmy traveled alone as one of the featured artists on the roster.

Hence, several more musicians were placed in the Rogers rotation, essentially creating three basic band configurations made up of musicians who seemed to mesh not only musically but also personally—an important ingredient not to be taken lightly when far away from home for extended periods of time. Roughly speaking, the bass/guitar tandem of Right Hand Frank and Rich Kirch worked well together, as did the team of Little Rich Yescalis and Dave Clark. For tours, Jimmy's harp choice was Madison Slim, with Little Joe Berson—who never had the opportunity to tour with Jimmy—doing most of the local and regional gigs.

One highlight of 1984 was Jimmy's performance at the Petrillo Band Shell in Grant Park on Friday, June 8, the first day of the first annual Chicago Blues Festival. This three-day event was officially designated as a "Tribute to Muddy Waters." In addition to featuring Jimmy, the event presented sets by Koko Taylor, James Cotton, Willie Dixon, Sunnyland Slim, Junior Wells, and Johnny Winter.[97] For lead guitar, Hip Linkchain or Rich Kirch were used on shorter tours. If lengthier tours allowed Jimmy to bring his own men, his first team for the rhythm section included Ted Harvey on drums, Bob Stroger on bass, and Pinetop Perkins on piano. This, of course, was all subject to availability, hence the need for multiple backup units for each position. The harp and piano chairs seemed to be the most volatile of the band, and over the years proved to be the areas that were more subject to change than any other roles in Jimmy's band.

According to Kirch, after Little Joe Berson died in December 1987, he was replaced by Wild Child Butler. That year, *Feelin' Good*, the LP Jimmy recorded with Rod Piazza and the Mighty Flyers, was released to positive reviews. It gave Jimmy's career a real boost, since he now had a new album to promote and take on tour. It was also a time of celebration for Rod Piazza and his band, which came out smelling like a rose for their excellent performance on the LP. Junior Watson weighed in with his verdict on how the finished product held up to scrutiny. While he was proud of the fact that "there were no overdubs; it was all live," he wasn't as pleased with the results sonically. "The mix on the album was a little tanky," he said. "The album sounded so much better when we were doing it."[98]

It wouldn't be Piazza's last encounter with Jimmy. "The next time I played with him was at the Dynamite Lounge, in a winter resort for Bruce Willis, called Sun Valley in Haley, Idaho," Rod said. "That was my band with Jimmy." Piazza then related a humorous story about a rare moment for him in the world of Jimmy Rogers: "We had been drinkin' pretty good. It was a short stage. Two of the guys standin' right up front was Bruce and Arnold Schwarzenegger. We were in the middle of the song and I looked down at Bruce. I gave him the harp mike. He started playing on the harp behind Jimmy. Jimmy said, 'Let me hear you, Rod!' Bruce was on the harp, he started blowin'. Jimmy didn't see it when I gave Bruce the mike. Arnold looked out and shook my hand and said, 'Awesome!'"[99]

Rod was always appreciative of the fact that Jimmy really liked his playing, and was not shy about letting others know about it. According to Piazza, "Madison

Slim—or Steve Guyger—said to me that when they were riding in the car, he'd have that album on in the car, he would say, 'Now you *see* that?—that's how you do it; that's it.'"[100] Indeed, the respect and musical admiration went both ways between Rogers and Piazza. Rod made great strides to ensure that he and his band gave their best performance whenever they backed Jimmy.

When asked about Jimmy's approach to recording that made the recording session so successful, Piazza became philosophical about how to deal with an artist of Jimmy's caliber, saying, "His voice was a mellow voice, a soothing voice. I always thought that the accompaniment needed to be sympathetic, dealt with a light hand, not too heavy-handed a backup. You wanted to weave it in and out and swing it, because he had that type of feel." Rod's attitude toward Jimmy's music was one that basically reflected the idea that sometimes it's what you leave out that's more important than what you put in.

> I've heard some cats that weren't playing sympathetic enough to coax the song into what he was trying to achieve. I think the record that we did had that kind of backing. That's where a lot of cats mess up: they're more interested in showing what they know how to *do* instead of giving him the best of what would make *him* sound the best. It's easy to run over the top of a singer, and everybody says, "Oh, man, you sound really good on that," but you might not have played the best thing for the cat *whose record it is.*[101]

Rod Piazza's obvious respect for Jimmy was yet one more indication that Rogers was well-loved from coast to coast. Jimmy's music had firmly taken root into the blues soil of the next generation, and his future plans were geared to inspire his offspring to bear even sweeter fruit in the upcoming year. He was feelin' good.

OUT ON THE ROAD

I had fun comin' right on up and I'm having
fun right today. When it gets to a place it ain't
no fun, I'll leave it go. I'll go and do somethin'
else—get my pole and go fishin'.

—Jimmy Rogers

Back in Boston, Jimmy was still rolling with his East Coast crew, gathering momentum up and down the coast. Local bassist Mudcat Ward was a permanent fixture among Boston's elite bluesmen. "With Jimmy, we played weddings and private parties—this is all during the middle '80s—they were good-paying gigs," Mudcat said. "He'd come two or three times a year." What Jimmy had now was a series of regular engagements that provided a stable income he could depend upon when he wasn't doing major tours. But it didn't start out that way. "At first he came up trying to find gigs; then we ourselves would [actually] get him gigs and he would come here to play with us," Ward reminisced. "We'd send him his flight money."[1]

Mudcat also recalls one particular visit in early 1984 when Jimmy was there for a brief tour, and Jimmy's wife, Dorothy, came visiting. After the band played at a place called No Tomatoes, she took the opportunity to demonstrate her cooking prowess at the home of Mudcat's parents, who lived in the Lewiston-Auburn area of Maine. She went out to the supermarket to buy some chicken for the evening meal, then went into the kitchen. "She went through the cupboards—she wanted to make her own barbecue sauce," Mudcat recalled. "She took stuff out of there that Mom hadn't used in years. She concocted this weird, gray mix. She said that it would keep it from burning on the grill." Although this home-made Southern recipe was something the Wards had never experienced, both

Jimmy and Dorothy applied the basting technique whenever they had outdoor barbecues, which was often. "They painted each piece," said Ward, "and there was actually a half-inch of space between the fire and the chicken—it was like the chicken was fire-proof . . . it was almost spooky how the flame wouldn't go near it, I was impressed."[2]

The partying went on for hours into the night. It was only after they'd gone to bed that someone noticed, at about 4:00 A.M., that the back-porch roof was on fire. The way Mudcat remembered it, Jimmy had been standing out there for a while; more than likely he was smoking a cigarette and didn't realize that something had caught a spark from his ashes. Mudcat and his family really had no idea how it could have happened. Luckily the flames were small enough to get under control in a matter of minutes. "We put it out. I don't know *what* he was doing out there!" he said with laughter.[3]

Jimmy was regularly working in the northeastern region of the country, but he was also protecting his turf in the southwestern region, where the reputation of Antone's was growing by leaps and bounds. By the early 1980s, several local groups in Austin began establishing strong reputations for playing at an exceptionally high level. A nucleus of players had formed a coalition of blues bands that allowed them to play in a variety of combinations to create multiple groups. The bustling scene was beginning to look very much like the one in Chicago during the 1950s. The Nightcrawlers, for example, had a young, hot sideman in Stevie Ray Vaughan; the Fabulous Thunderbirds had Stevie's older brother, Jimmie Vaughn; and Triple Threat Revue had Stevie Ray, Lou Ann Barton, and W. C. Clark, the elder statesman of Austin. Antone's co-owner at the club, Angela Strehli, had her own group, Southern Feeling, which featured Denny Freeman and W. C. Clark.[4] The Cobras and Double Trouble were other bands that had formed as a result of the breakdown and rebuilding of groups as personnel switched from one band to the next.

They all hung out at Antone's on a round-the-clock basis, and a family atmosphere was firmly established among the blues comrades who supported each other in every way. They all clamored over one another to get a chance to share the stage with blues pioneers like Jimmy Rogers whenever they came to town. Because Jimmy was treated so well, he was always generous about allowing the local Austin talent an opportunity to swap licks with him. He came regularly, often paired with Big Walter, Eddie Taylor, and Hubert Sumlin, who chose to live there permanently. "Hubert would do shows with Sunnyland and Big Walter and Eddie Taylor, Jimmy Rogers," Antone said proudly. "That's how I started doing it. I'd bring those guys and let them play together."[5]

As far as Chicago bluesmen were concerned, their relationship with Antone was a marriage made in heaven: good money, good food, and good music. In addition, there was the great appreciation by the club owner and total fan adulation. "I would imagine that between 1975 and 1985, we had more important blues than any club in Chicago," Antone said. "I don't think anyone, even in Chicago, had as many important blues shows as we did. I don't think they could match up . . . nobody was doing it for five days in a row."[6]

By 1981 the club had moved into what used to be Shakey's Pizza Parlor at 2915 Guadalupe Street. By then the word was out, and Antone's was not just thriving locally but was also earning a national reputation as the place to be if you wanted to hear good blues. For many of the elder blues veterans, Antone's wasn't just a place to play—it was a place to be loved and nurtured. Clifford so loved the blues and the men who made the music that he routinely went the extra mile, even making arrangements for the artists to have regular doctor appointments and seeing that their hospital bills were paid when they received medical attention in Austin. "He did that for all those guys," Kim Wilson recalled. "They got treated right; they had health care. As soon as they got there, they went to see Don Counts [the appointed local medical doctor chosen by Clifford Antone] to get a checkup. Any time anybody was sick, he'd take care of 'em."[7]

Kim stated emphatically that if there were any health issues, they didn't occur on Antone's watch. "When they got sick they would be gone from Austin," Wilson said.[8] Jimmy, Muddy, and others had to admit it: Clifford Antone was special. They hadn't been treated this well in Chicago for years—if ever. "That is someone who really cares about these blues legends," Kim said.[9] Antone's special brand of attention was paying off. Before he knew it, he had the largest draw of anyone in the country when it came to putting on an all-star blues extravaganza. As a result of his frequent visits, Jimmy Rogers's name became firmly cemented in the annals of Austin history.

Kim Wilson had been playing with Jimmy since the very beginning of the Antone era, and was the number one man whenever Jimmy came near Austin. "He was a big mentor of mine," Kim said. "He took me under his wing; he kept me in the business, treated me as an equal. He filled a void." With Kim's experiences as a record producer and bandleader, he knew how to take care of Jimmy's musical needs. "I would always put the best people with him—Ted Harvey, Bob Stroger, Pinetop, people I've known, all the guys, my whole life," Kim said proudly. This, of course, was the fuel Jimmy needed to take his music to new heights, which in turn forced Kim to play his harp even harder. That was exactly how Jimmy liked it. "He really gave me a cushion to take off and do my thing," Kim declared.

"He'd look over at me, sweating his ass off, and go, 'Muthafucka, you can *play* that thing!' There was no way anybody could top us when we played together."[10]

Clifford Antone had taken a special liking to Jimmy, booking him whenever he could. Jimmy was shifting musicians between two groups—his road band and his local band. By the mid-1980s he had made Austin one of his regular stops whenever he was traveling throughout the Southwest on tour, but most of the time he didn't take his Chicago band with him. The flexible lineup of backing musicians included Madison Slim, Barrelhouse Chuck, Hip Linkchain, Rich Kirch, Right Hand Frank, Little Rich Yescalis, and Ted Harvey. Former Rogers sideman, guitarist, and bassist Dave Clark had recently left the group to join an outfit led by his friend Ross Bon.

In the summer of 1985, Clifford Antone threw a bash at his club (by then located at 2928 Guadalupe Street) to honor the ten-year anniversary of its grand opening in July 1975. It was a weeklong celebration that stretched from Monday the eighth to Monday the fifteenth. The celebration featured several of Antone's favorite musicians from Chicago in an all-star tribute to Magic Sam. Guest performers were Buddy Guy, Jimmy Rogers, Albert Collins, James Cotton, Pinetop Perkins, Otis Rush, Junior Wells, Eddie Taylor, Hubert Sumlin, Sunnyland Slim, and Luther Tucker.

Antone loved pairing the musicians in a wide variety of combinations, often achieving spectacular results and stellar marathon jams that went on for hours. He also included many resident artists and local talents, including hometown favorites Derek O'Brien, Jimmie and Stevie Ray Vaughan on guitars, George Rains on drums, Sarah Brown on bass, Denny Freeman on piano, Mark Kazanoff and Joe Sublett on saxes, and Kim Wilson on harp. On that July 15, Jimmy sat in with Snooky Pryor and backed him up as he performed "How'd You Learn to Shake It Like That" (*"your daddy was a preacher, your mama was an alley cat!"*), with Eddie Taylor on guitar, Sunnyland Slim on piano, Bob Stroger on bass, Timothy Taylor on drums, and Derek O'Brien on guitar. Eddie Taylor then stepped up and performed "If You Don't Want Me Baby" with the same backing band, followed by Sunnyland Slim, who performed "Built Up from the Ground."

Jimmy was having a ball by this time. He joined harp veteran James Cotton to perform his early '50s debut hit on Sun Records, "Cotton Crop Blues," with another killer band of Luther Tucker, Pinetop Perkins, Bob Stroger, and Ted Harvey. After Pinetop took the lead on "Caldonia" with this same ensemble, it was Jimmy's turn to take charge. He chose "Walkin' by Myself" as his triumphant anthem, much to the delight of the crowd. Kim said, "He was great with songs in the key of E and A, he and Eddie Taylor."[11] Later he performed with local favorite Jimmie Vaughan on guitar. With Tim Taylor on drums, Jimmy grinned broadly as his homeboys James Cotton and Bob Stroger helped him drive home a swinging version of "You're Sweet."

Jimmy's laid-back style was a popular draw at Antone's. There were times, however, when Jimmy would tap into another bag just to prove a point. "One time I heard some stuff that sounded like B. B. King," Kim recalled. "I look up, and there's Jimmy smilin' with that big ol' Cheshire cat smile, when he was really enjoying himself . . . that gold tooth gleaming. He was smilin' his ass off. I was thinking, *look* at this guy!"[12] Kim's close kinship with Jimmy went well beyond the music. "I loved Jimmy as a person. Muddy was like my dad; Jimmy was like my uncle." Wilson, who had logged countless hours as a sideman for some of the best guitarists in the business who came through Austin, had a bird's-eye view of Jimmy's playing and came to appreciate his skills. According to Kim, "He could play very sophisticated things on the guitar. He didn't always do it, but he could whenever he wanted to. I loved backing him up."[13]

Kim also spent some quality time off the bandstand with Rogers, which was where he first learned about Jimmy's obsession with his favorite pastime—fishing.

One day I went to see him—they were staying at the Stephen F. Austin Hotel, when Antone's was on Sixth Street. I walk into the room—I couldn't believe the smoke alarm wasn't goin' off; the whole floor was covered in smoke and smelled like fish! There's Jimmy and Hubcap; they'd gone fishin' down over there in Lake Austin—which is polluted as hell—and caught a bunch of crappie or bluegill or somethin'. They drove down from Chicago and they brought a deep fryer with them. They were deep-fryin' all that fish in the hotel room. They were flushing the carcasses and oil down the toilet.[14]

The other favorite pastime, of course, was drinking, and there was plenty of that to go around, especially in a place like Antone's. During those weeklong stretches, the host created the perfect environment for his guests during nightly after-hours sessions. Everybody got to stay up late, gather in the back room and play blues, and drink at the bar well past closing time. Kim was right in the middle of it most of the time and admitted that many of his drinking adventures with Jimmy became the stuff of legend. "He was very much a night person," Wilson revealed. "Jimmy would always say, 'Yeah, get one for you, and one for *me!*' Somehow he could handle his shit, but I couldn't handle mine as well as those guys. I think he was a different guy at home; I don't think he drank as much."

Kim mentioned a strange sight that he encountered one evening when they were partying. "Jimmy used to carry this little gold coffin; he opened it up, and under the lid of the coffin was a picture of Little Walter in *his* coffin," Wilson declared.[15]

Of course, Austin, important as it was, was not home base to Jimmy. After each gig at Antone's, he headed back to the Windy City and to his local band-mates. The mid-1985 edition of Jimmy's lineup for the year had stabilized somewhat, with fewer musicians moving in and out. Wild Child Butler, Barrelhouse Chuck, Hip Linkchain, Rich Kirch, Right Hand Frank, and Ted Harvey remained as constants in his starting lineup. There was one notable change, however: Ariyo was gone, having taken a temporary gig as a "tour guide" of sorts in July as he made a special appearance as a pianist on the Japan tour of Robert Junior Lockwood. His sudden departure left an opening that Jimmy needed to fill quickly.

Dave Waldman was a multitalented, gifted musician and academic student who attended and taught at the University of Chicago. He played both the harmonica and the guitar quite capably and had an uncanny knack for copying certain blues legends' style with note-for-note precision. He could imitate Little Walter on the harp, then turn around and copy Jimmy Rogers's style on guitar with the same degree of accuracy. He'd been following Jimmy's career for a quite a while. "In the early to mid-'70s he was playing at the club Elsewhere," Waldman recalled. "So we went down there and we were so excited. Jimmy Rogers was one of my favorite artists of all time. And really, the way I play guitar, I really kind of modeled it after him [his older style]."[16]

Oddly enough, when Waldman actually met with Jimmy Rogers in 1985, neither of those talents were needed. "I was at a club, playing harp; I think probably with Big Smokey Smothers at the club B.L.U.E.S. located at 2519 North Halsted," Waldman recalled. "Eddie Taylor stopped by and said that he had mentioned my name to Jimmy Rogers about getting me a job. Jimmy Rogers showed up later. I was talking with him, along with Rich Yescalis, and Jimmy Rogers said that he was in the club looking for a piano player. At that point I said, 'Oh, I play piano!'"[17]

This statement was only partially true, as Waldman had no reputation or track record whatsoever as a blues pianist in Chicago, and he knew that. "I really had never played piano with a band or anything," he later confessed. Jimmy did not believe he was serious and said, "No, no—you're not a piano player. You're a harp player." Then Yescalis suddenly chimed in and said, "No, he really does play piano." "Oh, in that case, I'll hire you," Jimmy Rogers said, adding, "We're leaving tomorrow and then we will be in Atlanta the following day." According to Rich, at that point Dave's face turned absolutely white. "I had never played piano with a band," Waldman said. "I was sorta' thinking, 'Oh, my God, what have I gotten myself into?'" Before he knew it, Waldman had just been enlisted. He quickly tried to reverse the spell, backpedaling as fast as he could, trying to talk his way out of it. "Look, why don't you go around to the other clubs tonight and see if you can find another piano player. You really ought to hear me before you hire me." "No, no," Jimmy shot back. "If you say you can play, then you can play."[18] Dave's fate—or luck—was now sealed.

He went home and called up his friend Steve Cushing. "Oh, my God, Steve, what have I gotten myself into?" Cushing replied, "Come on, stop acting like an old man. This is just the kind of thing that you have been working towards!" After staying up all night worrying, Dave was awakened bright and early the next morning to the sound of a ringing phone. "I picked it up," Waldman said, "and a deep bass voice said, 'This is Jimmy Rogers and I am calling Dave Waldman just trying to speed him on his way.'" Once Waldman realized it wasn't a joke, he quickly got his gear and made his way to Jimmy's house, the traditional departure point for all tours. "We drove all night. I was very stressed and I thought, 'Oh, my God, he will just put me right back on the bus to Chicago.' So we got to the club and I sat down at the piano and I started playing . . . I had always tried to play like Otis Spann . . . The stuff I was playing just fit with the stuff he was playing like a hand in a glove, and then the next three weeks were absolutely great."[19]

Jimmy was pleased with the job that Waldman did, even if his personality was a bit quirky. Waldman, a self-admitted outspoken individual, was highly critical of almost everything musical—as a result of a particularly discerning ear, which served as both a blessing and a curse. On one hand, it allowed him to analyze and replicate with spooky precision practically any style he heard—a wonderful attribute for any musician, regardless of style. On the other hand, it made it damn near impossible for anyone, including himself, to live up to the high expectations that come with perfection.

Many musicians he worked with found his discriminating tastes—combined with his outspokenness—irksome, to say the least. Still, others swore that he had to be some kind of genius. Whatever the case, Waldman enjoyed his time with Jimmy and the guys, who duly impressed him. "I really thought that the music that we had then really came out pretty nicely," he admitted. "We had Big Smokey Smothers on guitar—he had a background with Muddy Waters and knew how to play the low bass runs that Muddy Waters had played with Rogers, so he was really playing the right 'second guitar' stuff behind Jimmy. And we had Wild Child Butler, who kind of stayed in the background; we didn't have an overbearing harp player. As for me, I was just kind of staying in the background."[20]

The "overbearing harp player" reference was a not-too-subtle jab at Little Joe Berson, whom Waldman absolutely detested. Theirs was an ongoing and well-publicized feud that played out repeatedly. According to Dave, "He was like a blustering, sort of insecure person. He tried to keep other harp players away from Jimmy Rogers. [He] felt threatened, you know . . . when [Berson] was playing, you could never sit in with Jimmy Rogers on harp, which was really a shame, because he was one of the greatest guys for backing a harp that there ever was in the music."[21] Obviously there were those who hated Little Joe's tactics and those who loved him as a person. Among those who loved him were Frank Bandy and Barrelhouse Chuck, Berson's longtime bandmates and Florida cronies. Both of them would staunchly defend their blustering friend. Barrelhouse once remarked admiringly, "He had the biggest sound; he was obsessed."[22]

Jimmy didn't allow himself to get too carried away with all the personal differences between bandmates; he was too busy tending to more pressing matters, like the itinerary for the road gigs they had to perform. Their current tour was fairly lightweight compared to some in the past, which allowed Waldman to relax a bit. "We played in Atlanta for a week," he recalled, "then we drove across the South. We went to a place called the Caravan of Dreams in Fort Worth. We played there, I think, for a week." (The Caravan gig was actually for only three nights.[23]) "Then we went down to Texas. We played one night at Antone's to begin; I think it was their tenth-anniversary festival. Then we went to San Antonio, we played a night, and returned again to Austin. Jimmy Rogers was going to be one of the stars there, so he really didn't need his band; he was going to be playing with the all-star group."[24]

Waldman, a harp player himself, was totally blown away by Kim Wilson's performance, saying that Kim was by far the best harp player around. "I mean, Kim Wilson is really a cut above everybody else," Dave admitted. "When I was down at Antone's I heard Kim Wilson backing up Jimmy Rogers and I thought that was just wonderful. Kim played all of these wonderful, hard-edged, angular licks behind Jimmy in Little Walter style, and it was just wonderful, just tremendous."[25]

Waldman got to see firsthand why Jimmy was so popular there and why he never refused an invitation from Clifford when asked to headline the show at Antone's. "Clifford Antone liked to do things in a big, out-sized way, so he just put a bunch of hotel rooms at Jimmy Rogers's disposal," said Dave. "So I was able to just stay for the rest of the week and see this great festival at Antone's with just about every major Chicago blues guy down there at one point or another during the week. They all played together and it was really wonderful." With both Pinetop Perkins and Jimmy as his heroes, watching them battle it out on the stage with the all-star lineup in Austin was a real thrill. Waldman hadn't seen anything like it. "It took me another week just to come back to reality," he said with a laugh.[26]

Dave seemed eternally grateful for the time he got to spend with Jimmy, whom he described as a leader who "was basically congenial; he was friendly to me. Musically, he was wonderful; he had that smooth voice." Dave also may have gotten a glimpse of something about Jimmy's music that most people didn't recognize at the time. "One time I was in B.L.U.E.S. after a gig and I was mingling around on the piano," Waldman remembered. "I was playing like Walter Davis, and Jimmy Rogers came out and he was starting to sing along, which was kind of unusual for him; it's hard to imagine him just coming out and singing. But then he said, 'Yeah, Walter Davis, he was my foundation when I was starting out in St. Louis.'"[27]

Jimmy did spend time in St. Louis before coming to Chicago, and it certainly is plausible that the legendary piano player may have played an instrumental role in helping shape Jimmy's musical concept of "I Used to Have a Woman." "I always thought there was a big connection between Jimmy Rogers's music and Walter Davis's music," Waldman said. When trying to sum up his experience in the band, he concluded, "It was great. I mean, he [Jimmy] was one of the greatest second guitar players in the history of blues, and he had a beautifully wistful way of playing with that great full sound where he would be playing on the bass strings and the upper strings."[28]

Jimmy was still doing gigs on the East Coast and having a great time traveling and playing with members of Steve Guyger's Excellos and Sugar Ray Norcia's Bluetones. Bassist Mudcat Ward recalls one particular weeklong engagement on Nantucket Island when the band had to take a ferry out of Woods Hole, Massachusetts, well beyond Martha's Vineyard. "We went to do a whole week at the same club," Ward said. "The entire gig was George Lewis's doing; he was providing Jimmy with a lot of money and work." Indeed, Lewis seemed to have limitless resources when it came to securing gigs for Jimmy and the band: Mudcat, George Lewis, Anthony Geraci, Ted Harvey, and Steve Guyger. "The gigs were at this jive restaurant that turned into a bar after hours," said Mudcat. "On Friday and Saturday we had a crowd, but Monday through Thursday, and Sunday, there was nobody at the club by nine o'clock when we got there."[29]

At least they were comfortable; they were ensconced in an expansive—and expensive—beach house, where they kicked up their heels. "We had this house and we stayed in it all week," recalled Ward. "Ted Harvey was the drummer for that gig. He handled the kitchen chores, and he was a great cook." The band found themselves with quite a bit of free time on their hands, "So we played cards all week long when we weren't at the gig—this endless card came called 'Tonk.'" Mudcat told a story about an event that occurred during one of those long, boring nights when they played this card game where the players needed two sets of three of a kind to win. Ted Harvey, known throughout the band as a very lucky person at cards, was well ahead of things as the weeklong marathon progressed. "The rest of us were coming out even," Mudcat recounted. What he describes next is absolutely hilarious.

> Jimmy cheats at cards, I'm sorry to tell you. We were playing for nickels and dimes; everybody had these coin jars. Jimmy kept losing. So Jimmy invents these rules out of nowhere. At one point he *slams* the cards down and yells, "*Tonk!* I win!" We go, "Whatd'ya mean, you won?" He goes, "What—don't you *know*? If you're dealt five face cards before anyone pulls a card to start the game, if you slam the cards down and yell, 'Tonk,' you win?" "No, nobody ever told us that!" "Well, I'm sorry nobody *told* ya, but those are the rules, and I win; this is *my* money!" Then someone else got five face cards, so they slam it down and yell, "*Tonk!*" Jimmy says, "Well . . . sorry—I win *again*, see . . . I got a forty-nine." We say, "What'n the hell's a *forty-nine!*" "Oh, it's when you get four face cards and a nine! Forty-nine can trump five face cards. I win again!" He rakes the pile across the table to himself with a big grin on his face . . . unbelievable, this guy![30]

Mudcat gave a hearty laugh and then finished the story by describing the next night when Jimmy was losing his nickels and dimes yet again. "Jimmy says, 'I'm tired of playing Tonk; now we're gonna play *my* game—Georgia Skin.' He was making up rules that changed every single time, making it up as he went and pulling cards off the bottom of the deck. It was hilarious."[31]

Once the East Coast tour was done, Jimmy headed back home to Chicago for a few weeks' rest. As the number of grandchildren increased, Jimmy and his family moved from the housing projects on the West Side and bought a new home located just off the corner of Sixty-third Street and Honore Avenue, on the South Side. Jimmy and Dorothy gave their full attention to their new home, and Jimmy quickly became known in the neighborhood as a pillar in the community. He was a highly respected individual whom even the local roughnecks honored, vowing to keep safeguard over his van full of equipment that always sat in the same open street lot on the corner of Sixty-fourth Street when he returned from long road trips. Street gang leaders loyally protected the turf on his behalf, putting the word out that the vehicle and its contents were permanently off limits, with a stiff penalty for anyone who dared cause an infraction. "You know whose van that is? Ya don't mess 'round wit' it." Head slowly nodding, with unblinking eyes—just to make sure the point was getting across to the thug pals, the leader confirms Jimmy's status in the 'hood: "Mr. Rogers's van, ya dig?"

Jimmy toured West Germany in the summer of 1985. The Bluesfest in Bonn saw Jimmy and Wild Child Butler back together again after Butler returned to the group for a spell. "While Jimmy Rogers was rather laid back, Butler sang very powerfully," wrote Klaus Kilian in *Living Blues* magazine.[32] Meanwhile, John Stedman released the third compilation in a trilogy of Jimmy Rogers/Left Hand Frank albums, this time milking the material for everything it was worth. Almost all of the songs were identical in content to the first album, released in 1979 as *Chicago Blues* (JSP 1090). This collection, titled *The Dirty Dozens,* had little new to offer, with the exception of a few items that deserve mentioning: the finally corrected title for "Honky Tonk" (previously identified incorrectly as "Oh Baby"); a slow version of "One Room Country Shack"; and "Cleo's Gone," an obvious tongue-in-cheek reference to "Cleo's Back," the ultra-funky instrumental made popular by tenor saxophonist Junior Walker and His All-Stars.

On February 7, 1986, Jimmy was asked by Jim O'Neal to come into Soto Sound Studio in Evanston, Illinois, and do overdubs on a few of tracks for Wild Child Butler's album *Lickin' Gravy*. Earlier versions of the songs contained on the 1986 album had been originally recorded on November 11, 1969, for Mercury, on an album called *Keep On Doing What You're Doing*. In June 1976 Butler had rerecorded the bulk of the tracks at the Music Factory in Wisconsin for M.C. Records. The music was now being scheduled for rerelease on Jim O'Neal's Rooster label, repackaged as *Lickin' Gravy*, with Jimmy's manager, Tom Radai, serving as the co-producer. O'Neal seemed to recall Butler approached him about overseeing the project. "He had the tapes for the album when it came out on the Roots label; he'd produced it himself in Milwaukee," O'Neal recalled. "I thought it needed a little more Chicago blues touch to it, so we hired Jimmy Rogers and Pinetop."[33]

Pinetop laid down eight tracks of overdubs; Jimmy, however, managed to get only three done. Evidently the jovial atmosphere maintained by the two men got the better of Jimmy on that day, a rare occurrence. "I remember Jimmy only played on a few songs; it didn't really go as well as I'd hoped; he was little tipsy," O'Neal said. Luckily, also accompanying Jimmy was his son Jimmy D. Lane, who was asked to rerecord portions of the sessions. "I first met Jimmy D. on the day of that session," said O'Neal. "We had him try to play along with some of the tapes, but he wasn't quite cutting it, so we didn't really use any of it."[34] When all was said and done, Jimmy Rogers was credited with supplying an overdubbed guitar solo on "Gravy Child," lead and rhythm guitars on "Rooster Blues," and lead guitar on "Speed."

Butler had now joined forces with Jimmy Rogers on tour, recently appearing with him at two blues festivals as part of Washington, D.C.'s Potomac Riverfest.[35] Rich Kirch recalled the festival because it was a rare occasion; John Wesley "Foots" Berry would play piano and joined on tours that took Jimmy's band to the West Coast. Berry was a piano player with Hank Ballard and the Midnighters. His real name was John Wesley Harding, "named after a gunfighter, I think," Kirch said. Little Rich Yescalis also remembers the festival well: "We drove all night to get to the gig. When Duke Robillard was finishing his set, the rains came." Promoters were in a bind. How could they pay Jimmy for not making an appearance? But he was there—his band had actually arrived. What to do? "We [only] had to go onstage and wave before they would pay us," Yescalis recalled with humor.[36]

Later the band went to a club and played an after set; then they loaded up the van and headed back to Chicago. Yescalis, meanwhile, went to Philadelphia to see a friend. He was probably glad he wasn't there when he found out about the mishap that occurred as the band made their return trip. "They had a flat on the way back, and Jimmy had the wrong jack," Rich was told by Barrelhouse Chuck. "Pinetop, Willie, and 'Fuzz' Jones just happened to drive by and saw them. They stopped, and 'Big Eyes' Willie Smith changed the tire for them."[37]

By 1986 several more personnel changes had taken place. Newcomer Scott Bradbury had entered the Rogers arena on harp, although Madison Slim still made appearances. Barrelhouse had quit the band temporarily and was replaced by Ariyo, who had returned to the band from his temporary Junior Lockwood gig. Newcomer guitarist Nick Moss was recommended on the strength of Dave Clark's word to Jimmy, although Rich Kirch was still doing part-time guitar work with Jimmy. "Jimmy Rogers was one of the greatest bandleaders to work for," Moss said. "I was just a kid in the band, and he treated me just like anyone else."[38] The bass chair still belonged to Right Hand Frank, with the ever present Ted Harvey on drums.

Back in Austin, Clifford Antone was gearing up for the eleventh anniversary at Antone's, dedicated to Eddie Taylor, who died on Christmas Day of 1985. Jimmy was excited about participating in the festivities. "Oh man, Antone's is the best spot in the world as far as I'm concerned." Jimmy declared. "I started coming here in the early '70s. I come three, maybe four times a year. Sometimes I would stay months at a time. Austin, Texas, is a second home for me because of this club." Since 1982 the club had moved to a new location on Guadalupe Street. About Clifford's decision to relocate, Jimmy said, "Every place he moves is just as hot as the others. I have a slogan, 'If you can't dig the blues you must have a hole in yo' soul.' Everybody here got good souls. That's the bottom line of it."[39]

Once back in Austin, Jimmy proceeded to participate in what was described in *Living Blues* magazine as "a hair-raising set on Saturday by Jimmy Rogers, Jimmie Vaughan, Pinetop Perkins and Kim Wilson, with bassist Sarah Brown and drummer Wes Starr."[40]Clifford Antone and Angela Strehli were now not only co-owners of the club but also co-producers of the record label that captured the music at Antone's. In 1986 they released the album, *Antone's Tenth Anniversary Anthology, Vol. 1*, which featured highlights from the previous year's event. Jimmy's music was prominently featured throughout the LP. His star was still riding high.

After returning to Chicago, Jimmy participated in an event that served as a fund-raiser for *Living Blues* magazine. The event was sponsored by Jim and Amy O'Neal to raise money to keep the magazine running. On July 20 the "8th Annual Blues Cookout, Blues Jam & Record Sale" was held by the magazine at B.L.U.E.S on Halsted Street. Meanwhile, several of Jimmy's former bandmates were going off in different directions. Madison Slim had just joined the Legendary Blues Band (a collection of veteran Muddy Waters sidemen). Barrelhouse Chuck was playing with his own band—the Blue Lights—with Johnny B. Moore, Barkin' Bill Smith, John Tanner, and S. P. Leary. Hip Linkchain was playing on the West Side at the Artesia Lounge, owned by harp ace Little Arthur Duncan.

Consequently, in the last part of 1986 Jimmy had to rebuild his band again. The lineup looked different on October 3–4 when Jimmy Rogers and Wild Child Butler were featured at the Blues Saloon (formerly called Wilebski's), located at the corner of Western Avenue and Thomas Street in St. Paul, Minnesota. Foots Berry was in the band for these gigs, and, according to reports, he was the life of the party. "Foots comes to life at the keyboards," wrote Paul Rossez. "He has undeniable charisma, and the audience picked up on it. They cheered the loudest for his solos, and he was clearly having as much fun as anybody that night." Bassist Rich Yescalis, rhythm guitarist Dave Clark, and drummer Ted Harvey rounded out the group, each of them thoroughly complimented for their musical support in the Rogers band.[41]

After this short road gig, the reconfigured band headed back home. Jimmy was always comfortable when he performed at his Chicago spots, and he customarily let a few people sit in each night. One night, however, things didn't work out too well. Local drummer Steve Cushing, widely known for the late Saturday night/early Sunday morning radio show *Blues Before Sunrise*, was close friends with Frank Bandy. Cushing was well respected in the field as being more than capable of handling a gig or jam session, having already played with several veterans, including Big Smokey Smothers, Magic Slim, Eddie Taylor, and Good Rockin' Charles. Given his musical credentials, it is not surprising that Bandy waved him up to the stage. "He wanted to sit in really bad," Bandy admitted. "Jimmy's attitude was, 'always give a guy a chance.' So I let him play."[42]

To everyone's surprise, things somehow didn't go too well. "For some reason, he [Cushing] didn't want to play a backbeat that night. He kept banging on the *side* of his drums . . . I think he was trying to recreate the old-time feel, like when Muddy was with Big Crawford, the way Elga played." Backstage, Jimmy chewed Bandy out about the situation, which no doubt triggered flashbacks of when he'd had to endure numerous past scenarios similar to this, like when Little Walter or John Littlejohn allowed various strangers to sit in, producing musical results that were usually dubious at best. "Jimmy got a little irritated with me . . . he really didn't want that kinda' sound." Jimmy, never one to lose his cool in public, gave Bandy a calm yet stern warning: "Don't do that to me, man . . . don't leave me out there hangin' like that."[43]

Indeed, Jimmy was all business when it came to his sidemen getting the sound right while they played behind him. He knew exactly what he wanted from each instrument. And he knew why he liked Bandy's bass lines. "Jimmy always said, 'Play my stuff like the record,'" Bandy said. "But, as the bass player, he did *not* want me to play the lines like Willie Dixon. Jimmy preferred more of a smooth line than the thumpy acoustic bass line. Jimmy could tell that I got my bass lines from Muddy's band—the Calvin Jones method. Jimmy would say, 'Play it like Calvin Jones.'" After further thought, Bandy clarified his position, saying, "My sound was a cross between Dave Myers and Calvin Jones. In my playing he liked that he could hear the turnaround." Dave Myers's influence on Bandy's style predated the invention of the Fender bass. "'Left Hand Frank Craig once told me that the way they would play before the electric bass came out, they would take a regular six string and tune it down to an A, then tune it in fourths, so they would have A-D-G-C," recalled Bandy.[44]

As time passed, Right Hand Frank learned more about Jimmy Rogers, who always seemed to have a few tricks up his sleeve. There was the time, for example, when they were doing a routine gig and Little Joe Berson decided to pull a fast one just for kicks after his harp solo. "Usually we opened with an instrumental, then Little Joe or Hip would sing one or two tunes, then Jimmy would play a set," Bandy remembered. "Then he'd come down off the stage, and there would be a rousing 'E' shuffle." This time, though, just for the fun of it, Berson thought he could catch Jimmy off guard. According to Bandy, "At one point, Little Joe handed Jimmy the mike—then handed Jimmy the *harmonica.*" Always up for a good laugh, Jimmy pulled a better stunt on Berson. "Jimmy played a few licks of music for about twelve bars," Bandy said. "When Joe took it back, the harp was upside down! That just made me and Joe get tear-welled, because we discovered right then that Jimmy played like Sonny Terry." That night Bandy realized just how unique Jimmy's style was. "I called Scott Dirks whether he thought something was different about that sound that Jimmy got on 'Round About Boogie,'" Bandy said, "and he said, yes, he thought something sounded really different about that."[45]

Jimmy wrapped up the year by playing the Abilene Café in New York on December 5, 1986, then started 1987 on the road by performing at Blues Harbor in Atlanta for a week from February 3 to February 8.[46] That summer he played the Chicago BluesFest, with invited guest James Cotton on harp.[47] Jimmy performed on Saturday, July 2, at the fourth annual Mississippi Valley Blues Festival in Davenport, Iowa. By the end of the first half of 1987, Jimmy's son Little Jimmy—known to many as "Jimmy D."—had already formed his own band, called Blue Train Running. Most of the time he performed with his dad, unless his own touring schedule took Blue Train Running to other locations. "I only opened for him with my full band at Buddy Guy's place," Jimmy D. said. (This was Legends, not the old Checkerboard Lounge on Forty-third Street.) Led by Jimmy D., this group included Bandy on bass, Neil Rose on drums, and Scotty Bradbury on harp and vocals. Rich Kirch still played in Big Jimmy's band.[48]

For the most part the Jimmy Rogers band took their touring gigs in stride, enjoying the playing, the after-hours jamming, and even some card playing. Occasionally, as with any group, things went sour. A highly negative incident occurred on their most recent overseas tour, involving a few band members who decided to "hijack" Jimmy over financial matters. A few of them threatened not to play if they didn't get more money. Not usually one to show his emotions, Jimmy wasn't furious at those who threatened to walk out on the tour; rather, he was devastated that any of his bandmates would instigate such a rebellion when he'd always tried to do his best by treating his musicians fairly. Now they were messing with his music.

According to Madison Slim, who immediately indicated that he wanted absolutely no part of the so-called coup, Jimmy took it very hard. Unfortunately, Jimmy D. wasn't there at the time. "It wasn't that I'd left the Rogers band," Lane said. "I had contractual obligations with my own band, which clashed with the dates that he had. The bands were going in two different geographical directions." However, this incident was serious—Jimmy D. had never known his dad to be so upset. Jimmy Senior asked his son to come in and protect the family's interests. When Jimmy D. heard about the clash, "I canceled everything I had, and we came on back with Pop."[49]

Basically, Jimmy needed someone to watch his back, and Jimmy D. was up to the challenge. "When it comes to me, I'm a straight shooter . . . and I'd like to think that I can spot bullshit," Jimmy D. said. "And then I started runnin' into these guys; I could smell it before I turned the corner. They kinda shied away from me, because they knew that if they were trying to take advantage of him, it wasn't gonna happen anymore when I got into traveling and touring with him. I joined right around the time when I did my first gig with him at Lilly's."[50] Of course, this meant Jimmy Senior had to retool his band all over again.

He reinstated Barrelhouse Chuck on piano, kept his good friend Madison Slim by his side, and had his son Jimmy on guitar full-time. He now needed a bass player. Jimmy D. recalled, "I think Bob Stroger was going back with Otis Rush, so I told Pop, 'Hey, I got a bass player that knows the stuff, because he plays with me already.'" The bassist, Fred Crawford, was a teenage friend and musical collaborator of Jimmy D. Their relationship went all the way back to one of Little Jimmy's first bands in Chicago. Now that the band was restructured, Jimmy D. had assumed the leadership role onstage, making sure things went smoothly. "We would do one number each before we brought him out," he said. "The harmonica player would do a number, the piano player would do one, then I would do a number, and then Dad would come out."[51]

Jimmy was the main attraction at the Abilene Café on September 5–6. After a smoking set that included "Walkin' by Myself" and his favorite closer, "Mojo," he performed a rare acoustic set. He did "Love Her with a Feeling," "Brown Skin Woman," and "Little Girl." John Campbell opened for him as acoustic guitarist. Campbell also opened for Johnny Littlejohn, who played two weeks after Jimmy. Steve Guyger was playing with the Excellos in May of that year, no longer in Jimmy's band for the time being.[52]

On December 2, 1987, Little Joe Berson passed away. No matter how hard some people found him to get along with, he was one of Jimmy's favorite harp players of all time; they'd played together on and off for around ten years. "Jimmy really loved Little Joe Berson's playing," Frank Bandy said. "He joined the band before me. Joe played from '78 right up until the end. He died a mysterious death."[53] Four hours before he died, he called his longtime friend, pianist Barrelhouse Chuck, who provided insight into Berson's last moments: "I talked to him; he wanted me to go out with him, and I couldn't go because I had food poisoning. It was winter. We talked for an hour and a half. He had a massive heart attack and died. I designed his headstone."[54] When Little Joe died he was replaced on tours by Wild Child Butler. "John Foots Berry on piano would also join us on tours," Rich Kirch remembered. "I recall traveling to Bozeman, Montana, for a weeklong gig and then on to Seattle, Washington, to play at the Ballard Firehouse in Washington State."[55]

After Berson's death, several people jockeyed for position to win the coveted harp chair. "Joe used to let Scott [Bradbury] sit in, and at one point he thought he was next in line to get the gig for Jimmy Rogers," said Bandy.[56] Interestingly, there were two Scotts positioning themselves for the role; Scott Dirks had also been close with Berson and had sat in with the band on occasion. The Rogers band had unfinished business, and Berson's unexpected death caught them all off guard. "We actually had a band job the next week," Bandy said. Joe Berson had befriended yet another harp player, Matthew Skoller, who also remembered the night Joe Berson died. "It was the same night Jimmy Johnson's band members were killed in that horrible automobile accident," he recalled.[57]

Skoller knew Berson well, and felt they had a close-knit relationship. "He was a tough New York Jew, and he'd kick a muthafucka's ass for lookin' at him wrong," Skoller said emphatically. "He liked me 'cuz I'm kind of a little tough New York Jew myself. But I'm a lover, not a fighter," he added with a laugh. Turning serious again, he said, "He took me under his wing. He was makin' a lotta money sellin' wine at the time [we met], and I was livin' in a hallway back then. He came up to me and shoved a hundred-dollar bill in my pocket and said, 'Don't fuckin' tell anybody about that or you're gonna have to have to pay it back.'" Skoller was well aware of Joe's reputation, but insisted, "He was really a sweet guy underneath all that bravado. And he was a soul man."[58]

In the end it was Jimmy's call as to who would be the replacement for Berson. And so he made it. "I got a phone call one evening," Skoller recalled. "I was taking a nap. I said, 'Hello?' He said in deep voice, 'Is Matt Skoller available; this is Jimmy Rogers.' I said, 'Yeah, and I'm Muddy Waters!' He said, 'No, this is *Jimmy Rogers!*' I said, 'Oh, excuse me, sir!' 'I hear you're a real good harp player. I'm playin' down at Lilly's—you wanna come down and blow?' I said, 'Yeah!'" Skoller was twenty-six years old, and his reputation as a fine harp blower had made the rounds. Several people had told Jimmy about him; Berson might have been one of them.

> I got my gig clothes on and went down to Lilly's. It was me, Little Jimmy, Big Moose Walker [who was taking Barrelhouse Chuck's place at the time], Ted Harvey on drums, "Right Hand" Frank Bandy. After I played that night,

he [Jimmy] looked at me after the end of the first set and said, "You jus' like Kim [Wilson]—you a *feedin' muthafucka* [implying that Matthew knew how to play off him and around him the way he liked it]. If you wanna be my harp player, you got the job." It was a huge compliment, I'll never forget that. I was in seventh heaven.[59]

Things went smoothly for the next few weeks.

Then I got a call from "Big Daddy" [Kinsey]. The Kinsey Report was the hottest thing in Chicago at that time. So Jimmy wasn't taking the band out on the road with him at that point; we were pretty much relegated to his local gigs. He was payin' us forty bucks a night, which was hard to live on. I told him, "I really wanna stay with you, but they wanna fly me to Florida to do an album, tour Europe . . ." He said, "Hey, listen—you gotta make a livin', so go ahead. That's good money and a good opportunity, and you should take it." He was very gracious and very paternal.

Skoller bowed out gracefully and was grateful for the brief but rewarding time period he spent inside the Rogers band. "I did eight or ten gigs over a couple of months. I wasn't a long-time veteran of his groups. Don't get me wrong; but the man *hired* me, and told me he loved my playing. That meant the world to me." Indeed, Skoller never had any aspirations about trying to be the favorite harp player. According to Skoller, "Steve Guyger was the cat that Jimmy really considered his man—he was really a monster player."[60]

At the beginning of the new year, 1988, Jimmy accepted an invitation to join Clifford Antone's blues bus tour, an all-star event that brought together many of the regular performers at Antone's for a cross-country jam session. Kim Wilson remembers how it all went down: "I devised a tour in 1988 that we called Antone's West. Jimmy, Luther Tucker, Buddy Guy, Albert Collins, James Cotton, Mel Brown, Derek O'Brien, Willie Smith, Calvin Jones—all of 'em. It was a huge revue. Buddy Guy sat on that stage every single night in his chair, watching Jimmy Rogers."[61]

The Antone's West Revue arrived in Sacramento in January 1988 to play at the Crest Theatre, the twelfth stop on a fourteen-city tour that had started in Tucson, Arizona, seventeen days earlier. This was Antone's second tour; the first tour, during the previous fall, had been shorter and with truncated performances. This time they gave Sacramento a three-and-a-half-hour concert. Miles Jordan described Jimmy's portion of the show as intense, stating that it was a "55-minute ambush on the blues that was very tight and gave plenty of solo space to the main men . . . Rogers was in excellent form, and, a bit earlier, he sang his own 'Gold Tailed Bird,' then brought the tempo up for a boogie that showcased the too rarely seen Tucker, who really stole the show on the succeeding 'Lemon Squeezing Daddy.'"[62] Reportedly, Antone's third and fourth tours were already in the planning; they conquered the Southwest in mid-July, with an eastern tour scheduled for August.

On January 23, 1988, the revue rolled into Portland, Oregon, and played at a club called Starry Night. The humongous tour was a blues fan's dream; one star after another formed a steady stream off the bus and into the club. From Muddy's old band were Pinetop Perkins, Willie Smith, James Cotton, and Calvin Jones. Also from the West and South Sides of Chicago were guitar gunslingers Buddy Guy and Luther Tucker. From Austin there was Kim Wilson, Mel Brown, Angela Strehli, and Jimmie Vaughan.[63] Wilson remembered when they went to San Francisco in the spring of that year, and Jimmy joined in to perform a gig with local guitarist Rusty Zinn, a West Coast guitar wizard who emulated Jimmy's style perfectly. "Jimmy was a huge influence on Rusty Zinn," Kim said. "When we went over there in '88, Rusty was sixteen years old [actually he was a year or two older]. He's one of the only guys left who can play that way, behind a harmonica player."[64]

At some point during the tour the band rolled into Seattle, Washington, where former Rogers bassist Rich Molina reunited with Jimmy and met the entire entourage before their gig at the Moore Theater. Molina had already established friendships with Luther Tucker and Eddie Taylor from the Chicago days of the late '70s, so the reunion was highly enjoyable for all.[65] After a brief rest, Jimmy was back on the road again. He played at the Lone Star on February 29 with a band called the Abilene Houserockers. A few days after the concert, on March 3 1988, Peter Watrous of the *New York Times* wrote a great piece on Jimmy, saying, "When he sings, instead of using a bleak Mississippi cry to break through the din of the instruments, he sings with a warm, well-rounded voice that implies friendliness ... [His] voice is as smooth and urbane as ever and his guitar playing, a roiling mass of zig-zagging rhythms and blues figures, was as distinct as it was when he worked out architectural accompaniments for Muddy Waters during the '50s."[66]

There were, however, a few negative comments thrown in as well. "His first set was a disappointment," Watrous wrote. "The problem lay in his thick-fingered backup band, which drowned out the nuance of Rogers's singing, effectively ending any chance for his subtle musicality to shine. Mr. Rogers isn't a shouter, or a high-volume bluesman, he is an intimate performer; the band, mistaking volume for intensity, steamrolled him ... they became the foreground and [he] became the background, exactly the opposite of how it should have been."[67]

Perhaps part of the problem was that Madison Slim had left Jimmy's band by then and was playing with guitarist Billy Flynn in a band called the Nite Crawlers. The band was going through a few changes, and Jimmy was doing his best to stabilize the situation to keep things rolling while conditions were getting rough out on the road. When asked about his longevity in the often harsh world of the blues musician, Jimmy told writer Tom Townsley, in June 1988, "You keep on keepin' on. That's the way I feel. Don't give up. You may give out, but just keep on keepin' on. If you's in a lake swimmin', and you get tired and stop, you'll sink and drown. But just keep on paddlin' . . . That's the way I did. Nothin' stopped me." It was almost as if Jimmy was giving himself a pep talk for all the public to see. He knew they had a long road ahead, but he also knew he was the fearless leader who couldn't show signs of weariness. "I've been fighting it—more 'ups and downs' than [just] 'ups,'—but . . . I just keep on tryin' to find the end of the tunnel."[68]

Jimmy traveled from the West Coast tour with the Antone's revue back to Chicago in order to resume his own band tour that was headed toward the opposite coast. As part of the New York festival of Chicago blues, Jimmy played at Tramps on June 3. "His quiet introspective blues was a welcome respite from the summer's heat," wrote Jack Hunter in *Living Blues*.[69] In Houston the Antone's revue played at Rockefeller's on July 18, with Jimmy having the honors of playing the first set.[70] On the east end of Long Island in New York, Jimmy played a club called the Stephen Talkhouse on July 31 and August 1.[71] At some point during this road tour, Jimmy caught word that his and Muddy's close musical companion Fred Below had died on August 13, 1988, just a month shy of his sixty-second birthday. Jimmy's old friends were leaving this earth slowly and steadily, each loss a reminder that life dealt out more "ups and downs" than just "ups." True to the philosophy shared with Tom Townsley, Jimmy bent his will to "keep on paddlin'."

On August 22 Jimmy returned to the Lone Star, which had a special night of Chicago blues featuring him and a couple of other old friends, Hubert Sumlin and Pinetop Perkins. According to the write-up in *Living Blues*, "They traded the most amazing stories in the dressing room between sets. It was almost as entertaining as the performances."[72] Later that fall, Jimmy would perform at the Turning Point in Piermont, New York, and then at the King Biscuit Blues Festival, a two-day event held on Friday night of October 7–8. This show closed with "A Tribute to Muddy Waters" that featured Jimmy along with Mojo Buford and the Legendary Blues Band.[73]

After October, Rich Kirch, who was sharing an apartment with Barrelhouse Chuck on Chicago's Augusta Avenue, had an opportunity for a change of scenery. "I left in 1988 to move to the San Francisco Bay Area to play with John Lee Hooker," Kirch said.[74] Bandy provided more details about the changes taking place: "When John Lee Hooker hired Rich and he left to go out to California, that's when Jimmy D. first officially entered the band: Big Moose, Little Joe, Ted, me, and Jimmy."[75] Bandy reminisced about how "Jimmy D. was rock-influenced at the time. It took him a few years to settle down to play more straight-ahead blues, but Jimmy always liked a fiery lead too, so it worked out well. Eventually Jimmy settled on hiring Scott 'Bad Boy' Bradbury in '88, 'til after I left in 1990."[76] Rich Kirch, although now with John Lee Hooker, had a few last hurrahs with Jimmy. "I did play with Jimmy a couple times after I moved to California" Kirch asserted. "Once at the Oakland Blues Festival [1989 or 1990] with the Luther Tucker band, and I backed him up. Then on June 17, 1995, at the Hayward/Russell City Blues and Brews Festival with Jimmy and his son Jimmy D. Lane, that was the last time I played with him."[77]

On Wednesday, November 9, 1988, Peter Watrous documented Jimmy's participation in the historic Saturday, November 5, performance at the Beacon Theatre in New York City. "It was a night of standing ovations at the Beacon Theatre on Saturday," Watrous wrote. "Five blues acts—John Hammond; an all-star group including Jimmy Rogers, Hubert Sumlin, Charlie Musselwhite and Pinetop Perkins; Albert Collins; Albert King, and Etta James—arrived."[78] Charlie Musselwhite remembered a humorous anecdote related to the gig, and shared the following story:

> [Drummer] Sam Lay was also there. I think Bob Stroger was on bass. While we were backstage waiting to go on, there was a discussion about what tunes we were going to do and what keys, and so on. Jimmy is telling Hubert how it's going to go and what tune he's going to sing first. Hubert is nodding his head and saying, 'okay. I got it. I'm with you.' We go out there and before Jimmy can even count off his first tune, Hubert just tears into a guitar instrumental of his OWN and the rest of us just had to fall in with him and back him up! After we got *that* out of the way, Jimmy took charge.[79]

The year 1989 was ushered in with another loss: Hip Linkchain, Jimmy's close friend and collaborator, died of cancer on February 13.[80] Jimmy soldiered on, continuing to play many venues. Jimmy's band played at Manny's Car Wash. On harp was Scott Bradbury, on piano was Big Moose Walker, whose recovery from a stroke allowed him to make a brief return to play with Jimmy, as a replacement for Barrelhouse Chuck, who'd quit yet again. The lead guitar was handled by Jimmy D., bass by Right Hand Frank, and drums by Ted Harvey.

Besides their local and road performances in 1989, Big Moose Walker and Jimmy Rogers shared recording space on a recording for Wolf Records in October. How Jimmy came to record for the Vienna, Austria–based label most likely had roots that stretched as far back as the 1972 American Folk Music Festival, where Jimmy teamed up with bassist Willie Kent to play with Moses "Whispering" Smith and Billy Davenport for the tune "Tricky Woman." Kent had a working relationship with label owner Hannes Folterbauer, who had met Kent when he first arrived in Chicago in 1982 to record guitarist Eddie Taylor. The band for the session that day was Tim Taylor on drums, Johnny B. Moore on guitar, and Kent on bass. Folterbauer swore it was the best West Side Chicago blues he'd ever heard.[81]

From that point on, Folterbauer's label strove to adopt what can best be described as the Berry Gordy–Leonard Chess approach to recording consistency: use the same musicians in the rhythm section for as many of the sessions as possible. The results were immediate and successful. After nearly scoring a W. C. Handy Award for their first project (a solo album for Johnny B. Moore), then actually winning the award in 1986 for producing a Magic Slim album, the four founding members of the label transformed what started out as a fan club in 1982 into a full-fledged label. They created a series of albums under the banner "Chicago Blues Session" and recruited the likes of Willie Kent, John Brisbin, Paul Smith, Brett Bonner, and others to be their stateside representatives for the company.[82]

Kent was chosen to persuade Jimmy to record on the label with Big Moose Walker, with whom Jimmy had already played together under countless circumstances over the years. The "house band" was already well established by this time to serve as the backup band for all recording sessions in the series: Tim Taylor, drums; Billy Branch, harp; John Primer, guitar; and Willie Kent, bass. This group, therefore, was the unit heard on the album Jimmy co-led with Moose Walker when they recorded on October 25, 1989. Jimmy D. Lane remembered how the project came about. "The guy [Folterbauer] contacted Tom Radai and said he wanted to do that project while he was in the States," Lane said. "So we went down there, loaded up, and we played. It was a fun project—we had a good time with that."[83]

For the Rogers-Walker partnership, the label scheduled a session at ACME Studios in Chicago, under the direction of Paul Smith. The session was dedicated to Muddy Waters. Jimmy offered a handful of his strongest tunes, opening the album with "Chicago Bound," which had a firm yet subtle shuffle for Jimmy's voice to cruise over. He followed with an even better vocal performance on "St. Louis," which showed the strength of Billy Branch. After Big Moose Walker recorded two tunes, "Do You Swear" and "Anna Lee," Jimmy countered with "Sloppy Drunk," "Lemon Squeezer," and "Last Time," the latter featuring a powerful, driving shuffle that was taken at a much quicker clip than the original. After two more tunes by Moose, "Whoopin' Foolin' with You," and "One Room Little Country Shack," Jimmy closed the album with "Going Away Baby," with more fantastic harp work from Billy Branch.

Overall the session was highly successful and stands comfortably on its musical merits. The one obvious drawback, however, was that there were three guitarists listed on the liner notes—Jimmy, John Primer, and Jimmy's son Jimmy D. Lane (who went by Jimmy Rogers Jr. at the time)—without offering any details as to who was soloing on what tunes. Because of the uniform mix provided for the players, it's a bit difficult to ascertain which man took which solos. Still, using the process of elimination, an educated guess leads one to deduce that Jimmy did not take any of them, a conclusion primarily based on the silky-smooth rhythm chords present on all five songs, typical of Rogers's accompaniment technique. Also, some solos had a relatively overaggressive, right-hand picking attack, creating a tone that was uncharacteristic of Jimmy's style; this points to John Primer. Other solos, like the hot one heard on "Last Time," use a fast flurry of notes that point to a younger, blues-rock approach that would later come to be associated with the rapidly developing musicianship of Jimmy D. Lane.

Besides the October 1989 recording session, Jimmy performed that month at a tribute to one of his strongest musical allies, Otis Spann. Billed as "Three Days of Indoor Blues," the Otis Spann Blues Festival was held Friday through Sunday, October 20–22, at a local club in Jackson, Mississippi, called Hal and Mal's, on 200 South Commerce Street.[84] Among the several bands that played, the festival featured the Legendary Blues Band, Pinetop Perkins (who fronted the East Coast blues band Little Mike and the Tornadoes), and Jimmy Rogers, who arrived without his own band. It was here that Jimmy first met pianist Willie O'Shawny, a blues enthusiast who grew up in Queens, New York, but who had also lived in the Midwest cities of Chicago, Madison, and Milwaukee.

O'Shawny, better known as Piano Willie, was touring with the Legendary Blues Band along with Willie Big Eyes Smith, Calvin Jones, and Madison Slim. Slim had recently left Jimmy to play harmonica for this group after Jerry Portnoy exited the band. "The first time I met Jimmy Rogers in Jackson, Mississippi, it was like at a mini-festival at a club," Piano Willie recalled. "He was the special guest with the Legendary Blues Band. I think at the time we had this album called *Keeping the Blues Alive* on the Ichiban label. We did a set and then Jimmy got up and we did Jimmy's stuff, behind Jimmy. He liked the way Slim and I played together because . . . he said it sounded like the old Chess brothers stuff."[85]

In 1989, when Jimmy returned home, he was booked for a series of gigs in his hometown, appearing on Friday, November 10, at B.L.U.E.S., Saturday at Rosa's Lounge, and November 17–18 at Lilly's on Lincoln Avenue. By this time he had fully initiated his son Jimmy D. Lane into the band. By the end of the decade, Jimmy Senior had come full circle, from retirement to restlessness. "It's been a long time since I had a week without gigging somewhere, he said. "If I sit around my house too long I start itching to get back on the road." Not that he was complaining; he well remembered the bad old days when he couldn't get some of these same club owners who now were clamoring for him to let him or his band come in to play for a few decent dollars. It wasn't all that long ago. But things were different now, and life was good; gigs were plentiful, and the band was an enjoyable lot. Jimmy never took these things for granted. "Every night I hit the stage I'm grateful for still being able to do it," he once admitted.[86]

He was now becoming the local hero, and the attention he was getting was at once unfamiliar and routine. He had come by it all honestly, through hard work and patience. He was simply beginning to enjoy the fruits of his labor. The local press coverage of his ongoing performances provided both recognition of his present work and many of the same questions asked about the heyday of the Waters era. As he sat comfortably—and shirtless—in his living room, Jimmy casually told a local reporter for the *Chicago Tribune* of his work with Muddy: "We always knew what each other was going to do on the bandstand. What we did would just click together like a padlock." He paused, then added with a sly grin, "There were a lot of musicians who just didn't know the combination to the lock."[87]

An early publicity photo of Jimmy Rogers for Chess Records. Photo courtesy of Jim O'Neal Collection.

Jimmy Rogers, circa 1955. (L-R: James Cotton, Rice Miller [aka Sonny Boy Williamson II], Jimmy Rogers, Muddy Waters, unidentified.) Photo courtesy of David Simmons.

Jimmy Rogers during the late 1950s. (L-R: Muddy Waters, Little Walter, Jimmy Rogers, Otis Spann.) Photo courtesy of Mary Katherine Aldin.

An early 1970s promo shot with Johnny Littlejohn and Jimmy Rogers. Photo courtesy of Mary Katherine Aldin.

Jimmy with the Bob Riedy
Chicago Blues Band, early
1970s. (L-R: Bob Riedy,
Frank Capek, Jimmy
Rogers, Sam Lay.) Photo
courtesy of Jim O'Neal
Collection.

Jimmy in the early 1970s. Photo
courtesy of Jim O'Neal Collection.

"Left Hand" Frank Craig and
Jimmy Rogers with JSP Records
producer John Stedman, 1979.
Photo courtesy of John Stedman.

Jimmy performing live with Johnny Littlejohn in Chicago's Old Town, early 1970s.
Photo courtesy of Jim O'Neal Collection.

Jimmy in the early 1970s.
Photo courtesy of
Jim O'Neal Collection.

Jimmy performing with Dave Myers on harp and guitar, early 1970s.
Photo courtesy of Jim O'Neal Collection.

Jimmy feeling the blues, mid-1970s. Photo courtesy of Jim O'Neal Collection.

Jimmy relaxing at home with a cold brew, late 1970s. Photo courtesy of Jim O'Neal Collection.

1979 Santa Fe Blues Festival at Golden Gate Park. (L-R: Luther Tucker, Jimmy Rogers, Louis Myers.) Photo courtesy of Jerry Haussler.

Luther Tucker, Jimmy Rogers, and Kim Wilson during the Antone's West Tour, Eureka, California, 1988. Photo courtesy of Derral Campbell.

Jimmy Rogers at the 1983 recording session with Rod Piazza for the *Feelin' Good* album. Photo taken by Honey Piazza; courtesy of James Nagel.

Jimmy performing with two of his regular touring bandmates, late 1970s. (L-R: Jimmy Rogers, unidentified guitarist, Rich Yescalis, George "Wild Child" Butler.) Photo courtesy of Jim O'Neal Collection.

Jimmy's road band in Bozeman, Montana, late 1989–early 1990. (L-R: unknown fan, Frank Bandy, George "Wild Child" Butler, Rich Kirch, Jimmy Rogers, "Foots" Berry, Ted Harvey.) Photo courtesy of Jim O'Neal Collection.

Backyard birthday party, early 1984 West Coast tour. (L-R: Rich Yescalis, Jimmy Rogers, Ariyo.) Photo courtesy of Jim O'Neal Collection.

Jimmy Rogers at the Lone Star in New York City, with "Tony O" on rhythm guitar, 1985. Photo courtesy of Tony Melio.

Jimmy Rogers with the original Aces, late 1989. (L–R: Dave Myers, Jimmy Rogers, Louis Myers.) Photo courtesy of Mary Katherine Aldin.

Jimmy Rogers backstage with the boys, circa 1984. (L–R: Pinetop Perkins, Jimmy Rogers, Hubert Sumlin.) Photo courtesy of David Horwitz.

Jimmy Rogers in Davenport, Iowa, 1988. Photo courtesy of David Horwitz.

Jimmy Rogers performing with William Clarke Band in Utrecht, Holland, April 22, 1990. Photo courtesy of Gordon Brown.

Jimmy onstage in Hollywood at the Spice Club with Rod and Honey Piazza at the "Tribute to Little Walter" concert in 1992 (not pictured is Luther Tucker, farther right). Photo taken by John DeLeon; courtesy of James Nagel.

Jimmy Rogers in Tucson, 1992. Photo courtesy of David Horwitz.

Jimmy Rogers at the 1992 San Francisco Blues Festival. (L-R: Jimmy Rogers, Mark Hummel, Rusty Zinn.) Photo courtesy of Mark Hummel.

1992 San Francisco Blues Festival, backstage with Mark Hummel's infant. Photo courtesy of Mark Hummel.

Jimmy backstage with Rich Yescalis, mid-1990s. Photo courtesy of Jim O'Neal Collection.

Jimmy's European tour band, November–December 1992. (L-R: "Piano Willie" O'Shawny, Ted Harvey, Jimmy D. Lane, Steve Guyger, Jimmy Rogers, Rich Yescalis.) Photo courtesy of Jim O'Neal Collection.

Father and son: Jimmy and Jimmy D. (with Ted Harvey on drums), Utrecht, Holland, 1996. Photo courtesy of Charlie Hussey.

Jimmy and Joe Harley at Jimmy's last recording session during his son Jimmy D. Lane's *Legacy* album, mid-October 1997. Photo courtesy of Joe Harley.

PART III

FATHERS AND SONS
(1989–1997)

12

CHANGING LANES

I hope within [the sound of] my voice here, all the
blues players that's up and comin' will listen to
the lyrics and the phrases that I'm doin' now, and
you'll get a helluva lot out of it. I'll tell you.

—Jimmy Rogers

In November 1989 *Chicago Tribune* newspaper reporter Dan Kening mentioned that a new Jimmy Rogers LP would be forthcoming.[1] Indeed, Clifford Antone had decided to make his club the centerpiece for Jimmy's next album project. He put Kim Wilson in charge of producing the record. Clifford clearly thought Wilson was the perfect choice to oversee the project, and Kim was ecstatic to be the chosen one. "Jimmy's and Muddy's music—even more than the Thunderbirds—that was my stompin' grounds," Kim said. "Because it was harmonica music."[2]

Kim gave the project his full attention and produced one of the finest LPs ever recorded under Jimmy's name. The album was appropriately titled *Ludella*, the name of the cherry-red Gibson ES 355 Jimmy played. "Antone gave him that guitar," Kim Wilson proudly revealed, saying that Clifford gave it to Jimmy as a personal gift after seeing the one Jimmy had brought with him for the first concert in 1975, which was badly in need of an upgrade.[3] Jimmy played his new guitar for years afterward to show Clifford that the present meant as much to him as the song that brought him fame. With Pinetop Perkins on harmonica, Hubert Sumlin on guitar, and Kim Wilson on harmonica, the album was sure to please. About making *Ludella*, Jimmy said, "A lot of the cuts is real nice and tight, which reminds me of back in the good old Muddy Waters and Little Walter days. Kim Wilson is a fantastic harmonica player, boy. Yes he is."[4]

On January 1, 1990, Antone's record label officially released the album. Kim Wilson chose to show two sides of Jimmy. Half the album was recorded in the studio, with Pinetop Perkins on piano, Kim Wilson on harp, Derek O'Brien on rhythm guitar, Bob Stroger on bass, and Ted Harvey on drums. The second half was captured live at Antone's. Wilson discussed how he developed the project: "On *Ludella*, I had to really work hard on that record. I didn't have enough to make a record from the studio stuff. We had done an Antone's anniversary album with Pinetop, Ted Harvey, Derek O'Brien, Calvin Jones, and Willie 'Big Eyes' Smith. So half of it was from the studio, and half was live."[5]

The album opened with a studio version of "You're Sweet," followed by two live cuts: "Rock This House" and "Can't Sleep for Worrying." Kim steps up as the outstanding performer on this pair, with "in-your-face" solos that reflect the fearless personality that he became known for when it came to harp blowing. He goes back to the studio with "Why Did You Do It" and "Sloppy Drunk," both of which possess an incredibly tight lock-step groove from Pinetop, Harvey, and Stroger. The music then shifts back to a live setting at Antone's, where Jimmy performs "Gold Tailed Bird" and a rousing rendition of "Chicago Bound" that prominently features an air-tight groove formed between bassist Calvin "Fuzz" Jones and Willie "Big Eyes" Smith on drums. While drummer Ted Harvey's studio groove is unmatched, Willie Big Eyes offers one of the hardest-driving shuffles on record. Stroger's classically carved bass lines serve as the perfect foundation for the recording, and Jones's free-wheeling patterns continually push this particular ensemble deeper into the groove.

"Monkey Faced Woman," a St. Louis Jimmy tune, is a studio version of a rare recording of Jimmy singing romantically about a lady who has a face like a monkey, hair like a teddy bear, and skin as smooth as an elephant's hide. The tune has a perfectly executed, Muddy-inspired slide guitar from Derek O'Brien. "Ludella" is a live cut with Jones, Smith, and Pinetop as Jimmy's rhythm foundation. In typical fashion Rogers closes the live portion of the set with "Got My Mojo Working." This time, though, he shows a rare glimpse of sentimentality in his spoken acknowledgment of the closeness he felt with Muddy. He prefaces the tune by saying, "Now, here's one I'm gonna try to do a little bit of . . . [to] commend a very good friend of mine . . . [who] was like a father once upon a time; they call him the 'Hoochie Coochie Man'—the Muddy Water[s]!"[6] Jimmy then delivers the rowdiest version of "Got My Mojo Workin'" that he could muster, the tune ending—as always—to roaring applause.

When *Ludella* was released the LP was universally praised, with positive reviews from most critics. Paul Frenzy, who wrote in *Blues Access* magazine, gave the album a generally positive rating, although he found drawbacks. "Unfortunately, there are a few disappointments as well," Frenzy wrote. "Probably the biggest is that we only get a small taste of Rogers'[s] stinging guitar. In fact, the album almost seems to be a showcase for Wilson's powerful harp playing . . . Some of Jimmy's greatest songs are all harmonica with Rogers taking a back seat. And two of the live performances, 'Ludella' and 'Got My Mojo Workin'', are rather uninspired."[7]

In discussing the absence of fresh material, Frenzy argued with a touch of wistfulness that "almost all the songs are Jimmy Rogers standards and have been released before on other albums. This seems like a shortcut." Frenzy may have crossed the line when he took things a step further with the following commentary: "Even though they are still active today, people like Rogers, Otis Rush, or Pinetop Perkins will end up being remembered for songs they penned in the '50s and '60s. This is a shame, since their creative influence is sorely needed today for the younger musicians who are spiraling away from good blues to rock and pop-flavored package sounds."[8]

Perhaps Frenzy has a point; then again, maybe not. An established artist like Jimmy—at the age of sixty by the time the article was written—had already built the foundation more than thirty-five years earlier. What more could one ask for? With regard to pop or rock styles, Jimmy's influence was well established in the hearts and minds of the younger generation, including Kirch, Bandy, Waldman, Yescalis, and several other young musicians who worked with Rogers. One reason Rogers had such influence was because his own unique style was so easily identifiable and adaptable to what was becoming the modern R & B and pop guitar sound, one that still can be heard in the music today.

Nine months later, when the CD version of *Ludella* was released, fans would find three added bonus tracks. The first was an alternate studio take of "Why Did You Do It?" featuring both a classic solo from Pinetop (who rolls the low end of the piano with unmatched authority) and a Kim Wilson harp solo that serves as the best performance on this take, with phrasing that would make Big Walter beam with pride. The second track was a live version of "You're Sweet," and added for extra measure was a third track, a studio take of the upbeat instrumental "Naptown."

Jimmy was in New York City on Wednesday, April 4, and Thursday, April 5, 1990, to perform at Tramps for a concert called "A Chicago Blues Tribute to Muddy Waters." Muddy would have been seventy-five on that Wednesday, and the tribute concert featured Jimmy, Hubert Sumlin, and Jerry Portnoy, with Little Mike and the Tornadoes serving as backup. Soon after, in England, blues-rock guitarist Gary Moore's most popular album, *Still Got the Blues*, was released in

May. Among the impressive set of tunes on this well-produced LP was a hard-driving cover version of Jimmy's "Walkin' by Myself." Moore's version would eventually earn Jimmy a substantial amount of money in royalties.

Jimmy's popularity was definitely on the rise now. The next generation of players was beginning to take note of his status among the blues veterans who were still active. He was asked by "Steady Rollin'" Bob Margolin to be a special guest on his newest album project, and Jimmy gladly accepted the offer to lend support to Muddy's longtime guitarist, who had officially filled Jimmy's role in Muddy's musical career until the end. Margolin's album for Powerhouse Records, aptly titled *Chicago Blues*, had a few songs that were recorded in the "old school" manner that Muddy had passed directly to Margolin—"just two guitars, harp, and minimal drums, no bass," Margolin said. The band was loaded with veterans: Jimmy and Bob on guitars, Kim Wilson on harp, and Willie Big Eyes Smith on the deliberately bare-bones setup of a kick, snare, and high hat. "Jimmy participated on three of the album's tracks—"She's So Pretty," "She and the Devil," and "Steady Rollin' Man." About Jimmy's work on the this last tune, Margolin said, "His guitar intro on 'Steady Rollin' Man' is amazing."[9] When the CD version of the album was released, it included a few bonus tracks, one of which was Jimmy playing with the band on "Sugar Sweet."[10]

By the time May rolled around, Jimmy had already embarked on an extensive overseas tour, which included dates in Scotland, Norway, Finland, and Scandinavia. After a northern tour that included Canada and Alaska, Jimmy flew in from Alaska to get to Glasgow, where he crossed paths with Bob Margolin, who was traveling with his band, now with Tom "Mookie" Brill on bass and harp and Chuck Cotton on drums. Jimmy used Margolin's band as his backup group during the tour and rode with them in a truck from Glasgow to Edinburgh, where the next gig was located, then proceeded on to Norway.[11]

On July 11, 1990, Shelter Records rereleased the material recorded for the June 4, 1973, album *Gold Tailed Bird*. The disc served as a bearer of both good and bad news. On the positive side, this new edition not only included five previously unreleased tunes but also featured an extended version of "Brown Skinned Woman" that was unveiled for the first time, an obvious bonus for Rogers fans. The bad news, however, was much more severe for those same fans: the liner notes carried over all of the mistakes from the original LP. The misspelled names for Louis and Dave Myers, Bob Riedy, and Fred Below remained uncorrected. Even worse, the musical contribution of the entire band from side A of the album—Bill and Steve Lupkin, Jim Kahr, Richard Hubcap Robinson, Frank Capek, and Jim Wydra—were never listed, which was a real insult, since they were the ones who put in hard time, traveling all the way to California with Jimmy for the Freddie King sessions. To still not receive proper credit after almost twenty years must have been agonizing for them.

The liner notes correctly indicate that the first six songs from side A—the Aces rhythm section plus Riedy—were produced in February 1972 by J. J. Cale, with Stu Black as the engineer. However, the notes incorrectly identify the side B music of the Riedy band as being recorded on January 28, 1972, not in Hollywood, California, at Paradise Recording Studios, but in Disney, Oklahoma, by John Lemmay (listed incorrectly as LeMay on the original LP). To add further confusion, four of the six extra tracks were identified as having been produced at a third recording session on December 8, 1973, in Nashville, by Owen Bradley (at his own studio called Bradley's Barn) by an unknown engineer. The album did not do as well as expected.

On the fifteenth of July, Jimmy participated in the fifteenth anniversary of Antone's blues club in Austin, Texas. The usual all-star roster showed up to perform, with Jimmy as one of the main attractions. When the LP from the celebration was released the following year, Jimmy was featured on the first track, playing the tune "Chicago Bound" with the backup band of Chester King on rhythm guitar, Calvin Jones on bass, Willie Smith on drums, Pinetop Perkins on piano, and Hubert Sumlin on guitar.

One month later Jimmy's manager, Tom Radai, booked a tour package called the Chicago Blues Heritage that sent the James Cotton band, Robert Junior Lockwood, and Jimmy Rogers and the Legendary Blues Band on a brief excursion through Japan. The Legendary Blues Band included "Tony O" Melio on guitar, Calvin Fuzz Jones on bass, Willie Big Eyes Smith on drums, "Piano Willie" O'Shawny on keys, and Madison Slim on harp.[12] From July 22 to July 24, the three groups performed at the flower festival in Osaka, the Gargoyle Coliseum in Tokyo, and Club Tacu Tacu in Kyoto. "Jimmy Rogers was featured as our special guest," O'Shawny recalled.[13]

Madison Slim, who had played with Rogers sporadically over the last few years, was already a well-traveled musician by this time, having played at the Zoo Bar in Lincoln, Nebraska, with the Heart Murmurs, as well as performing and recording with the Legendary Blues Band, featuring Willie Big Eyes Smith, Pinetop Perkins, Calvin Fuzz Jones, and Billy Flynn.[14] O'Shawny had impressed Jimmy in October '89 at the Otis Spann tribute in Jackson. Jimmy decided then and there to make his move. He approached O'Shawny and Madison Slim about their augmenting his own group. Luckily for him there was a bit of instability inside the Legendary Blues Band, at least according to O'Shawny, who stated the following:

Calvin Jones, the bass player that played with Muddy Waters—he retired, and then there was some management problems and there wasn't a lot of work coming in. Then Willie Big Eyes got an Ichiban recording contract, so he started doing his thing . . . It was really slow. But Jimmy had a lot of work, so he said, "I know there's not a lot of work with them, why don't you guys come with me?" It was like a no-brainer! We're musicians, we've got to survive! He had Bob Stroger and Ted Harvey at the time. From then on, Madison Slim and I started accompanying Jimmy. We ended up going to Japan together; we ended up doing a *whole* bunch of things![15]

Once inside the group, O'Shawny adapted quickly to Jimmy's method of handling his sidemen. One of the cardinal rules of the Rogers band was that you had to have the music down cold at all times, which meant Jimmy fully expected each individual to be responsible for himself on the bandstand when it was showtime. "We never rehearsed," O'Shawny remembered. "He expected musicians to know his music. He just called the key off and we just went and did it. It was very spontaneous like that. That's how we worked."[16] Jimmy D. agreed, saying about his dad, "As long as I played in the old man's band, I don't ever recall rehearsing—you either knew the stuff or you didn't. That's just the way it was with the old guys. I'm the same way with my band."[17]

A typical Rogers set was filled with quick segues that flowed seamlessly, with little wasted time in between tunes and even less talk. "He wouldn't tell you what tune was comin up; he would just play licks in the key the tune was going to be in," Piano Willie said. "Then we all would know from the little intro licks. When he kind of knew that everyone knew what key it was in, then he'd kick off the actual guitar riff. We wouldn't come in like gangbusters, so we always kind of eased in to every tune. It's not like rock 'n' roll, where 1–2–3–4 *boom,* everybody's in. It started really laid back, and we eased into it."[18] It didn't take long for Willie to appreciate Jimmy's bandleading style. He recognized that Jimmy's leadership skills were identical to his playing style, and Jimmy's musicianship, in turn, matched his approach to interacting with people in general. "He was extremely congenial," O'Shawny said.

Jimmy's gentle humor also meshed well with the pianist's love for a good-natured ribbing. According to O'Shawny, "He also liked fucking with people—not in a sadistic way, ya know. He liked joking around and teasing people. He'd joke around with someone a little bit, and then he'd have that cartoon laugh, like a Hanna-Barbera cartoon kind of way . . . he would . . . [mimics laughing] 'hehehehehe!' like that dog Smedley from those old Sunday morning *Wacky Racers* cartoons."[19] The laughs didn't stop there. Jimmy's comic sense was evidently a big part of his everyday appeal, as illustrated in this hilarious exchange of dry wit, witnessed by Willie, who said, "Another thing, if he wasn't so thrilled about a scenario, or what was happening . . . or if he wasn't so thrilled about someone's company—underneath his breath he'd go '*eehhhh boy*.' Like Fred Flintstone, or like something Jackie Gleason would do. He was really subtle with it, ya know? So if you didn't know, you wouldn't catch on that he was doing it! If you *knew*, though, you'd catch that something was getting on his nerves."[20]

O'Shawny, over the years, would eventually get to know not only Jimmy but also his wife, Dorothy, and their children. At forty years old, O'Shawny was older than most of the musicians upon their entry into Jimmy's band. While he wasn't as old as Harvey or Stroger, the relatively closer proximity in age led to a slightly different dynamic for him and Jimmy, as opposed to the one Jimmy had with younger members of the band like Bandy or Kirch. O'Shawny was given a crash course on the history of Chess piano players back in the day when Jimmy and Muddy had created the classic literature. Jimmy made sure that O'Shawny had the straight facts. "Eddie Ware was given little credit on Chess brothers records and was mistaken for Otis Spann many times but was an early mainstay of Jimmy Rogers," O'Shawny revealed. "I know this because some of the licks I was playing that I thought were Otis's Jimmy told me were actually Eddie Ware's!"[21]

An idea that was supposedly a one-time event for the Japanese tour became a regular feature, and the Legendary Blues Band continued to use Jimmy as a guest artist after the tour was over. Guitarist "Tony O" Melio explained the hierarchy within the band with regard to who got top billing, and he also clarified when and where it occurred. According to his recollection, "For two years—from 1990 to 1992—most of the shows were 'Jimmy Rogers and the Legendary Blues Band.' Once in a while we would do some shows without Jimmy and then it was just the 'Legendary Blues Band.' On the late July 1990 Japan tour it was 'Jimmy Rogers and the Legendary Blues Band.'"[22] All three groups that traveled through Japan stayed at the same hotels.

When showtime arrived they delivered the concerts in the same format as Jimmy's home band would do: each person was given his own chance to shine in the spotlight before the main attraction. According to Tony, "On these shows, the band would open up, each one of us would sing a song. It was a mandatory requirement that everyone in the Legendary Blues Band had to be a singer and front man as well. Then after five numbers we would bring up Jimmy Rogers, either on 'Sweet Home Chicago' or 'She's Sweet' or 'Walkin' by Myself.' It was so authentic."[23]

There was also another special guest who appeared regularly with the band, and was even captured posing for pictures with them. His face was familiar.

"The photos with Ariyo were taken when we were on that tour," Tony explained. "He came to all the shows we played in Osaka, Tokyo, and Kyoto. He was sitting in with us; he was living in Japan at that time."[24] Ariyo had been caught trying to enter the States after going on a tour with Otis Rush back in 1988 and had been stopped at the gate, jailed, and deported back to his own country. He was thrilled to be able to play with Jimmy again.

Tony sat next to Jimmy as they rode the bullet train at two hundred miles per hour. He had some great memories of being with Jimmy during the Asian experience: "When we were in Japan, Jimmy called me on the phone from his room to mine and said, 'Meet me at my room; I am going to take you to a good place for breakfast.'" When Tony got to his room, Jimmy had a bottle of Hennessy cognac and two shot glasses filled to the top. They had a shot to celebrate the first morning in Japan, then they went to the restaurant. After they finished eating, Jimmy picked up the tab and went to the register with it while Tony left a nice amount of yen on the table for a tip for the waitress. "On the way out the door, all the workers in the restaurant were talking about us in Japanese and giving us dirty looks." Jimmy said to Tony, "You didn't leave a *tip* on that table did you?" Tony replied, "Yeah, I did—and a *good* one too. Do you think it was enough?" Jimmy first laughed and then started walking fast toward the door. When they got outside, he said to Tony, "Didn't you know if you leave a tip in Japan they take that as an *insult*?" "No," Tony cried, "should I go back and get it?" Jimmy responded, "Are you crazy? Let's get *outta here!*"[25]

At one point during the tour, Tony's and Jimmy's groups got separated from each other during a midday stroll through the busy city of Kyoto. The situation caused a bit of fright for Tony. "We were all walking together in a pack, and I dropped my Walkman radio," Melio recalled. "It broke into a lot of pieces, and by the time I picked it all up, the entourage of three bands and promoters had vanished. I was actually lost then, and no one there spoke English." Panic set in, and Tony thought he'd been left behind for good. "I was walking around in Kyoto for hours, and finally I saw Jimmy on the street, waving and laughing his head off. He was worried though, but it was funny. To be honest, I was a little scared."[26]

Tony's musical friendship and experience with Jimmy began well before the Japanese tour, as Tony attests in this humorous story:

Once in 1988, we were on the road somewhere up in the mountains of New York State, a very windy, stormy night. We used to travel in a big touring truck with beds in the back; I was driving before Jimmy fell asleep. When Jimmy woke up, the truck was wobbling from side to side and getting blown around by the wind—it could hardly stay on the road. Jimmy looked at everybody sleeping, then he came to my bed and said, "Tony, who the fuck is driving?" and I said, "I don't know, go see." When he went up front to see, I heard him yell, "Oh, no—fuck no! Pull over right now!" It was my girlfriend, driving this big rig in the storm, struggling to keep it on the road. When she finally pulled over and I started driving again, Jimmy said, "I'm *never* going to sleep when you're driving ever again; can't *trust* ya, man!"[27]

Tony and Jimmy formed a lasting friendship that had a significant impact on Tony's life, even after he left the band. "When I play a show, I play a lot of Jimmy's songs, and I play them just like he showed me how to," Tony said with pride and humility. "He was my favorite of them all; he had a smile and a sense of humor that was awesome."[28]

During the first week of September 1990, Jimmy's hometown Chicago band went on the road to play at Manny's Car Wash in New York City. By all accounts the gig was a success, in spite of the sadness that accompanied the event. "This was the first weekend after Stevie Ray Vaughan passed away," said bassist Frank Bandy. The Texas-born guitarist had died an untimely death in a helicopter crash on August 27. Bandy remembered seeing a side of Jimmy he hadn't seen before: "Jimmy loved Stevie Ray Vaughan as a person and as a player. The dressing room was behind the stage. We could hear every song that every band was playing. Some band on the stage cranked up one of Stevie Ray's tunes, and immediately tears came out of his eyes; he was crying. He said, 'They're playing Stevie's shit.'"[29]

This would be one of the last memorable gigs Bandy would have with Jimmy. "I played until November 1990, eleven years," said Bandy. "The last gig was in Salt Lake City, Utah. I flew out there and drove back. Madison Slim, Ted [Harvey], and Little Jimmy was in the band. After I left the band, Barrelhouse and Steve [Guyger] went to Europe with him."[30] This was a huge letdown for Bandy, because it was a rare opportunity to go overseas with Jimmy and see a part of the world he hadn't yet visited. "Near the end of 1990, early '91, it was the first time they let him take his own band. I didn't go, because I just got a mortgage and needed to make the payments . . . It was emotionally disappointing, because I played with him eleven years; they were going three weeks to the East Coast and three weeks to Europe, and since I couldn't afford to go, basically I was replaced." Jimmy asked Bob Stroger to replace Bandy for this tour. "Before I'd left," Bandy said, "Stroger filled in for me sometimes, and he did all the local stuff after I left in November '90."[31]

Bandy was upset not only that he couldn't go but also that he never got to make tracks with his longtime boss. "Jimmy was not well recorded during the eleven years I worked with him," he said regretfully. Still, when it was all over, Bandy felt nothing but gratitude and love for his bandleader, and said, "Jimmy— he was a really sweet guy. He had a very sweet persona; I don't know how else to describe it. He was very cool."[32] Bandy's work with the Rogers family was not yet done. "When I left in 1990, me and Jimmy D. played together for about a year," Bandy recalled. After that, Bandy would go on to play with J. B. Ritchie, with whom he stayed for fifteen years running.[33] Meanwhile, O'Shawny was trying to get comfortable in his new surroundings after leaving the Legendary Blues Band. Although the core of the band was Ted Harvey on drums and Bob Stroger on bass, there was a high level of interchange within the group. "Harmonica players were mostly Madison Slim, but sometimes Steve Guyger and Scotty Bradbury," O'Shawny said. "Sometimes Jimmy's son James Lane [Jimmy D.] would play guitar and also sometimes Nick Moss was on guitar and bass. Dave Myers from the original Little Walter band would also play bass and sing from time to time."[34]

From April 24 to May 23, 1991, the Jimmy Rogers band toured Europe. The traveling band was Harvey, Stroger, Bradbury, Jimmy D., and O'Shawny. Madison Slim was originally supposed to make the gig but somehow missed the opportunity. More than likely he went back temporarily to the Legendary Blues Band. For the April 24–30 leg the road manager was Morten Bosy, and for the May 1–13 leg, Frank Svarholt was road manager.

The band played on Wednesday, April 24, in Stockholm, Sweden, at the *Daily News* at 10:00 P.M., then proceeded to play either two forty-five-minute sets or one hour-long performance for each of the following nights in the Swedish cities of Uppsala, Vasteras, Delsbo, and Karlstad. By April 30 they crossed into Norway, where they delivered evening sets in Oslo, Tromso, Bergen, Fredrickstad, Trondheim, and Horten. Although Little Jimmy experienced several memorable moments, one particular performance stood out among all others.

> We played somewhere in Norway, right around the time that Gary Moore cut "Walkin' by Myself." We came out, there was an ocean of heads, as far as you could see. We started out with "Walkin'" and the audience didn't know a lick of English, but they knew that song! They were singing the words with their foreign accents. I looked over at him [Jimmy Senior] and he looked at me. We smiled at each other and kept playing; I was very proud of him. That will always stand out in my mind as one of the most precious moments onstage with him.[35]

Once they got to England, they played the Langbaurgh International Blues Festival in Redcar, then on to London, where they performed at the 100 Club.

By Thursday, May 9, they made one stop for a gig in Ruiselede, Belgium, then wrapped up their tour in Holland, with the last three shows in Rotterdam, Ospel, and Amsterdam. They boarded KLM Airlines on May 13 and arrived back in Chicago at 2:40 in the afternoon.

In early June, Jimmy Rogers gave a concert at the Breminale Festival in Bremen, Germany, with Ronnie Earl and the Broadcasters. This June 7 performance would be released as a live album titled *Jimmy Rogers with Ronnie Earl and the Broadcasters*. Mudcat Ward provided details about how it all came together, saying, "Crosscut Records is in Germany. The president of the label and [guitarist] Ronnie [Earl] put that together. As we were flying over, I had no idea we were playing with Jimmy Rogers. When we got to Bremen, I knocked on the door of his trailer; he greeted me, 'Hey, Mudcat!' We did a set, then Jimmy came on."[36] Ronnie Earl and the Broadcasters opened up the set with four house-rocking numbers. Earl delivered a blistering version of "Okie Dokie Stomp" on his scorching Stratocaster. Earl, in rare form that night, peeled off a series of smoked rockabilly-riffs dripped in barbecue sauce. After letting things simmer down a little with "Blues in D Natural," Earl's harp player, Sugar Ray Norcia, stepped up to the mike to sing "Same Old Blues." The band then proceeded to play Jimmy's set with the same level of intensity, even though they'd had no rehearsal.

On the LP of this performance, Jimmy comes on with a hard-shuffling "Rock This House," in which Sugar Ray Norcia takes a howling solo, Big Walter–style. The band settles things down again with "Gold Tailed Bird," where Jimmy acknowledges Continental Airlines as the reference source of one of his most popular, purely original tunes. "He told me numerous times that he always thought they would want to use that tune as an advertisement for their airline," said Frank Bandy.[37]

Jimmy speeds things up with "Why Did You Do It?" then shifts downward into "Can't Sleep for Worrying." The highlight of the set, "Walkin' by Myself," has the band playing an exceptionally tight shuffle, with Ronnie Earl playing a Rogers-inspired solo. The audience's response, a loud and lengthy applause, shows their appreciation. Jimmy cools things off with "Left Me with a Broken Heart," set at the patented honey-dripping tempo of which he was so fond. The Broadcasters hold it perfectly as Ronnie cranks out a gut-wrenching solo that again met with the audience's wholehearted approval. Jimmy dedicates the next tune to Muddy Waters, singing with such energy and passion that he seems to be trying to conjure Muddy's spirit right then and there.

Jimmy closes with "Shake Your Money Maker," which includes inspired solos by both Sugar Ray and Ronnie. The crowd yells louder and louder for each subsequent tune, and Ronnie asks Jimmy to come back for an encore. They crank up "You're Sweet" with a groove that captures the Chicago blues feel better than any other that night. As Mudcat Ward drives the bass pedal point in the key of E, drummer Per Hanson conjures Fred Below's vibes, Dave Maxwell spits out Spann-ish piano riffs, and Ronnie digs deep to get Muddy's low-down sound underneath Jimmy's groove.

At some point during the tour, Jimmy was booked to perform on another gig, one that featured three groups. Mudcat Ward was in one of the groups. "Those three bands—Ronnie Earl, Lonnie Mack, and Jimmy Rogers—we traveled in Norway, flying from gig to gig," Ward remembered. "We did three shows in Norway, and Jimmy had his own band with Stroger, Ted, Jimmy D., and Piano Willie."[38] Ward recalled a situation that would have been funnier if it hadn't been so scary.

North of the Arctic Circle, we went to a place called Tromso. On our way back, they had a bus to take us back. Ronnie looked out the window and saw a billboard that advertised L. Mack Beer. Ronnie, says, "Oh that's great!" So they had the bus driver stop, they go into this place, they're all happy; they got cases of beer and souvenirs. The bus takes off. I go, "Hey, where's Piano Willie?" Jimmy and Lonnie goes, "Oh, well, he'll find his way . . ." I go, "No, he won't!" They'd left him. I had to talk the bus driver into going back and getting him. He had just stepped out to have a smoke.[39]

Not one to rest for too long a stretch, by July 27 Jimmy was doing a weeklong stint in Edmonton, Alberta, while on the Canadian portion of his tour. As he had on previous gigs, he once again dropped by his old friend Holger Peterson's radio station, CKUA, where he gave a thirty-minute radio interview for Peterson's show, *Natch'l Blues*. Just as he'd stated on Jimmy's last visit in October 20, 1982, Peterson said "the live show was fantastic."[40]

Jimmy Rogers was in the midst of one of the greatest triumphs of his career. His popularity was soaring around the world. The public accolades were coming in, one after the other. In mid-October, Antone's Records issued a press release advertising the happy news that on October 11, 1991, Jimmy Rogers won the W. C. Handy Award from the Blues Foundation for *Ludella*. A celebration for this honor was held on Beale Street in Memphis, Tennessee. Then on February 8, 1992, Jimmy was invited by Milwaukee Blues Unlimited and the Wisconsin Blues Society to perform at Shank Hall in Milwaukee, Wisconsin at 9:00 P.M.[41] He allowed himself little time to rest. "I still enjoy playing for the people," Jimmy later explained to Tom Townsley in a 1994 interview.[42] Clearly he'd had a complete turnaround from his attitude toward being in the business in the late 1950s.

Back then he rarely wanted anything to do with touring the world, country, or even the city. Of course, his negative attitude then had to do mainly with the lack of gigs available and the low pay, which affected his family life. Now things were totally reversed; with a stable family life and reasonable monetary gains, he was much more amenable to the touring life. As the last of the Headhunters, he was more in demand than ever; so much, in fact, that he had very few days off to spend with his family or to enjoy his favorite pastime—fishing.

On Monday, May 25, 1992, Jimmy played the inaugural Santa Cruz Blues Festival, which was then and continues to be held on Memorial Day.[43] Meanwhile, one of Jimmy's longtime piano sidemen, Barrelhouse Chuck, was traveling through Europe in 1992 with his own band when he had an experience that he thought should be brought to Jimmy's attention immediately. "From '89 to '92, I wasn't working with Jimmy," Barrelhouse said. "I was in Denmark. I told him that Gary Moore had recently recorded 'Walkin' by Myself.' Every airport, bathroom, hotel, I heard Gary Moore's version of the *Still Got the Blues* album. It was like Michael Jackson's *Thriller* or something—it was everywhere. I told Jimmy, 'You gotta find out who this guy is.'"[44]

Chuck wasn't aware that Jimmy had already been in Europe himself earlier that year. None other than rock guitar god Eric Clapton had personally asked for Jimmy's participation at a huge outdoor festival. He then flew Jimmy from Chicago to England to perform at Wembley Stadium in June 1992, where Jimmy played in front of one hundred thousand people. About the arena experience, Jimmy glowed when he said, "That was about the biggest indoors festival that I ever did in my life and I really enjoyed that. We'll do that again. Soon as the opportunity knocks, I'll do it."[45]

In September 1992 Jimmy was invited to come to San Francisco by blues festival organizer Tom Mazzolini to play with harp player Mark Hummel and his band, the Blues Survivors. "Jimmy rarely stopped in San Francisco from Chicago," Hummel mused. "When I was able to book a tour with Jimmy Rogers and Billy Boy Arnold in 1992, it was a dream come true. Jimmy had long been my idol, thanks to his great Chess sides with [Little] Walter." With the quintet of Hummel on harp, Tom Mahon on acoustic piano, Rusty Zinn on rhythm guitar, Mark Bohn on drums, and Ronnie James on acoustic bass, the group did a warm-up gig at Moe's Alley in nearby Santa Cruz on Friday night and got up the next day to play their 12:30 afternoon gig at the festival in San Francisco, where Jimmy ran into his childhood friend and musical comrade Honeyboy Edwards. Rogers and Hummel's band then played in San Jose at J. J.'s Downtown later that night and hit the road the next morning to play yet another festival in Sacramento on Sunday.[46]

On the last stop, Jimmy played in San Francisco at a club called Slim's, where he played an impressive set, including "Tricky Woman," "Can't Sleep for Worrying," "You're the One," "Big Boss Man," and "Ludella." Hummel was thrilled at Zinn's guitar work with Jimmy. "Rusty was also in awe of Jimmy and has his guitar down so pat it's hard to tell them apart," Mark commented.[47]

After leaving San Francisco, Jimmy traveled across the state to get to Arizona for a concert at the Rhythm Room, the hippest blues club in Phoenix. Harp player and radio show producer Bob Corritore had created one of the most exciting blues scenes in the country. Corritore was born in Chicago on September 27, 1956, and was raised in the suburb of Wilmette. He said his life changed when he heard "Rolling Stone" by Muddy Waters at the age of twelve or thirteen. Subsequently, he saw Muddy and Jimmy Rogers play in his high school gymnasium and wrote his junior class theme paper on Muddy Waters.[48] He began exploring the streets in search of blues players by the age of eighteen. Corritore saw the Bob Riedy Blues Band when he snuck into Biddy Mulligan's, located on the North Side. That band included Carey Bell, Johnny Littlejohn, and Eddy Clearwater.[49] He left the Windy City and moved to Scottsdale, Arizona, in 1981 to try his luck as a harmonica player on there. "I moved right after my 25th birthday, which I spent watching Smokey Smothers, then Big Walter."[50]

Corritore established a stronghold in the Phoenix area, and then he convinced Louisiana Red and blues drummer and singer Chico Chism to make the exodus from Chicago and join him. Next, he started the Blues Over Blues label in the Phoenix area, where he established himself as a premier harp player. He then lured even more artists to join in the fun, including Henry Gray, Li'l Ed Williams, the Fabulous Thunderbirds, Paul Oscher, and Jimmy Rogers, among dozens of others. "I was friends with so many of these great Chicago bluesmen," Corritore reminisced. "I used to hang around Louis Myers all the time. I knew Freddy Below, Floyd Jones, Jimmy Rogers, Eddie Taylor, Hip Linkchain, Bob Stroger . . . I knew them all and was part of that family in a small way."[51]

By 1991 Corritore was booking the best blues artists in the country to join his house band for show-stopping performances at the Rhythm Room, as well as featuring the artists and their music for *Those Lowdown Blues*, his weekly radio show on KJZZ. On October 13, 1992, Bob booked a session for Jimmy. They recorded "Out On the Road" in a laid-back, slow-paced tempo for Corritore's label, HMG Records. Jimmy's backing band included Bob Corritore on harp, Buddy Reed on guitar, S. E. Willis on piano, Paul Thomas on bass, and Chico Chism on drums.

To better serve the slower groove of "Out on the Road," Jimmy chose to sing in a lower key than in the original recording. Corritore takes a wickedly greasy solo that permeates the cloth of the rhythm section, perfectly defining the mood of the song. Meanwhile, Buddy Reed does a wonderful job of capturing the dual-guitar effect pioneered by Rogers and Waters, which inspired Jimmy to sing with the kind of passion that matched his August 12, 1952, Chess session.

In late October, Jimmy would return to San Francisco to play the San Francisco Blues Festival, along with several other outstanding artists on the bill, including a cadre of Texans: Albert Collins, Kim Wilson, and Antone's Women Texas Blues Revue (featuring Lou Ann Barton, Sue Foley, and Angela Strehli). As the months passed by, the gigs continued to increase. By the following summer of 1993, Jimmy was the headliner for the Legendary Blues Band, had appeared on the *Conan O'Brien Show*, and had also performed at Dan Ackroyd's House of Blues. He was fully enjoying life, and although he worked harder than ever, he still managed to find a little time for simple pleasures, like his family, his favorite foods, and, of course, fishing.

Surprisingly, he even found time to return to his first love—the harmonica. Steve Guyger was shocked when he realized that Jimmy was doing a little moonlighting on the harp. "Jimmy was taking my harmonicas in the early '90s," Guyger confessed. "Yeah, he was playing! Not on gigs or anything, but if I blew a harp out or something, he'd take it." Guyger recalled the day when he confronted Jimmy: "We were in Atlanta one day and I blew out an F harp. He said, 'What're you gonna do with that?' I said, 'What are YOU going to do with it?'"[52]

Steve squinted his eyes, and said, accusingly, "You're *playin'* again, aren't you?" Jimmy started smiling. "Yeah." Guyger was amazed at the revelation, saying,"When I got back home to Philly again, I called up Angela [Jimmy's youngest daughter], and asked, 'Your old man's playing again, isn't he?' She said, 'Heh, yup.' He was playing everybody's stuff!" When asked what Jimmy sounded like on harp after all those years, Guyger, without missing a beat, commented, "From what little I heard, he sounded like a cross between Snooky Pryor, John Lee [Williamson], and early Little Walter."[53]

The music from Jimmy's concert at the Breminale Festival (in Bremen, Germany) with Ronnie Earl and the Broadcasters was finally released in 1993 by Bullseye Blues (a subsidiary of Rounder Records). Supposedly a videotape of that album exists. "I saw it when I played in Geneva, Switzerland," said Mudcat. "There was a guy who ran the Geneva Blues Festival who showed it to me. Sugar Ray knows his name." Around the same time, Evidence Records, which had bought out the ESP label, revived the material that was released on Jimmy by Jaques Morgantini for his French label, Black & Blue.

The old 1976 LP with the cartoon drawing on the cover, titled *Sloppy Drunk* (ECD 26036), was now being released on CD for the first time, with five bonus tracks added. The first four extra tunes were taken live from the December 8 concert at the Biarritz Casino. The fifth bonus track was a previously unreleased version of "Ludella," taken from that same concert. The dashing new CD cover shot, taken by noted blues photographer James Fraher, caught Jimmy smiling from ear to ear, with the title of the CD highlighted in an eye-popping pink Day-Glo color, coolly reflecting off his tinted shades. It was enough to make the American audiences think they were actually getting an entirely new album.

Jimmy received one of the highest honors ever bestowed upon a blues musician when his music was inducted into the Blues Hall of Fame. His first Chess album, *Chicago Bound*, was nominated in the "Classics of Blues Recordings" category.[54] Producer John Koenig convinced label owner Chad Kassem that Jimmy was a national treasure and that he needed to be properly recorded for a superb album befitting such a legend. That album was *Bluebird*, and Koenig set out to hire the best studios and sidemen available in order to create the strongest Rogers album in recent years. Such a product would thrust Jimmy even more firmly into the national spotlight, securing his rightful place as a leader among the living legends—a pool that was shrinking by the month.

In an ironic twist, "The Iceman" Albert Collins, who was supposed to be there for the Kassem recording session, would be the next victim of time and age. "The *Bluebird* project is when I first met Chad Kassem," Jimmy D. recalled soberly. "I was on that session accidentally. They were supposed to get Albert Collins, but he was sick and couldn't make the session, so Pops said, 'Since he's right here, I want Little Jimmy to play,' because he knew that I knew the music."[55] Kassem also knew that time was of the essence, so he shifted gears quickly to make sure the dream became a reality not only for himself but for Jimmy too.

It was November 1993 when Jimmy arrived in Chicago for the recording session, the first he'd done in Chicago as a leader in thirty years. The sessions were booked for the seventeenth and eighteenth in studio D of the Chicago Recording Company. Scott Dirks, who was there to supply a few amps and microphones for Carey Bell, recalled that the sessions were recorded early in the day. "I got there just after lunchtime on the second day, Dirks said. "John Koenig was very concerned about getting the sound perfect."[56] This album would include a fresh batch of tunes that Jimmy had written, something he hadn't offered to a studio in years. About the new music for that album, Little Jimmy said, "He had a lot of stuff under his sleeve that he hadn't laid out. A lot of Muddy's songs were credited to Willie Dixon, but the old man wanted credit for the songs that he wrote."[57]

Jimmy's purpose was clear—he'd started a new publishing company that he named after his grandson, Cordero, the son of his second daughter, Jacqueline. All the publishing rights for the original tunes slated for this project would go to Cordero Music Inc., affiliated with BMI. Jimmy would also rename some of his previously written tunes and place them under the new holding corporation once they were rerecorded for these sessions. "It was time for him to get his own publishing together, after experiencing that whole Chess thing," Jimmy D. said. "Those guys were raised at a time when they weren't the most educated. They took people at their word, and there was a lot of ripping off later on, so he was advised by his lawyer."[58]

Little Jimmy had quite a busy schedule of his own, but was glad to be there for the occasion. "I was getting ready to go out on a tour with my band heading out West," Lane said. "We started out in Wichita, and we set it up to do the recording. Then my band headed out to Los Angeles. I played at B. B. King's club in Universal City and reconnected with John [Koenig] to let him hear what the band sounded like. So we finished, came back to Chicago, joined Pop's band again."[59] The studio band for the session included harp player Carey Bell and legendary pianist Johnnie Johnson (of Chuck Berry fame and who also played with Albert King.) The first installment of new arrangements for the *Bluebird* sessions was "I'm Tired of Crying for You" (previously recorded by Fats Domino for Imperial and by Morris Pejoe for Checker). This hard shuffle worked as an ideal vehicle for the band to get things kick-started. The straightforward lyrics lamented Jimmy's lost love:

Oh baby, I'm tired of crying over you (repeat)
I cried for you so, I thought that your love was true
Oh baby, your time to cry for me (repeat)
I cried you a river it's your turn to cry me a sea
I cried last night I cried the night before
You know pretty baby you gotta reap just what you sow
Oh baby, your time to cry for me
I cried you a river it's your turn to cry me a sea

For the entire session, Jimmy let Jimmy D. take the lion's share of the lead work. Throughout the proceedings, his solos clearly indicated that the roadwork with his father had paid off—he had truly arrived. On "Blue Bird" Jimmy sings about a bird sending a letter down to Shannon Street in Jackson, Mississippi. Johnnie Johnson rolls on the piano keys in his own inimitable way, while Carey howls on harp with his dark chocolate tone. Jimmy calls out proudly, "Little Jimmy—gimme the blues, son!" Jimmy D. proceeds to lay down the purest of blues licks, sending official notice that he can play it as straight as anyone whenever he chooses.

An up-tempo version of "Walkin' by Myself" is next, the quickest tempo on record from Jimmy for this tune. The band is tight, and while Carey borrows liberally from Big Walter's approach, he still manages to insert his own personality into the mix. Jimmy then sings the classic "Rock Me (Baby)," with a very subdued singing style, adequately reflecting the comfortable key and groove that the band has set for him to massage his patented vocal phrasing. With Johnnie Johnson more subdued on this one, veteran bassist Dave Myers and longtime drummer Ted Harvey use the opportunity to lock down the tightest rhythm possible underneath Jimmy, with Carey percolating on the harp. Far in the background, you can hear faint traces of Jimmy D's deft arpeggios—just enough to add the ideal foundation for his son's perfected *lumpty-lump* rhythm guitar shuffle, no doubt an inherited trait from Jimmy.

Jimmy offers "I Lost a Good Woman," and "Blue and Lonesome" as medium-slow blues tunes in G, both taken from the *Gold Tailed Bird* album (the latter tune was originally listed as "Lonesome Blues"). Jimmy even found time to give a nod to Howlin' Wolf and the year he spent with him in 1960 by recording "Howlin' for My Darlin'," where Jimmy D. does a dead-on impression of Hubert Sumlin's wicked vibrato and edgy tone from Wolf's July 1959 recording.

"Why Are You So Mean to Me?" is a revamped original taken from Jimmy's 1991 concert with Ronnie Earl and the Broadcasters in Bremen, Germany. While the Bremen version (listed on the LP as "Why Did You Do It?") was served up as a swinging jump-blues in the key of A, this studio version is a medium-slow cooker in the key of G with an entirely different set of verses. Johnnie Johnson lets loose on a solo that sounds like he hasn't lost a step since the classic Chuck Berry sessions, while Jimmy D. has the last word, offering a short but stylistically sweet solo that surely made his father beam with pride.

"Blues Falling" uses an infectious, galloping groove that makes it the funkiest tune on the album. Ted Harvey and Dave Myers drive the boogie beat, and there are brief but tasty solos by both Carey and Jimmy D. The main attraction here is the lyrics, expertly crafted by Jimmy in three verses:

When my blues start fallin' my trouble begin to rise (repeat)
When your woman stops lovin' you she's lovin' some other guy
When your woman stops lovin' you its just like an old true sayin' (repeat)
When she don't wash and iron your clothes she's in love with another man
I'm not gonna start no fight, I'm not gonna fuss and clown (repeat)
You better get yourself together if you want poor Jimmy around

"Lemon Squeezer" is another tune Rogers inserted as rare encore performance. Originally from the October 1989 session for the LP *Chicago Bound*, this recording was co-led with Big Moose Walker for Wolf Records. "That Ain't It (Baby I Need Your Love)" was revived from the October 29 Chess session in 1956. Originally titled "If It Ain't Me (Who Are You Thinking Of)," the piece was in the higher-pitched key of G with a heavy drum shuffle provided by Fred Below. Here the tune is dropped to the key of open E and delivered with a slightly slower gait, with Ted Harvey gently prodding the tune along over Dave Myers's smooth bass lines.

The ultimate highlight of the entire album is "Smokestack Lightning," with Jimmy singing verses that even Wolf didn't include on his January 1956 session. A smooth groove in the flavor of "Rock Me Baby" is provided for Jimmy as he smartly blends Wolf's words with Muddy's methodology of the earlier September 1954 session that Jimmy recorded when he was a central figure in the Waters band. Jimmy's choice to use Muddy's version was clearly meant as a paean to his former bandleader, whose singing style on this number is closely copied here. Rogers even goes through the trouble of dropping the guitars down to the key of E flat, just like the original. When asked about the song's inclusion on the album, Jimmy D. said, "Maybe he resorted back to that as a tribute, because they did so many things together. Maybe that was his way of giving props to his friend."[60]

The song has some of the most incredible lyrics ever written, and that Jimmy revived Muddy's original version with such exquisite detail is a stroke of genius.

The woman I love, she got long black curly hair (repeat)
She's a married woman her husband don't allow me there
Train I ride, sixteen coaches long (repeat)
Sittin' here wonderin' if it'll bring my baby home
Smokestack lightnin', the bells all shine like gold (repeat)
How much I love her don't nobody know
Meanest people, that I've ever seen
I asked her for water, she gave me gasoline (what kinda woman is that?)
Church bell toll, the hearse was rolling slow (now don't you hear me cryin!)
Sometimes I wonder where did my baby go

In "Big Boss Man," Jimmy D. does his absolute best imitation of Jimmy's accompaniment style of the '50s, showing that the apple never fell too far from the tree. This tune was more than likely chosen as a good-time piece, chosen just for the fun of it. The frolicking continues until the very last track on the album—a jam session captured by producer John Koenig, who caught the guys in a moment when they were keeping it loose and letting it fly.

By the time they wrapped things up, there was enough material on the CD for two albums, and one wonders if that wasn't the plan all along. The artwork for both the cover and the CD shows Jimmy in a black cowboy hat, posing with a guitar that he hadn't been seen with before; he usually had his beloved Gibson ES 355 with him. "The guitar on the cover—that belonged to producer John Koenig," said Joe Harley.[61] Koenig concurred, saying, "We brought Jimmy to L.A. to shoot the cover because world-renowned jazz photographer Bill Claxton agreed to do it, but we'd just had a big earthquake in early 1994 and Jimmy was afraid to come. He braved the trip, but he didn't want to subject his guitar to the risk of aftershocks, so we used mine for the cover shot." A wonderful group photo was taken by Scott Dirks, which showed a band that appeared to be quite pleased with each other's company.[62]

While there was certainly joy in making the album, things weren't as joyous outside the studio. Jimmy had lost his mother, Grossie Jackson, on November 2, 1993 at 10:00 A.M., just a couple of weeks before the recording sessions began. The loss had devastated him. The two had grown very close since she'd come to Chicago to live with him during the '80s. Jimmy had been thrilled to be reunited with her after all the years of their separation, having been raised by his grandmother, who served as his surrogate mother. Nowhere is Jimmy's grief more evident than on the cover of the *Bluebird* album; his mournful expression tells everything about how much he missed his mother, affectionately known by all of her children as "Little Bit." It was one of the few times in his entire life that he'd sat for a picture that didn't display that classic Jimmy Rogers smile, with his gleaming gold tooth. He just couldn't hide the pain; the image conjures up Jimmy's own haunting lyrics, "You left me with a broken heart."

By June 3, 1994, Jimmy was feeling a whole lot better. He celebrated his seventieth birthday in front of thousands of adoring fans at the Chicago Blues Festival. The city turned the atmosphere into a party by honoring Jimmy with a birthday cake that ran nearly the length of the stage. Jeff Johnson wrote the following notes in the Sunday edition of the *Chicago Sun-Times*: "There were no candles to blow out on the giant birthday cake given to him onstage by the city during one of the longest artist introductions on record. Instead, he and his bandmates nearly blew the roof off the Petrillo Music Shell as the opening-night headliners for the 11th annual Chicago Blues Festival."[63]

After a short statement thanking the crowd and acknowledging the honor bestowed upon him by the mayor, Jimmy and the band got down to business. "There was no doubting Rogers'[s] sincere feeling for the blues," wrote Johnson. "The always impeccably dressed Mississippi native played classic Chicago blues tunes, ably supported by a band that includes his son, Jimmy D., keyboardist Piano Willie, and harpist Madison Slim."[64] It was Fred Crawford on bass and

Ted Harvey on drums. Muddy Waters's alumni members appeared as special guests, with Pinetop Perkins on piano, Jerry Portnoy handling the harmonica duties, and Bob Margolin was there to blow the crowd away with his slide guitar work on "Blow Wind Blow." Old friend Snooky Pryor emerged to entertain the throngs with his "Snooky and Moody Boogie." The Rogers celebration also featured the Chicago Soul Revue, a local ten-piece horn and rhythm section ensemble led by Willie Henderson.

Jimmy received another huge boost when Eric Clapton released a new album, *From the Cradle*, which instantly became a million-seller. Clapton's goal was to record an album that signaled his return to the hard-core Chicago blues and to pay tribute to the pioneers that created the music. As a public nod to Jimmy's influence on his own career, Clapton included two of Jimmy's best tunes, "Blues Leave Me Alone" and "Going Away Baby." The mega-hit CD generated a huge windfall of money in royalties for Jimmy and his family. His popularity soared after Clapton's album struck worldwide.

Now at the age of seventy, Jimmy was playing more than two hundred dates a year, moving between gigs of his own as a leader and as a veteran in the Muddy Waters tribute band, which toured heavily after the success of the *I'm Ready* album.[65] Jimmy, who always enjoyed having a strong harp underneath him, had Waters veteran Paul Oscher blowing on the tribute tour. Meanwhile, the 1994 edition of Jimmy's own band consisted of his son Jimmy D. on guitar, Willie O'Shawny on keys, Bob Stroger on bass, and Ted Harvey on drums. With Steve Guyger's recent exit from the band, "Madison Slim" Mark Koenig was back on harmonica.

That year Atomic Records released an album under the leadership of harp player Big Bill Hickey. *Bill's Blues* listed Jimmy and former Howlin' Wolf guitarist Hubert Sumlin as co-leaders of the album. Producer and label owner Willie Murphy was a guitarist who nurtured early albums in the careers of Bonnie Raitt and John Korner. The LP was developed, oddly enough, at rock star Prince's purple home and personal recording facility in Chanhassen, Minnesota, called Paisley Park Studio. The rhythm section included Bob Stroger on bass, Robert Covington on drums, and Charles Lewandowsky, who sat in on keyboards for a few cuts.

The album opens with Jimmy's "Slick Chick," set at a leisurely swinging pace, with a guitar solo from Jimmy's son Jimmy D. Lane, followed by Willie Murphy's guitar work. The tune is easily the LP's strongest offering. Later in the album Jimmy appears again on "Crazy Woman," with Jimmy D. supplying background licks on guitar. After the elder Jimmy sings two verses, Junior steps up to solo, followed by an even more distorted solo from Sumlin.

"When It Comes to Love" and "Feed Me" are funk-jam workouts, the latter featuring Sumlin on lead vocals and guitar. According to the liner notes, Sumlin was a close friend of Bill Hickey and took on the role of mentor and "musical father" to him, which accounts for his presence at the session. "I Am the Blues" was a six-minute-plus instrumental excursion that allowed for Jimmy to flaunt his Stevie Ray Vaughan–influenced blues-rock chops. Unfortunately, it eventually gives way to a rambling introspective dialogue from Hickey that does little to enhance the music.

"Talk to Me Baby" gives more solo space to Jimmy D. than to Hickey, who doesn't seem too interested in using the album as a showcase for his own talents. "Easy" (a tune with chord changes similar to Ivory Joe Hunter's "I Almost Lost My Mind") is credited to Big Walter and features Sam Burkhart taking a sax solo. A forgettable "Shake, Rattle, and Roll" uses a New Orleans groove that shifts down to a shuffle, while "Put the Kettle On" is probably included as filler for this relatively short album. All in all the record probably did more for Jimmy D.'s image as an upcoming gun-slinging guitarist than for Hickey's as a hot harp player.

Jimmy Rogers had befriended journalist Tom Townsley in the late 1980s. Townsley, a novice harp player, played with Jimmy when Rogers sat in with Tom's band a few times in New York. Jimmy was Tom's house guest on his second trip to Syracuse when he flew in especially to play with Tom's band. When Tom came to Chicago, Jimmy returned the favor, letting him sit in with his band on Tom's wedding night. Tom remembered the event this way:

> My wife Kathy and I had been making annual pilgrimages to the Chicago Blues Festival for several years prior to our marriage, so we decided it would be fun to get married during the festival—something borrowed, something Blue . . . That night making the club rounds, we came to Lilly's, where Jimmy and his band were holding court. Jimmy greeted us warmly, congratulated us, and offered me a spot onstage for a set. What a rush. Bob Stroger on bass, Ted Harvey on drums, and Jimmy [Lane], Jr. on guitar! I'll never forget Jimmy's graciousness on that special night.[66]

Although Jimmy was getting to the age where he should have seriously considered declining the ever increasing requests for interviews, he still took the time and energy to sit and share his experiences in life, love, and music. He and Tom eventually became very close friends, with Jimmy regaling Tom with personal stories about the good old days, including tales about Muddy, Walter, Wolf, Dixon, the Chess brothers, and others. He shared with Tom intimate details about the traumatic experience of the death of Henry Strong at the hands of Strong's wife. Even after all these years, the memory remained clear. Strong's wife was never indicted, he told Tom, and thus did no jail time for the vicious and blatant crime, in which Muddy himself was slightly injured while trying to help Strong escape with his life.

On a lighter note, Jimmy also told Tom a story about the hilarious wrestling match between Willie Dixon and Howlin' Wolf as they battled each other in the Chess Studios, "like two elephants rolling around." He mentioned the rare, unexpected event that occurred when Good Rockin' Charles completely lost his nerves in the studio and had to be replaced by Big Walter Horton, who promptly stepped up to the plate and hit a home run with the solo work he contributed to the sides that were cut that day, laying down the tracks for the single, "Walkin' by Myself."[67]

As the last of the Headhunters, Jimmy understood his obligation to keep the blues tradition alive. And as he grew older, he became more philosophical, more introspective; he began to look at his life from a historical perspective. Jimmy said to Townsley, "So now they've passed on, you know, but I'm still here, doin' the blues, holding that style in portion as best I can and teachin' the younger blues players what it's all about. It's very simple to me 'cause it's just soul and feelin' that's deep down in your heart. A desire, you know?"[68]

Clearly Jimmy was trying to deal with several issues that have always been relevant: whether blues can be taught, whether whites can or have the right to play the blues, and whether blacks should go out of their way to pass the mantle on to whites, lest they lose their legacy. Jimmy's response appears to have been that he was not worried about losing the legacy; in fact, he was passing it on to whoever wanted to pick up the cross, black or white. He never worried about anyone outdoing him on the guitar. By the mid-1990s there were a slew of white gunslingers trying to play the blues, and much of it was sounding more like rock than the blues. Maybe some things can't be taught, regardless of color.

"I see a lot of up-and-coming blues players is tryin' to get it, but you know in my style of blues right now, it's gonna be hard," Jimmy said. "Where you gonna find a musician? They can outplay me, as far as execution and runnin' up and down the neck and stuff. But the soul is hard to beat, yeah."[69] Reflecting back, Jimmy seemed a bit nostalgic as he fondly remembered his life before Muddy Waters, when he would run the Chicago streets and play blues down on Maxwell Street with his regular cronies: Little Walter; Claude "Blue Smitty" Smith; John Henry Barbee; Eddie "Porkchop" Hines; Johnny "Stovepipe" Watson; Ed Newman; and Moody Jones. They were all dead and gone by now. These were the guys he'd relied upon to help form his first Chicago blues band.[70]

Jimmy was happy with the way his life turned out. He was surrounded by his children, whom he loved dearly. He was also actively involved in managing real estate properties.[71] His wife, Dorothy, was his constant companion. Whenever Jimmy finally returned home from the many long road gigs, fishing was still among the couple's favorite recreational activities. Pinetop Perkins, his lifelong piano player and good old friend, was his "number two" fishing buddy, and the two of them would meet as regularly as they could and go to one of several select spots to catch whatever was biting, hoping they'd get lucky. As with everything else he did, Jimmy pursued the art of fishing with gusto. "When I'm goin' after a fish, I don't care how big he is," Jimmy asserted. "I'll keep at it. I go to different places. I go to different places around Illinois, places I usually have a chance to run out there for three or four hours. I fish for cats, crappies, bass and stuff like that. Sometimes we goes out to Aurora and stay all night . . . We go out there maybe twelve, one o'clock durin' the day. We'd stay out there till four or five in the morning next day."[72] He got great pleasure out of getting away from it all, just sitting there with his pole and bait. More often than not there was the added bonus of enjoying the comfort of his beloved companion. "Dorothy hangs right there with me," Jimmy said adoringly. "She *loves* to fish. We stay out there, away from the kids. They don't even know where we are."[73]

While Jimmy may have been closest to Muddy when the Headhunters first roamed the streets, it was the bond between Jimmy and Pinetop that endured the years. While there is little or no evidence of Muddy being an avid fisherman while in Chicago, Jimmy and Pinetop always found time to get out on the water and try to catch whatever was biting. It was another way to enjoy each other's company when they were off the bandstand, while still enjoying something they both loved. "Me and Jimmy goes fishing together. I love to fish," Pinetop remarked. "But the people looks like they ain't gonna fish none this year. They workin' us old men to death. Sometimes we catch a right smart one, sometimes we don't. We always have a good time."[74]

Both men seemed to find a common thread between the art of catching a good fish and the art of capturing a good groove. "Just like the music," Pinetop once noted. "Sometimes you do pretty good at it, and sometimes you don't." Jimmy would go on to make a statement about being in the water and continually stroking to stay afloat; no doubt he used his affinity for the water several times as metaphors to be applied in other aspects of his life. "That was lots of fun," Pinetop concurred. "Me and Jimmy, we work good together. We know what each is going to do before we do it."[75] Pinetop, knowingly or not, in this description, used almost the exact same words when describing his relationship with

Jimmy as Jimmy himself had used in an earlier interview when explaining his unique relationship with Muddy.

In that same interview Jimmy also spoke about his son Jimmy D. and the new generation's ability to replicate the sounds of the classic blues of the '50s. "The unit I have now, my son and the rest of the guys, they play as close to the traditional sounds as they can," Jimmy said. "It's nothing like the regular sound that we had. But they do the best they can. I appreciate them coming as close as they do." It was clear that he held no grudges against the youth for their personal preferences. Just like everyone else, they were merely products of their own environment. "The younger guys, they are not really related with what you're thinking when you're on stage," Jimmy admitted. "They play soul and funk and what have you. When they came through that's what they heard."[76]

In a later interview Jimmy had all but resigned himself to the idea that the next generation was generally ill-equipped to adequately replicate the blues style, saying, "The heavy stuff that we're playing, to the average young blues player, that stuff is too hard. It's too much work. They're changing the blues. It's like church ballads or something. They're not driving them, it's more like spirituals than blues." Unlike the days when he and Muddy sat on stage and carefully coaxed the music out to the people, Jimmy realized that the youngsters just wanted to hurl the sounds at the public, who seemed to prefer it that way as well. "They're screaming and preaching because that seems easier to play," Rogers lamented. "When we played it was more like harmonizing, more of a piano sound . . . its different now, but I know where they're coming from, and they know where I'm coming from."[77]

Still, Jimmy knew that at least his own son was not purely one-dimensional. Little Jimmy could play the blues as deep as the next guy anytime he felt like it. Indeed, he had learned the history firsthand from the legends. Over the years he'd amassed a treasure trove of tunes, forming a vast reservoir of knowledge that went far deeper than that of a lot of his contemporaries. Jimmy said of his father, "He would call off some song that most of the cats, they would have no idea of where he was going. He'd be going off into a riff, and I'd jump right on it, and he'd look over at me and chuckle, like, 'I can't believe you remembered that.' We'd smile at each other and go on."[78]

Back on the road in September 1994, Jimmy played the Long Beach Blues Festival in California on Saturday and Sunday of Labor Day weekend. The festival honored the legacy of Leonard and Phil Chess with an "All-Star Chess Records Tribute" that featured Jimmy, along with Junior Wells, Bo Diddley, Lowell Fulson, Johnnie Johnson, Sam Lay, Dave Myers, and Hubert Sumlin. Toward the end of the year, Jimmy's fans were treated to a little surprise when the CD version of Blues Queen Sylvia's 1983 LP, *Midnight Baby,* was released. There were three bonus tracks added to the eight previously issued tracks, two of which were borrowed from the November 11, 1983, concert for the American Folk Blues Festival, produced by Horst Lippman for the L + R label. Embry's strong bass lines and vocal performance (backed by Jimmy, Louisiana Red, Lovie Lee, Charles "Honey Boy" Otis, and Carey Bell) led the group as they stormed through "I Love You," and "Baby, What Do I Do," ending the set on a high note.

Jimmy would have good fortune in 1995, the year he was inducted into the Blues Hall of Fame. The Saturday, May 13 performance by Jimmy Rogers and the Chicago Blues All-Stars at the fifteenth annual Fountain Blues Festival in San Jose, California, marked another high note. On the bill that day was Jimmy's St. Louis pal Johnnie Johnson (backed by the Tommy Castro Band), as well as his old friend Mark Hummel and his Blues Survivors. Two months later Jimmy arrived at his old familiar stomping grounds in Austin, Texas, for the twentieth anniversary of Antone's on July 15. The following year the Antone's label produced a two-CD set with selected cuts from that anniversary celebration, featuring Jimmy on the first two tunes. For "Got My Mojo Working," Jimmy's backup band was Bill Campbell on guitar, Bob Stroger on bass, Ted Harvey on drums, Pinetop Perkins on piano, and Hubert Sumlin on guitar. "Chicago Bound" had James Cotton on harp, Bob Stroger on bass, Ted Harvey on drums, Pinetop Perkins on piano, and Luther Tucker on guitar.

Still another highlight of the year came on October 24, 1995, when Capitol Records released a CD titled *Chicago Blues Masters: Volume Two.* As a second compilation in this series, the two-disc set was dedicated to the music of Jimmy Rogers and the three separate sessions that had yielded the music for *Gold Tailed Bird.* This new and definitive version corrected the previously mislabeled song titles, performers, dates, and locations of recording. Finally the musicians in the Bob Riedy Blues Band were properly credited for their accomplishments. Pianist Bob Riedy, bassist Jim Wydra, drummer Richard Hubcap Robinson, guitarists Frank Capek and Jim Kahr, and harp man Bill Lupkin were appropriately acknowledged in print for being the actual musicians on the first side of the original album, and for the fact that they did record the music in Hollywood at Paramount Studios.

In addition to the original tracks from *Gold Tailed Bird,* this release offered four extra tracks, along with more corrections (at long last) regarding the three recording sessions that took place from January 1972 through mid-1973. "Dorcie Bell," "Slick Chick," and "Blues (Follow Me All Day Long)," while not necessarily inspiring as far as performances go, do provide a bit more insight into what Jimmy was interested in recording during this period of his life. The tune "Dorcie Bell" was discussed briefly in the 1972 interview Jimmy gave shortly after the original session was recorded. He revealed that the song's title was given as a reference to his guitar, much in the same way the title "Ludella" was conceived. Another of the album's tracks, "I Lost a Good Woman," has horns overdubbed on the tune. According to Frank Capek, who'd replaced Jim Kahr for the extra session, the horns were overdubbed during the Tulsa, Oklahoma, session of 1973. Liner notes on the CD hint otherwise, suggesting they were added later on in Nashville by producer Owen Bradley.

But there was still more drama left to complete the picture of the Capitol Records release. In his excellent liner notes, blues scholar Bill Dahl revealed that although Owen Bradley was previously given credit by Shelter Records for being the producer for four of the outtake tunes—"Slick Chick," "Blues Follow Me All Day Long," "I Lost a Good Woman," and "Dorcie Bell," guitarist Frank Capek had told Dahl that those tunes were recorded in neither Nashville, Tennessee, nor in Disney, Oklahoma. According to Capek, the songs were recorded in Tulsa. Leon Russell, previously credited with producing the session, was not even present for that particular session.[79] As it turns out, Capek's memory was more accurate than Shelter's liner notes. In the autumn 1973 issue of *Living Blues* magazine, Jim O'Neal reported "Jimmy Rogers recorded a second LP for Shelter on June 4–5 in Tulsa."[80] Unfortunately, the horn overdubs on "I Lost a Good Woman" still remain a mystery—no one is sure when or where that happened.

During two days in October 1995 and two others in January 1996, Jimmy D. took even more major steps in securing his own blues legacy beyond his father's shadow. He'd already established himself as a legitimate artist in his own right, and nowhere was his strength more evident than on the last Kassem-Koenig project that yielded Jimmy's *Bluebird* in 1994 (Koenig produced and Kassem financed it). Jimmy D. thoroughly respected John's ability to produce an album and appreciated how well he had done on the most recent Jimmy Rogers album. "Koenig was very exacting on a lot of points in the studio," Lane said. "If a guitar went out of tune, he heard it, and all the other little things that we were too involved to notice. I'd work with him any day and twice on Sunday. He was an excellent producer."[81]

While *Bluebird* was all about the music of Jimmy Senior, this time Jimmy D. was the center of attention, and Chad Kassem put his entire weight behind the project, just as he had for the elder Rogers. The supporting musicians chosen for the recording were deliberately stripped down in order to deliver the hard, power-trio sound that Jimmy D. preferred for getting his message across. Seasoned veteran Jim Keltner was brought in on drums, a real coup for the Rogers family. "In between Pop's dates, we set up the studio dates for my album," Jimmy D. said. 'We would have had to fly my drummer all the way out from Chicago. We knew that Jim Keltner was at Ocean Way, so we just hired him—he's a legendary drummer there anyway."[82] John Koenig provided more specific details, saying, "I thought Jimmy D. needed a top-flight drummer . . . Keltner was available and excited about the project. He [Jim] told me later that of all the albums he did that year, he was most proud of Little Jimmy's and one he did with guitarist Bill Frisell." The bass chair was left to Jimmy D.'s longtime friend Fred Crawford, who'd recently been hired as a permanent replacement in the Jimmy Rogers band for Bob Stroger.

Jimmy D. wasted no time establishing his individuality and personal sound on this new album. Armed with a snow-white Fender Stratocaster, jet-black Afro hairdo, moccasin boots, and wide-brimmed Texas hat, he opened with "Hear My Train A-Comin'," the quintessential Hendrix manifesto of the late 1960s. Beautifully distorted, overdrive-drenched soul music of the '60s was mixed with the modern mind-set, meant to match Stevie Ray Vaughan's band Double Trouble. Simply put, the music on this album was not his father's sound. It wasn't meant to be, either. Still, tucked neatly underneath the rock was a warm spot held for the old-school blues. Indeed, Jimmy D. strategically placed musical markers throughout the repertoire to remind listeners that he never intended to fully abandon the blues.

"Rolling Stone," for example, was inserted as an obvious nod to the legacy of Muddy Waters (albeit via Hendrix); "Boom Boom" was offered as an homage to John Lee Hooker, a personal friend of Jimmy's family. And then there was the moving gesture of Jimmy D.'s inclusion of the Jimmy Rogers piece "I'm in Love." Jimmy D. went out of his way to get that one; after all, it was an original tune that, surprisingly enough, would not be found on any of the Chess sides. Predating the legendary Chess years, Jimmy had recorded it only once, with Sunnyland Slim on August 26, 1949, for Apollo, nearly fifty years before this specially prepared, all-acoustic treatment for Junior's own album.

He may have been long gone, but Jimmy D. was never *too* far gone.

13

THAT'S ALL RIGHT

I think Muddy and me contributed quite a bit to
the blues . . . I'm well pleased to be in history for
this thing. I guess the timing must have been right.

—Jimmy Rogers

The year 1996 turned out to be another exciting one for Jimmy. He was seventy-two years old and still going strong. In early February he and his band had a gig in St. Louis. John May, a prominent local club owner, was instrumental in serving as liaison between local musicians and blues acts that came through the city of St. Louis. It was May's idea to hire harp player Keith Doder and his Blue City Band to open for Jimmy at a club called Off Broadway. Doder wanted to be a part of Jimmy's group, but the harp chair was occupied at the time by Madison Slim, who was in the "on" phase of his on-off relationship with Jimmy and the band.[1]

Dave Krull was a member of the band Cryin' Shame, the band that opened up for Jimmy when he performed at Off Broadway that night. Krull, raised in Kansas City, Missouri, had grown up listening to his father's piano music and his record collection, which ranged from Count Basie to Duke Ellington and from Otis Spann to George Shearing. He eventually moved to St. Louis and had been living there for nearly ten years before he was approached by Jimmy that lucky day. John May, the bass player for Krull's band, was also serving as a liaison between the big-name artists and the local musicians. When the spotlight turned to Dave for his feature number, he ripped it up, delivering a performance that left Jimmy duly impressed. Not only was Jimmy awestruck, but so was piano legend Johnnie Johnson, who had performed with Krull in a few amazing piano duels at a club called the Sheldon. Backstage, Jimmy approached Dave and coolly asked, "Does that piano travel?"

A few months later, in a visit to St. Louis in May, pianist Dave Krull would be hired to play with Jimmy. Madison Slim, because of his tempestuous relationship with alcohol, had shifted to the "off" phase with Jimmy and would eventually get fired. Once Slim was relieved of his duties, Doder believed he'd be chosen to go with Jimmy. When Krull was selected on this second visit to St. Louis, Doder got his hopes up. But it didn't happen—Jimmy decided to stick with his then current harp player, Bill Hickey, and Doder was disappointed.

Between those two St. Louis appearances in the early months of 1996, Jimmy went on an extensive world tour, his biggest yet. For this trip abroad he took his own musicians. The band was led by Jimmy D., who had Fred Crawford playing a six-string bass; Barrelhouse Chuck on piano; Ted Harvey on drums; and, for this trip, Scotty "Bad Boy" Bradbury on harp. They arrived in Europe on February 29 and traveled through six countries. In the first ten days they played a series of gigs located mainly in cities throughout Holland, including Haarlem, Amsterdam (where their second set was recorded and was also broadcast live for national radio), Laren, Groningen, Sneek (where Jimmy and Little Jimmy also gave a blues master class at a music academy during the day), and Rotterdam. They hit Brussels in Belgium; did two gigs in Ireland, in Dublin and Belfast; and played at the 100 Club in London, where Jimmy had recorded his live sets with Left Hand Frank back in the mid-1970s. Of this tour, Barrelhouse would remember, "After Clapton and Gary Moore recorded those tunes, Jimmy was treated like a rock star, and we all had really nice dressing rooms, too."[2]

They went from Belfast to Utrecht, where they performed in Vredenburg on March 16. The next day they traveled back to Amsterdam, where after a day off they performed a gig in Haltern. Jimmy did an after-dinner interview the evening of March 18 with Uli Lemke for *Blues Rhythm* magazine. The next day they were off again, traveling eight long hours before putting on shows in the small towns on Hunziken and Rubigen, near Bern, Switzerland. They then went to Paris and had dinner at a Lebanese club across the street from New Morning, the venue they were playing. After shows at the Cricketer in Bordeaux on March 22, and at La Mounede in Toulouse on the twenty-third, they drove directly back to Paris for a flight home to Chicago.

"We played at Legends [Buddy Guy's blues club in Chicago]; it was one of the last gigs I played with him," recalled Barrelhouse Chuck, who had been in and out of the band several times by now. "He had a gig in St. Louis coming up and he wanted me to go."[3] Due to some mix-up, Chuck never made that May trip and was out of the band once again. Piano Willie O'Shawny returned to the group just as the band began another lengthy tour. He'd already seen quite a few places over the years with Rogers. "During the time I was with him, Jimmy

Rogers toured all of the USA, Canada, South America, Japan, United Kingdom, and Europe," O'Shawny said. "I was in Spain in 1996 with Rogers's band. I can't recall how many times; we traveled so much. We went to Barcelona, Toledo, and Cordoba. He also played festivals internationally and in the USA. We played both the Chicago Blues Fest and the American Folk Blues Fest."[4]

Piano Willie played a major role in making sure the old man was comfortable these days. "Madison Slim and myself was the leader of the band when Rogers wasn't on the stage," Willie said. He and Jimmy got closer during that trip, and Willie came to better understand the reason behind Jimmy's work ethic. "Jimmy came up in the Depression and had great strength of character as anyone from the greatest generation," said Willie. O'Shawny also came to appreciate the cool and calm manner with which Jimmy dealt with all things in life, a trait that always gave a Buddha-like appearance to his demeanor. In O'Shawny's opinion, "Little things—and even big things—did not upset him. He was very soft-spoken and low-key. He was also very personable and friendly even under the worst conditions."[5] Jimmy led his band tirelessly from one tour to another, bringing the Chicago blues to the world. His efforts were approved not only by his audiences but by critics as well. In 1996 Jimmy received another great honor among blues artists. He won the W. C. Handy Award for Best Male Traditional Blues Artist.

During this successful run a few more personnel changes occurred, but the band situation did not ruffle Jimmy's calm demeanor. He not only knew his music, but he also knew musicians. When the recently hired Hickey suddenly got fired, it didn't create a hole in the band; rather, it opened the door for Doder's opportunity to play with Jimmy. By February 1997 Doder had been asked to temporarily substitute for Hickey and play with Jimmy in Champaign, Illinois, at the Malibu Lounge, which led to an eventual mini-tour from Ft. Wayne, Indiana, at the Hot Spot to the Trolley Stop in Dayton, Ohio, and then east to Massachusetts, where they played in Worcester and at the House of Blues in Cambridge.[6]

On April 8, 1997, MCA released *Jimmy Rogers: The Complete Chess Recordings* (CHD2–9372), part of a series labeled "The Chess 50th Anniversary Collection." According to producer Andy McKaie, who compiled the music for the album, the collection essentially represented "every master Jimmy Rogers recorded for Chess as well as the best available alternate takes still extant."[7] This two-disc set had fifty-one tunes, which fell into three basic categories: twenty-six released as singles between 1950 and 1959; twenty-two songs that were shelved during Jimmy's active career at Chess but later released on reissue albums or other compilations; and twelve alternate takes of recorded tunes, nine of which were previously unreleased.

The set is beautifully packaged, with Jimmy's black-and-white cover picture taken from the standard photo shoot required whenever Chess Records signed an artist. A fifteen-page booklet was included with exceptionally well-written liner notes by Mary Katherine Aldin, a blues scholar and historian who interviewed Jimmy late in 1996 to gather material for the release of the project. Inside the jewel case is an impressive color photo of Jimmy sporting a cool pair of shades and a dark suede jacket. His trimmed mustache, goatee, and tight Afro hint at the mid-1970s period. For the back panel of the insert, Aldin supplied a beautiful updated shot of Jimmy comfortably settled in between Louis and Dave Myers, the three of them smiling. In typical fashion, Jimmy has the biggest, brightest smile of all.

As wonderful as the collection was, to some it seemed like a gesture that arrived too little, too late in Jimmy's career. Indeed, such a sentiment was reflected in Aldin's comment as she wrote, "Today he is at last achieving the recognition he deserves."[8] So many of those who knew Jimmy and had followed his career had long felt he had been seriously underrated when it came to his place in the pantheon of blues greats. The release of the Chess collection represented a great stride toward restoring Jimmy's image among blues fans as an artist who rightfully deserved every accolade that should be afforded a living legend.

When Aldin contacted Jimmy to gather notes regarding his thoughts about the impending release of the Chess collection, she observed that he seemed somewhat preoccupied with his current affairs, which seemed to be steadily mounting as a result of his increasing popularity. By Aldin's account, her phone interview "was done at a time when he was on the road and really busy, so it was just a short conversation . . . I only asked a few questions. When we spoke about it, he wasn't particularly excited one way or the other, because at the same time we were speaking, he was also in the studio working on one of his brand new albums, and he was really more excited about THAT."[9]

Although he rarely had time to spend thinking about the old days, Jimmy took a trip down memory lane as he shared a few thoughts with Aldin. "It was Sunnyland Slim who introduced me to Chess," Muddy told her. "Chess did so much for the blues, you know, they were the only ones at that time who were really getting it out there." Rogers was putting a positive spin on what he had sometimes felt was not always a fair and balanced world of blues and business. He found his own way of making his equality statement regarding just who helped whom by adding wryly, "and then I guess you could say, the blues did so much for them, too!" Still, he always found a way to get in a good word for Sunnyland Slim, saying, "[He] did so much for me and for many musicians at that time. And he got me together with Muddy."[10] He went on to tell Aldin, "When

I came here to record, I had my own material written for the most part. I knew [Willie] Dixon, of course, he played on some of my records, but I never could see doing his type of material, nothing wrong with them but it seemed as if my own songs just suited me better. So I went on with my own songs."[11]

Jimmy also shared some memories of his former bandleader and greatest collaborator. "Well, now, let me tell you about Muddy; he was never a binding man or a selfish man," he told Aldin. "Just like today, I have these guys here in my band, my son and everyone, but they are with me because they want to be with me. And I have always told them, if an opportunity comes up down the road, you go on, I'm not holding them back. Well, Muddy was the same way. When I had the opportunity to make records on my own, that was all there was to it. I never did leave Muddy, you know."[12] Clearly his respect and affection for his friend and mentor never wavered.

Jimmy reflected on the experiences he'd had and how his career slowly yet steadily blossomed out of the rich soil that both he and Muddy created. The tag-team effort that those two thrived upon led directly to his solo career, and in the initial stages he was allowed generous helpings of star time on Muddy's bandstand. "My biggest records, without question, were 'Ludella' and 'That's All Right,' and they were the ones that first got my name known," Jimmy said. "So when I would be playing with Muddy, naturally the audience would know my records and ask me to play them, so I would step forward, within the show Muddy was doing, and take my numbers."[13]

He also told Aldin that he had found those sessions as leader fairly difficult because he was always placed in the position as the "closer," with his tunes always reserved for being recorded after Muddy had taken the lions' share of the time allotted. All these years later, after scores of songs and sessions, Jimmy said of the cover versions of his tunes, "I've heard a lot of cover versions of my songs. I don't have any particular ones that are my favorites; they all try to put their own sound on them you know. Some of them try to copy me, and some try their own sound, but sometimes they hit and sometimes they don't!"[14]

Even at the age of seventy-two, Jimmy's spirit was as vibrant as ever, and his career was reaching new heights. He was beginning to get the royal treatment, including tributes, high-profile concerts, and star-status accommodations whenever and wherever he performed. His tunes were being covered by more and more artists. In addition to Eric Clapton's versions of Jimmy's tunes, Gary Moore's rendition of "Walkin' by Myself" (on his 1990 album *Still Got the Blues*) created a major surge in popularity and record sales for Jimmy overseas, which not only gave Jimmy's career and reputation a huge boost but also boosted his bank account. Aldin soon realized that Jimmy wasn't just dwelling on the past—he was too busy making other plans for the future. "Tracks that he had laid down forty years ago were not in the forefront of his mind to the same extent as brand-new tracks that he had just finished yesterday," she said. "He was certainly *interested* to know that his Chess material was being reissued; but again, it just wasn't as immediate to him as the project he was currently involved with."[15] When word finally hit the streets about this previously undisclosed "project" that demanded so much of Jimmy's time and attention, an immediate buzz was in the air, and everyone understood why Jimmy was excited about the future. The seeds of the project were planted when John Koenig, who'd recently produced albums for Jimmy and his son, played "Blue Bird" for his friend, legendary Atlantic Records co-founder Ahmet Ertegun. "Ahmet was crazy about the blues and loved the feel of the record," said Koenig.

Koenig and his wife, Elaine, mused that it would be a coup for Jimmy if they could get Ahmet to go for the idea of doing a record with Jimmy paired with a number of the luminaries of the rock world who had been influenced by Jimmy. They'd all grown up on the Chess sides that Jimmy animated with the rhythm guitar style that he'd virtually invented, so it seemed to Koenig like a natural fit.

"John and Elaine mentioned wanting to do something with Pop to Ahmet," Jimmy D. said. "And Ahmet knew him way back in '55 when Pop recorded with T-Bone Walker. Jerry Wexler, all those guys at Atlantic knew him." Ertegun, a powerhouse in the industry who had relationships with virtually everyone important in music, called in a few favors to put the wheels in motion. He was pleased to see that everyone was more than willing to participate in the festivities. "Ahmet called up all those guys who loved Pop; they said they'd wanted to do it for years," Jimmy D. said proudly. "They always talked about him—especially Mick [Jagger], Keith Richards, and Eric Clapton."[16]

When Jimmy first heard word about Koenig and Ertegun's mammoth undertaking, "we were on tour," said Jimmy D. "So we came out during one of the breaks in the schedule while we were already on the West Coast." All the other stars came out too. The sessions took place at Ocean Way Studios in Hollywood, California. From stateside, a wide array of blues guitar guests showed up, including Taj Mahal, Stephen Stills, Jeff Healey, and Lowell Fulson. From the British side, rock royalty emerged, including England's biggest guitar hero, Eric Clapton; Rolling Stones legends Mick Jagger and Keith Richards; and Led Zeppelin's rock superstars, Jimmy Page and Robert Plant. Jimmy Rogers and his band returned to the studio for a second session to finish what they started. "The next time we came out was a couple of months later," Jimmy D. recalled. "Eric [Clapton] was working on a project—I think it was the one he produced with Kenneth 'Baby Face' Edmonds. He [Eric] came over."[17] (John Koenig recalled it this way: "We started with Lowell Fulson and Eric Clapton in the fall of '97. Then we did Jeff Healey and Stephen Stills and a few weeks later, Mick and Keith in early '98. I forget where Taj fit in, but I think it was between Healey/Stills and Mick/Keith, although it may have been before.") Clapton knew Jimmy well, having already beckoned for him to join Clapton's band in London for the Wembley Stadium concert.

In order to keep things feeling like normal, co-producers John and Elaine Koenig made sure Jimmy was surrounded by his "home team" players, those who'd been in his starting lineup for years. With Ted Harvey on drums, Jimmy D. on guitar, Johnnie Johnson on piano, Carey Bell and Kim Wilson on harps, and Fred Crawford on bass, Jimmy felt more at ease in an environment that had so much talent in one room that conditions in the studio could have easily gotten out of control. John Koenig did manage to keep everything in hand and even managed to leave a few tracks open for himself to sneak in a bit of rhythm guitar ("Bright Lights, Big City"). Koenig reflected on how he wanted to make things perfect for Jimmy. "My job was to put together a context where people would be able to be comfortable and do their thing," said Koenig. "I worked with Little Jimmy on putting the grooves together on all these songs. We would get together, get our guitars out, and work out the grooves, because they're not exactly the same as the original recordings."[18]

As soon as they began recording, they realized they were not alone in the building laying down tracks. "The Stones were working on *Bridges to Babylon* during the first sessions we did," Jimmy D. recalled. "They were in studio 1; we were in the next studio room over in 2."[19] It was not just a coincidence. Koenig said, "I booked the rooms adjacent to the rooms they were working in. Eric and the Stones were in Ocean Way Studio 1, and then I booked Studio 2. Elaine worked *very* hard to make that happen!" "We were running back and forth, visiting each others' sessions. It was fun; it was like a party," said Jimmy D. Jagger described the sensation of leaving the high-tech atmosphere of the Stones' *Babylon* sessions and going down the hall to join in the blues session taking place nearby. According to Mick, "The two experiences were completely different—like walking out of some electronic thing and into Chicago in the other room."[20]

Jagger had always wanted to work with Jimmy. He told a London reporter, "I wasn't aware of Jimmy Rogers until I went to see him in a club many years ago [the West Coast gig at the Ash Grove in 1970]. I never saw him play with Muddy Waters or anything, but I connected that he was one of the guys who backed Howlin' Wolf, Little Walter and Sonny Boy Williamson."[21] Jagger ran into Jimmy again when the two of them were on the same bill at the inaugural event called National Music Day, which occurred in the summer of 1992 at the Hammersmith Odeon in London.[22] Jagger admitted that he used to perform

"Sloppy Drunk" at his earlier concerts with the Stones. Now he had his chance to work side by side with Jimmy. About his participation on the session, Mick said, "I was there to sing. I just did whatever they wanted me to do really."[23]

John Koenig remembers one special moment with Jagger that truly indicated how unique the session was. The last verse that Mick sings was censored from the original record, Koenig said. On the album, Jagger croons, *"He stopped his car / said baby get in / didn't stop drivin' 'til he hit the 40 mile bend / took the back seat out/ and put it on the ground / I don't need to tell you what he was putting down."* It was the first time the words had been captured on vinyl. Koenig recalled, "Jimmy remembered the words—that's how we got them!"[24] Said Koenig, "When I showed the lyric sheet to Mick and explained about the lost verse, he said, 'That really is quite good, isn't it?'"

Jagger was having the time of his life, but he did observe a certain strain that seemed to constantly crease Jimmy's face. Jagger was one of the first people to notice this. Looking back, we know now that he had good reason to be concerned: Jimmy's health was apparently beginning to slowly reveal visible signs of decline, although he was not confessing to having any pain or injuries, at least not publicly. But at the time, no one knew anything about a serious health condition in Jimmy Rogers.

Jimmy's naturally upbeat, easygoing manner came through at the session, but Jagger seemed to see something well beyond the positive attitude and happy facade Jimmy tried to exude that day. "Jimmy was pretty game but he was really ill," Mick said. "We were doing the vocals in the booth and I didn't know he was pretty sick. No one said anything. You make allowances for people his age and he was pretty good considering how ill he was."[25] Jagger was right about one thing: no one (if *anyone* knew) was commenting about what they saw regarding Jimmy's physical condition—not Jimmy, his son Jimmy D., nor anyone else in the Rogers family or band. It worried Mick, but he tried not to draw attention to the situation, not wanting to ruin Jimmy's efforts.

He and Jimmy collaborated on a few numbers, including "Going Away Baby" and the Muddy Waters tune "Trouble No More." Both men seemed to be thoroughly enjoying themselves. "The trickiest was the Sonny Boy Williamson one, 'Don't Start Me to Talkin'." It was fun trading the verses around . . . It was all done live," Mick said. Of all the tunes he participated on in the session, he concluded, "I think ['Talkin''] is the most interesting track. It just sounds really good . . . The timing is really odd, it's the only one I had to do again. The other ones I knew really well."[26]

Jagger was pleasantly surprised at the level of musicianship among members of Jimmy's "home team" players. Referring to Ted Harvey, Jagger said, "That drummer is incredibly quiet, whatever his name is. I'm not exaggerating. I walked into that studio and I didn't know whether they were playing or not. I could hardly hear them. I thought, [Stones guitarist] 'Keith [Richards] likes to play really loud, how's he going to manage?' But it's a good reminder of how those guys used to record."[27] Richards, who played on several tracks, had gone on record as saying, "I recognize myself in there between Chuck Berry, Muddy Waters and Jimmy Rogers."[28]

Lowell Fulson exchanged verses with Jimmy on "Ev'ry Day I Have the Blues," which had a brief but chilling piano solo from Johnnie Johnson. Jeff Healey and Jimmy traded verses of "Blow Wind Blow," and Healey took a blistering solo, as did Kim Wilson, who sounded so intense on every one of his solos, it was as if Little Walter himself had risen from the dead and decided to show up, since seemingly everybody else was there. Robert Plant and Jimmy Page teamed up with Jimmy to do John Lee Hooker's "Gonna Shoot You Right Down (Boom Boom)," with Plant howlin' toward the end just like Chester Burnett, the "original Wolf."

Stephen Stills alternated verses with Jimmy on two classics, "Sweet Home Chicago" and "Worried Life Blues," while Taj Mahal traded verses with him on "Ludella" and gave a perfect imitation of Jimmy Reed on harp after singing harmony to Jimmy Rogers's lead vocals on "Bright Lights, Big City." (Taj had asked John Koenig what part would he sing, to which Koenig replied, "The Mama Reed part.") Clapton swapped verses on "That's All Right" and "Blues All Day Long," supplying well-crafted solos for both tunes. Jimmy surprised everyone toward the end of "That's All Right" when he threw in an extra verse that no one had heard before. Jimmy's son was also having the time of his life, flanked by superstars, many of whom had been his childhood idols. "Eric was really knocked out by Little Jimmy and Ted," Koenig recalled. Even as he was surrounded by legends, Jimmy D. had a chance to get a few of his own licks in. "I played lead on 'Ludella' and 'Going Away Baby,'" he said proudly. "And there was a track that Jeff Healey and I did—they didn't release it, it didn't make the cut, but we were trading solos on it."[29] (Koenig says it was because the rehearsal take for that tune had a much better groove.)

"The album is full of magic moments," said producer Ahmet Ertegun. "And although everybody says, 'Wow, all those names,' that's good because it leads people to listen to it. What's really good about the album is not the famous people on it, but that they play the blues so well." As executive producer and pioneer of the project, Ertegun said with pride, "These people did not do it because they are great friends of mine. They did it because they are all real fine blues people and they loved Jimmy Rogers. We never got a turndown. Whomever we asked was very happy to play with Jimmy Rogers."[30]

On February 14–15, 1997, Jimmy Rogers brought his group to St. Paul, Minnesota. The band Inside Straight opened up for Jimmy at a place called Orrie's Blues Club on Valentine's Day, after which Jimmy came on and played two sets. Before the show Jimmy was seen sitting in a corner booth, signing autographs and taking pictures. He was feelin' good—having a ball and enjoying his life. No doubt he was proud of Jimmy D.'s performance that night. One reporter at the show observed, "Jimmy [D.] Lane is carrying on the family business—playing great electric Chicago blues guitar. He is an outstanding player in his own right, playing anything from hot licks to tasteful slow blues. He was burning the place up!"[31] The band played their typical set, including "Walkin' by Myself," "That's All Right," "Ludella," and "Mojo," but the elder Jimmy still had a few old-school tricks left up his sleeve, which included Lowell Fulson's "Every Day I Have the Blues" (most likely inspired by Fulson's rendition of the tune recorded for Jimmy's upcoming album), and a fast version of Freddie King's "Hideaway."

"He was sounding good tonight," reviewer Ray Stiles wrote. "His voice was as strong and as sweet as ever. He was also showing some of his old form on guitar—playing some nice rhythm and bass lines that was very enjoyable to watch."[32] Nearly three months later, Jimmy appeared at the Beale Street Music Festival on May 2, 1997, where he played a late-night set at 10:50 P.M., after Big Daddy Kinsey and the Kinsey Report. He played until ten past midnight. Jimmy was scheduled to return to Memphis later that year, but his concert was quickly canceled. (It was later discovered that Jimmy had gotten ill.)[33]

It was also in May that harp man Keith Doder finally and officially joined the band after receiving a phone call from Jimmy's daughter Angela Lane, who was working as an assistant to his business manager, Tom Radai. Doder joined Jimmy D., Ted Harvey, Fred Crawford, and David Krull as the band began a monthlong tour that started in New Orleans at Tipitina's and B. B. King's club in Memphis. Doder, who kept a road diary, recalled that the band then went on a more substantial tour in Europe, playing in Switzerland for about ten days, then going to Italy and several hits in San Sebastian, Spain, and Castilla y Leon. The tour ended in the southern part of Switzerland at the Piazza Blues Festival in Bellinzona, Italy, where Jimmy shared the bill with Johnny Adams and Eddie Floyd. Unfortunately, the show was cut short by a tumultuous rainstorm.[34]

In Rome the last gig of the tour was also cut short by a storm, just as Jimmy was ending the tune "My Little Machine." The band exited from the stage and barely made it to the airport in time for their flight from Milan that returned them back home to the States.[35] During the late summer months of 1997, Jimmy worked as much as ever, including tours throughout the South and Southwest, where they played in Phoenix, Arizona, and Albuquerque, New Mexico. In the West, they played in Denver, Colorado, and in a San Francisco club called Blues and Biscuits, with opening acts Chris Cain and Curtis Salgado. They then traveled through the Canadian Rockies across British Columbia.[36]

Jimmy once again participated in the Labor Day engagement at the Long Beach Blues Festival, in Long Beach, California, during the first two days of September 1997. He joined the "Chess All-Stars" featuring Hubert Sumlin, Billy Boy Arnold, and Johnnie Johnson for a special reunion performance. Three days later, on September 5, he played a show at Yoshi's in Oakland, California. According to an article written in the January/February '98 issue of *Blues Revue*, "When he came onstage, he seemed to be moving a bit slow and was lovingly assisted to his chair by his sidemen. But the fiery light in his eyes told the story before he hit his first number. He loves the blues and lives to play his old guitar."[37] The observation about Jimmy's slow approach to the stage and obvious need of assistance confirmed Mick Jagger's earlier suspicion that Jimmy's health condition was seriously heading in a negative direction.

A few days later, on September 8, Jimmy was scheduled to perform at the Mystic Theater in Petaluma. Before the concert he expressed his satisfaction with his career to Greg Cahill, a newspaper reporter for the *Sonoma Independent*, saying, "Everything is working out pretty nice." The constant surge in activity toward the end of his career surprised even Jimmy, as he commented with a chuckle, "They waited until I got to be an old man and then they started me to workin' real hard."[38] Still, he wasn't really complaining—after all, he loved his work. And there was always the relaxation at home and fishing to look forward to whenever a spate of road work was done.

When asked about his family life, Jimmy responded, "My kids are grown up and I'm a grandfather now. They all appreciate what I do, so I'm just having a lot of fun." With the Atlantic Records all-star album completed and only months away from being released, Jimmy was totally optimistic about his future prospects, especially since the Atlantic Records project stood to be the biggest event in his entire career. Many involved in the project eagerly anticipated its release, feeling as though the best was yet to come. "Everything is shaping up real good," Jimmy said. "I've just got to keep on rolling, that's the way I do it."[39]

Jimmy also played the King Biscuit Blues Festival in Helena, Arkansas, where he performed on the riverbank in front of ten thousand adoring fans. Evidently, Jimmy's condition took a serious turn for the worse, and he was coming to realize there wasn't much time left for him to lead his band out on the road. Still, he wasn't complaining outwardly when he did perform. Nevertheless, one can only speculate that at some point he must have begun the process of either declining future engagements or canceling preexisting ones. By now he had to have known that his time wasn't long.

When Jimmy played what turned out to be his last festival—in Atlanta, Georgia—the harp man Keith Doder had made previous commitments with his own band, and it saddened Doder when he realized he wouldn't be able to make that gig. But he was present for the very last gig that Jimmy ever performed on tour, which was at the Up and Under in Milwaukee. "Jimmy was gracious to me. By now the physical signs of disability were clearly visible. [He] was suffering and had a loss of weight," Doder said. "But he fought the good fight and toured regularly in his last year." Looking back, Doder remembered just how attentive Jimmy was toward every member of the band. "Jimmy listened closely to the music as we toured on the long road trips," Keith recalled. "He was very generous in acknowledging his sidemen and giving us plenty of room to stretch out and solo."[40]

Little Jimmy confirmed Doder's statement that the Milwaukee gig was indeed the last hurrah for Jimmy. "The Up and Under in Milwaukee was the last live performance he ever gave," Lane said sadly. "He was on . . . it was a good night. We played, had fun, the people enjoyed it."[41] Recently, Piano Willie O'Shawny had been missing a few of Jimmy's engagements. "I played until 1997 but was busy with my own band. I toured internationally with William Clarke and did my own solo acts while in Jimmy's band, too, so I missed some with Jimmy in the end," Willie said.[42] Jimmy knew he was going to have to find a replacement for Willie, but the two parted on excellent terms. Like Frank Bandy, Willie had done great things with Jimmy, except in one major area. "The only recording I did with Jimmy was for the BBC out of London, England. Can't remember what year that was," he said.[43] O'Shawny was worried, because he knew Jimmy was really showing signs that he was gradually getting sicker. "He did not write a lot of new songs in these years that I knew of. Jimmy worked a lot and was very strong until the bitter end," O'Shawny said. But he reiterated what many others believed at the time: "No one—including family members—knew really how sick Jimmy was."[44]

Jimmy D. had been featured routinely as part of the opening act before his dad played his set. Whenever there weren't specific dates booked with his dad's band, Jimmy D. booked shows and traveled with his own group, Blue Earth, a power trio that leaned heavily on the Hendrix/Vaughan–flavored repertoire. Trying to serve two masters made for a tough schedule. "We drop one van and trailer in the garage and load up the other van. We pick up my drummer in Chicago and we're off on the road again . . . I got 100 dates with my dad and probably 150 with mine."[45]

Jimmy D. developed his work ethic under the microscope of the heavyweights who set the standard for the hard-knocks lifestyle that comes with the territory of being a bluesman. Lane recalled that "Louis and Dave Myers would say, 'Boy, put that thing down. You don't know what you're doing!' That was their way of making me work that much harder . . . the old man, too. He'd talk about me. 'Son, you're not doin' that right. You're never gonna get that.' . . . James Cotton told me, 'Nobody gonna give it to you, you gotta get it for yourself.'" About Jimmy's style, Jimmy D. put it simply: "My dad's music is not fancy stuff. It's real simple-sounding notes, but it's not easy to play."[46]

To his credit, Jimmy Rogers understood, appreciated, and respected not only his son's musical pursuits but also the music of Stevie Ray Vaughan. On July 16, 1997, APO Records had released *Long Gone* (APO 2003), Jimmy D.'s first fully produced CD, to enthusiastic reviews. *Living Blues* reviewer Jim DeKoster wrote, "No matter how well Jimmy D. Lane plays his father's music, he is entitled to play his own style when he's on his own."[47]

After that final live appearance in Milwaukee, Jimmy immediately got off the road and came straight home to Chicago to help Little Jimmy complete his second album for producer Chad Kassem at APO Records. "The next day we headed back, drove right up to the studio from Milwaukee. We unloaded Dave's piano and all the rest of the equipment," said Little Jimmy. "The old man went on to the house, and we started laying tracks for the record. He came in a couple of days after we started the session and laid his two tracks." They recorded at Chicago Recording Company, where Jimmy had recorded *Bluebird*. Jimmy D.'s band for the session was a mixture of his and his father's band members: Freddie Crawford on bass, David Krull on keyboards, Per Hanson on drums (who had played on the live Ronnie Earl album with Jimmy), and Carey Bell on harp.

Chicago veterans Hubert Sumlin and Sam Lay appeared as guest artists. The biggest guest, of course, was the old man himself; in what was documented on record as his bravest show of support in the descent of his life, Jimmy found the strength—one last time—to come to the studio and make an appearance on wax for his beloved son. He surely was suffering from physical pain by this point, but Jimmy Rogers was not going to let that stop him; he had a legacy to sustain 'til the very end.

From October 13 to October 15 the band settled into the studio, cranking out nine of Junior's hard-hitting originals like "Little Girl," "Clue Me," and "It's All Good," one of the more outstanding tracks from the session. Of course, Jimmy D. couldn't resist the opportunity to pay his respects to the pioneers. They eased their way through Memphis Slim's minor-moded "Four O'Clock in the Morning" and shuffled their way through Howlin' Wolf's "Big House," with Little Jimmy doing a Sumlin-flavored solo that kicked the tune into high gear. Little Jimmy then handed the reins over to his dad, who sat gingerly in his chair, positioned his mike in front of him, and counted off a downright funky version of "Another Mule Kickin' in My Stall," a title that triggered memories of the last line of Muddy Waters's "Long Distance Call." He saved his best vocal performance, however, for "One Room Country Shack," which he sang with true passion, even managing to get off a short but subtle solo.

At one point during the session Jimmy's energy flagged and he needed some attention from his daughter Angela, who was at the session. His body was no doubt in agony, even as he soldiered on. His apparent internal pain distracted him, and he began to lose focus. He gradually found it more difficult to use his hands to run the patented chords and lead riffs that he normally executed without fail. Then, after a couple of faltering notes on his Gibson, he was overheard to say, "Ohh. . . . whew!" Jimmy D., alert to the situation, quickly encouraged his dad to forge ahead, saying, "It's all right, it's just the old blues, baby." This was an incredibly touching moment, caught on tape—the child as father to the man in the twilight of what was, by all measures, a stellar career. Joe Harley reflected on the moments captured at the October 15 session:

> It was my honor to produce a session featuring Jimmy D. Lane and his father, Jimmy Rogers . . . [who] sang his heart out . . . We all commented on how relaxed and happy Jimmy Sr. seemed. His performances that day were so powerful and strong! The last track he performed that day was "One Room Country Shack." He said, "We're reaching WAY back on this one!!" There was a particular passage that he was having trouble remembering so we left the main studio while Jimmy Sr. and his daughter Angela Lane slowly worked over the lyrics. Jimmy Sr. was determined to get this song right for his son's album. We came back in and he performed brilliantly.[48]

Jimmy was elated to work beside his son on such a monumental project in Junior's career, even though there was a brief snag that needed untangling before they could commence with the sessions. "He was apprehensive because he didn't know if it would disturb his contract with Atlantic," Jimmy D. said. "But he said 'I'm gonna go ahead and do it, to help my boy out.'" A few phone calls between Chad Kassem and legal personnel were exchanged, and the problem was resolved. "Chad Kassem—that's my guy, he's good people," Jimmy said.[49]

During a brief intermission, Chad Kassem had the ingenious idea to ask Jimmy about how he was feeling about the evening's proceedings. Jimmy expressed his emotions while the tape was rolling. At the end of "One Room Country Shack," he said, "It's nice being here in the studio with Little Jimmy and the whole gang.

He's, uh . . . on his own. I'm trying my best to give him something to go on. He's got to grab this ball and keep it rolling. That all I want him to do—just grab it and keep it rolling; till somebody comes along and picks it up." Kassem made sure that the touching comments were included on the album. James Fraher was there to photograph the sessions and took several great shots of Jimmy D. with his dad. Kassem also filmed a portion of the session, with the camera panning between the leading man, Jimmy D., and the living legend—James A. Lane, aka Rogers—the last man standing among the Headhunters. No one knew that these would be the last photos ever taken of Jimmy in the studio. He was seventy-three years old, and it was also the last time he played guitar in any recording studio.

Looking back on the comments Jimmy made right after they recorded "One Room Country Shack," it is apparent that he knew the end was near and wanted to leave a comment for posterity for all to hear. Undoubtedly there were those in the blues community who weren't sure about just how much Jimmy was willing to endorse his son's rock-influenced style. Some folks say that blood is thicker than water. For Jimmy Rogers, blood was always thicker than blues. A few days after his birthday, Jimmy sat for a lengthy interview with David Jaffe, who was impressed with the Jimmy's demeanor. "I caught him in an outstanding mood," Jaffe said. "He was quite jovial throughout the interview even when I asked tougher questions. What struck me most was his tireless appreciation for those people who were interested in him and his music. At certain points in the interview I actually wished he would become moody or angry. Instead he just thanked everyone."[50]

Neither Jaffe nor any other interviewer would ever get a rise out of Jimmy; it was not his nature, especially at that point in his life. Jaffe couldn't have known then, but Jimmy knew that he was pretty sick, and he was being extremely pleasant—not in a condescending way, but in a way that showed he was already on his way to achieving the peaceful, serene state when one realizes that everything in life is sweet, just because life still exists.

When asked about whether he was surprised at the reaction of fans and critics who embraced the award-winning *Bluebird* LP, Jimmy calmly said, "No, I wasn't surprised; I be proud whenever they catch ahold to it. Sometimes they don't and sometimes they do, so I be glad when it happens, I be proud. I appreciate that." Jimmy told Jaffe about his hectic tour schedule that seemed to have no end, saying, "I just got off tour, and I'm fixin' to head back out [referring to their departure on June 20]. I've got a couple of weeks [vacation] here and I'm goin' back out to Europe again for two more weeks . . . in the last part of June . . . I've got some spots I've got to do here in the States. So I'm pretty well tied up right now."[51]

Jaffe mentioned the Atlantic project, which was rumored at the time to have included female vocalists Tina Turner and Bonnie Raitt. Jimmy responded,

"Yeah, I got a pretty good deal with Atlantic, they found a pretty good thing. I appreciate it." When asked about Jimmy D.'s career and artistic direction with Chad Kassem and APO Records, Jimmy said, "I'm glad they're taking the time out to get him in there . . . You know he's working hard, he is, and I appreciate it, them doin' it. He works with me and he [does] things on his own. We'll be gone for a couple of weeks and then I'll turn him loose again and let him do what they [Jimmy's D.'s band, Blue Earth] want to do . . . He likes that Jimi Hendrix style. But it's okay, you know. It's rock 'n' roll, or whatever they call it. He likes that."[52]

It was clear that Jimmy had arrived at a place where he had come to accept and appreciate Jimmy D.'s role in being a full and active supporter of his dad's music; in turn, Jimmy had come to appreciate and respect Jimmy D.'s talent and tastes in music. At one point Jaffe's phone interview with Jimmy was interrupted by his subject's grandchildren, who were tearing around the house, oblivious to the interview he was trying to take part in. Where some might have gotten upset at the distraction, Jimmy, consistent with his serene state of mind, merely took it in stride. "Excuse them, they just my little grandkids," he said with a laugh. "They just playin' around here. I've got a little crowd over here." The children of Jimmy's daughter Marilyn had company over, and they were inventing house games, chasing each other around, doing what kids do when it's summer and they need to get out and play. "I've got two grandkids. Two little girls, one's about eleven and one's about four. They's up there tryin' to do something, I don't know . . . It's just a lot of fun to have them around."[53]

It was becoming more and more apparent to Jaffe that Jimmy was finding joy in literally everything he experienced. In these last months, nothing could upset him. Life was beautiful. Other questions followed: "What would you be doing if you had not been a blues singer?" "Maybe gambling!" Jimmy countered, followed by hearty laughter. "What's your favorite of your own recordings?" "The one that sells the most!" More laughter. "Is there a favorite part of the country or world that you like to play in?" "It doesn't matter where I go now. I go so many places that one is just like the other. The people come to have fun and it turns out good. We just have fun, that's the way I do."[54] In the end, when asked if he had any final thoughts, all Jimmy really wanted to say was, "I've tried to make a decent life for my children and the people that I'm involved with. That's what I try to do."[55] No one could have described his life's journey any better. While the contents of the Jaffe WWOZ radio interview never made it to the pages of a magazine (it was released online for a limited time), the contents of another feature-length interview were published in *Living Blues* magazine, with Jimmy as the cover story in the premier blues journal. It happened one month before Jimmy died.[56]

By November, Dave Krull had returned to St. Louis before making an extensive two-week tour of Europe. While enjoying some time off, he gave an interview to a guy known as "Big Dave," a writer for a local blues website, and discussed all the great fun he'd been having for the last twenty-seven days while being on tour with Jimmy's band. When asked where he'd been since mid-June, Krull replied, "The Southwest, California, Colorado, Texas, Hawaii, and Canada early last summer . . . I was scared but found I liked it . . . I'm gonna hang with the old man as long as I've got a job . . . If I'm so lucky as to still be with these people, it might prove to be something real good for me."[57]

Krull, of course, had no idea that things would take a sudden turn for the worse. Jimmy D. picks up the story:

> I played some shows around in Indiana, Wisconsin, and a few other places. I got back from one of those and I was laying down and the phone rang. It was my mother. She said, "You gotta get your dad to the hospital; he won't go unless you take him." I said, "Okay, I'm on my way." We got in my Lincoln Town Car—just he and I—and I took him over. But I remember, when we left the house, he turned back and looked at the building like he was never gonna see it again. He closed the gate, just stood there, looking up at the walls.[58]

Jimmy D. drove as fast as he could to Holy Cross Hospital. "We picked that hospital because it was the closest one to the house," he said. Once the family had arrived, they waited to see what the doctors had to say about Jimmy's condition. No one could tell beforehand just how serious it might be. "They did tests on him," Jimmy D. recalled. "We thought it was emphysema." While everyone was concerned about Jimmy Senior's health, he of course had music on his mind— a bluesman all the way to the end. "We had a tour for Japan scheduled; he was worried about that tour," Lane said. "I told him, 'Don't worry about that.'"[59]

Jimmy was insisting on going on the trip, so they had to find some kind of way to accommodate him, or at least to discuss the possibilities. The most immediate concern was Jimmy's shortness of breath. They tried to figure out how they could deal with the situation if Jimmy was on the plane and needed medical attention. "They said, 'Well, we can just get you an oxygen tank,'" Jimmy D. recalled. When the tests were all done, the news was a bit more serious than just a case of shortness of breath. Jimmy D. was shocked at what the doctors told him. "We had no idea it was full-blown cancer," Lane said. "They kept him overnight. It was the first time in his entire life that he spent the night in a hospital."[60]

The word was spreading pretty quickly that Jimmy Rogers was deathly ill. Many of his closest friends began reminiscing about their own memories of the great man who had brought so much joy to millions of fans for so many years. Maxwell Street historian Steve Balkin said, "I saw him playing early this year at Buddy Guy's with the Muddy Waters Revival Band. He had real energy and soul; it was authentic. I loved hearing him." Balkin had recently opened the Maxwell Street Museum at 1318 South Halsted, just around the corner from Abrams Music (formerly Maxwell Street Radio), where Jimmy had recorded his first sides in 1947 with Little Walter.[61]

Longtime sideman Steve Guyger, one of Jimmy's favorite harp players, was trying to get in touch with all those in the blues fraternity whom he knew loved Jimmy and would want to know about Jimmy's condition. He contacted his hero and former Rogers bandmate James Cotton. Guyger provided the following details:

> In '97 James Cotton was playing in Philly, and I went up and told Cotton that Jimmy was really sick, and he went off on me. He said, "Jimmy Rogers, man, that guy there is a harmonica player!" He told me that he was the closest thing to Little Walter. He literally told me that if Jimmy had stayed on harp, he would've been right there with Little Walter. Jimmy's the one who showed Cotton to play behind Muddy! He showed Little Walter how to play behind Muddy. Cotton said, "Yeah, Jimmy had his own thing going on harp, though, he was not like you or me." It was insane! It was the last thing that I think I would hear from Cotton.[62]

On November 10 Mary Katherine Aldin spoke with Jimmy D., who had told her a week earlier that his dad was having some chest pains and that they'd gone to the hospital then for tests. Jimmy was checked into the hospital under his given name of James A. Lane.[63] Jimmy D. confirmed that he had been diagnosed with early stage emphysema but that his doctors had also found some tumors in his colon. They did surgery to remove the tumors and thought they had gotten all of it. Jimmy told Aldin that, at the time, his dad was up and about, although he still had plans to remain in the hospital for another week. Jimmy had just watched a Chicago Bears football game—the Bears lost. Jimmy D. also added that Jimmy hadn't had a cigarette since he'd been admitted to Holy Cross, a major change in habit, since he'd been a habitual smoker for roughly sixty years. As the days passed, Jimmy's health seemed to be improving; then everything suddenly took a turn for the worse. Well-wishers were advised to send their contributions to Holy Cross Hospital.

Maxwell Street legend Jimmie Lee Robinson, a frequent visitor at the hospital, was one of the last people to have a chance to see Jimmy. "He had his family there. We had to put on gloves and masks. He was unconscious. When I saw him a month ago, he could sit up and talk. He told me I was his ham. When you gambling and lose your money they say, 'you ain't nothin' but a ham.' I hate to be called that. We was joking. He also told me he wanted oxtails—to eat for soup, or whatever his wife made from that." Robinson was already reflecting on the good old days he'd had with Jimmy when they shared one of their favorite activities—going to the movies. "I remember we used to go to the Irvin Theater on Halsted together with Johnny Shines," Robinson remembered fondly. "That was the closest theater to us. We went to see cowboy pictures."[64]

Jimmy Rogers passed away at 6:15 A.M. on December 19, 1997. The official cause of death was colon cancer. The official medical jargon used was "complications after surgery for an intestinal infection," Tom Radai told *New York Times* reporter Ben Ratliff, who posted an article in the paper on December 20.[65] Radai, assisted by Rita McHann, handled phone, faxes, and emails, working in accordance with the family's wishes. On December 21 he sent out a worldwide Internet release from his Milwaukee office detailing the specifics of the funeral arrangements. At the time, the release date for Jimmy's final album had not yet been announced.

The *Chicago Tribune* delivered the sad news to the Chicagoland fans on December 21, quoting Dorothy as saying, "He kept wanting to do more music. He didn't want to retire." She then quoted Jimmy's final words of wisdom to his adoring fans, saying in tribute to the music he loved, "If you can't dig the blues, you must have a hole in your soul."[66] Besides his wife, Dorothy, Jimmy was survived by his sons, Willie, James Darrel, and Jimmy D.; his daughters, Vera, Debra, Marilyn, Jacqueline, and Angela; and nineteen grandchildren. His four remaining sisters were Iguster Brown, Elizabeth Hunter, Mary Shipp, and Gertrude Taylor.

The viewing of the body was held on the afternoon of Friday, December 27, at the William W. Jackson Metropolitan Funeral Home. The wake was held the next day, and then Jimmy was buried at Restville Cemetery.[67] Kim Wilson said, "I was honored when they asked me to be a pallbearer. I played and sang there. It was very upsetting to me; I was very tight with him; the family knew it. He led by example. He was a fun hang."[68]

Of his own legacy, Jimmy Rogers told John Brisbin in 1997, "What I made people recognize as the Jimmy Rogers sound was that sound of 'That's All Right.' Always, after that, I kept my groove, my foundation. That's it. The bridge is built." Then, like the great blues leader of so many followers, he declared, "Peoples, you can cross it now. You can go from side to side."[69] Looking back, his prophetic words—delivered so close to the end of his life—may have been his own subtle way of signaling that he had already made peace with himself and the work he had done in this realm; he was prepared for the moment when his time came to cross over to the other side.

14

LONG GONE

I think about the fact that the last time
he ever played was in an attempt to
help me out. I miss him, man.

—Jimmy D. Lane

Jimmy D. Lane's album *Legacy* was released in 1998, just months after Jimmy's passing. The lengthy liner notes accompanying the CD read like an autobiography. The homage to his beloved father was bittersweet, with Jimmy D. reminiscing about growing up in a household where blues legends routinely dropped by. "When I grew up, Louis and Dave Myers, Robert Junior [Lockwood], Johnny Littlejohn, Muddy, Big Walter, and Wolf would all come over to the house, set up and jam. They'd have jam sessions, chicken sessions and fish sessions [laughs]. I feel real proud and lucky that I was able to be raised around those guys. Hell, they raised me."[1]

Jimmy D. would definitely miss the road work with the "old man" and the routine that Rogers and son had when they finally unloaded the van and relaxed at home. Lane described his father by saying, "He loved smoking his More cigarettes, loved fishing, watching his baseball games and certain movies he loved—old westerns like *Red River*." Jimmy D. was remembering the stories he'd heard from his dad about spending time watching movies together with Jimmie Lee Robinson. "They would go down in the theater with some Vanilla Wafers and Pet milk, or cheese and lunchmeat," Lane said. "He'd sit down and watch John Wayne ride that horse."[2]

On January 5, 1999, more than a year after Jimmy Rogers's death, Atlantic Records released the long awaited *Blues Blues Blues* to widespread acclaim, although some were critical of how much star power was on the album. Indeed, Stephen Thomas Erlewine wrote, "That's a lot of star power—too much, as a matter of fact—since they occasionally overwhelm Rogers himself. . . It's likely that it would have broken Rogers'[s] career wide open, if he had lived to see its release. Knowing that makes 'Blues' a little bittersweet. Yes, it's enjoyable, but it would have been great to hear Rogers tear it up on his final record."[3] The truth was, Jimmy was never one of those "tear-it-up" kind of people. He was more a master of subtlety and finesse—highly melodic, tasteful, and laid back. "Tearin' it up" is always the job of the designated second guitarist when experienced veterans like Jimmy, Buddy Guy, or B. B. King shift downward and gradually ease into the twilight of their careers, enjoying the luxury of no longer having to prove themselves on the bandstand.

John Koenig aptly summarized Jimmy Rogers's lifetime contributions in his liner notes for Blues Blues Blues, saying, "His influence, reflected in the work of those who followed him, will carry on into the next millennium." The fact that Jimmy had so many of the most important blues artists of the day wanting to play beside him "was a source of great personal satisfaction for this modest man who spent his years quietly advancing the art form that has been so important to them all," Koenig said.[4]

On July 5, 1999, the Jimmy Rogers Tribute Band contributed a stellar performance at the Montreaux Jazz Festival in Switzerland. The all-star lineup included Taj Mahal on vocals and harp (singing "Paint My Mailbox Blue"), Lucky Peterson on vocals and guitar (singing "I'm Ready"), Kim Wilson on vocals and harp (singing "I Got a Woman in Helena"), Van Morrison on vocals and harp (singing "Forty Days" and "Young Fashioned Ways"), Johnny Johnson on piano, Jimmy D. Lane on guitar, Bob Stroger on bass, Ted Harvey on drums, and John Koenig on guitar. The festival event was produced by Claude Nobs, with the music produced by Ahmet Ertegun.[5]

On August 10, 1999, Bob Corritore had released his compilation of recorded sessions with a wide variety of blues artists. The album, Bob Corritore All-Star Blues Sessions (HMG1009), boasted an impressive sixteen tracks with an array of performers from across the country: Jimmy Rogers, former Rogers pianist Henry Gray, Bo Diddley, Pinetop Perkins, Robert Junior Lockwood, and a host of others. Jimmy's contribution, "Out on the Road," was placed prominently in the rotation, as the second track.

Also in 1999 the French label Black & Blue had released a fourth version of the 1974 album That's All Right (PCD5516) that captured Jimmy's live and studio sessions when Jacques Morgantini had the Aces (Dave and Louis Myers and

Fred Below) plus Willie Mabon as Jimmy's backing band. Using the same cover as the original LP, this expanded edition on CD contained the same material as the third version in 1993, with three previously released bonus tracks. "I Can't Sleep for Worrying," "Pretty Baby" and "Sloppy Drunk (III)," all of which were taken from the December 13 studio session at Condorcet in Toulouse, France.

On February 11, 2001, Bonnie "Queen Bee" Stebbins, writer for the *Blues Ambassador* newsletter, met Jimmy's eldest son, J. D. Mosley, along with Jimmy's manager, Tom Radai; local city and district alderman Theodore Thomas from the 15th Ward; and blues guitarist Jimmie Lee Robinson. A small gathering of friends, companions, business associates, and family members came together near a street corner on Chicago's South Side to honor the late Jimmy Rogers by permanently renaming the twelve-block stretch of Honore Avenue between Fifty-fifth and Sixty-seventh Streets as Honorary Jimmy Rogers Street. Approximately forty people were in attendance, including Shirley and Robert Jr. Whitall from *Big City Blues* magazine. Former manager Tom Radai gave a short speech, followed by J. D., Dorothy, and then other family members.

The alderman said a few final words and then pulled the sign out of the trunk of his car. The special-colored brown street sign (Chicago street signs are traditionally green) read "Honorary Jimmy Rogers Street" in capital letters. J. D. joked about having to hang all the signs himself. Then they all went to Dorothy Lane's house for food and refreshments and were treated to a huge spread she had prepared. Stebbins especially recalled the warm atmosphere that enveloped the household.

About an hour into the festivities, someone noticed that one of the new signs had already been posted on the street corner, but the wrapping hadn't been removed. So everyone rose up and quickly returned outside to witness the unveiling, and J. D. Mosley pulled the string that unveiled the shiny new street sign, gleaming in the Chicago sunlight. Stebbins joked with J. D. that it was one less sign to have to take down. Later she held an impromptu interview with Jimmie Lee Robinson, who had recently held an eighty-one-day fast and vigil to protest the tearing down of Maxwell Street.[6]

On December 14, 2002, APO record label owner and studio producer Chad Kassem used his Blue Heaven studio in Salina, Kansas, to record a live concert that hosted an all-star blues band of Muddy Waters sidemen. As guitarist and former right-hand man to Muddy, Steady Rollin' Bob Margolin took the opportunity to pay tribute to Jimmy in a big way. "I had written a song called 'Mean Old Chicago' on the way to Jimmy's funeral and recorded it in '99," he said, "but with Jimmy D. there, I realized that he would be the ultimate musician for me to play my song with. We performed it live at my concert for the recording. We [me and Jimmy D.] stood onstage with just the two guitars, and a big photo of Jimmy smiling between us."[7] The 1999 version Margolin is referring to is the third track on his *Hold Me To It* album (Blind Pig BPCD5056). The live recording was captured at the 2002 Salina concert and is also included as the sixth track on *All-Star Blues Jam* (Telarc CD-83579), an album that features Carey Bell on harp, Willie Big Eyes Smith on drums, Hubert Sumlin on guitar, Pinetop Perkins on piano, and Tom Mookie Brill on bass. Both versions of "Mean Old Chicago" are absolutely spine-chilling, with Margolin doing a dead-on Muddy guitar style and Tad Walters sounding as much like Little Walter as anyone has ever recorded.

On August 29, 2003, a Jimmy Rogers Headstone Tribute Show was arranged to raise money for a grave marker. Billy Flynn drove down from Green Bay, Wisconsin; Steve Guyger came from Philadelphia; Eddie Taylor Jr. and Bob Stroger were also in attendance. Piano Willie came from Milwaukee. Tony Mangiullo of Rosa's Lounge paid the expenses for the event, and Chuck Winans from Chicago documented it. Personality conflicts between Jimmy D. and certain former band members led to his refusal to attend the tribute—he said they hadn't been in his dad's corner when he needed them. Still, "It was an excellent night of music and a very nice turnout," Dick Shurman recalled.[8] Guitarist Billy Flynn agreed, saying, "The mood that night was great because we all loved Jimmy so much. I played with Dave Waldman; we did Muddy's 'Still a Fool' and Jimmy's 'Goin' Away Baby.' I was also very happy to meet Dorothy [Jimmy's wife]; she was very touched by the tribute."[9]

In the wake of Jimmy's absence, Jimmy D. soldiered on, continuing his working relationship with Chad Kassem and APO Records. He left Chicago for good, moving to Salina, Kansas, to work as musical director of Kassem's Blue Heaven studios. Over the next several years, he helped to produce and perform on a wide variety of recording projects, including albums for Wolf's guitarist Hubert Sumlin, harp player and former Chicago bandmate Eomot RaSun, and Maxwell Street legend Jimmie Lee Robinson.

For his own next project Chad pulled out all the stops, providing Jimmy D. with what can only be described as his personal "dream team." Kassem hired the rhythm section of Tommy Shannon on bass and Chris "Whipper" Layton on drums from the Stevie Ray Vaughan's famed Double Trouble band. With the addition of Mike Finnegan on organ and none other than Eddie Kramer as engineer, the album had all the ingredients for success. Jimmy D. rose to the occasion, writing an entire album full of original tunes (except one, a Hendrix-inspired version of "Bleeding Heart") and delivering his most inspired guitar playing to date. Steady Rollin' Bob Margolin wrote the liner notes for the CD, titled, *It's Time*, released on October 12, 2004.

Jimmy Rogers's contribution to the blues cannot be overstated. His influence on the younger generation of blues guitarists stretched far and wide. Players ranging from veterans like Jimmie Vaughan, Ronnie Earl, and Duke Robillard to the next generation of Rusty Zinn, Junior Watson, and Nick Moss built a significant portion of their careers on the foundation of the patented Rogers sound. For example, when blues lovers listen to Junior Watson's licks on Kim Wilson's *Tiger Man* (Watson dances around Kim exquisitely) or Moss's *First Offense* ("She Keeps Me Worried" is one of the absolute best Rogers-influenced performances on record), it's readily apparent that the baton has successfully been passed. Bob Margolin says, "Jimmy called it 'filling in the cracks.'" But, he adds, "It was not simply playing rhythm guitar while another instrument was featured. Jimmy's parts wove in and out of the others, informed by knowledge of the style and players and some creative extrasensory perception."[10] Like all great masters of their craft, Jimmy mastered the art of making it look easy.

About the dozens of Chess sessions he logged, it was no secret that Jimmy was sometimes harsh in his criticism of the Chess brothers as they gradually documented the history of the Chicago blues. In an interview with Dan Kening of the *Chicago Tribune*, Jimmy said, "They got me like they got the rest of 'em. They made lots of hits out of the people in our unit—Muddy, myself, [and] Walter; and they died owing a lot of people money . . . I just got tired of being ripped off."[11]

There are those who might contend that the choices Leonard Chess made regarding his steadily decreasing release of sides produced by Jimmy was based primarily (if not solely) on the charting statistics—or lack thereof—of Jimmy's songs and their placement on *Billboard* magazine's closely monitored and highly regarded mechanism. Indeed, it can be said that, relatively speaking, Jimmy did not produce the kind of figures that rivaled, say, Chuck Berry's meteoric and sustained rise or the well-established and prolonged presence on the charts of Muddy Waters. And it is true that of all the creative output Jimmy produced, he yielded only one chart hit—"Walkin' by Myself," which peaked at number fourteen in 1957 and stayed on the charts for only one week.

A few other comments, however, can also be made about this issue. First, it is quite possible to achieve success at both local and regional levels without denting the charts. Second, the Chess brothers allowed Jimmy to stay on their label for what essentially amounted to a ten-year run as a solo artist before they officially parted ways. The Chess brothers were not necessarily known for their "charity" among the musicians on their roster, so they must have seen both value and promise in Jimmy Rogers and his ability to produce.

Third, merely making the charts doesn't necessarily represent or guarantee sustained success, productivity, or security with the label—or the public, for that matter. There are numerous cases that support this notion. Indeed, Willie Mabon, as an example, charted a number one hit on Billboard with "I Don't Know" in 1952, number one in 1953 with "I'm Mad," and number 7 with "Poison Ivy." Yet he had significantly fewer recording sessions and released sides than Jimmy Rogers had. And when all was said and done, Mabon was still released from the label despite having obviously better chart success than Jimmy Rogers.

Finally, there were many cases of those sides recorded by a wide variety of artists on the Chess roster whose output never even saw the light of day. So when looking at the totality of it all in this light, one has to concede that—everything being relative—Jimmy might have had it better than some and worse than others.

Mudcat Ward stated emphatically, "Jimmy didn't make any serious money until Eric Clapton recorded songs of Jimmy's. Jimmy told me he got a check for three hundred thousand dollars."[12] Toward the end of his life, Jimmy did get money back after some serious legal wrangling that began when the Chess masters were sold to MCA, with Scott Cameron demanding that MCA get their books straight with Jimmy's catalog and royalties before they released the next round of reissues. According to Jimmy's longtime manager, Tom Radai, Jimmy reportedly got at least some of what was due to him.[13]

Blues writer Tom Townsley made an observation that could serve as a universal theme to sum up Jimmy Rogers: "Here is a man who remembers all the people he encounters in his career and who treats them all, the well known and the insignificant, with courtesy and respect . . . I know I'm not an exception; there are hundreds across the country who could testify to his character, hundreds who have been made to feel they have a friend in Jimmy Rogers."[14]

There, in a nutshell, is the most pristine summation of the character and integrity of Jimmy Rogers, a man who walked among kings, all the while playing the role of servant to the blues. From a career perspective it might have looked as if his life was dedicated to playing second fiddle, but in reality he was making others look better while he deflected the spotlight away from himself and onto those around him. Bassist Bob Stroger testifies to this fact, saying, "I don't care how big Jimmy Rogers got, he always wanted to be with his boys. He never got big enough to want separate dressing rooms and all that. He was always with us."[15]

Fellow blues writer Sandra Pointer-Jones provided what is probably the most succinct summation of Jimmy Rogers's enormous and continuing impact on the blues: "Rogers is not merely a piece or section of the blues . . . Of the three original members of the band, Rogers was the one to bridge the gap between the rough, raw-edge Delta sound of Waters and the almost futuristic sound of Walter. Between a great grizzly and a roaring lion sat a calm calculating cougar."[16]

Yes, indeed, Jimmy went out swinging; no one was a greater champion for the blues. In what may have been his greatest statement, he gave the charge to the next generation as he compelled one reporter to pass his words on to the blues people of the future:

> You tell the people, man—I don't want the younger people to give up the blues. Blues will always be here because someone'll *always* have the blues, man—li'l babies get the blues! Of course, blues don't mean you're down in the dumps all the time! You can have happy blues! Listen, everybody gets to a point in life, they don't know what it's all about. Well, the blues *will* carry you through! That's why I'm not ashamed of the blues, I've sung 'em from Europe to Japan to all over America. It's an old slogan—but it's true—*if you can't dig the blues, you must have a hole in your soul!*[17]

CODA

THE LAST TIME

> When we think of Jimmie Rodgers in Mississippi, we
> automatically think of the father of country music, but
> when people in Chicago think of Jimmy Rogers, they think
> of the great Jimmy Rogers of the blues . . . I want us to be
> the same as the folks in Chicago—that here in Ruleville
> when people say Jimmy Rogers, you'll know that he is the
> great bluesman that came from Sunflower County.
>
> —Alex Thomas

The words above were delivered by Alex Thomas at the dedication of a Mississippi Blues Trail marker on behalf of Jimmy Rogers in Ruleville on Friday, November 4, 2011. In a fitting gesture, the Film and Tourism Development Bureau of the Mississippi Development Authority placed the 144th marker on the Mississippi Blues Trail in Sunflower County in Jimmy's honor.[1]

Thomas, program manager for the bureau, began the ceremonies by saying, "The blues trail gives us an opportunity to learn about this history and heritage that has happened in our own backyard. This is another historic day for Mississippi." After Ruleville Development Council president Rodney Clark offered attendees a brief history of Jimmy's illustrious career, state senator Willie Simmons commented, "Today, we come to unveil this marker in honor of a man who has contributed so much to music and the blues."

Sadly, none of the Rogers family members were in attendance. Thomas did, however, mention that he'd received a message from Jimmy D. Lane, who had an album cover photo placed on the marker right below one of his father's images. "He said he really wanted to be here, but he is doing a lot of traveling," Thomas said. "He wanted to express his gratitude on behalf of the family that we were placing this marker here. He said he hoped to be here in Mississippi very soon to see the marker."

Jimmy D. won't be alone in his journey. Over the upcoming years, tourists from around the world will, without a doubt, be arriving in untold numbers to visit the place where it all began. Jimmy Rogers's place in blues history is now secure and on display for all to see.

NOTES

CHAPTER 1. MONEY, MARBLES, AND CHALK

Epigraph. John Brisbin, "Jimmy Rogers: I'm Havin' Fun Right Today," *Living Blues* 135 (September/October 1997): 15.

1. Ibid.

2. Ibid.

3. Robert Gordon, *Can't Be Satisfied: The Life and Times of Muddy Waters* (Boston: Little, Brown, 2002), 73.

4. Jim O'Neal and Bill Greensmith, "Living Blues Interview: Jimmy Rogers," *Living Blues* 14 (Autumn 1973): 11.

5. Brisbin, "Jimmy Rogers: Havin' Fun," 15.

6. Ibid.

7. Ibid.

8. O'Neal and Greensmith, "Living Blues Interview," 11.

9. Brisbin, "Jimmy Rogers: Havin' Fun," 16.

10. John Brisbin, "Pryor Arrangements," *Blues Access* (Winter 1999): 52.

11. Tim Schuller, "Jimmy Rogers: Not Giving Up on the Blues," *Blues Access* 5 (Spring 1991): 12.

12. Ibid., 5.

13. O'Neal and Greensmith, "Living Blues Interview," 11.

14. Ibid.

15. Ibid.

16. Ibid.

17. Ibid.

18. Jim O'Neal, Steve Wisner, and David Nelson, "Snooky Pryor: I Started the Big Noise around Chicago," *Living Blues* 123 (September/October 1995): 11.

19. Brisbin, "Jimmy Rogers: Havin' Fun," 15.

20. Frank Voce, "Jimmy Rogers," *Blues Unlimited* 44 (September 1972): 5–7.

21. Gordon, *Can't Be Satisfied,* 73.

22. Voce, "Jimmy Rogers," 5.

23. John Hubner, "Keeping the Blues Alive—Jimmy Rogers: More Than History," *Boston Phoenix*, July 22, 1980, 2.

24. O'Neal and Greensmith, "Living Blues Interview," 11.

25. Brisbin, "Pryor Arrangements," 52.

26. O'Neal and Greensmith, "Living Blues Interview," 11.

27. Amy O'Neal, "Snooky Pryor," *Living Blues* 6 (Autumn 1971): 4–5.

28. Brisbin, "Jimmy Rogers: Havin' Fun," 16.

29. Ibid.

30. O'Neal, Wisner, and Nelson, "Snooky Pryor," 10.

31. Ibid., 11.

32. Brisbin, "Pryor Arrangements," 52.

33. O'Neal, Wisner, and Nelson, "Snooky Pryor," 10.

34. Brisbin, "Jimmy Rogers: Havin' Fun," 17.

35. O'Neal and Greensmith, "Living Blues Interview," 11.

36. Ibid.

37. Brisbin, "Jimmy Rogers: Havin' Fun," 17.

38. Ibid., 18.

39. Robert Palmer, *Deep Blues* (New York: Penguin Books, 1982), 191.

40. Ibid., 178.

41. Mike Rowe, *Chicago Blues: The City and the Music* (New York: Da Capo Press, 1973), 83–84.

42. Gordon, *Can't Be Satisfied,* 85.

43. O'Neal and Greensmith, "Living Blues Interview," 11.

44. Tony Glover, Scott Dirks, and Ward Gaines, *Blues with a Feeling: The Little Walter Story* (New York: Routledge, 2002), 24.

45. Palmer, *Deep Blues*, 175.

46. Hubner, "Keeping the Blues Alive," 2.

47. O'Neal and Greensmith, "Living Blues Interview," 11.

48. Brisbin, "Jimmy Rogers: Havin' Fun," 17.

49. Ibid.

50. Ibid.

51. Brisbin, "Jimmy Rogers: Havin' Fun," 18.

52. Ibid.

53. Ilene Melish, "The Man Who Shaped a Sound," *Melody Maker*, October 6, 1979, 38.

54. Brisbin, "Jimmy Rogers: Havin' Fun," 18.

55. Ibid., 19.

56. O'Neal and Greensmith, "Living Blues Interview," 11.

57. Ibid.

58. Melish, "Man Who Shaped a Sound," 38.

59. O'Neal and Greensmith, "Living Blues Interview," 12.

60. Ibid.

61. Ibid.

CHAPTER 2. CHICAGO BOUND

Epigraph. Barney Tabor, "Jimmy Rogers: Still Burnin' 'Em Up and Going Strong at 70," *Blues Revue* 14 (Fall 1994): 22.

1. Robert Gordon, *Can't Be Satisfied: The Life and Times of Muddy Waters*, (Boston: Little, Brown, 2002), 74.

2. John Brisbin, "Jimmy Rogers: I'm Havin' Fun Right Today," *Living Blues* 135 (September/October 1997): 19.

3. Robert Palmer, "Muddy Waters: The Delta Son Never Sets," *Rolling Stone* 275 (October 5, 1978): 55.

4. Sandra B. Tooze, *Muddy Waters: The Mojo Man* (Toronto: ECW Press, 1997), 58.

5. Palmer, "Muddy Waters: Delta Son," 55.

6. Gordon, *Can't Be Satisfied,* 69.

7. Tooze, *Muddy Waters: Mojo Man,* 59.

8. Gordon, *Can't Be Satisfied,* 74.

9. Brisbin, "Jimmy Rogers: Havin' Fun," 20.

10. Gordon, *Can't Be Satisfied,* 73.

11. Tamara Chapman, "Learning to Hurt Brings Out the Blues," *El Paso Times*, September 4, 1983.

12. John Hubner, "Keeping the Blues Alive—Jimmy Rogers: More Than History," *Boston Phoenix*, July 22, 1980, 12.

13. Gordon, *Can't Be Satisfied,* 84.

14. Brisbin, "Jimmy Rogers: Havin' Fun," 84.

15. Ibid.

16. Jim O'Neal and Bill Greensmith, "Living Blues Interview: Jimmy Rogers," *Living Blues* 14 (Autumn 1973): 13.

17. Brisbin, "Jimmy Rogers: Havin' Fun," 13.

18. Ibid., 21.

19. Gordon, *Can't Be Satisfied,* 75.

20. Brisbin, "Jimmy Rogers: Havin' Fun," 21.

21. Gordon, *Can't Be Satisfied*, 72.

22. Palmer, "Muddy Waters: Delta Son," 55.

23. Tom Townsley, "Jimmy Rogers: His Legacy Still Lives On," *Blues Revue* 14 (Fall 1994): 24.

24. Gordon, *Can't Be Satisfied*, 75.

25. Brisbin, "Jimmy Rogers: Havin' Fun," 75.

26. O'Neal and Greensmith, "Living Blues Interview," 13.

27. Jimmy Rogers, quoted in Tony Glover, Scott Dirks, and Ward Gaines, *Blues with a Feeling: The Little Walter Story* (New York: Routledge, 2002), 39.

28. Townsley, "Jimmy Rogers: Legacy," 24.

29. Gordon, *Can't Be Satisfied*, 72.

30. Brisbin, "Jimmy Rogers: Havin' Fun," 19.

31. O'Neal and Greensmith, "Living Blues Interview," 20.

32. Mike Rowe, *Chicago Blues: The City and the Music* (New York: Da Capo Press, 1973), 43.

33. Muddy Waters, quoted in Gordon, *Can't Be Satisfied*, 73.

34. Brisbin, "Jimmy Rogers: Havin' Fun," 21.

35. Rogers quoted in Glover, Dirks, and Gaines, *Blues with a Feeling*, 44.

36. O'Neal and Greensmith, "Living Blues Interview," 13.

37. Brisbin, "Jimmy Rogers: Havin' Fun," 19.

38. Palmer, "Muddy Waters: Delta Son," 55.

39. Jim O'Neal, phone interview with Jimmy Rogers, February 26, 1982, O'Neal's private collection.

40. Gordon, *Can't Be Satisfied*, 77.

41. Ibid., 76.

42. Ibid., 77.

43. Townsley, "Jimmy Rogers: Legacy," 24.

44. Gordon, *Can't Be Satisfied*, 77.

45. Palmer, "Muddy Waters: Delta Son," 155.

46. Claude Smith, quoted in Glover, Dirks, and Gaines, *Blues with a Feeling*, 44.

47. Palmer, "Muddy Waters: Delta Son," 155.

48. Ibid.

49. Glover, Dirks, and Gaines, *Blues with a Feeling*, 44; Palmer, "Muddy Waters: Delta Son," 155.

50. David "Honeyboy" Edwards, *The World Don't Owe Me Nothing: The Life and Times of Delta Bluesman Honeyboy Edwards* (Chicago: Chicago Review Press, 1997), 149.

51. Ibid., 150.

52. Glover, Dirks, and Gaines, *Blues with a Feeling*, 27.

53. Ibid., 28.

54. Ibid., 42.

55. Jimmy Rogers, quoted in Ilene Melish, "The Man Who Shaped a Sound," *Melody Maker* (October 6, 1979): 38.

56. Townsley, "Jimmy Rogers: Legacy," 23.

57. Brisbin, "Jimmy Rogers: Havin' Fun," 20.

58. O'Neal and Greensmith, "Living Blues Interview," 13.

59. Glover, Dirks, and Gaines, *Blues with a Feeling,* 39.

60. Brisbin, "Jimmy Rogers: Havin' Fun," 20.

61. Glover, Dirks, and Gaines, *Blues with a Feeling,* 29.

62. O'Neal and Greensmith, "Living Blues Interview," 11.

63. John Brisbin, "Pryor Arrangements," *Blues Access* (Winter 1999): 52.

64. Jim O'Neal, Steve Wisner, and David Nelson, "Snooky Pryor: I Started the Big Noise around Chicago," *Living Blues* 123 (September/October 1995): 13.

65. Brisbin, "Pryor Arrangements," 54.

66. Ibid.

67. O'Neal, Wisner and Nelson, "Snooky Pryor: Big Noise," 14.

68. Ibid.

69. Ibid.

70. O'Neal and Greensmith, "Living Blues Interview," 13.

71. Brisbin, "Jimmy Rogers: Havin' Fun," 27.

72. Ibid., 20.

73. Ibid.

74. Ibid.

75. Glover, Dirks, and Gaines, *Blues with a Feeling,* 48.

76. O'Neal and Greensmith, "Living Blues Interview," 14.

77. Ibid.

78. Glover, Dirks, and Gaines, *Blues with a Feeling,* 44.

79. Palmer, "Muddy Waters: Delta Son," 156.

80. Transcribed unpublished phone recording with Jimmy Rogers about Blue Smitty, January 3, 1980, Jim O'Neal personal collection.

81. Brisbin, "Jimmy Rogers: Havin' Fun," 22.

82. O'Neal, unpublished interview.

83. Edwards, *World Don't Owe Me Nothing,* 154.

84. O'Neal and Greensmith, "Living Blues Interview," 13.

85. Ibid.

86. Ibid.

87. O'Neal, Wisner and Nelson, "Snooky Pryor: Big Noise," 34.

88. Glover, Dirks, and Gaines, *Blues with a Feeling,* 34.

89. O'Neal and Greensmith, "Living Blues Interview," 20.

90. Ibid.

91. O'Neal, Wisner and Nelson, "Snooky Pryor: Big Noise," 15.

92. Gordon, *Can't Be Satisfied,* 88.

93. Brisbin, "Jimmy Rogers: Havin' Fun," 22.

94. Hubner, "Keeping the Blues Alive," 2.

95. Palmer, "Muddy Waters: Delta Son," 209.

96. Gordon, *Can't Be Satisfied,* 86.

97. Robert Palmer, *Deep Blues* (New York: Penguin Books, 1982), 209.

98. Townsley, "Jimmy Rogers: Legacy," 24.

99. Hubner, "Keeping the Blues Alive," 2.

100. Melish, "Man Who Shaped a Sound," 38.

101. Ibid.

102. O'Neal and Greensmith, "Living Blues Interview," 13.

103. Ibid.

104. Melish, "Man Who Shaped a Sound," 38.

CHAPTER 3. CHESS MOVES

Epigraph. John Brisbin, "Jimmy Rogers: I'm Havin' Fun Right Today," *Living Blues* 135 (September/October 1997): 19.

1. Ibid., 24.

2. Ibid.

3. Ibid., 20.

4. Jim O'Neal, Steve Wisner, and David Nelson, "Snooky Pryor: I Started the Big Noise around Chicago," *Living Blues* 123 (September/October 1995): 14.

5. John Brisbin, "Pryor Arrangements," *Blues Access* (Winter 1999): 52.

6. Brisbin, "Jimmy Rogers: Havin' Fun," 20.

7. Jim O'Neal and Bill Greensmith, "Living Blues Interview: Jimmy Rogers," *Living Blues* 14 (Autumn 1973): 14.

8. Jim O'Neal, phone interview with Jimmy Rogers, February 26, 1982.

9. Ibid.

10. O'Neal and Greensmith, "Living Blues Interview," 13.

11. Chris Smith, "Words, Words, Words," *Blues & Rhythm* 228 (April 2008): 22.

12. O'Neal, phone interview with Rogers, February 26, 1982.

13. *Down Home Blues Classics Chicago, 1946–1954* [Disc 1], Boulevard Vintage (BVB DC1014S-UK), 2005.

14. George Paulus, "Rare Jams: George Paulus Discovers Jimmy Rogers' First Record," *Blues & Rhythm* 18 (1993): 167.

15. Les Fancourt and Bob McGrath, *The Blues Discography, 1943–1970* ([West Vancouver] Canada: Eyeball Productions, 2006), 468.

16. George Paulus, Robert Campbell, Robert Pruter, Robert Stallworth, Dave Sax, and Jim O'Neal, "Ebony, Chicago, Southern, and Harlem: The Mayo Williams Indies,"

June 13, 2011, revised April 2, 2014, http://myweb.clemson.edu/~campber/ebony
.html.

17. Norman Darwen, "The Chess Boys Got to It and It Exploded," *Blues and Rhythm* 82 (1993): 6.

18. Tony Glover, Scott Dirks, and Ward Gaines, *Blues with a Feeling: The Little Walter Story* (New York: Routledge, 2002), 40.

19. Justin O'Brien, "The Dark Road of Floyd Jones," *Living Blues* 58 (Winter 1983): 5.

20. Ibid., 11.

21. Fancourt and McGrath, *Blues Discography,* 468.

22. O'Neal and Greensmith, "Living Blues Interview," 14.

23. Mike Rowe, *Chicago Blues: The City and the Music* (New York: Da Capo Press, 1973), 52.

24. Brisbin, "Jimmy Rogers: Havin' Fun," 22.

25. O'Neal and Greensmith, "Living Blues Interview," 14.

26. Wayne Goins, phone interview with Jim O'Neal, January 9, 2008.

27. O'Neal and Greensmith, "Living Blues Interview," 14.

28. Glover, Dirks and Gaines, *Blues with a Feeling,* 40.

29. O'Neal and Greensmith, "Living Blues Interview," 14.

30. O'Neal, phone interview with Rogers.

31. Robert Palmer, *Deep Blues* (New York: Penguin Books, 1982), 82.

32. O'Neal, phone interview with Rogers.

33. O'Neal and Greensmith, "Living Blues Interview," 20.

34. Ibid.

35. Brisbin, "Pryor Arrangements," 54.

36. O'Neal, Wisner, and Nelson, "Snooky Pryor," 15.

37. Tim Schuller, "Jimmy Rogers: Not Giving Up on the Blues," *Blues Access* 5 (Spring 1991): 12.

38. Ibid., 6.

39. Robert Palmer, "Muddy Waters: The Delta Son Never Sets," *Rolling Stone* 275 (October 5, 1978): 54.

40. Brisbin, "Jimmy Rogers: Havin' Fun," 23.

41. Robert Gordon, *Can't Be Satisfied: The Life and Times of Muddy Waters* (Boston: Little, Brown, 2002), 91.

42. Brisbin, "Jimmy Rogers: Havin' Fun," 23.

43. Gordon, *Can't Be Satisfied,* 93.

44. Ibid., 96.

45. Nadine Cohodas, *Spinning Blues into Gold: The Chess Brothers and the Legendary Chess Records* (New York: St. Martin's, 2000), 49.

46. Tom Townsley, "Jimmy Rogers: His Legacy Still Lives On," *Blues Revue* 14 (Fall 1994): 24.

47. Ibid.

48. Ibid., 25.

49. Ibid.; emphasis added.

50. Brisbin, "Jimmy Rogers: Havin' Fun," 23.

51. Mary Katherine Aldin, liner notes to "Muddy Waters: The Chess Box" (MCA Records 1989), 4.

52. Ibid.

53. Cohodas, *Spinning Blues into Gold,* 43.

54. Malcolm Chisholm, quoted in Palmer, *Deep Blues,* 162.

55. Glover, Dirks and Gaines, *Blues with a Feeling,* 57.

56. Palmer, *Deep Blues,* 162.

57. Palmer, "Muddy Waters: Delta Son," 55.

58. Brisbin, "Jimmy Rogers: Havin' Fun," 26.

59. Ibid., 24.

60. Townsley, "Jimmy Rogers: Legacy," 25.

61. Glover, Dirks, and Gaines, *Blues with a Feeling,* 60.

62. Palmer, *Deep Blues,* 208.

63. Robert Pruter and Robert Campbell, "Tempo-Tone," June 16, 2009, revised October 25, 2013, http://myweb.clemson.edu/~campber/tempotone.html.

64. Ibid.

65. Glover, Dirks, and Gaines, *Blues with a Feeling,* 47.

66. Brisbin, "Jimmy Rogers: Havin' Fun," 22.

67. Ibid.

68. O'Neal and Greensmith, "Living Blues Interview," 13.

69. Gordon, *Can't Be Satisfied,* 87.

70. O'Neal and Greensmith, "Living Blues Interview," 13.

71. Brisbin, "Jimmy Rogers: Havin' Fun," 22.

72. Robert Campbell, "JOB," Red Saunders Research Foundation, October 8, 2011, revised September 10, 2013, http://myweb.clemson.edu/~campber/rsrf.html.

73. *Sunnyland Slim: House Rent Party.* Apollo Series. (Delmark DD-655), 1992.

74. Mary Katherine Aldin, liner notes to *The Aristocrat of the Blues: The Best of Aristocrat Records.* MCA/Chess (CHD2–9387), 1997, 22.

75. Michel Ruppli, *The Chess Labels: A Discography,* Vol. 1. (Westport, CT: Greenwood Press, 1983), 9.

76. Mary Katherine Aldin, liner notes to *Muddy Waters—Rollin' Stone: The Golden Anniversary Collection.*

77. Bob Eagle, "Big Town Playboy: Johnnie Jones," *Living Blues* 12 (Spring 1973): 28.

78. Author e-mail interview with Dick Shurman, December 23, 2011.

79. O'Neal and Greensmith, "Living Blues Interview," 12.

80. Glover, Dirks, and Gaines, *Blues with a Feeling,* 58.

81. O'Neal and Greensmith, "Living Blues Interview," 12.

82. Dan Forte, "Jimmy Rogers and the Pioneers of Chicago Blues," *Guitar Player* 21 (August 1987): 67.

83. Brisbin, "Jimmy Rogers: Havin' Fun," 26.

84. Ibid.

85. Ibid.

86. Peter Guralnick, *Feel Like Going Home* (New York: Bay Back Books, 1971), 72.

87. Gordon, *Can't Be Satisfied,* 95.

88. Glover, Dirks, and Gaines, *Blues with a Feeling,* 56.

89. Bob Margolin, "What Was Muddy Like?" July 2003, http://bobmargolin.com/327–2.

90. Glover, Dirks, and Gaines, *Blues with a Feeling,* 56.

CHAPTER 4. HEADHUNTERS AND WOLFMEN

Epigraph. Dan Forte, "Jimmy Rogers and the Pioneers of Chicago Blues," *Guitar Player* 21 (August 1987): 69.

1. Robert Gordon, *Can't Be Satisfied: The Life and Times of Muddy Waters* (Boston: Little, Brown, 2002), 99.

2. John Brisbin, "Jimmy Rogers: I'm Havin' Fun Right Today," *Living Blues* 135 (September/October 1997): 22.

3. Robert Pruter and Robert Campbell, "The Legendary Parkway Label," June 16, 2009, revised October 25, 3013, http://myweb.clemson.edu/~campber/parkway.html.

4. Brett Bonner, liner notes to *Memphis Minnie: Early Rhythm and Blues 1949 from the Rare Regal Sessions.* Biograph Records (COL-CD 6937), 2007.

5. Pruter and Campbell, "Legendary Parkway Label."

6. D. Thomas Moon, "All About the Beat: The Elga Edmonds Story," *Living Blues* 136 (November/December 1997): 37.

7. Ibid., 36.

8. Ibid., 38.

9. Ibid., 41.

10. Elga Edmonds II, quoted in ibid., 40.

11. Ibid., 38.

12. Unpublished interview portions from Jim O'Neal and Bill Greensmith, "Living Blues Interview: Jimmy Rogers," *Living Blues* 14 (Autumn 1973).

13. Gordon, *Can't Be Satisfied,* 87.

14. Moon, "All About the Beat," 38.

15. Ibid.

16. Gordon, *Can't Be Satisfied,* 88.

17. John Hubner, "Keeping the Blues Alive—Jimmy Rogers: More Than History," *Boston Phoenix*, July 22, 1980, 2.

18. Ibid.

19. Charlie Musselwhite, email to author.

20. Brisbin, "Jimmy Rogers: Havin' Fun," 24.

21. Ibid.

22. Ibid.

23. Nadine Cohodas, *Spinning Blues into Gold: The Chess Brothers and the Legendary Chess Records* (New York: St. Martin's Griffin, 2000), 52.

24. Ibid.

25. Brisbin, "Jimmy Rogers: Havin' Fun," 23.

26. Ibid., 24.

27. *Chicago Defender* (national edition) (1921–1967), November 25, 1950.

28. Tony Glover, Scott Dirks, and Ward Gaines, *Blues with a Feeling: The Little Walter Story* (New York: Routledge, 2002), 63.

29. Brisbin, "Jimmy Rogers: Havin' Fun," 24.

30. O'Neal and Greensmith, "Living Blues Interview," 14.

31. Ibid.

32. Brisbin, "Jimmy Rogers: Havin' Fun," 25.

33. Robert Gordon, "Jimmy Rogers," in *Encyclopedia of the Blues*, ed. Edward Komara (New York: Routledge, 2006), 877.

34. Pete Welding, "Interview: Johnny Shines," *Living Blues* 16 (Spring 1974): 32.

35. James Segrest and Mark Hoffman, *Moanin' at Midnight: The Life and Times of Howlin' Wolf* (New York: Thunder's Mouth Press, 2004), 64.

36. Ibid., 65.

37. Ibid., 64.

38. Peter Guralnick, *Feel Like Going Home* (New York: Bay Back Books, 1971), 156.

39. Mike Rowe, *Chicago Blues: The City and the Music* (New York: Da Capo Press, 1973), 85.

40. Brisbin, "Jimmy Rogers: Havin' Fun," 24.

41. Glover, Dirks, and Gaines, *Blues with a Feeling,* 73.

42. Moon, "All About the Beat," 39.

43. O'Neal and Greensmith, "Living Blues Interview," 16.

44. Glover, Dirks, and Gaines, *Blues with a Feeling,* 66.

45. Segrest and Hoffman, *Moanin' at Midnight,* 87.

46. Ibid., 92.

47. Glover, Dirks, and Gaines, *Blues with a Feeling,* 67.

48. Michel Ruppli, *The Chess Labels: A Discography,* Vol. 1 (Westport, CT: Greenwood Press, 1983), 20.

49. Cohodas, *Spinning Blues into Gold,* 68.

50. Gordon, *Can't Be Satisfied,* 115.

51. Brisbin, "Jimmy Rogers: Havin' Fun," 25.

52. Tom Townsley, "Jimmy Rogers: His Legacy Still Lives On," *Blues Revue* 14 (Fall 1994): 26.

53. Brisbin, "Jimmy Rogers: Havin' Fun," 25.

54. Glover, Dirks, and Gaines, *Blues with a Feeling,* 76.

55. Ibid., 77.

CHAPTER 5. THE WORLD'S IN A TANGLE

Epigraph. Robert Gordon, *Can't Be Satisfied: The Life and Times of Muddy Waters* (Boston: Little, Brown, 2002), 147.

1. Tom Townsley, "Jimmy Rogers: His Legacy Still Lives On," *Blues Revue* 14 (Fall 1994): 26.

2. Jim O'Neal, "Houston Stackhouse," in Jim O'Neal and Amy Van Singel, *The Voice of the Blues: Classic Interviews from* Living Blues *Magazine* (New York: Routledge, 2002), 108.

3. Ibid.

4. Peter Guralnick, *Feel Like Going Home* (New York: Bay Back Books, 1971), 223.

5. John Brisbin, "Jimmy Rogers: I'm Havin' Fun Right Today," *Living Blues* 135 (September/October 1997): 25.

6. Townsley, "Jimmy Rogers: Legacy," 26.

7. Brisbin, "Jimmy Rogers: Havin' Fun" 25.

8. Ibid.

9. Robert Palmer, *Deep Blues* (New York: Penguin Books, 1982), 211.

10. Brisbin, "Jimmy Rogers: Havin' Fun," 25.

11. Palmer, *Deep Blues,* 211.

12. Brisbin, "Jimmy Rogers: Havin' Fun," 25.

13. Townsley, "Jimmy Rogers: Legacy," 26.

14. Ibid., 25.

15. Ibid., 26.

16. Ibid., 25.

17. Brisbin, "Jimmy Rogers: Havin' Fun," 25.

18. Tony Glover, Scott Dirks, and Ward Gaines, *Blues with a Feeling: The Little Walter Story* (New York: Routledge, 2002), 75.

19. Townsley, "Jimmy Rogers: Legacy," 25.

20. Bob Margolin, "What Was Muddy Like?" July 2003, http://www.bobmargolin.com/muddylike.html.

21. Jim O'Neal and Bill Greensmith, "Living Blues Interview: Jimmy Rogers," *Living Blues* 14 (Autumn 1973): 13.

22. Jean-Luc Varbes, "ABS Magazine English Interview," Bob Corritore, http://bobcorritore.com/news/news-articles/abs-magazine-france-feature-article/abs-magazine-english-interview.

23. Townsley, "Jimmy Rogers: Legacy," 26.

24. Ibid.

25. O'Neal and Greensmith, "Living Blues Interview," 13.

26. Townsley, "Jimmy Rogers: Legacy," 26.

27. Margolin, "What Was Muddy Like?"

28. Brisbin, "Jimmy Rogers: Havin' Fun," 26.

29. O'Neal and Greensmith, "Living Blues Interview," 16.

30. Brisbin, "Jimmy Rogers: Havin' Fun," 26.

31. Although Little Walter had quit the band, he continued to record with them.

32. Glover, Dirks, and Gaines, *Blues with a Feeling,* 82.

33. Ibid., 88.

34. O'Neal and Greensmith, "Living Blues Interview," 17.

35. Robert Palmer, "Muddy Waters: The Delta Son Never Sets," *Rolling Stone* 275 (October 5, 1978): 54.

36. Gordon, *Can't Be Satisfied,* 119.

37. Michel Ruppli, *The Chess Labels: A Discography,* Vol. 1 (Westport, CT: Greenwood Press, 1983), 27.

38. O'Neal and Greensmith, "Living Blues Interview," 17.

39. Brisbin, "Jimmy Rogers: Havin' Fun," 25.

40. Glover, Dirks, and Gaines, *Blues with a Feeling,* 140.

41. Ibid., 144.

42. O'Neal and Greensmith, "Living Blues Interview," 14.

43. Muddy Waters, quoted in Palmer, "Muddy Waters: Delta Son," 55.

44. Ilene Melish, "The Man Who Shaped a Sound," *Melody Maker,* October 6, 1979, 37.

45. Nadine Cohodas, *Spinning Blues Into Gold: The Chess Brothers and the Legendary Chess Records* (New York: St. Martin's Griffin, 2000), 117.

46. O'Neal and Greensmith, "Living Blues Interview," 16.

47. Melish, "Man Who Shaped a Sound," 37.

CHAPTER 6. BLUES LEAVE ME ALONE

Epigraph. Jim O'Neal and Bill Greensmith, "Living Blues Interview: Jimmy Rogers," *Living Blues* 14 (Autumn 1973): 15.

1. Ibid.

2. Ibid.

3. Ibid.

4. Ibid.

5. Ibid.

6. Ibid.

7. Ibid.

8. Ibid.

9. Ibid.

10. Ibid.

11. Ibid.

12. John Brisbin, "Jimmy Rogers: I'm Havin' Fun Right Today," *Living Blues* 135 (September/October 1997): 25.

13. O'Neal and Greensmith, "Living Blues Interview," 15.

14. Ibid., 16.

15. Ibid.

16. Ibid.

17. Ibid., 17.

18. Ibid.; emphasis added.

19. Ibid.

20. Ibid.

21. Ibid., 16.

22. Ibid.

23. Ibid., 17.

24. Ibid.

25. Ibid., 16.

26. Ibid., 15.

27. Nadine Cohodas, *Spinning Blues into Gold: The Chess Brothers and the Legendary Chess Records* (New York: St. Martin's, 2000), 131.

28. O'Neal and Greensmith, "Living Blues Interview," 16.

29. Ilene Melish, "The Man Who Shaped a Sound," *Melody Maker* (October 6, 1979): 38.

30. Will Romano, *Incurable Blues: The Troubles and Triumph of Blues Legend Hubert Sumlin* (San Francisco: Backbeat Books, 2005), 63.

31. *Chicago Defender* (1910–1975), 18.

32. Brisbin, "Jimmy Rogers: Havin' Fun," 26.

33. Author email interview with Scott Dirks, January 6, 2008.

34. Brisbin, "Jimmy Rogers: Havin' Fun," 27.

35. Robert Palmer, *Deep Blues* (New York: Penguin Books, 1982), 168.

36. Ibid.

37. D. Thomas Moon, "All about the Beat: The Elga Edmonds Story," *Living Blues* 136 (November/December 1997): 39.

38. Ibid., 41.

39. Ibid., 39.

40. Jim O'Neal, liner notes to *Big Leon Brooks: Let's Go to Town* (Earwig CD4931), 1994, 2.

41. Ibid., 1.

42. *Chicago Defender*, 15.

43. O'Neal and Greensmith, "Living Blues Interview," 18.

44. Ibid., 17.

45. Ibid.

46. Author phone interview with Iguster Brown, April 2, 2008.

47. O'Neal and Greensmith, "Living Blues Interview," 18.

48. *Chicago Defender*, 18.

49. Author phone interview with Scott Dirks, December 28, 2007.

50. *Chicago Defender*, 18.

51. Ibid., 10.

52. "This Has Never Been," track 22 on *Jimmy Rogers: Complete Chess Recordings,* MCA (1997).

53. Neal Slaven, liner notes to *The OKeh Rhythm and Blues Story, 1949–1957.* Vol. 3, OKeh, (SPV 42532 CD 1993), 4.

54. O'Neal and Greensmith, "Living Blues Interview," 19.

55. Ibid., 18.

56. Brisbin, "Jimmy Rogers: Havin' Fun," 27.

57. Jim O'Neal and Bill Greensmith, original transcript, "Living Blues Interview: Jimmy Rogers," *Living Blues* 14 (Autumn 1973): 28.

58. Ibid.

59. Author email interview with Scott Dirks, January 6, 2008.

CHAPTER 7. WALKIN' BY MYSELF

Epigraph. John Brisbin, "Jimmy Rogers: I'm Havin' Fun Right Today," *Living Blues* 135 (September/October 1997): 27.

1. Jim O'Neal and Bill Greensmith, "Living Blues Interview: Jimmy Rogers," *Living Blues* 14 (Autumn 1973): 19.

2. Ibid., 18.

3. James Segrest and Mark Hoffman, *Moanin' at Midnight: The Life and Ties of Howlin' Wolf,* (New York: Thunder's Mouth Press, 2004), 45.

4. Willie Dixon and Don Snowden, *I Am the Blues: The Willie Dixon Story* (New York: Da Capo Press, 1989), 81.

5. Ibid., 85.

6. Ibid., 194.

7. Ibid., 96.

8. Segrest and Hoffman, *Moanin' at Midnight,* 45.

9. Dixon and Snowden, *I Am the Blues,* 147.

10. Segrest and Hoffman, *Moanin' at Midnight,* 177.

11. Ibid., 182.

12. Ibid., 184.

13. Ibid., 185.

14. O'Neal and Greensmith, "Living Blues Interview," 18.

15. John Brisbin, "Jimmy Rogers: I'm Havin' Fun Right Today," *Living Blues* 135 (September/October 1997): 27.

16. Tim Schuller, "Jimmy Rogers: Not Giving Up on the Blues," *Blues Access* 5 (Spring 1991): 13.

17. O'Neal and Greensmith, "Living Blues Interview," 18.

18. Ibid.

19. Schuller, "Jimmy Rogers: Not Giving Up," 13.

20. Author phone interview with Jimmy D. Lane, January 23, 2008.

21. Brisbin, "Jimmy Rogers: Havin' Fun," 27.

22. Ibid.

23. O'Neal and Greensmith, "Living Blues Interview," 18.

24. Schuller, "Jimmy Rogers: Not Giving Up," 13.

25. Peter Guralnick, *Feel Like Going Home* (New York: Bay Back Books, 1971), 73.

26. Chuck Berry, *Chuck Berry: The Autobiography* (New York: Harmony Books, 1987), 218.

27. Mike Rowe, liner notes to *The American Folk-Blues Festival: The British Tours 1963–1966,* Hip-O Records (B0008353–09, 2007), 8.

28. Ibid., 3.

29. Ibid., 8.

30. Will Romano, *Incurable Blues: The Troubles and Triumph of Blues Legend Hubert Sumlin* (San Francisco: Backbeat Books, 2005), 75.

31. Kim Field, *Harmonicas, Harps, and Heavy Breathers: The Evolution of the People's Instrument* (New York: Cooper Square Press, 1993), 171.

32. Ibid., 190.

33. Author email interview with Charlie Musselwhite, December 30, 2011.

34. Ibid.

35. Field, *Harmonicas, Harps,* 192.

36. Musselwhite interview, December 30, 2011.

37. Romano, *Incurable Blues,* 83.

38. Ibid.

39. D. Thomas Moon, "All About the Beat: The Elga Edmonds Story," *Living Blues* 136 (November/December 1997): 41.

40. O'Neal and Greensmith, "Living Blues Interview," 12.

41. Nadine Cohodas, *Spinning Blues into Gold: The Chess Brothers and the Legendary Chess Records* (New York: St. Martin's Griffin, 2000), 321.

42. Field, *Harmonicas, Harps,* 177.

43. Guralnick, *Feel Like Going Home,* 77.

44. John J. Broven, "Walking by Myself: A Commentary on Jimmy Rogers, Blues Singer," *Blues Unlimited 23* (June 1965): 3.

45. Schuller, "Jimmy Rogers: Not Giving Up," 13.

46. Brisbin, "Jimmy Rogers: Havin' Fun," 27.

47. Bob Riedy, personal diary (private collection), 12.

48. Author phone interview with Bob Riedy, January 13, 2008.

49. Ibid., November 14, 2007.

50. Ibid.

51. Cohodas, *Spinning Blues into Gold,* 267–68.

52. Riedy phone interview, November 14, 2007.

53. Cohodas, *Spinning Blues into Gold,* 277.

54. Ibid., 294.

55. Ibid., 292–93.

56. Ibid., 290.

57. Guralnick, *Feel Like Going Home,* 96.

58. Jim O'Neal, "Record Review," *Living Blues 1* (Spring 1970): 27.

59. Romano, *Incurable Blues,* 84.

60. Riedy phone interview, November 14, 2007.

61. Ibid., January 13, 2008.

62. Ibid., November 14, 2007.

63. Ibid., January 13, 2008.

64. O'Neal and Greensmith, "Living Blues Interview," 18.

CHAPTER 8. SHELTER FROM THE STORM

Epigraph. Jim O'Neal and Bill Greensmith, "Living Blues Interview: Jimmy Rogers," *Living Blues* 14 (Autumn 1973): 18.

1. John Brisbin, "Jimmy Rogers: I'm Havin' Fun Right Today," *Living Blues* 135 (September/October 1997): 27.

2. Tim Schuller, "Jimmy Rogers: Not Giving Up on the Blues," *Blues Access* 5 (Spring 1991): 13.

3. Brisbin, "Jimmy Rogers: "Havin' Fun," 27.

4. John Hubner, "Keeping the Blues Alive—Jimmy Rogers: More Than History," *Boston Phoenix*, July 22, 1980, 12.

5. Author phone interview with Bob Riedy, January 13, 2008.

6. Author phone interview with Bob Riedy, November 14, 2007.

7. Ibid.

8. Riedy interview, January 13, 2008.

9. Jim O'Neal, "Blues News," *Living Blues* 2 (Summer 1970): 2.

10. Bruce Iglauer, "Record Review," *Living Blues* 1 (Spring 1970): 27.

11. Ibid., 29.

12. Frank Scott, liner notes, *Chicago Blues at Home,* Testament Records (TCD 5028), 1995.

13. Riedy interview, November 14, 2007.

14. Riedy interview, January 13, 2008.

15. Riedy interview, November 14, 2007.

16. Ibid.

17. Ibid.

18. Ibid.

19. Schuller, "Jimmy Rogers: Not Giving Up," 13.

20. Ibid.

21. Jim O'Neal and Bill Greensmith, "Living Blues Interview: Jimmy Rogers," *Living Blues* 14 (Autumn 1973): 16.

22. Ibid.

23. Ibid.

24. Jim O'Neal, "Blues News," *Living Blues* 6 (Autumn 1971): 48.

25. Author phone interview with Jimmy D. Lane, January 23, 2008.

26. Ibid.

27. Ibid.

28. O'Neal, "Blues News," *Living Blues* 6, 15.

29. Lane interview, January 23, 2008.

30. Ibid.

31. Robert Gordon, *Can't Be Satisfied: The Life and Times of Muddy Waters* (Boston: Little, Brown, 2002), 229–30.

32. Riedy interview, November 14, 2007.

33. Lane interview, January 23, 2008.

34. Ibid.

35. Author interview with Bill Lupkin, December 17, 2007.

36. Ibid.

37. Riedy interview, November 14, 2007.

38. Ibid.

39. Ibid.

40. Mary Katherine Aldin, Bob Hite promotional flyer (private collection).

41. O'Neal and Greensmith, "Living Blues Interview," 19.

42. David J. Russell, "Jimmy Rogers, Band Performs Tight Blues," *College Times* (January 21, 1972).

43. Riedy interview, November 14, 2007.

44. Russell, "Jimmy Rogers, Band."

45. Frank Voce, "Jimmy Rogers," *Blues Unlimited* 44 (September 1972): 18.

46. O'Neal and Greensmith, "Living Blues Interview," 19.

47. Ibid.

48. Schuller, "Jimmy Rogers: Not Giving Up," 5.

49. Author email interview with Jim Kahr, January 30, 2008.

50. Riedy interview, November 14, 2007.

51. Ibid.

52. Voce, "Jimmy Rogers," 6–7.

53. Riedy interview, November 14, 2007.

54. Ibid.

55. Ibid.

56. Jim O'Neal, "Blues News," *Living Blues* 8 (Spring 1972): 29.

57. Amy Van Singel, "Blues News," *Living Blues* 17 (Summer 1974): 11.

58. Author phone interview with Bob Riedy, November 14, 2007.

59. Jimmy Rogers, introduction to track 3 on the LP *Lake Michigan Ain't No River.*

60. O'Neal and Greensmith, "Living Blues Interview," 19.

61. Ibid.

62. Ibid.

63. Schuller, "Jimmy Rogers: Not Giving Up," 5.

64. Jim O'Neal and Cary Baker, "Chicago Blues Label Guide," *Living Blues* 12 (Spring 1973): 9.

65. Jim O'Neal and Wesley Race, "Chicago Blues Club Guide," *Living Blues* 11 (Winter 1972–73): 8–10.

66. Ibid., 8, 9.

67. Ibid., 10.

68. Riedy interview, November 14, 2007.

69. O'Neal and Greensmith, "Living Blues Interview," 19.

70. Ibid.

71. Ibid.

72. Ibid.

73. Riedy interview, November 14, 2007.

74. Schuller, "Jimmy Rogers: Not Giving Up," 13.

75. Brisbin, "Jimmy Rogers: "Havin' Fun," 27.

76. Riedy interview, November 14, 2007.

77. Norbert Hess, "American Folk Blues Festival '72," *Living Blues* 11 (Winter 1972–73): 6.

78. David Walters, Laurence Garman, and John Matthews, "Jimmy Rogers" *Blues Unlimited* 105 (December 1973–74): 13.

CHAPTER 9. GOLD TAILED BIRD

Epigraph. Jim O'Neal and Bill Greensmith, "Living Blues Interview: Jimmy Rogers," *Living Blues* 14 (Autumn 1973): 19.

1. Ibid., 18.

2. Ibid., 19.

3. Kip Lornell, "Blues News," *Living Blues* 7 (Winter 1971–72): 36.

4. Jim O'Neal, "Blues News," *Living Blues* 14 (Autumn 1973): 3.

5. Author phone interview with Bob Riedy, November 14, 2007.

6. Ibid.

7. Jim O'Neal and Cary Baker, "Chicago Blues Label Guide," *Living Blues* 12 (Spring 1973): 9.

8. "Blues News," *Living Blues* 17 (Summer 1974): 51.

9. *Chicago Daily Defender* (Daily Edition) (1960–1973), February 14, 1973.

10. Jim O'Neal, "Blues News," *Living Blues* 17, 5.

11. Jim O'Neal, "Blues News," *Living Blues* 13 (Summer 1973): 40.

12. Jim DeKoster, "Blues News," *Living Blues* 15 (Winter 1973–74): 40.

13. Author email interview with Jim Kahr, January 30, 2008.

14. Ibid.

15. O'Neal and Greensmith, "Living Blues Interview," 19.

16. Ibid., 20.

17. Ibid.

18. Ibid., 19.

19. Jim O'Neal, "Blues News," *Living Blues* 13, 6.

20. DeKoster, "Blues News," *Living Blues* 15, 34.

21. John Kally, "Blues News," *Living Blues* 14 (Autumn 1973): 34.

22. Ibid.

23. Ibid.

24. Ibid., 39.

25. Riedy interview, November 14, 2007.

26. Jimmy Rogers, quoted in Ilene Melish, "The Man Who Shaped a Sound," *Melody Maker* (October 6, 1979): 38.

27. Jim O'Neal, "Obituaries: Johnny Young," *Living Blues* 17 (Summer 1974): 6.

28. Jim O'Neal, "Blues News," *Living Blues* 20 (March/April 1975): 8.

29. Tim Schuller, "Jimmy Rogers: Not Giving Up on the Blues," *Blues Access* 5 (Spring 1991): 13.

30. Norbert Hess, "Blues News," *Living Blues* 19 (January/February 1975): 6.

31. Jim O'Neal, "Blues News," *Living Blues* 21 (May/June 1975): 7.

32. Ibid., 8.

33. Jim O'Neal, "45s," *Living Blues* 20 (March/April 1975): 54.

34. Jim O'Neal, "Blues News," *Living Blues* 23 (September/October 1975): 8.

35. O'Neal, "Blues News," *Living Blues* 20: 8.

36. Wesley Race, "LPs," *Living Blues* 21 (May/June 1975): 47.

37. Christopher Gray, "TCB News: Blues for Clifford," *Austin Chronicle, May 26, 2006,* http://www.austinchronicle.com/music/2006–05–26/368456.

38. Ibid.

39. Will Romano, *Incurable Blues: The Troubles and Triumph of Blues Legend Hubert Sumlin* (San Francisco: Backbeat Books, 2005), 117.

40. Ibid.

41. Gray, "TCB News."

42. Author phone interview with Kim Wilson, November 5, 2007.

43. Ibid.

44. Ibid.

45. Ibid.

46. Ibid.

47. Mike Callahan and David Edwards, "The Chess Story," *Both Sides Now Publications*, November 4, 2005, www.bsnpubs.com/chesscheck.html.

48. "Blues News." *Living Blues 24* (November/December 1975): 49.

49. Pete Welding, liner notes to *Jimmy Rogers: Chess Masters Blues Series*. Chess (2ACMB-207), 1976.

50. Ibid.

51. Bob Margolin, liner notes to Muddy Waters, *I'm Ready*, Epic/Legacy (EK90565), 1978, 4.

52. Ibid., 5.

53. Ibid.

54. Ibid., 8.

55. That's All Right" is one of three bonus tracks (#11) on the Muddy Waters *I'm Ready* CD (released by Sony in 2004).

56. Margolin, liner notes, 10.

57. Sandra Pointer-Jones, "Jimmy Rogers: The Long Road to the Top," *Blues Revue* 14 (Fall 1994): 27.

58. Robert Gordon, *Can't Be Satisfied: The Life and Times of Muddy Waters* (Boston: Little, Brown, 2002), 73.

59. Bob Margolin, "What Was Muddy Like?" July 2003, BobMargolin.com, http://www.bobmargolin.com/muddylike.html.

60. Ibid.

61. David Nelson, "Obituaries: Hip Linkchain," *Living Blues* 87 (July/August 1989): 36.

62. Herbert Pessiak, liner notes to *Jimmy Rogers & Big Moose Walker: Chicago Bound*, Wolf Records (CD 120.861), 1986.

63. Schuller, "Jimmy Rogers: Not Giving Up," 113.

64. Melish, "Man Who Shaped a Sound," 38.

65. Jim O'Neal, caption indicating band lineup in a Chicago 1978 photo (private collection).

66. Author email interview with Richard Molina, January 9, 2012.

67. Ibid.

68. Melish, "Man Who Shaped a Sound," 37.

69. Ibid.

70. Ibid., 38.

71. Author phone interview with Jim O'Neal, January 9, 2008.

72. Track 4, "Fishin' in My Pond," *The Dirty Dozens*, by Jimmy Rogers and Left Hand Frank, JSP Records PCD-23890, 2007.

73. Track 5, "Crazy Woman Blues," *The Dirty Dozens*.

74. Author phone interview with Frank Bandy, January 27, 2008.

75. Ibid.

76. Ibid.

77. Bandy interview, November 19, 2007.

78. Ibid.

79. Ibid.

80. Ibid.

81. Bandy interview, January 27, 2008.

82. Bandy interview, November 19, 2007.

83. Ibid.

84. Ibid.

85. Author email interview with Jerry Haussler, February 22, 2008.

86. Tom Mazzolini, liner notes to *San Francisco Blues Festival, Vol. 2,* Solid Smoke (SS-8010), 1981.

87. Haussler interview, February 22, 2008.

88. Ibid.

CHAPTER 10. FEELIN' GOOD

Epigraph. John Hubner, "Keeping the Blues Alive—Jimmy Rogers: More Than History," *Boston Phoenix*, July 22, 1980, 12.

1. Author phone interview with Mudcat Ward, January 12, 2008.

2. Mel Cramer and Peter Ward, "Blue Notes," *Bay State Banner*, March 6, 1980, 15.

3. Ward interview, January 12, 2008.

4. Cramer and Ward, "Blue Notes," 15.

5. Louis X. Elanger, "Blue 'n' Boogie," *Weekly Soho News*, March 12–18, 1980, 24.

6. Robert Palmer, "The Blues: Jimmy Rogers," *New York Times*, February 25, 1980.

7. Ibid.

8. Elanger, "Blue 'n' Boogie," 24.

9. Ward interview, January 12, 2008.

10. Elanger, "Blue 'n' Boogie," 24.

11. Norman Darwen, "I Wrote Jimmy Rogers a Letter (Chats with Steve Guyger)," *Harmonica World* (June/July 1993): 15.

12. Author phone interview with Steve Guyger, December 4, 2007.

13. Ibid.

14. Author phone interview with Ola Dixon, January 15, 2008.

15. Guyger interview, December 4, 2007.

16. Ward interview, January 12, 2008.

17. Ibid.

18. Ibid.

19. Jim O'Neal, "Paul Kahn 1980 tour itinerary (Concerted Efforts)," private collection.

20. Hubner, "Keeping the Blues Alive," 12.

21. Ibid.

22. Tony Lioce, "Music," *Providence Journal*, July 11, 1980.

23. Ibid.

24. Mike Joyce, "Jimmy Rogers," *Washington Post*, July 24, 1980, Performing Arts Section, B-6.

25. Guyger interview, December 4, 2007.

26. Author phone interview with Frank Bandy, November 19, 2007.

27. Ibid.

28. Ibid.

29. David Whiteis, "Floyd Jones, By Himself," *Chicago Reader*, January 24, 1986, 45.

30. Bandy interview, November 19, 2007.

31. Author phone interview with Barrelhouse Chuck Goering, January 6, 2008.

32. Ibid.

33. Ibid.

34. Ibid.

35. Ibid.

36. Ibid.

37. Bandy interview, November 19, 2007.

38. Tom Townsley, "Jimmy Rogers: His Legacy Still Lives On," *Blues Revue* 14 (Fall 1994): 25.

39. Bandy interview, November 19, 2007.

40. Ibid.

41. "The 1983 W. C. Handy International Blues Awards," *Living Blues* 58 (Winter 1983): 16.

42. Bandy interview, November 19, 2007.

43. Ibid.

44. Author phone interview with Holger Peterson, November 9, 2007.

45. Goering interview, January 6, 2008.

46. Ibid.

47. Ibid.

48. Ibid.

49. Ibid

50. Ibid.

51. Tamara Chapman, "Learning to Hurt Brings Out the Blues," *El Paso Times*, September 4, 1983.

52. D. Thomas Moon, "Bob Stroger: First Call Bass," *Living Blues* 158 (July August 2001): 33–34.

53. Goering interview, January 6, 2008.

54. Ibid.

55. Dan Lambert, "Blues in El Paso: The Border Blues Festival and Señor Blues," *Living Blues* 58 (Winter 1983): 23.

56. Ibid., 24.

57. Chapman, "Learning to Hurt."

58. Russ Parsons, "Bluesman Gets Down to Basics," *Tribune Accent*, September 9, 1983, B-1, B-5.

59. Ibid.

60. Author phone interview with Rod Piazza, December 28, 2007.

61. Ibid.

62. Author phone interview with Junior Watson, December 20, 2007.

63. Tim Schuller, "Jimmy Rogers: Not Giving Up on the Blues," *Blues Access* 5 (Spring 1991): 12.

64. Bandy interview, November 19, 2007.

65. Goering interview, January 8, 2008.

66. Bandy interview, November 19, 2007.

67. Ibid.

68. Ibid.

69. Goering interview, January 8, 2008.

70. Piazza interview, December 28, 2007.

71. Watson Interview, December 20, 2007.

72. Piazza interview, December 28, 2007

73. Ibid.

74. Ibid.

75. Ibid.

76. Watson interview, December 20, 2007.

77. Ibid.

78. Ibid.

79. Bandy interview, November 19, 2007.

80. Dan Forte, "Jimmy Rogers: Feelin' Good," *Guitar Player* (April 1984): 120.

81. Author phone interview with Tony Mangiullo, March 28, 2008.

82. Elizabeth Winkowski, "Blues with a Feeling: Meet Sumito Ariyoshi," Gapers Block, June 11, 2007, http://www.gapersblock.com/detour/blues_with_a_feeling.

83. Ibid.

84. Ibid.

85. Ibid.

86. Ibid.

87. Ibid.

88. Bandy interview, November 9, 2007.

89. Author phone interview with Rich Kirch, November 6, 2007.

90. Ibid.

91. Author phone interview with Rich Kirch, February 2, 2008.

92. Bandy interview, November 19, 2007.

93. Author phone interview with Rich Kirch, January 7, 2008.

94. Ibid.

95. Ibid.

96. Ibid.

97. Jim O'Neal, "Chicago Blues Festival," *Living Blues* 62 (Winter 1983): 17.

98. Watson interview, December 20, 2007.

99. Piazza interview, December 28, 2007.

100. Ibid.

101. Ibid.

CHAPTER 11. OUT ON THE ROAD

Epigraph. John Brisbin, "Jimmy Rogers: I'm Havin' Fun Right Today," *Living Blues* 135 (September/October 1997): 27.

1. Author phone interview with Mudcat Ward, January 12, 2008.

2. Ibid.

3. Ibid.

4. Christopher Gray, "TCB News: Blues for Clifford," *Austin Chronicle*, May 26, 2006, http://www.austinchronicle.com/music/2006–05–26/368456.

5. Will Romano, *Incurable Blues: The Troubles and Triumph of Blues Legend Hubert Sumlin* (San Francisco: Backbeat Books, 2005), 127.

6. Ibid., 129.

7. Author phone interview with Kim Wilson, November 5, 2007.

8. Romano, *Incurable Blues*, 128.

9. Ibid.

10. Wilson interview, November 5, 2007.

11. Ibid.

12. Ibid.

13. Author phone interview with Kim Wilson, November 8, 2007.

14. Ibid.

15. Ibid.

16. Author phone interview with Dave Waldman, December 19, 2007.

17. Ibid.

18. Ibid.

19. Ibid.

20. Ibid.

21. Ibid.

22. Author phone interview with Barrelhouse Chuck Goering, January 6, 2008.

23. Tim Schuller, "Living BluesLetter," *Living Blues* 67 (1986): 4.

24. Waldman interview, December 19, 2007.

25. Ibid.

26. Ibid.

27. Ibid.

28. Ibid.

29. Ward interview, January 12, 2008.

30. Ibid.

31. Ibid.

32. Klaus Kilian, "Living BluesLetter," *Living Blues* 68 (1986): 8.

33. Author in-person interview with Jim O'Neal, January 12, 2008.

34. Ibid.

35. Tim Schuller, "Jimmy Rogers: Not Giving Up on the Blues," *Blues Access* 5 (Spring 1991): 10.

36. Author phone interview with Rich Yescalis, January 10, 2008.

37. Ibid.

38. Karen Hanson, *Today's Chicago Blues* (Chicago: Lake Claremont Press, 2007), 180.

39. Jonathan Foose, "Antone's Lights Eleven Candles," *Living Blues* 73 (1987): 20.

40. Ibid., 21.

41. Paul Rossez, "Living BluesLetter," *Living Blues* 73 (1987): 10.

42. Author interview with Frank Bandy, February 28, 2008.

43. Author phone interview with Frank Bandy, November 19, 2007.

44. Ibid.

45. Ibid.

46. Eric King, "Living BluesLetter," *Living Blues* 75 (1987): 10.

47. Helen Doob Lazar, "Interview: James Cotton," *Living Blues* 76 (1987): 29.

48. Bandy interview, November 19, 2007.

49. Author phone interview with Jimmy D. Lane, January 5, 2008.

50. Ibid.

51. Ibid.

52. Helen Doob Lazar, "BluesLetter," *Living Blues* 74 (1987): 4.

53. Bandy interview, November 19, 2007.

54. Author phone interview with Barrelhouse Chuck Goering, January 6, 2008.

55. Author phone interview with Rich Kirch, February 2, 2008.

56. Bandy interview, November 19, 2007.

57. Author phone interview with Matthew Skoller, March 28, 2008.

58. Ibid.

59. Ibid.

60. Ibid.

61. Author phone interview with Kim Wilson, March 20, 2008.

62. Miles Jordan, "BluesLetter," *Living Blues* 81 (1987): 6.

63. Chris Roth, "BluesLetter," *Living Blues* 83 (1987): 3.

64. Wilson interview, March 20, 2008.

65. Author email interview with Rich Molina, January 9, 2012.

66. Peter Watrous, "Cabaret: Jimmy Rogers," *New York Times*, March 3, 1988. Available online at http://www.nytimes.com/1988/03/03/arts/cabaret-jimmy-rogers.html.

67. Ibid.

68. Tom Townsley, "Jimmy Rogers: His Legacy Still Lives On," *Blues Revue* 14 (Fall 1994): 23.

69. Jack Hunter, "BluesLetter," *Living Blues* 82 (September/October 1988): 10.

70. Ibid., 11.

71. Lazar, "BluesLetter," *Living Blues* 83, 7, 8.

72. Ibid.

73. Brett J. Bonner, "Festivals: Putting the Blues Back Where It Oughta Be," *Living Blues* 84 (1988): 14–15.

74. Author phone interview with Rich Kirch, November 6, 2007.

75. Author phone interview with Frank Bandy, January 27, 2008.

76. Bandy interview, November 19, 2007.

77. Author phone interview with Rich Kirch, February 2, 2008.

78. Peter Watrous, "Reviews/Music; The Heart of the Blues, in 5 Acts." *New York Times* online. November 9, 1988. http://www.nytimes.com/1988/11/09/arts/reviews-music-the-heart-of-the-blues-in-5-acts.html.

79. Author e-mail interview with Charlie Musselwhite, December 30, 2011.

80. David Nelson, "Obituaries: Hip Linkchain," *Living Blues* 87 (August 1989): 36.

81. "Wolf Story," Wolf Records International, www.wolfrec.com/wolf-story.html.

82. Ibid.

83. Author phone interviews with Jimmy D. Lane, March 17, 19, 2008.

84. Advertisement, *Living Blues* 88 (September/October 1989): 65.

85. Author phone interview with "Piano Willie" O'Shawny, December 7, 2007.

86. Dan Kening, "Quiet Giant," *Chicago Tribune*, November 7, 1989, 53.

87. Ibid.

CHAPTER 12. CHANGING LANES

Epigraph. Tom Townsley, "Jimmy Rogers: His Legacy Still Lives On," *Blues Revue* 14 (Fall 1994): 23

1. Tim Schuller, "Jimmy Rogers: Not Giving Up on the Blues," *Blues Access* 5 (Spring 1991): 5.

2. Author phone interview with Kim Wilson, November 8, 2007.

3. Ibid.

4. Tom Townsley, "Jimmy Rogers: His Legacy Still Lives On," *Blues Revue* 14 (Fall 1994): 25.

5. Author phone interview with Kim Wilson, November 8, 2007.

6. Jimmy Rogers, "Got My Mojo Working," track 10, *Ludella,* Antone's Records (ANT0012), 1990.

7. Frenzy record review in Schuller, "Jimmy Rogers: Not Giving Up," 12.

8. Ibid.

9. Author email interview with Bob Margolin, November 22, 2007.

10. Bob Margolin, *Chicago Blues,* Powerhouse Records (POW 4105), 1991.

11. Author email interviews with Tom "Mookie" Brill, February 1, 2008, and January 2, 2012.

12. Author email interview with "Tony O" Melio, March 27, 2008.

13. Author phone interview with "Piano Willie" O'Shawny, December 7, 2007.

14. Roberto Prieto Ruguera, "Email interview with 'Piano Willie' O'Shawny, May 12, 2005," (private collection).

15. O'Shawny interview, December 7, 2007.

16. Ibid.

17. Author phone interview with Jimmy D. Lane, March 17, 2008.

18. O'Shawny interview, December 7, 2007.

19. Ibid.

20. Ibid.

21. Ibid.

22. Melio interview, March 27, 2008.

23. Ibid.

24. Ibid.

25. Ibid.

26. Ibid.

27. Ibid.

28. Author email interview with "Tony O" Melio, February 20, 2008.

29. Author phone interview with Frank Bandy, November 19, 2007.

30. Author phone interview with Frank Bandy, January 27, 2008.

31. Bandy interview, November 19, 2007.

32. Bandy interview, January 27, 2008.

33. Bandy interview, November 19, 2007.

34. Ruguera, O'Shawny interview.

35. Author phone interview with Jimmy D. Lane, January 20, 2008.

36. Author phone interview with Mudcat Ward, January 12, 2008.

37. Bandy interview, January 27, 2008.

38. Ward interview, January 12, 2008.

39. Ibid.

40. Jimmy Rogers interviews, October 20, 1982, and July 27, 1991, from Holger Peterson's Saturday night blues show, *Natch'l Blues.*

41. Pete Welding, "Jimmy Rogers," *Blues Mentor (Milwaukee Blues Unlimited)* (February/March 1992): 1, Mary Katherine Aldin, private collection.

42. Barney Tabor, "Jimmy Rogers: Still Burnin' 'Em Up and Going Strong at 70," *Blues Revue* 14 (Fall 1994): 21.

43. Mike Garner, "Jimmy Rogers," Blues News, January 6, 1994, www.santacruzblues .com/info.php.

44. Author phone interview with Barrelhouse Chuck Goering, January 8, 2008.

45. Transcript of interview with Jimmy Rogers by David Jaffe on WWOZ 90.7, New Orleans radio show, from personal collection of Mary Katherine Aldin.

46. Mark Hummel, *Big Road Blues : 12 Bars on I-80* (San Mateo, CA: MountainTop Publishing, 2012), 182–84.

47. Author phone interview with Mark Hummel, December 10, 2007. Mark Hummel's CD release, *Chicago Blues Party* (tracks 1–5), recorded 1992 at Slim's in San Francisco, California, Mountain Top Productions (MTP-0013), 2009.

48. Jean-Luc Varbes, "ABS Magazine English Interview," *Bob Corritore,* http:// bobcorritore.com/news/news-articles/abs-magazine-france-feature-article/abs -magazine-english-interview.

49. Ibid.

50. Ibid.

51. Ibid.

52. Author interview with Steve Guyger, December 4, 2007.

53. Ibid.

54. Tabor, "Jimmy Rogers: Still Burnin' 'Em Up," 22.

55. Lane interviews, March 17, 19, 2008.

56. Author email interview with Scott Dirks, December 5, 2007.

57. Lane interviews, March 17, 19, 2008.

58. Ibid.

59. Ibid.

60. Ibid.

61. Author phone interview with Joe Harley, January 27, 2008.

62. Dirks interview, December 5, 2007.

63. Jeff Johnson, "Still Going Strong at 70: For Rogers, Blues Fest Is a Party," *Chicago Sun-Times,* June 5, 1994, 47.

64. Ibid.

65. Tabor, "Jimmy Rogers: Still Burnin' 'Em Up," 22.

66. Townsley, "Jimmy Rogers: His Legacy," 23–24.

67. Ibid., 24.

68. Ibid.

69. Ibid., 25.

70. Ibid.

71. Mike Garner, "Jimmy Rogers" Blues News, January 6, 1994, www.blues.co.nz/features/article/.php?id=1.

72. John Brisbin, "Jimmy Rogers: I'm Havin' Fun Right Today," *Living Blues* 135 (September/October 1997): 27.

73. Ibid.

74. Sandra Pointer-Jones, "Jimmy Rogers: The Long Road to the Top," *Blues Revue* 14 (Fall 1994): 27.

75. Ibid.

76. Ibid.

77. Ibid.

78. Lane interview, March 17, 2008.

79. Bill Dahl, "Blues Follow Me All Day Long," liner notes to *Chicago Blues Masters, Volume Two: Jimmy Rogers*, Capitol CDP7243.

80. Jim O'Neal, "Blues News," *Living Blues* 14 (Autumn 1973): 3.

81. Lane interview, March 17, 2008.

82. Ibid.

CHAPTER 13. THAT'S ALL RIGHT

1. *Epigraph*. John Brisbin, "Jimmy Rogers: I'm Havin' Fun Right Today," *Living Blues* 135 (September/October 1997): 27.

1. Roberto Prieto Ruguera, "Email interview with 'Piano Willie' O'Shawny, May 12, 2005," private collection.

2. Author phone interview with Barrelhouse Chuck Goering, January 6, 2008.

3. Ibid.

4. Author phone interview with "Piano Willie" O'Shawny, December 7, 2007.

5. Ruguera, "O'Shawny interview."

6. Ibid.

7. Mary Katherine Aldin, liner notes to "Jimmy Rogers: The Complete Chess Recordings," Chess 50th Anniversary Collection, Chess Records (CHESS 2ACMB 207) January 1997, 15.

8. Author email interview with Mary Katherine Aldin, March 21, 2008.

9. Ibid.

10. Aldin, liner notes to "Jimmy Rogers: The Complete Chess Recordings," 4.

11. Ibid., 5.

12. Ibid., 6.

13. Ibid.

14. Ibid., 8.

15. Aldin interview, March 21, 2008.

16. Author phone interview with Jimmy D. Lane, March 17, 2008.

17. Ibid.

18. Author phone interview with John Koenig, January 18, 2008.

19. Ibid.

20. Pierre Perrone, "Jagger Sings the Blues," *London Independent*, March 5, 1999. http://www.independent.co.uk/arts-entertainment/jagger-sings-the-blues-1078429.html.

21. Ibid.

22. Greg Cahill, "Blues Legend Jimmy Rogers on a Roll," *Sonoma County Independent: MetroActive Central*, September 4–10, 1997, www.metroactive.com/papers/sonoma/09.04.97/music-9736.html.

23. Perrone, "Jagger Sings the Blues."

24. Mary Katherine Aldin, Atlantic Records promotional press kit release for *Blues Blues Blues*, private collection.

25. Perrone, "Jagger Sings the Blues."

26. Ibid.

27. Ibid.

28. "Jimmy Rogers," Blind Pig Records, http://www.blindpigrecords.com/index.cfm?section=artists&artistid=51.

29. Author in-person interview with Jimmy D. Lane, January 25, 2007.

30. Mike Zwerin, "Dodging Danger in Music Business: Record Nabob Sets the Tempo," *International New York Times*, February 10, 1999, http://www.nytimes.com/1999/02/10/style/10iht-ahmet.t.html.

31. Ray Stiles, "Jimmy Rogers @ Orrie's February 14–15, 1997," www.mnblues.com/review/j_rogers.html.

32. Ibid.

33. "Blue Farewell," Weekly Wire, weeklywire.com/ww/01–12–98/Memphis_mus.html.

34. Ruguera, "O'Shawny interview."

35. Ibid.

36. Ibid.

37. Listserv email announcement from *Blues Revue*, Mary Katherine Aldin (private collection).

38. Cahill, "Blues Legend Jimmy Rogers."

39. Ibid.

40. Ruguera, "O'Shawny interview."

41. Lane interview, March 17, 2008.

42. O'Shawny interview December 7, 2007.

43. Ibid.

44. Ruguera, "O'Shawny interview."

45. John Brisbin, liner notes to *Jimmy D. Lane: Legacy*, APO Records (APO 2005), 1998.

46. Ibid.

47. Jim DeKoster, "Record Reviews: Jimmy D. Lane Long Gone," *Living Blues* 137 (January/February 1998): 65.

48. Joe Harley, notes, in Mary Katherine Aldin, private collection.

49. Author phone interview with Jimmy D. Lane, January 25, 2008.

50. David Jaffe, "Jimmy Rogers Interview," *SoulBot.* http://www.Soulbot.com/jimmyrogers.

51. Ibid.

52. Ibid.

53. Ibid.

54. Ibid.

55. Brisbin, "Jimmy Rogers: Havin' Fun, 27.

56. Ibid.

57. Big Dave, "David Krull," StLBlues. www.stlblues.net/Krull.html.

58. Lane interview, January 25, 2008.

59. Ibid.

60. Ibid.

61. Listserv email announcement, Mary Katherine Aldin (private collection).

62. Author phone interview with Steve Guyger, December 4, 2007.

63. "Jimmy Rogers Update," Blues Music listserv email, November 10, 1997, Mary Katherine Aldin (private collection).

64. Jimmie Lee Robinson quote sent from Steve Balkin to Jimmy Rogers Memorial homepage on December 20 1997, Mary Katherine Aldin (private collection).

65. Ben Ratliff, "Jimmy Rogers, 73, Guitarist Specializing In Electric Blues," *New York Times*, December 20, 1997, 12. Available online at
http://www.nytimes.com/1997/12/20/arts/jimmy-rogers-73-guitarist-specializing-in-electric-blues.html.

66. Teresa Puente, "Jimmy Rogers, Bluesman Who Teamed with Waters," *Chicago Tribune*, December 21, 1997. Available online at http://articles.chicagotribune .com/1997−12−21/news/9712210287_1_muddy-waters-mr-rogers-jimmy-rogers.

67. Ibid.

68. Author phone interview with Kim Wilson, March 20, 2008.

69. John Brisbin, " Obituaries: Jimmy Rogers," *Living Blues* 138 (March/April 1998): 74.

CHAPTER 14. LONG GONE

Epigraph. Author phone interview with Jimmy D. Lane, January 25, 2008.

1. Jimmy D. Lane, quoted in John Brisbin, liner notes to *Jimmy D. Lane: Legacy,* APO Records (APO 2005), 1998.

2. Lane interview, January 25, 2008.

3. Stephen Thomas Erlewine, "Blues Blues Blues: Review," All Music Guide, http://www.allmusic.com/album/blues-blues-blues-r379569.

4. John Koenig, liner notes, "Blues Blues Blues: The Jimmy Rogers All-Stars" (Atlantic 83148−2), 1999.

5. Unreleased CD recording from John Koenig private collection.

6. Bonnie Stebbins, "Honoring Jimmy Rogers," Geoff Wilbur's Renegade Newsletter, http://membrane.com/renegade/spring01/rogers.html. Originally published in April 2001 issue of "Blues Ambassador" (monthly newsletter of the Capital Area Blues Society [CABS], Lansing, Michigan).

7. Author email interview with "Steady Rollin'" Bob Margolin, November 27, 2007.

8. Dick Shurman, liner notes, *Bob Corritore All-Star Blues Sessions* (HMG 1009), 1999.

9. Author email interview with Billy Flynn, January 23, 2008.

10. Margolin interview, November 27, 2007.

11. Dan Kening, "Quiet Giant: Blues Guitarist Jimmy Rogers Is Reclaiming His Legend," *Chicago Tribune*, November 7, 1989, Tempo section, 53, quoted in Barney Tabor, "Jimmy Rogers: Still Burnin' 'Em Up and Going Strong at 70," *Blues Revue* 14 (Fall 1994): 22.

12. Author phone interview with Mudcat Ward, January 12, 2008.

13. Author phone interview with Tom Radai, November 24, 2007.

14. Tom Townsley, "Jimmy Rogers: His Legacy Lives On," *Blues Revue* 14 (Fall 1994): 24.

15. D. Thomas Moon, "Bob Stroger: First Call Bass," *Living Blues* 158 (July August 2001): 33–34.

16. Sandra Pointer-Jones, "Jimmy Rogers: The Long Road to the Top," *Blues Revue* 14 (Fall 1994): 27.

17. Tim Schuller, "Jimmy Rogers: Not Giving Up on the Blues," *Blues Access* 5 (Spring 1991): 13.

CODA

1. Source for all quotes in this chapter is Emily Peacock, "Rogers Honored by Blues Marker," *Bolivar [Mississippi] Commercial,* November 26, 2011, http://www.bolivarcom .com/view/full_story/16302875/article-Rogers-honored-by-blues-marker.

A SELECTED JIMMY ROGERS DISCOGRAPHY

JIMMY ROGERS CHESS RECORDS RELEASED SINGLES

Date	Matrix	Title	Release #
August 15, 1950	U7269	Ludella	1435
	U7270	That's All Right	1435
October 20, 1950	U7277	Going Away Baby	1442
	U7278	Today, Today, Blues	1442
January 23, 1951	U7309	World in a Tangle	1453
	U7310	Loves Another Man	1453
	U7308	I Used to Have Woman	1506[a]
July 11, 1951	U7361	Money, Marbles, and Chalk	1476
	U7364	Chance to Love	1476
February 11, 1952	U7424	Back Door Friend	1506
August 12, 1952	U7445	The Last Time	1519
	U7447	Out on the Road	1519
May 4, 1953	U7503	Left Me with a Broken Heart	1543
	U7504	Act Like You Love Me	1543
January 7, 1954	U7591	Blues All Day Long	1616[b]
	U7592	Chicago Bound	1574
April 13, 1954	U7632	Sloppy Drunk	1574
December 1955	U7970	You're the One	1616

Date	Matrix	Title	Release #
October 29, 1956	U8304	If It Ain't Me	1643
	U8305	Walkin' by Myself	1643
December 1, 1956	U8394	I Can't Believe	1659
	U8395	One Kiss	1659
September 18, 1957	U8597	What Have I Done	1687
	U8599	Trace of You	1687
February 1959	U9241	Rock This House	1721
	U9242	My Last Meal	1721

Chess Records released thirteen singles for Jimmy Rogers [26 sides], with "Walkin' by Myself" as the only tune that made the charts, reaching #14 on the R&B rankings.

[a] Shelved until released as B side to February 11 recording of "Back Door Friend"

[b] Shelved until released as B side to December 1955 recording of "You're the One"

JIMMY ROGERS WITH THE MUDDY WATERS BAND: CHESS RECORDINGS

Date	Matrix	Title	Release #
Summer 1949	U7215	Screamin' and Cryin'	406[a]
	U7216	Where's My Woman Been	406[a]
October 20, 1949	U7306	Honey Bee	1468
December 29, 1951	U7413	They Call Me Muddy Waters	[c]
	U7415	Stuff You Gotta Watch	[c]
	U7416	Lonesome Day	[c]
May 12, 1952	U7437	Juke	758[b]
	U7438	Can't Hold on Much Longer	758[b]
	U7439	Please Have Mercy	1514
September 17, 1952	U7476	Who's Gonna Be Your Sweet Man	1542
	U7477	Standing Around Crying	1526
	U7478	Gone to Main Street	1526
	U7479	Iodine in My Coffee	1527
December 1952	U4332	Flood	[c]
	U4333	My Life Is Ruined	[c]
	U4334	She's All Right	1537
	U4335	Sad, Sad Day	1537
May 4, 1953	U7501a	Turn the Lamp Down Low	1542
	U7502	Loving Man	1585
September 24, 1953	U7551	Blow Wind Blow	1550
	U7552	Mad Love	1550
January 7, 1954	U7589	Hoochie Coochie Man	1560
	U7590	She's So Pretty	1560

Date	Matrix	Title	Release #
	U7591	Blues Leave Me Alone	c
	U7592	Memphis Blues	c
April 13, 1954	U7630	I Just Want to Make Love to You	1571
	U7631	Oh Yeah	1571
September 1, 1954	U7697	I'm Ready	1579
	U7698	Smokestack Lightnin'	c
	U7699	I Don't Know Why	1579
	U7670	Shake It Baby	c
September 1954	U7746	I'm a Natural Born Lover	1585
	U7747	Ooh Wee	1585
February 3, 1955	U7783	This Pain	c
	U7784	Young Fashioned Ways	1602
	U7785	I Want to Be Loved	1596
March 9, 1955	U7797	My Eyes Keep Me in Trouble	1596
May 24, 1955	U7846	Mannish Boy	1602

[a] Muddy Waters session for the Aristocrat label
[b] Little Walter session for the Checker label
[c] Released not as a single but later on LP or CD

JIMMY ROGERS ON OTHER ARISTOCRAT/CHESS RECORDINGS

Date	Matrix	Title	Release #
September 1949[a]	U7213	Big Town Playboy	405
	U7214	Shelby County Blues	405
October 23, 1950[b]	U7279	Joliet Blues	1443
	U7280	So Glad I Found You	d
December 29, 1951[c]	U7417	Overseas	d
	U7418	Playhouse	d
(acquired from JOB)	F1006	Dark Road	d
	F1007	Big World	d
September 17, 1952[c]	U7480	You Can't Live Long	1527
	U7481	Early Morning	d

[a] Session for Little Johnny Jones. Released on *The Aristocrat of the Blues: The Best of Aristocrat Records*, MCA (CHD2–9327).
[b] Session for Johnny Shines ("Shoe Shine Johnny"). Released on *Drop Down Mama*, MCA (CHD-93002).
[c] Session for Floyd Jones. Released on *Drop Down Mama*, MCA (CHD-93002).
[d] Released not as a single but later on LP or CD

JIMMY ROGERS ON PRE-CHESS RECORDINGS

Date	Matrix	Title	Release #
September 1946[a]	C 112a	Round About Boogie	1021
Month Unknown 1947[b]	—	Little Store Blues	+
December 22, 1948[c]	—	You Don't Have to Go	+
	—	I'm in Love with a Woman	+
August 26, 1949[d]	R-1398	I'm in Love	+
	R-1397	That's All Right	+
January 1950[e]	R-1218-2	Ludella	+

+ Originally unreleased

[a] Session with Sunnyland Slim on J. Mayo Williams's Harlem label, although the title is attributed to "Memphis Slim & His Houserockers."

[b] Session for Bernard Abrams's Ora Nelle label; released on Barrelhouse Records (BHO4) and on the *Chicago Boogie!* CD on P-Vine (PCD-1888).

[c] Session for Irving Taman's Tempo-Tone label. Both sides went unreleased.

[d] Session recorded with Sunnyland Slim for Joe Brown/Jimmy Burke Oden's JOB label. Sides were sold several times to Apollo, Regal, and Delmark. Released on Sunnyland Slim's *House Rent Party* for Delmark (DD-665)

[e] Session recorded for Monroe Passis for Parkway label. Session was sold to Regal and was hidden in obscurity for years until this author discovered it under a Memphis Minnie session. Previously thought to be recorded by Regal, but now known to be part of the historic marathon Parkway session that included Jimmy, Muddy, Baby Face Leroy, Sunnyland Slim, Little Son Joe, Little Walter, and Ernest "Big" Crawford. Released on Biograph label's *Memphis Minnie Early Rhythm & Blues 1949* (COL-CD-6937).

JIMMY ROGERS LP AND CD RECORDINGS

American Folk Blues Festival '72 (1980 CD) / L + R Records / LR CD 2018
(Billy Davenport, drums; Jimmy Rogers, guitar & vocals; Lightnin' Slim, guitar & vocal; T-Bone Walker, guitar & vocals; Whispering Smith, harp; Willie Kent, bass)
Tracks: Tricky Woman; Goin' Back to Church

American Folk Blues Festival '83 (1984 CD) / L + R Records / LR CD-2063
(Blues Queen Sylvia, vocals & bass guitar; Carey Bell, harp; Honeyboy Otis, drums; Jimmy Rogers, guitar; Louisiana Red, guitar; Lovie Lee, piano)
Tracks: I Love You; Baby, What Do I Do; Red's Tribute to Muddy Waters

Antone's 10th Anniversary (1986 LP) / Antone's Records / ANT0004LP
(Bob Stroger, bass; Derek O'Brien, guitar; Eddie Taylor, guitar; James Cotton, harp & vocals; Jimmy Rogers, guitar & vocals; Jimmie Vaughan, guitar; Luther Tucker, guitar; Pinetop Perkins, piano & vocals; Sunnyland Slim, piano & vocals; Ted Harvey, drums; Timothy Taylor, drums)

Tracks: Cotton Crop Blues; How'd You Learn to Shake It Like That; You're Sweet; If You Don't Want Me Baby; Built Up from the Ground; Cold Cold Feeling; Bad Boy; Look on Yonder's Wall; Things I Used to Do; Caldonia; Double Trouble

Antone's 10th Anniversary (1986 CD) / Antone's Records / ANT0004CD
(Bob Stroger, bass; Derek O'Brien, guitar; Eddie Taylor, guitar; James Cotton, harp & vocals; Jimmy Rogers, guitar & vocals; Jimmie Vaughan, guitar; Luther Tucker, guitar; Pinetop Perkins, piano & vocals; Sunnyland Slim, piano & vocals; Ted Harvey, drums; Timothy Taylor, drums)
Tracks: Cotton Crop Blues
How'd You Learn to Shake It Like That; Walkin' by Myself; You're Sweet; If You Don't Want Me Baby; Built Up from the Ground; Cold Cold Feeling; Sad Letter Blues; Bad Boy; Look on Yonder's Wall; Things I Used to Do; Caldonia; Double Trouble

Antone's 20th Anniversary (1986 LP) / Antone's Records / 74703
(Bill Campbell, guitar; Bob Stroger, bass; Hubert Sumlin, guitar; James Cotton, harp & vocals; Jimmy Rogers, guitar & vocals; Luther Tucker, guitar; Pinetop Perkins, piano; Ted Harvey, drums)
Tracks: Chicago Bound; Got My Mojo Working

Antone's Anniversary Anthology Vol. 2: 15th Anniversary (1991 CD) / Antone's Records / PCD-1817
(Willie Big Eyes Smith, drums; Bob Stroger, bass; Chester King, guitar; Derek O'Brien, guitar; Calvin Fuzz Jones, piano; Hubert Sumlin, guitar; James Cotton, harp & vocals; Jimmy Rogers, guitar & vocals; Matt Murphy, guitar; Mel Brown, harp; Pinetop Perkins, harp; Snooky Pryor, harp & vocals; Ted Harvey, drums)
Tracks: Chicago Bound; Sloppy Drunk; Trouble Blues; Shake for Me; Everything Is Going to Be All Right; Natural Ball; Moanin' at Midnight; Evan's Shuffle; Black Cat Bone; Same Thing Could Happen to You; High Jack

Big Moose Walker: Chicago Bound (1989 CD) / Wolf Records / CD 120.861
(Big Moose Walker, piano; Billy Branch, harp; Jimmy D. Lane, guitar & vocals; Jimmy Rogers, guitar & vocals; John Primer, guitar; Luther Adams, guitar; Timothy Taylor, drums; Willie Kent, bass)
Tracks: Anna Lee; Chicago Bound; Going Away Baby; Last Time; Lemon Squeezer; One Room Little Country Shack; Sloppy Drunk; St. Louis; Whoopin' Foolin' with You

Bill Hickey & Hubert Sumlin: Bill's Blues (1994 CD) / Atomic Theory Records / ATD 1112
(Bill Hickey, harp; Bob Stroger, bass; Charles Lewandowsky, piano; Hubert Sumlin,

guitar; Jimmy D. Lane, guitar & vocals; Jimmy Rogers, guitar & vocals; Robert Covington, drums; Sam Burkhardt, saxophone; Willie Murphy, guitar)

Tracks: Crazy Woman; Slick Chick; When It Comes to Love; Feed Me; I Am the Blues; Talk to Me Baby; Easy; Shake, Rattle, and Roll; Put the Kettle On

Bluebird (1994 CD) / Analogue Productions Originals / APO 2001

(Carey Bell, harp; Dave Myers, bass; Jimmy D. Lane, guitar & vocals; Jimmy Rogers, guitar & vocals; Johnnie Johnson, piano; Ted Harvey, drums)

Tracks: Big Boss Man; Blue and Lonesome; Blue Bird; Blues Falling; Howlin' for My Darling; I Lost a Good Woman; I'm Tired of Crying over You; Jammin' with Johnnie; Lemon Squeezer; Rock Me; Saint Louis Blues; Smokestack Lightning; That Ain't It (Baby I Need Your Love); Walkin' by Myself; Why Are You So Mean to Me

Blues Blues Blues (1999 CD) / Atlantic / 83148–2

(Big Crawford, bass; Carey Bell, harp; Eric Clapton, guitar; Jeff Healey, vocals; Jimmy D. Lane, guitar & vocals; Jimmy Page, guitar; Jimmy Rogers, guitar & vocals; John Koenig, guitar; Johnnie Johnson, piano; Keith Richards, guitar; Kim Wilson, harp; Lowell Fulson, guitar & vocals; Mick Jagger, vocals; Robert Plant, vocals; Stephen Stills, vocals; Taj Mahal, vocals & harp; Ted Harvey, drums)

Tracks: Going Away Baby; Ludella; That's All Right; Blow Wind Blow; Blues All Day Long; Trouble No More; Bright Lights Big City; Ev'ry Day I Have the Blues; Sweet Home Chicago; Don't Start Me to Talkin'; Worried Life Blues; Gonna Shoot You Right Down (Boom Boom)

Blues Queen Sylvia w/Jimmy Dawkins: Midnight Baby (1994 CD) / Evidence Music / ECD 26057

(Carey Bell, harp; Honeyboy Otis, drums; Jimmy Rogers, guitar; Louisiana Red, guitar; Lovie Lee, piano)

Tracks: I Love You; Baby, What Do I Do

Bob Corritore: All-Star Blues Sessions (1999 CD) / HGM Sound Recordings / HGM1009

(Bob Corritore, harp; Buddy Reed, guitar; Chico Chism, drums; Jimmy Rogers, guitar & vocals; Paul Thomas, bass; S. E. Willis, piano)

Track: Out on the Road

The Bob Riedy Chicago Blues Band: Lake Michigan Ain't No River (2004 CD) / Chicago Sound Enterprises / CSR 2005

(Bob Riedy, piano; Carey Bell, harp; Frank Capek, guitar; Richard "Hubcap" Robinson, drums; Jim Wydra, bass; Jimmy Rogers, guitar & vocals; John Littlejohn, guitar & vocals; Johnny Young, mandolin; Sam Lay, drums)

Tracks: Back at the Chicken Shack; Dust My Broom; Have You Ever; House Rocker;
Johnny's Jump; Keep on Looking; Mandolin Boogie; My Eyes (Keep Me in Trou-
ble); Pig Ear Rag; Reconsider Baby; Slick Chick; Sloppy Drunk; Walkin' by Myself;
Why Did You Break My Heart

Chicago Blues at Home (1977 LP) / Advent Productions / ADVENT 2806
(Andrew McMahon, guitar; Bob Myers, vocal & harmonica; Eddie Taylor, vocal &
guitar; Homesick James Williamson, vocal & guitar; Jimmy Rogers, guitar & vo-
cals; John Littlejohn, guitar & vocals; Johnny Shines, vocal & guitar; Louis Myers,
vocals & guitar; Lou Ella Smith, conga drum; Phillip Walker, guitar)
Tracks: Back Door Friend; Ludella; Mean Old World; What Have I Done; The Moon
Is Rising; Slidin'; Going Back to the Ghetto; Greyhound Bus; Stop Breaking Down;
Train Fare Home; Ramblin'; Tell Me Who; Short Haired Woman; Right Kind of
Life; Mean Red Spider; Jackson Town; Tell Me Baby

Chicago Blues at Home (1995 CD) / Testament Records / TCD 5028
(Andrew McMahon, guitar; Bob Myers, vocal & harmonica; Eddie Taylor, vocal &
guitar; Homesick James Williamson, vocal & guitar; Jimmy Rogers, guitar & vo-
cals; John Littlejohn, guitar & vocals; Johnny Shines, vocal & guitar; Louis Myers,
vocals & guitar; Lou Ella Smith, conga drum; Phillip Walker, guitar)
Tracks: Back Door Friend; Ludella; Mean Old World; What Have I Done; The Moon
Is Rising; Slidin'; Going Back to the Ghetto; Greyhound Bus; Stop Breaking Down;
Train Fare Home; Ramblin'; Tell Me Who; Short Haired Woman; Right Kind of
Life; Mean Red Spider; Jackson Town; Tell Me Baby

Chicago Blues Masters Volume 2: Jimmy Rogers (1995 CD) / Capitol Records / CDP
742383391622
(Bob Riedy, piano; Dave Myers, bass; Frank Capek, guitar; Fred Below, drums; Fred-
die King, guitar; Richard "Hubcap" Robinson, drums; Jim Kahr, guitar; Jim Wydra,
bass; Jimmy Rogers, guitar & vocals; Louis Myers, guitar)
Tracks: Act Like You Love Me; Bad Luck Blues; Blues (Follow Me All Day Long);
Broken Hearted Blues; Brown Skinnned Woman; Dorcie Belle; Gold Tailed Bird;
House Rocker; I Lost a Good Woman; Information Please; Live at Ma Bea's;
Lonesome Blues; Pretty Baby; Slick Chick; Sloppy Drunk; That's All Right; You're
Sweet; You're the One

Chicago Boogie 1947 (1993 CD) / St. George Records / STG 1888
(Jimmy Rogers, guitar & vocals; Little Walter, harp)
Tracks: Little Store Blues (Take 1); Little Store Blues (Take 2)

Chicago's Jimmy Rogers Sings the Blues (1990 CD) / Shelter Records / SRZ 8016
(Jimmy Rogers, guitar & vocals; Bob Riedy, piano; Dave Myers, bass; Fred Below,
    drums; Freddie King, guitar; Jimmy Dawkins, guitar & vocals; Louis Myers, guitar)
Tracks: Bad Luck Blues; Blues (Follow Me All Day Long); Broken Hearted Blues;
    Brown Skinnned Woman; Dorcie Belle; Gold Tailed Bird; House Rocker; I Lost
    a Good Woman; Information Please; Lonesome Blues; Pretty Baby; Slick Chick;
    Sloppy Drunk; That's All Right; You're Sweet; You're the One; Live at Ma Bea's

Down Home Blues Classics: Chicago 1946–1954 (1999 CD) / Secret Records Limited /
    BVBCD1014
(A. J. Gladney, drums; Big Crawford, bass; Eddie Taylor, guitar; Elga Edmonds,
    drums; Fred Below, drums; Henry Gray, piano; Hubert Sumlin, guitar; Jimmy
    Rogers, guitar & vocals; Jimmy Rogers, harp & vocals; Leroy Foster, guitar; Little
    Walter, harp; Muddy Waters, guitar; Otis Spann, piano; Po' Bob Woodfork, guitar;
    S. P. Leary, drums; Shoe Shine Johnny, guitar & vocals; Sunnyland Slim, piano &
    vocals; Willie Dixon, bass)
Tracks: Act Like You Love Me; Left Me with a Broken Heart; Out on the Road; Blow
    Wind Blow; Round About Boogie; Joliet Blues; You Can't Live Long; Dark Road;
    Early Morning; Who's Gonna Be Your Sweet Man; Turn the Lamp Down; Mad
    Love; Going Back to Memphis; Devil Is a Busy Man; So Glad I Found You

Drop Down Mama (1970 LP) / Chess Records / Chess LP 411
(Big Crawford, bass; Elga Edmonds, drums; Floyd Jones, guitar & vocal; Jimmy Rog-
    ers, guitar; Little Walter, harp; Willie Coven, drums)
Tracks: Joliet Blues; You Can't Live Long; Playhouse; Dark Road

Drop Down Mama (1990 CD) / Chess Records / CHD-93002
(Big Crawford, bass; Elga Edmonds, drums; Floyd Jones, guitar & vocal; Jimmy Rog-
    ers, guitar; Little Walter, harp; Willie Coven, drums)
Tracks: Joliet Blues; You Can't Live Long; Playhouse; Dark Road

Feelin' Good (1984 LP) / Murray Brothers Blues Records / MP 1006
(Bill Stuve, bass; Bill Swartz, drums; Honey Alexander-Piazza, piano; Jimmy Rogers,
    guitar & vocals; Junior Watson, guitar; Rod Piazza, harp)
Tracks: Angel Child; Blue and Lonesome; Chicago Bound; Rock This House; Slick
    Chick; St. Louis; Tricky Woman; You Don't Know; You're Sweet

Feelin' Good (1994 CD) / Murray Brothers Blues Records / BPCD 5018
(Alex Schultz, bass; Bill Stuve, bass; Bill Swartz, drums; Honey Alexander-Piazza,
    piano; Jimi Bott, drums; Jimmy Rogers, guitar & vocals; Junior Watson, guitar;
    Rod Piazza, harp; Steve Killman, guitar)

Tracks: Angel Child; Blue and Lonesome; Chicago Bound; Harp Throb; Rock This House; Rock with You Baby; Slick Chick; St. Louis; Tricky Woman; You Don't Know; You're Sweet; Sharp Harp

Gold Tailed Bird (1973 LP) / Shelter Records / SW-8921
(Bob Riedy, piano; Dave Myers, bass; Fred Below, drums; Freddie King, guitar; Jimmy Rogers, guitar & vocals; Louis Myers, guitar)
Tracks: Act Like You Love Me; Bad Luck Blues; Broken Hearted Blues; Brown Skinnned Woman; Gold Tailed Bird; Information Please; Live at Ma Bea's; Lonesome Blues; Pretty Baby; That's All Right; You're Sweet; You're the One

Jimmy Rogers and Left Hand Frank: The Dirty Dozens! (1985 LP) / JSP Records / JSP 1090
(Bob Brunning, bass; Jimmy Rogers, guitar & vocals; Left Hand Frank, guitar; Ray Weston, drums)
Tracks: Baby Please; Cleo's Gone; Crazy Woman Blues; Dirty Dozens; Fishing in My Pond; Honky Tonk; Information Please; Mean Red Spider; Oh Baby; One Room Country Shack; Take a Walk; You're Sweet

Jimmy Rogers and Left Hand Frank: The Dirty Dozens! (2007 CD) / Blues Interactions Inc. / PCD 23890
(Bob Brunning, bass; Jimmy Rogers, guitar & vocals; Left Hand Frank, guitar; Ray Weston, drums)
Tracks: Baby Please; Blue and Lonesome; Chicago Bound; Cleo's Gone; Crazy Woman Blues; Dirty Dozens; Fishing in My Pond; Honky Tonk; Information Please; Mean Red Spider; Oh Baby; One Room Country Shack; Rock This House; Take a Walk; You're Sweet

Jimmy Rogers and Left Hand Frank: The Dirty Dozens! 30th Anniversary Reissue (2009 CD) / Blues Interactions Inc. / JSP8817
(Bob Brunning, bass; Jimmy Rogers, guitar & vocals; Left Hand Frank, guitar; Ray Weston, drums)
Tracks: Baby Please; Blue and Lonesome; Chicago Bound; Cleo's Gone; Crazy Woman Blues; Dirty Dozens; Fishing in My Pond; Honky Tonk; Information Please; Mean Red Spider; Oh Baby; One Room Country Shack; Rock This House; Take a Walk; You're Sweet

Jimmy Rogers: Chess Blues Masters (1976 LP) / Chess Records / 2ACMB-207
(A. J. Gladney, drums; Big Crawford, bass; Big Walter Horton, harp; Eddie Ware, piano; Elga Edmonds, drums; Ernest Cotton, tenor sax; Francis Clay, drums; Fred Below, drums; Fred Robinson, guitar; George Hunter, drums; J. T. Brown, tenor sax; Jimmy Rogers, guitar & vocals; Johnny Jones, piano; Little Walter, harp; Lu-

ther Tucker, guitar; Mighty Joe Young, guitar; Muddy Waters, guitar; Odie Payne, drums; Otis Spann, piano; Po' Bob Woodfork, guitar; S. P. Leary, drums; Wayne Bennett, guitar; Willie Dixon, bass)

Tracks: Left Me with a Broken Heart; Mistreated Baby; Rock This House; What Have I Done; You Don't Know; Blues All Day Long; The World Is in a Tangle; Trace of You; Cryin' Shame; My Baby Don't Love Me No More; Give Me Another Chance; I Can't Believe; One Kiss; Don't You Know My Baby; This Has Never Been; My Last Meal; My Little Machine; Today, Today, Blues; She Loves Another Man; Hard Working Man; Chance to Love; What's the Matter?; You're the One (First Version); If It Ain't Me (Who Are You Thinking Of); Can't Keep from Worrying

Jimmy Rogers: The Complete Chess Recordings (1997 CD1) / Chess (MCA) / CHD2–9372 CD1

(Jimmy Rogers, guitar & vocals A. J. Gladney, drums; Big Crawford, bass; Big Walter Horton, harp; Eddie Ware, piano; Elga Edmonds, drums; Ernest Cotton, tenor sax; Francis Clay, drums; Fred Below, drums; Henry Gray, piano; J. T. Brown, tenor sax; Johnny Jones, piano; Little Walter, harp; Muddy Waters, guitar; Odie Payne, drums; Po' Bob Woodfork, guitar; Robert Lockwood Jr., guitar; S. P. Leary, drums; Willie Dixon, bass)

Tracks: Act Like You Love Me; Back Door Friend; Chicago Bound; Going Away Baby; I Used to Have a Woman; Last Time; Left Me with a Broken Heart; Ludella; Mistreated Baby; Money, Marbles, and Chalk; Out on the Road; Sloppy Drunk; That's All Right; You're the One; Blues All Day Long; The World Is in a Tangle; Cryin' Shame; My Little Machine; Today, Today, Blues; She Loves Another Man; Hard Working Man; Chance to Love; What's the Matter?; You're the One (First Version); If It Ain't Me (Who Are You Thinking Of)

Jimmy Rogers: The Complete Chess Recordings (1997 CD2) / Chess (MCA) / CHD2–9372 CD2

(Jimmy Rogers, guitar & vocals; A. J. Gladney, drums; Big Crawford, bass; Big Walter Horton, harp; Elga Edmonds, drums; Francis Clay, drums; Fred Below, drums; Fred Robinson, guitar; George Hunter, drums; Jody Williams, guitar; Little Walter, harp; Luther Tucker, guitar; Margaret Whitfield, vocals; Mighty Joe Young, guitar; Odie Payne, drums; Otis Spann, piano; Reggie Boyd, guitar; Robert Lockwood Jr., guitar; S. P. Leary, drums; Willie Dixon, bass)

Tracks: Act Like You Love Me; Can't Sleep for Worrying; Can't Sleep for Worrying (Alternate); Rock This House; Walkin' by Myself; What Have I Done; You Don't Know; Don't Turn Me Down; Trace of You; My Baby Don't Love Me No More; I Can't Believe; One Kiss; Don't You Know My Baby; Looka Here; This Has Never Been; My Last Meal; What Have I Done (Alternate); My Baby Don't Love Me No More (Alternate); Trace of You (Alternate); Don't You Know My Baby (Alternate); Don't Turn Me Down (Alternate); This Has Never Been (Alternate); Rock This House (Alternate); My Last Meal (Alternate); You Don't Know (Alternate); Ludella (Alternate)

Jimmy Rogers w/Ronnie Earl & the Broadcasters (1994 CD) / Bullseye Blues/Crosscut Records / CD BB 9544
(Dave Maxwell, piano; Jimmy Rogers, guitar & vocals; Mudcat Ward, bass; Per Hanson, drums; Ronnie Earl, guitar; Sugar Ray Norcia, harp)
Tracks: Gold Tailed Bird; Got My Mojo Working; Can't Sleep for Worrying; Left Me with a Broken Heart; Rock This House; Shake Your Money Maker; Walkin' by Myself; Why Did You Do It; You're Sweet; Okie Dokie Stomp; Blues in D-Natural; Same Old Blues

Koko Taylor: Southside Lady (1992 CD) / Evidence Music Inc. / ECD 26007–2
(Dave Myers, bass; Fred Below, drums; Jimmy Rogers, guitar; Koko Taylor, vocals; Louis Myers, guitar; Willie Mabon, piano)
Tracks: Big Boss Man; Black Nights; Got My Mojo Working; I Got What It Takes; I Love a Lover Like You; I'm a Little Mixed Up; I'm Gonna Get Lucky; Love Me to Death; Twenty-Nine Ways; Twenty-Nine Ways (Live); Wang Dang Doodle; What Kind of Man Is This?; Wonder Why; I Got What It Takes (Live)

Left Hand Frank: Chicago Blues (1979 LP) / JSP Records / JSP 1008
(Bob Brunning, bass; Jimmy Rogers, guitar & vocals; Left Hand Frank, guitar; Ray Weston, drums)
Tracks: Baby Please; Blue and Lonesome; Chicago Bound; Crazy Woman Blues; Dirty Dozens; Fishing in My Pond; Information Please; Mean Red Spider; Oh Baby; Rock This House; Take a Walk; You're Sweet; You Don't Have to Go

Left Hand Frank: Live (1998 LP) / JSP Records / JSP 1043
(Bob Brunning, bass; Jimmy Rogers, guitar & vocals; Left Hand Frank, guitar; Ray Weston, drums)
Tracks: Brown Skinnned Woman; Can't Sleep for Worrying; Ludella; Sloppy Drunk; That's All Right; Walkin' by Myself; Linda Lu; Frank's Blues; Blues for Freddie

Legacy w/Jimmy D. Lane (1998 CD) / APO / APO2005
(Big Crawford, bass; Carey Bell, harp; Dave Krull, piano; Hubert Sumlin, guitar; Jimmy D. Lane, guitar & vocals; Jimmy Rogers, guitar & vocals; Sam Lay, drums)
Tracks: Another Mule Kickin' in My Stall; One Room Country Shack; Clue Me; Four O'Clock in the Morning; Going Downtown; In This Bed; Call It Blues; Big House; Baby's Mule; Dem Blues; Pride; It's All Good

Little Walter & Muddy Waters: Chicago Bound (1970 LP) / Chess Records / Chess LP 407
(Big Crawford, bass; Big Walter Horton, harp; Eddie Ware, piano; Elga Edmonds, drums; Ernest Cotton, tenor sax; Fred Below, drums; Henry Gray, piano; J. T. Brown, tenor sax; Jimmy Rogers, guitar & vocals; Little Walter, harp; Muddy Waters, guitar; Otis Spann, piano; Willie Dixon, bass)
Tracks: Act Like You Love Me; Back Door Friend; Blues Leave Me Alone; Chicago Bound; Going Away Baby; I Used to Have a Woman; Last Time; Ludella; Money, Marbles, and Chalk; Out on the Road; Sloppy Drunk; That's All Right; Walkin' by Myself; You're the One

Little Walter & Muddy Waters: Chicago Bound (1990 CD) / Chess Records / CHD 93000
(Big Crawford, bass; Big Walter Horton, harp; Eddie Ware, piano; Elga Edmonds, drums; Ernest Cotton, tenor sax; Fred Below, drums; Henry Gray, piano; J. T. Brown, tenor sax; Jimmy Rogers, guitar & vocals; Little Walter, harp; Muddy Waters, guitar; Otis Spann, piano; Willie Dixon, bass)
Tracks: Act Like You Love Me; Back Door Friend; Blues Leave Me Alone; Chicago Bound; Going Away Baby; I Used to Have a Woman; Last Time; Ludella; Money, Marbles, and Chalk; Out on the Road; Sloppy Drunk; That's All Right; Walkin' by Myself; You're the One

Ludella (1990 LP) / Antone's Records and Tapes / ANT0012LP
(Willie Big Eyes Smith, drums; Bob Stroger, bass; Derek O'Brien, guitar; Calvin Fuzz Jones, bass; Hubert Sumlin, guitar; Jimmy Rogers, guitar & vocals; Kim Wilson, harp; Pinetop Perkins, piano; Ted Harvey, drums)
Tracks: Chicago Bound; Gold Tailed Bird; Got My Mojo Working; Can't Sleep for Worrying; Ludella; Monkey Faced Woman; Rock This House; Sloppy Drunk; Why Did You Do It; You're Sweet

Ludella (1990 CD) / Antone's Records and Tapes / ANT0012 CD
(Willie Big Eyes Smith, drums; Bob Stroger, bass; Derek O'Brien, guitar; Calvin Fuzz Jones, bass; Hubert Sumlin, guitar; Jimmy Rogers, guitar & vocals; Kim Wilson, harp; Pinetop Perkins, piano; Ted Harvey, drums)
Tracks: Chicago Bound; Gold Tailed Bird; Got My Mojo Working; Can't Sleep for Worrying; Ludella; Monkey Faced Woman; Naptown; Rock This House; Sloppy Drunk; Why Did You Do It; You're Sweet; You're Sweet (Alternate); Why Did You Do It (Alternate)

Muddy Waters: I'm Ready (1978 LP) / Epic / K 90565E-S1
(Willie Big Eyes Smith, drums; Big Walter Horton, harp; Bob Margolin, bass; Jerry Portnoy, harp; Jimmy Rogers, guitar; Johnny Winter, guitar; Muddy Waters, guitar; Pinetop Perkins, piano)

Tracks: 33 Years; Copper Brown; Good Morning Little School Girl; I'm Ready; I'm Your Hoochie Coochie Man; Mamie; Rock Me; Screamin' and Cryin'; Who Do You Trust

Muddy Waters: I'm Ready (2004 CD) / Epic / EK 90565E
(Willie Big Eyes Smith, drums; Big Walter Horton, harp; Bob Margolin, bass; Jerry Portnoy, harp; Jimmy Rogers, guitar; Johnny Winter, guitar; Muddy Waters, guitar; Pinetop Perkins, piano)
Tracks: 33 Years; Copper Brown; Good Morning Little School Girl; I'm Ready; I'm Your Hoochie Coochie Man; Lonely Man Blues; Mamie; No Escape from the Blues; Rock Me; Screamin' and Cryin'; That's All Right; Who Do You Trust

San Francisco Blues Fest (1981 LP) / Solid Smoke Records / SS-8010
(Byron Sutton, bass; Jimmy Rogers, guitar & vocals; Lee Hildebrand, drums; Louis Myers, guitar; Mark Naftalin, piano)
Tracks: House Rocker; Ludella; That's All Right; Walkin' by Myself; You're Sweet

Sloppy Drunk (1976 LP) / Blues Interactions Inc. / (1976) R-9930507
(Dave Myers, bass; Fred Below, drums; Jimmy Rogers, guitar & vocals; Louis Myers, guitar; Willie Mabon, piano)
Tracks: Can't Sleep for Worrying; I Lost a Good Woman; Last Time; Left Me with a Broken Heart; Mistreated Baby; Pretty Baby; Shelby County; Slick Chick; Sloppy Drunk; Tricky Woman; You're Sweet

Sloppy Drunk (1993 CD) / Blues Interactions Inc. / (1993) PCD-5516
(Dave Myers, bass; Fred Below, drums; Jimmy Rogers, guitar & vocals; Louis Myers, guitar; Willie Mabon, piano)
Tracks: Gold Tailed Bird; Can't Sleep for Worrying; I Lost a Good Woman; Last Time; Left Me with a Broken Heart; Ludella; Mistreated Baby; Pretty Baby; Shelby County; Slick Chick; Sloppy Drunk; Sloppy Drunk II; That's All Right; Tricky Woman; Walkin' by Myself; You're Sweet

Steady Rollin' Bob Margolin: Chicago Blues (1991 CD) / Powerhouse Records / POW 4105
(Willie Big Eyes Smith, drums; Bob Margolin, guitar & vocals; Calvin Fuzz Jones, piano; Jimmy Rogers, guitar; Kim Wilson, harp; Pinetop Perkins, harp)
Tracks: She's So Pretty; She and the Devil; Sugar Sweet; Steady Rollin' Man

Stickshift (1982 LP) / Teardrop Records / VPA TR-2002
(Hip Linkchain, guitar; Jimmy Rogers, guitar & vocals)
Tracks: Dorcie Belle; Going Down Slow; Blow Wind Blow; Somebody Stole My Mule; Don't Your Peaches Look Mellow; I Don't Know; 61092973; Find Myself; Floating Bridge; Cold Chills; Rock Me Baby

T-Bone Walker: T-Bone Blues (1989 CD) / Atlantic Jazz / 8020–2
(Francis Clay, drums; Jimmy Rogers, guitar; Junior Wells, harp; T-Bone Walker, guitar
    & vocals; Willie Dixon, bass)
Tracks: Play On Little Girl; T-Bone Blues Special

That's All Right (1974 LP) / Blues Interactions Inc. / (1974) R-9930507
(Dave Myers, bass; Fred Below, drums; Jimmy Rogers, guitar & vocals; Louis Myers,
    guitar; Willie Mabon, piano)
Tracks: Gold Tailed Bird; I Lost a Good Woman; Last Time; Ludella; Shelby County;
    Sloppy Drunk; That's All Right; Tricky Woman; Walkin' by Myself; You're Sweet

That's All Right (1999 CD) / Blues Interactions Inc. / (1999) PCD-5516
(Dave Myers, bass; Fred Below, drums; Jimmy Rogers, guitar & vocals; Louis Myers,
    guitar; Willie Mabon, piano)
Tracks: Gold Tailed Bird; Can't Sleep for Worrying; Can't Sleep for Worrying (Alter-
    nate); I Lost a Good Woman; Last Time; Left Me with a Broken Heart; Ludella;
    Mistreated Baby; Pretty Baby; Pretty Baby II; Shelby County; Slick Chick; Sloppy
    Drunk; Sloppy Drunk II; Sloppy Drunk III; That's All Right; Tricky Woman;
    Walkin' by Myself; You're Sweet

Wild Child Butler: Lickin' Gravy (1998 CD) / M.C. Records / MC0036
(Aaron Burton, bass; Jimmy Rogers, guitar; Joe Kelly, guitar; Joe Zaklan, guitar; Pine-
    top Perkins, piano; Sam Lay, drums; Wild Child Butler, harp)
Tracks: Gravy Child; Rooster Blues; Speed; Spoonful; Everybody Got a Mojo; Funky
    Butt Lover; None of Nothing; Built for Comfort; I Love You from Now On; My Baby
    Got Another Man; Love Like a Butterfly

You're the One: The Chicago Blues Masters (1984 LP) / MCA/Chess Records / CH2–92505
(A. J. Gladney, drums; Big Crawford, bass; Big Walter Horton, harp; Eddie Ware,
    piano; Elga Edmonds, drums; Ernest Cotton, tenor sax; Francis Clay, drums; Fred
    Below, drums; Fred Robinson, guitar; George Hunter, drums; J. T. Brown, tenor
    sax; Jimmy Rogers, guitar & vocals; Johnny Jones, piano; Little Walter, harp; Lu-
    ther Tucker, guitar; Mighty Joe Young, guitar; Muddy Waters, guitar; Odie Payne,
    drums; Otis Spann, piano; Po' Bob Woodfork, guitar; S. P. Leary, drums; Wayne
    Bennett, guitar; Willie Dixon, bass)
Tracks: Left Me with a Broken Heart; Mistreated Baby; Rock This House; What Have
    I Done; You Don't Know; Blues All Day Long; The World Is in a Tangle; Trace of
    You; Cryin' Shame; My Baby Don't Love Me No More; Give Me Another Chance;
    I Can't Believe; One Kiss; Don't You Know My Baby; This Has Never Been; My
    Last Meal; My Little Machine; Today, Today, Blues; She Loves Another Man; Hard
    Working Man; Chance to Love; What's the Matter?; You're the One (First Version);
    If It Ain't Me (Who Are You Thinking Of); Can't Keep from Worrying

BIBLIOGRAPHY

BOOKS

Cohodas, Nadine. *Spinning Blues into Gold: The Chess Brothers and the Legendary Chess Records.* New York: St. Martin's, 2000.

Dixon, Willie, and Don Snowden. *I Am the Blues: The Willie Dixon Story.* New York: Da Capo Press, 1989.

Edwards, David "Honeyboy." *The World Don't Owe Me Nothing: The Life and Times of Delta Bluesman Honeyboy Edwards.* Chicago: Chicago Review Press, 1997.

Fancourt, Les, and Bob McGrath. *The Blues Discography, 1943–1970.* [West Vancouver] Canada: Eyeball Productions, 2006.

Field, Kim. *Harmonicas, Harps, and Heavy Breathers: The Evolution of the People's Instrument.* New York: Cooper Square Press, 1993.

Forte, Dan. "Jimmy Rogers." In *Blues Guitar: The Men Who Made the Music,* edited by Jas Obrecht, 160–67. San Francisco: GPI Books, 1993.

Glover, Tony, Scott Dirks, and Ward Gaines. *Blues with a Feeling: The Little Walter Story.* New York: Routledge, 2002.

Gordon, Robert. *Can't Be Satisfied: The Life and Times of Muddy Waters.* Boston: Little, Brown, 2002.

———. "Jimmy Rogers." In *Encyclopedia of the Blues,* edited by Edward Komara, 843–45. New York: Routledge, 2006.

Guralnick, Peter. *Feel Like Going Home: Portraits in Blues and Rock 'n' Roll.* Boston: Bay Back Books, 1999.

Hummel, Mark. *Big Road Blues : 12 Bars on I-80*. San Mateo, CA: Mountain Top Publishing, 2012.

O'Neal, Jim, and Amy Van Singel. *The Voice of the Blues: Classic Interviews from* Living Blues *Magazine*. New York: Routledge, 2002.

Palmer, Robert. *Deep Blues*. New York: Penguin Books, 1982.

Romano, Will. *Incurable Blues: The Troubles and Triumph of Blues Legend Hubert Sumlin*. San Francisco: Backbeat Books, 2005.

Rowe, Mike. *Chicago Blues: The City and the Music*. New York: Da Capo Press, 1973.

Ruppli, Michel. *The Chess Labels: A Discography*. Vol. 1. Westport, CT: Greenwood Press, 1983.

Segrest, James, and Mark Hoffman. *Moanin' at Midnight: The Life and Times of Howlin' Wolf*. New York: Thunder's Mouth Press, 2004.

Tooze, Sandra B. *Muddy Waters: The Mojo Man*. Toronto: ECW Press, 1997.

MAGAZINES

Brisbin, John. "Jimmy Rogers: I'm Havin' Fun Right Today." *Living Blues* 135 (September/October 1997): 12–27.

——. "Obituaries: Jimmy Rogers." *Living Blues* 138 (March/April 1998): 74.

——. "Pryor Arrangements." *Blues Access* (Winter 1999): 52–54.

Broven, John J. "Walking by Myself: A Commentary on Jimmy Rogers, Blues Singer." *Blues Unlimited 23* (June 1965): 3.

Cappuccio, Robert. "Blues News." *Living Blues* 15 (Winter 1973–74): 6.

Darwen, Norman. "I Wrote Jimmy Rogers a Letter (Chats with Steve Guyger)." *Harmonica World* (June/July 1993): 15.

——. "The Chess Boys Got to It and It Exploded." *Blues & Rhythm* 82 (1993): 4–7.

DeKoster, Jim. "LPs." *Living Blues* 15 (Winter 1973–74): 35.

Elanger, Louis X. "Blue 'n' Boogie." *Weekly Soho News*, March 12–18, 1980, 24.

Forte, Dan. "Jimmy Rogers and the Pioneers of Chicago Blues." *Guitar Player* 21 (August 1987): 67–78.

——. "Jimmy Rogers: Feelin' Good." *Guitar Player* (April 1984): 120.

Hammond, Scott. "Blues News." *Living Blues* 16 (1974): 3.

Hess, Norbert. "American Folk Blues Festival '72." *Living Blues* 11 (Winter 1972–73): 6.

——. "Blues News." *Living Blues* 7 (Winter 1971–72): 36.

——. "Blues News." *Living Blues* 17 (Summer 1974): 7.

——. "Blues News." *Living Blues* 19 (January/February 1975): 6.

Hunter, Jack. "BluesLetter," *Living Blues* 82 (September/October 1988): 10.

Iglauer, Bruce. "Blues News." *Living Blues* 2 (Summer 1970): 12.

——. "Live Chicago Blues." *Living Blues* 4 (Winter 1970–71): 24.

——. "LPs." *Living Blues* 4 (Winter 1970–71): 33.

——. "Record Review." *Living Blues* 1 (Spring 1970): 27–29.

Jordan, Miles. "BluesLetter," *Living Blues* 81 (1987): 6

Kilian, Klaus. "Living BluesLetter," *Living Blues* 68 (1986): 8

King, Eric. "Living BluesLetter," *Living Blues* 75 (1987): 10.

Lambert, Dan. "Blues in El Paso: The Border Blues Festival and Señor Blues." *Living Blues* 58 (Winter 1983): 23.

Lazar, Helen Doob. "BluesLetter," *Living Blues* 74 (1987): 4.

——. "Interview: James Cotton. " *Living Blues* 76 (1987): 29.

Leiser, Willie. "Down in the Alley (Part 2)." *Blues Unlimited* 101 (May 1973): 17.

Lornell, Kip. "Records." *Living Blues* 7 (Winter 1971–72): 36.

Margolin, Bob. "Muddy Waters—Can't Be Satisfied." *Blues Review* 20.

Mazzolini, Tom. "Blues News." *Living Blues* 15 (Winter 1973–74): 40.

Melish, Ilene. "The Man Who Shaped a Sound." *Melody Maker*, October 6, 1979, 37–38.

Moon, D. Thomas. "All about the Beat: The Elga Edmonds Story." *Living Blues* 136 (November/December 1997): 36–41.

——. "Bob Stroger: First Call Bass." *Living Blues* 158 (July/August 2001): 26–35.

Nelson, David. "Obituaries: Hip Linkchain." *Living Blues* 87 (July/August 1989): 36.

O'Brien, Justin. "The Dark Road of Floyd Jones." *Living Blues* 58 (Winter 1983): 11.

O'Neal, Amy. "Snooky Pryor." *Living Blues* 6 (Autumn 1971): 4–5.

O'Neal, Jim. "Blues News." *Living Blues* 6 (Autumn 1971): 15, 48.

——. "Blues News." *Living Blues* 8 (Spring 1972): 28.

——. "Blues News." *Living Blues* 9 (Summer 1972): 22.

——. "Blues News." *Living Blues* 13 (Summer 1973): 40.

——. "Blues News." *Living Blues* 14 (Autumn 1973): 3.

——. "Blues News." *Living Blues* 20 (March/April 1975): 8.

——. "Blues News." *Living Blues* 21 (May/June 1975): 7.

——. "Blues News." *Living Blues* 23 (September/October 1975): 8.

——. "Blues News." *Living Blues* 24 (November/December 1975): 49.

——. "45s." *Living Blues* 20 (March/April 1975): 54.

——. "Interview: Houston Stackhouse." *Living Blues* 17 (Summer 1974): 30.

——. "Obituaries: Johnny Young." *Living Blues* 17 (Summer 1974): 6.

——. "The 1983 W.C. Handy International Blues Awards." *Living Blues* 58 (Winter 1983): 14–17.

O'Neal, Jim, and Bill Greensmith. "Living Blues Interview: Jimmy Rogers." *Living Blues* 14 (Autumn 1973): 11–20.

O'Neal, Jim, and Cary Baker. "Chicago Blues Label Guide." *Living Blues* 12 (Spring 1973): 8–9.

O'Neal, Jim, and Wesley Race. "Chicago Blues Club Guide." *Living Blues* 11 (Winter 1972–73): 8–10.

O'Neal, Jim, Steve Wisner, and David Nelson. "Snooky Pryor: I Started the Big Noise around Chicago." *Living Blues* 123 (September/October 1995): 11.

Palmer, Robert. "Muddy Waters: The Delta Son Never Sets." *Rolling Stone* 275, October 5, 1978, 53–56.

Paulus, George. "Rare Jams: George Paulus Discovers Jimmy Rogers' First Record." *Blues & Rhythm* 18 (1993): 167.

Pointer-Jones, Sandra. "Jimmy Rogers: The Long Road to the Top." *Blues Revue* 14 (Fall 1994): 27.

Race, Wesley. "LPs." *Living Blues* 21 (May/June 1975): 46–47.

Rossez, Paul. "Living BluesLetter." *Living Blues* 73 (1987): 10.

Roth, Chris. "BluesLetter." *Living Blues* 83 (1987): 3.

Schuller, Tim. "Jimmy Rogers: Not Giving Up on the Blues." *Blues Access* 5 (Spring 1991): 112–13.

———. "Living BluesLetter." *Living Blues* 67 (1986): 4.

Smith, Chris. "Words, Words, Words." *Blues & Rhythm* 228 (April 2008): 22.

Tabor, Barney. "Jimmy Rogers: Still Burnin' 'Em Up and Going Strong at 70." *Blues Revue* 14 (Fall 1994): 21–22.

Townsley, Tom. "Jimmy Rogers: His Legacy Still Lives On." *Blues Revue* 14 (Fall 1994): 23–26.

Van Singel, Amy. "Blues News." *Living Blues* 17 (Summer 1974): 11.

Voce, Frank. "Jimmy Rogers." *Blues Unlimited* 44 (September 1972): 5–7.

Walters, David, Laurence Garman, and John Matthews. "Jimmy Rogers." *Blues Unlimited* 105 (December/January 1973–74): 13, 18.

Welding, Pete. "Blues News." *Living Blues* 16 (1974): 32.

———. "Interview: Johnny Shines." *Living Blues* 16 (Spring 1974): 32.

———. "Jimmy Rogers." *Blues Mentor* (Milwaukee Blues Unlimited) (February/March 1992): 1–2.

———. "LPs." *Living Blues* 16 (Spring 1974): 34.

NEWSPAPERS

Chapman, Tamara. "Learning to Hurt Brings Out the Blues." *El Paso Times*, September 4, 1983.

Chicago Defender. (1921–1967). November 25, 1950, 20.

———. (1910–1975). 18. ProQuest Historical Newspapers.

Cramer, Mel, and Peter Ward. "Blue Notes." *Bay State Banner* (Boston), March 6, 1980, 15.

Hubner, John. "Keeping the Blues Alive—Jimmy Rogers: More Than History." *Boston Phoenix*, July 22, 1980, 2, 12.

Johnson, Jeff. "Still Going Strong at 70: For Rogers, Blues Fest Is a Party." *Chicago Sun-Times*, June 5, 1994, 47.

Joyce, Mike. "Jimmy Rogers." *Washington Post*, July 24, 1980: Performing Arts Section, B-6.

Kening, Dan. "Quiet Giant." *Chicago Tribune*, November 7, 1989, 53.

Lioce, Tony. "Music." *Providence Journal*, July 11, 1980.

Palmer, Robert. "The Blues: Jimmy Rogers." *New York Times*, February 25, 1980.

Parsons, Russ. "Bluesman Gets Down to Basics." *Tribune Accent* (Albuquerque), September 9, 1983, B-1, B-5.

Perrone, Pierre. "Jagger Sings the Blues." *London Independent*, March 5, 1999. Available online at http://www.independent.co.uk/arts-entertainment/jagger-sings-the -blues-1078429.html.

Puente, Teresa. "Jimmy Rogers, Bluesman Who Teamed with Waters," *Chicago Tribune*, December 21, 1997. Available online at http://articles.chicagotribune.com/1997 -12-21/news/9712210287_1_muddy-waters-mr-rogers-jimmy-rogers.

Ratliff, Ben. "Jimmy Rogers, 73, Guitarist Specializing in Electric Blues." *New York Times*, December 20, 1997, 12.

Russell, David J. "Jimmy Rogers, Band Performs Tight Blues." *College Times* (Los Angeles), January 21, 1972.

Watrous, Peter. "Cabaret: Jimmy Rogers." *New York Times*, March 3, 1988.

Whiteis, David. "Floyd Jones: All by Himself." *Our Town* (Chicago), January 24, 1986, 45.

CD LINER NOTES

Aldin, Mary Katherine. *The Aristocrat of the Blues: The Best of Aristocrat Records*. MCA/ Chess (CHD2–9387), 1997.

———. *Jimmy Rogers: The Complete Chess Recordings The Chess 50th Anniversary Collection*. Chess Records (CHESS 2ACMB 207), January 1997.

———. *Muddy Waters: The Chess Box*. MCA/Chess (CHD3–80002), 1989.

———. *Muddy Waters—Rollin' Stone: The Golden Anniversary Collection*. Chess Records (MCA/Chess 088112301–2), 2000.

Bonner, Brett. *Memphis Minnie. Early Rhythm & Blues 1949 from the Rare Regal Sessions*. Biograph Records (COL-CD6937), 2007.

Brisbin, John. *Sunnyland Slim: House Rent Party*. Apollo Series (Delmark DD-665), 1992.

Koenig, John. *Blues Blues Blues: The Jimmy Rogers All-Stars*. (Atlantic 83148–2), 1999.

Margolin, Bob. *Chicago Blues*. Powerhouse Records (POW 4105), 1991.

———. *Muddy Waters: I'm Ready*. Epic/Legacy (EK90565), 1978.

Mazzolini, Tom. *San Francisco Blues Festival. Vol. 2*. Solid Smoke (SS-8010), 1981.

O'Neal, Jim. *Big Leon Brooks: Let's Go to Town*. Earwig (CD4931), 1994.

Pessiak, Herbert. *Jimmy Rogers & Big Moose Walker: Chicago Bound*. Wolf Records (CD 120.861), 1986.

Rowe, Mike. *The American Folk-Blues Festival: The British Tours, 1963–1966*. Hip-O Records (DVD). (B0008353–09), 2007.

———. *Down Home Blues Classics: Chicago, 1946–1954*. Disc 1. Boulevard Vintage (BVB DC1014S-UK), 2005.

Scott, Frank. *Chicago Blues at Home*. Testament Records (TCD 5028), 1995.

Shurman, Dick. *Bob Corritore All-Star Blues Sessions* (HMG 1009), 1999.

Slaven, Neal. *The OKeh Rhythm & Blues Story, 1947–1957. Vol. 3.* OKeh (SPV 42532 CD), 1993.

Welding, Pete. *Jimmy Rogers: Chess Masters Blues Series.* Chess (2ACMB-207), 1976.

ONLINE ARTICLES

Beardsley, David. "Jimmy Rogers." *StLBlues.* http://www.stlblues.net/rogers.html.

Big Dave. "David Krull." *StLBlues.* www.stlblues.net/Krull.html.

"Blue Farewell." Weekly Wire. weeklywire.com/ww/01–12–98/Memphis_mus.html.

Blues News. "Chicago Street to Be Named after Jimmy Rogers." December 24, 2000. www.blues.co.nz/news/article.php?id=414.

Cahill, Greg. "Blues Legend Jimmy Rogers on a Roll." *Sonoma County Independent: MetroActive Central.* September 4–10, 1997. www.metroactive.com/papers/sonoma/09.04.97/music-9736.html.

Callahan, Mike, and David Edwards. "The Chess Story." *Both Sides Now Publications.* November 4, 2005. www.bsnpubs.com/chess/chesscheck.html.

Campbell, Robert, et al. "JOB." "Red Saunders Research Foundation." October 8, 2011. Revised September 10, 2013. http://myweb.clemson.edu/~campber/rsrf.html.

Erlewine, Stephen Thomas. "All Music Guide: Review. *Blues Blues Blues.*" http://www.allmusic.com/album/blues-blues-blues-r379569.

Garner, Mike. "Jimmy Rogers." *Blues News,* January 6, 1994. www.blues.co.nz/features/article/.php?id=1.

Gray, Christopher. "TCB Music News: Blues for Clifford." *Austin Chronicle.* May 26, 2006. http://www.austinchronicle.com/music/2006–05–26/368456.

Jaffe, David. "Jimmy Rogers Interview." *SoulBot.* http://www.Soulbot.com/jimmyrogers.

"Jimmy Rogers." Blind Pig Records. http://www.blindpigrecords.com/index.cfm?section=artists&artistid=51.

Lange, Charlie. "In Memory of Jimmy Rogers." *Santa Cruz Blues Festival.* http://www.santacruzblues.com/info.php.

Margolin, Bob. "What Was Muddy Like?" July 2003. http://bobmargolin.com/327–2.

Meekings, John. "Jimmy Rogers: 1924 to 1997." *Blues and Two J's.* www.john-meekings.co.uk/jalane.html.

O'Brien, Justin. *Bill Lupkin Artist Bio.* http://www.bluebellarecords.com/Pages/artists_lupkin.html.

Paulus, George, Robert Campbell, Robert Pruter, Robert Stallworth, Dave Sax, and Jim O'Neal. "Ebony, Chicago, Southern, and Harlem: The Mayo Williams Indies." June 13, 2011. Revised June 15, 2003. http://myweb.clemson.edu/~campber/ebony.html.

Peacock, Emily. "Rogers Honored by Blues Marker." *Bolivar Commercial.* November 26, 2011. http://www.bolivarcom.com/view/full_story/16302875/article-Rogers-honored-by-blues-marker.

Pruter, Robert, and Robert Campbell. "The Legendary Parkway Label." June 16, 2009. Revised October 25, 2013. http://myweb.clemson.edu/~campber/parkway.html.

———. "Tempo-Tone." June 16, 2009. Revised October 25, 2013. http://myweb .clemson.edu/~campber/tempotone.html.

Radai, Tom. "Steve Guyger." *Blues Management Group*. 2008.http://www .bluesmgtgroup.com/pub/clients/Steve_Guyger/index.html.

Rusky, Craig. "Building an Essential Blues Collection: Part Three; Jimmy Rogers: The Chess 50th Anniversary Collection." *Blues On Stage*. http://www.mnblues.com/ cdreview/2002/essentialblues3-jimmyrogers-cr.html.

Stebbins, Bonnie. "Honoring Jimmy Rogers." *Geoff Wilbur's Renegade Newsletter*. http:// membrane.com/renegade/spring01/rogers.html. Originally published in April 2001 issue of "Blues Ambassador" (monthly newsletter of the Capital Area Blues Society [CABS]).

Stiles, Ray. "Jimmy Rogers @ Orrie's February 14–15, 1997." www.mnblues.com/ review/j_rogers.html.

Varbes, Jean-Luc. "ABS Magazine English Interview." *Bob Corritore*. http://bobcorritore .com/news/news-articles/abs-magazine-france-feature-article/abs-magazine -english-interview.

Watrous, Peter. "Cabaret: Jimmy Rogers. " *New York Times*, March 3, 1988. Available online at http://www.nytimes.com/1988/03/03/arts/cabaret-jimmy-rogers.html.

———. "Reviews/Music: The Heart of the Blues, in 5 Acts." *New York Times* online. November 9, 1988. http://www.nytimes.com/1988/11/09/arts/reviews-music-the -heart-of-the-blues-in-5-acts.html.

Winkowski, Elizabeth. "Blues with a Feeling: Meet Sumito Ariyoshi." *Gapers Block*. June 11, 2007. http://www.gapersblock.com/detour/blues_with_a_feeling.

"Wolf Story." Wolf Records International. http://www.wolfrec.com/wolf-story.html.

Zwerin, Mike. "Dodging Danger in Music Business: Record Nabob Sets the Tempo." *International New York* Times online. February 10, 1999. http://www.nytimes .com/1999/02/10/style/10iht-ahmet.t.html.

PRIVATE COLLECTIONS

Mary Katherine Aldin (photos, email correspondences, newspaper and magazine articles)

Scott Dirks (personal photos; Rogers recordings, email correspondences)

Jim O'Neal (Living Blues magazine catalog; personal Rogers photos, articles,

Bob Riedy (photos, recordings, email correspondences, newspaper and magazine articles)

Roberto Prieto Ruguera (Willie O' Shawny & Keith Doder material, unfinished biographical material on Jimmy Rogers [written in Spanish])

Rich Yescalis (photos, email correspondences, newspaper and magazine articles)

INTERVIEWS

Mary Katherine Aldin (email, November 14, 2007)

Susan Antone (in-person, Austin, Texas, May 29, 2008; phone, April 14, 2008)

Frank "Right Hand" Bandy (phone, November 15, 19, 2007, February 28, 2008)

Scotty "Bad Boy" Bradbury (phone, December 19, 2007; in-person, December 21, 2007, January 27, 2008)

Billy Branch (phone, January 30, 2008)

Tom "Mookie" Brill (phone, email, February 1, 2008)

Gordon "Buzz" Brown (email, January 28–30, 2008)

Iguster Brown (phone, April 2, 2008)

Mike Buck (in-person May 27, 2008)

"Good Rockin'" Derral Campbell (email, February 1, 24, 2008)

Robert Campbell (phone, November 12, 2007; email, November 11, 2007)

George Case (email, September 29, 2008)

Edward Chmelewski (phone, email, February 5, 2008)

Randy Chortkoff (email, April 14, 24, 2008)

Dave Clark (phone, January 10, 2008)

Bob Corritore (phone, January 22, 2008; email January 27–30, February 25, April 14, 2008)

Steve Cushing (in-person, November 2, 2007; phone, January 15–16, 2008)

Norman Darwen (email, February 1, 2008)

John DeLeon (phone, January 15, 2014)

Scott Dirks (phone, December 28, 2007; email, January 6, 2008)

Ola Dixon (phone, January 15, 2008)

Keith Doder (letter, July 10, 16, 2008)

Steve F'dor (email, January 28, 2008; phone, January 24, 2008)

Billy Flynn (phone, May 8, 2008; December 27, 2007)

James Fraher (email, January 30, 2007)

"Barrelhouse Chuck" Goering (phone, January 6, 8, 2008)

Henry Gray (phone, March 17, 2008)

Adam Gussow (email, October 18, 22, 2010)

Steve Guyger (phone, December 3–4, 2007)

Joe Harley (phone, email, January 18, 27, 2008)

Jerry Haussler (email, February 21, 2008)

David Horwitz (phone, email, January 30, 2008)

Andrew Huff & Gapers Block (email, March 30, 2008)

Mark Hummel (phone, December 10, 2007; email, December 7, 2007)

Charlie Hussey (email, January 28, 2008)

Bruce Iglauer (email, November 25–26, December 2, 2007, January 15, 2008)

Paul Kahn (phone, February 29, 2008; email, March 1, 2008)

Jim Kahr (email, January 30, 2008)

Chad Kassem (in-person, December 29, 2007; phone, December 25, 2007; email January 2, 2008)

Rich Kirch (phone, November 6, 2007, January 21, 2008; email, February 2, May 22, 2008)

John Koenig (email, February 24, 2008, November 12, 2013)

Mark "Madison Slim" Koenig (phone, March 31, April 1, June 1, 2008)

Bob Koester (in-person, November 3, 2007)

Ed Komara (email, December 18, 2007)

Dave Krull (phone, December 27, 2007)

Angela Lane (phone, November 4, 2007; in-person, December 16, 2007)

Cordero Lane (in-person, November 22, 2007)

Deborah Lane (phone, April 8, 2008)

Jackie Lane (in-person, November 22, 2007)

Jimmy D. Lane (in-person, January 25, 2008; phone, January 23, March 17, 19, 2008)

Sam Lay (phone, January 18, 2008)

Willy Leiser (email, January 23, 2008)

Andy Loesche (email, January 23, 2008)

Bill Lupkin (phone, Monday, December 7, 2007)

Tony Mangiullo (phone, March 28, 2008)

Ben Manilla (email, January 30, 2008)

Eli Marcus (email, January 25, 2008)

"Steady Rollin'" Bob Margolin (email, November 23–27, 2007)

John May (phone, March 26, 2008)

"Tony O" Melio (phone, February 4, March 27, 2008)

Willie Miller (phone, January 17, 2008)

Richard Molina (email, January 9, 2012)

Danny Morrison (email, February 5, 2008)

James D. Mosley (in-person, December 16, 2007; phone, January 3, April 2–3, 2008)

Nick Moss (in-person, November 3, 2007)

Charlie Musselwhite (email, October 29, November 14, December 27, 2007)

James Nagel (email, February 5, 2008; phone, February 20, 2008)

Derek O' Brien (phone, March 28, 2008)

Jim O'Neal (in-person, January 12, 2008; phone, November 9, 2007, January 9, 2008)

Paul Oscher (phone, January 25, 2008; email, January 29, 2008)

"Piano Willie" O'Shawny (email, December 7, 2007)

Holger Peterson (email, January 25, March 3–4, 2008)

Rod and Honey Piazza (phone, December 28, 2007)

Robert Pruter (email, November 8, 15, 2007)

Tom Radai (phone, November 16, 18, 24, December 25, 2007)

Eomot RaSun (phone, January 18, 2008)

Bob Riedy (phone, November 14, 2007, January 11, 2008; email, November 15–19
   2007, March 7–11, 2008)

Dave Rubin (email, December 24, 2007)

Roberto Prieto Ruguera (email, November 17, 21, 2007)

Dick Shurman (phone, June 2, 2008; email, December 2–10, 2007, June 4 2008)

Matthew Skoller (phone, March 28, 2008)

John Stedman (email, February 2, 8, 2008)

Bob Stroger (phone, January 15, 25, 2008)

Richie Untenberger (email, December 26, 2007)

Dave Waldman (phone, December 18–19, 2007)

Michael "Mudcat" Ward (phone, January 10, 12, 2008)

Michael "Junior" Watson (phone, December 20, 2007)

Jody Williams (phone, December 20, 2007, January 3, 2008)

Kim Wilson (phone, November 5, 7, 8, 12, 18, 2007, March 20, 2008)

Richie "Little Rich" Yescalis, (phone, January 10, 29–30, 2008)

Rusty Zinn (phone, December 13, 2007)

INDEX

WAYNE EVERETT GOINS is a Professor of Music and Director of Jazz at Kansas State University. He is author of *Pat Metheny's Secret Story* and co-author of *Charlie Christian: Jazz Guitar's King of Swing*.

MUSIC IN AMERICAN LIFE